Sacred Place and Sacred Time in the Medieval Islamic Middle East

Edinburgh Studies in Classical Islamic History and Culture
Series Editor: Carole Hillenbrand

A particular feature of medieval Islamic civilisation was its wide horizons. The Muslims fell heir not only to the Graeco-Roman world of the Mediterranean, but also to that of the ancient Near East, to the empires of Assyria, Babylon and the Persians; and beyond that, they were in frequent contact with India and China to the east and with black Africa to the south. This intellectual openness can be sensed in many interrelated fields of Muslim thought, and it impacted powerfully on trade and on the networks that made it possible. Books in this series reflect this openness and cover a wide range of topics, periods and geographical areas.

Titles in the series include:

Arabian Drugs in Early Medieval Mediterranean Medicine
Zohar Amar and Efraim Lev

The Abbasid Caliphate of Cairo, 1261–1517: Out of the Shadows
Mustafa Banister

The Medieval Western Maghrib: Cities, Patronage and Power
Amira K. Bennison

Keeping the Peace in Premodern Islam: Diplomacy under the Mamluk Sultanate, 1250–1517
Malika Dekkiche

Queens, Concubines and Eunuchs in Medieval Islam
Taef El-Azhari

The Kharijites in Early Islamic Historical Tradition: Heroes and Villains
Hannah-Lena Hagemann

Medieval Damascus: Plurality and Diversity in an Arabic Library – The Ashrafiya Library Catalogue
Konrad Hirschler

A Monument to Medieval Syrian Book Culture: The Library of Ibn ʿAbd al-Hādī
Konrad Hirschler

The Popularisation of Sufism in Ayyubid and Mamluk Egypt: State and Society, 1173–1325
Nathan Hofer

Defining Anthropomorphism: The Challenge of Islamic Traditionalism
Livnat Holtzman

Making Mongol History: Rashid al-Din and the Jamiʿ al-Tawarikh
Stefan Kamola

Lyrics of Life: Saʿdi on Love, Cosmopolitanism and Care of the Self
Fatemeh Keshavarz

Art, Allegory and The Rise of Shiism In Iran, 1487–1565
Chad Kia

The Adminstration of Justice in Medieval Egypt: From the Seventh to the Twelfth Century
Yaacov Lev

A History of the True Balsam of Matarea
Marcus Milwright

Ruling from a Red Canopy: Political Authority in the Medieval Islamic World, From Anatolia to South Asia
Colin P. Mitchell

Islam, Christianity and the Realms of the Miraculous: A Comparative Exploration
Ian Richard Netton

Sacred Place and Sacred Time in the Medieval Islamic Middle East: A Historical Perspective
Daniella Talmon-Heller

Conquered Populations in Early Islam: Non-Arabs, Slaves and the Sons of Slave Mothers
Elizabeth Urban

edinburghuniversitypress.com/series/escihc

Sacred Place and Sacred Time in the Medieval Islamic Middle East

A Historical Perspective

Daniella Talmon-Heller

EDINBURGH
University Press

Edinburgh University Press is one of the leading university presses in the UK. We publish academic books and journals in our selected subject areas across the humanities and social sciences, combining cutting-edge scholarship with high editorial and production values to produce academic works of lasting importance. For more information visit our website: edinburghuniversitypress.com

Edinburgh University Press Ltd
The Tun – Holyrood Road
12 (2f) Jackson's Entry
Edinburgh EH8 8PJ

First published in hardback by Edinburgh University Press 2020

Typeset in 11/15 Adobe Garamond by
Servis Filmsetting Ltd, Stockport, Cheshire

A CIP record for this book is available from the British Library

ISBN 978 1 4744 6096 5 (hardback)
ISBN 978 1 4744 6097 2 (paperback)
ISBN 978 1 4744 6099 6 (webready PDF)
ISBN 978 1 4744 6098 9 (epub)

Contents

List of Figures vii
Acknowledgements ix
Map of the Middle East xi

Introduction 1

1 Etic Concepts and Emic Terms 9

2 The State of the Art 17

PART ONE A Sacred Place: The Shrine of al-Husayn's Head

Introduction 27

3 From Karbala to Damascus: A Relic with Multiple Shrines 29

4 The Commemoration of al-Husayn in Fatimid Ascalon 42

5 Excursus: Donations to Mosques and Shrines 55

6 Why Ascalon? Christian Martyrs and Muslim *Murābiṭūn* (Defenders) 61

7 Excursus: Medieval Pilgrimage – Victor Turner's Input 70

8 From Ascalon to Cairo: The Duplication of Sacred Space 73

9 Excursus: Arabic Treatises in Praise of Ascalon 85

10 The Shrine in Cairo under the Sunni Ayyubids and Mamluks 87

11 Excursus: al-Husayn and Saladin in Palestinian Lore 97

12 The Shrine in Ascalon under the Ayyubids and Mamluks 101

13 Excursus: Ibn Taymiyya on the Veneration of the Head of al-Husayn 112

14 Summary 119

PART TWO A Sacred Time: The Month of Rajab

Introduction 127

15 Rajab in Pre-Islamic Arabia and in Early Islam 134

16 Excursus: The Founding of an Islamic Lunar Calendar 151

17 Rajab under Fatimid Rule 154

18 Excursus: *Istighfār* (Seeking Divine Forgiveness) 179

19 Rajab under the Ayyubids and Mamluks 182

20 Excursus: Arabic Treatises in Praise of the Sacred Months 218

21 Summary 221

Final Comments: Spacial and Temporal Sanctity 227

Works Cited 235

Index 265

Figures

3.1	Shemr about to murder al-Husayn and sever his head, at Karbala	30
3.2	Mu'awiya's troops parading al-Husayn's severed head	31
3.3	The Umayyad Great Mosque of Damascus – floor plan	34
3.4	The Shrine of Yahya b. Zakariya (John the Baptist) in the Umayyad mosque	35
3.5	Gateway to the shrine of Husayn's Head in the Umayyad Mosque	36
3.6	Route of al-Husayn's head from Karbala to Damascus and Cairo	37
4.1	Masjid al-Juyushi (Badr al-Din) in Cairo, north-eastern façade	45
4.2	Badr al-Din's minbar, front view	47
4.3	Badr al-Din's minbar, side view	48
4.4	Inscription on the minbar's gate	48
5.1	Mosque lamp	56
5.2	Madrasa lamp, Cairo, fourteenth century	58
6.1	Madaba Map	63
8.1	Map of the Latin Kingdom of Jerusalem (524/1130 and 555/1160)	75
8.2	Wooden casket of the head, c. 550/1154	78
10.1	Restored cenotaph at Masjid al-Husayn, Cairo, illuminated by lanterns	89
10.2	Masjid al-Husayn with elevated view of Ayyubid minaret and gate	92
11.1	The Shrine of Seyid Hussein, April 1943, from the northeast	98
11.2	Courtyard of the shrine, April 1943	99

11.3 Symbolic open mosque commemorating the shrine of al-Husayn 99
12.1 Ruins of Ascalon in 1875, view from east wall 104
17.1 Map of Fatimid Cairo (al-Qāhira) 156
17.2 Map of Greater Cairo in the twelfth century 160
19.1 Titles of manuscripts from the Ashrafiyya Library catalogue 184
19.2 Fourteenth-century miniature of the Mosque of Medina 190
19.3 Drawing of the Kaʿba, sixteenth century 202
19.4 Map of Mamluk Cairo 207
19.5 Muslim pilgrims departing from Egypt for Mecca 208

Acknowledgements

Over the years of my work on this project, I shared my ideas and worries with many people, whose questions and comments undoubtedly enhanced its development. I cannot list them all, but I will mention with gratitude friends with whom it was equally pleasurable and beneficial to discuss history, religion and personal life: Elisheva Baumgarten, Efrat Ben-Zeev, Daphna Ephrat, Shaun Marmon, Iris Shagrir, and particularly Raquel Ukeles. I am also grateful to my erstwhile teachers and mentors, Benjamin Z. Kedar and Michael Cook, who gave me wise advice; Yoram Bilu, who read a draft of Part One, Yaacov Lev, who read a draft of Part Two; and the lectors of Edinburgh University Press.

Parts of this research were presented at conferences, workshops and seminars over the course of the past decade. For those opportunities to move my research forward, I thank my hosts and audiences at Middle East Studies Annual (MESA) meetings, the International Medieval Congress at Leeds, the Annemarie Schimmel Kolleg in Bonn, Ruhr-Universität of Bochum, Ben-Gurion University of the Negev, Bar-Ilan University, the School for Mamluk Studies in Ghent, Edinburgh University, the Near Eastern Studies Department at Princeton University, the Institute for Advanced Study in Princeton, and the Middle East and Islamic Studies Department of New York University. Collaboration with Johannes Pahlitzsch and Youval Rotman resulted in a fruitful international workshop entitled 'Sacred Time in Medieval Societies of the Middle East', at Johannes Gutenberg University, Mainz (2016).

Most of my research was conducted at the National Library of Israel, my favourite working place. I would like to thank the librarians of the Islam and Middle East Reading Room for their unfailing service. This is also an opportunity to acknowledge the silent support of fellow readers, who likewise engage, day after day, in study and academic production, inadvertently creating the proper ambiance for this particular ritual. For a supportive environment I also owe a debt of gratitude to my colleagues and students in the Middle East Studies Department at Ben-Gurion University of the Negev.

While writing and rewriting this book was a long and sometimes agonising process, correspondence with Edinburgh University Press editors Nicola Ramsey, Kirsty Woods, Eddie Clark and copy-editor Nina Macaraig was immediate. Their friendly attitude and efficient work are indeed admirable.

The Israel Science Foundation (ISF) generously supported my work with two research grants: grant no. 1676/09 for the study of 'The Foundation of a Muslim Society in Palestine (c. 600–1500 AD)', and grant no. 676/15 for the study of 'The Sanctification of Space, Time and Object in the Muslim Middle East (7th–15th centuries)'. Those endowments enabled me to enjoy the help of four devoted research assisstants: Or Amir, Aseel Fatafta, Oren Hendel and Salama Kohla. I thank them all.

Last but not least, I thank my husband, Dror Heller, for his help with the maps and images for this book, and, more importantly, for having endured my preoccupation with its preparation. Dror, Amit, Ayelet and Uri – the end product is dedicated to you, with love.

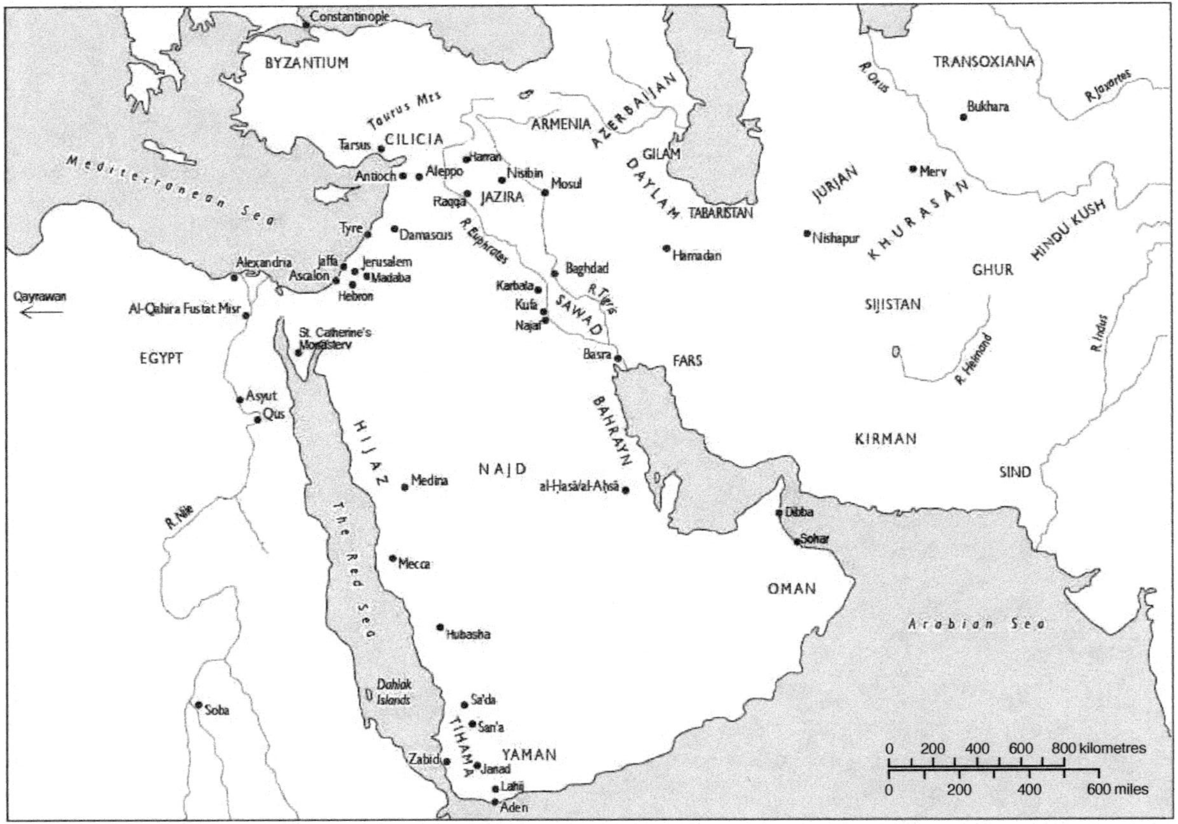

Map of the Middle East, with locations mentioned in the text.

Introduction

> God, the Sublime, assigned an angel known as the Summoner [*al-dāʿī*] to the seventh sky. On each and every night of the month of Rajab, from nightfall to sunrise, that angel calls out: 'Blessings [*ṭūbā*] to those who remember God, blessings to those who worship [Him]'. And God answers: 'I am one with those who seek Me, accommodating with those who obey Me, forgiving to those who ask for My forgiveness. The month [of Rajab] is My month, the worshipper is My worshipper, and the mercy is My mercy. On this month, I answer those who beseech Me, I fulfill the requests of those who entreat Me, and I guide those who ask for My guidance. I have made this month a rope that connects between Me and My devotees. Those who cling to it will reach Me'.
>
> Ibn Tawus (d. 664/1266)[1]

The way Ibn Tawus uses this vivid Qurʾanic image of a physical link between God and the faithful[2] calls to mind Mircae Eliade's depiction of holy places as symbolic ladders, pillars, or mountains that connect the earth to heaven; the *axis mundi* in the imagined sacred geography of various cultures.[3] In the quotation above, it is a sacred time rather than a sacred place that bridges the enormous gap between heaven and earth, using the image of *ḥabl Allāh* (the rope of God). It is included in chapter seven of Ibn Tawus's *al-Iqbāl bi-l-Aʿmāl al-Ḥasana* (Devoting Oneself to Good Works), a bulky compendium of supererogatory prayers and devotions for special days on the Islamic calendar, arranged by month. With respect to Rajab, the author, a renowned Shiʿi Imami scholar,[4] recommends visiting shrines (*ziyārat al-mashāhid*), particularly those associated with al-Husayn (the martyred grandson of the Prophet), on the first and fifteenth of the month. He considers these days no less than God's 'most blessed and cherished time (*aḥabb al-awqāt*)', as well as the anniversary of seminal events, such as the beginning of the Prophet's mission[5] and the marriage of his daughter Fatima to ʿAli. Hence, he offers his readers a rather lengthy text for personal supplication *at* Husayni shrines *on* those particular days of Rajab (*fī hādhā al-mīqāt*). The supplication opens with the following words: 'Praise to God for allowing us to witness the shrine of His saintly friends (*awliyāʾihi*) on Rajab, and obliging us to fulfill our duties towards them'.[6]

Although it is impossible to ascertain whether the rituals prescribed by Ibn Tawus were in fact observed on a regular basis – he claims that his grandfather used to perform them, but also admits the need to urge other believers to do so – we can piece together his outlook on the merits of visiting shrines (*mashhads*) on special days. Various other medieval Shiʿi and Sunni Arabic sources, both pre- and post-dating *al-Iqbāl*, allow a detailed study of particular shrines in honour of al-Husayn and a reenactment of multiple rites of Rajab. Whereas some authors, like Ibn Tawus, encouraged the veneration of these sites and days, others bitterly opposed such practices. Their polemical works bare controversial doctrines and customs, thereby opening a window onto intra- and inter-faith competition, religious hierarchies and social tensions, as well as actual praxis.

The choice of a peripheral 'secondary' shrine[7] and a 'second-tier' holy month, rather than of the prototypical cases of the Kaʿba and the month of Ramadan,[8] as case-studies for an investigation into how medieval Muslims constructed sanctity seems to promise a more stimulating discussion. Rajab, like the shrines of the head of al-Husayn, was informed by an elusive, fluid, and disputed sanctity. While the practice of the hajj at the Meccan Sanctuary and the rites of fasting throughout Ramadan were fairly standardised at an early stage,[9] there was much more leeway for devotional creativity at non-consesual shrines of saints and martyrs, and during Rajab. Moreover, ironic as it may be, I discovered that, although prescriptive works naturally devoted greater attention to the major rituals of Islam and mapped out every detail of their correct observance, they were rarely documented by medieval historians, biographers, geographers, and travellers. Such authors were more likely to record less common practices than the 'standard fare'.[10]

Part One of this book is devoted to expanses that were sanctified by virtue of their association with the severed head of al-Husayn b. ʿAli Ibn Abi Talib, the Prophet's grandson. Al-Husayn was also the second son of the fourth caliph ʿAli and the most illustrious martyr of Karbala in 61/680. He was to become the third of the twelve imams of the Imami (or *Ithnā ʿasharī*) Shiʿis and the second of the seven imams of the Ismaʿilis. Towards the end of the eleventh century, a shrine purportedly holding al-Husayn's head was established in the Palestinian coastal town of Ascalon, a town with an earlier halo of sanctity, then under Fatimid Ismaʿili rule. As Ascalon fell to the Crusaders in the mid-twelfth century, the Fatimids transferred the relic to Cairo and interred it in a new shrine. In Part One, I reconstruct the various narratives concerning the establishment of these two shrines and the artifacts that they housed. This part also describes the itineraries and rituals of visitors to the sites as 'thickly' as the sources allow, and it discusses the devotional and polemical discourses concerning the shrines' authenticity. Both shrines continued to be revered under the Sunni Ayyubids (1172–1250), Mamluks (1250–1517), and Ottomans (1517–1918). They have retained their sanctity also throughout the twentieth century and in contemporary Egypt and Israel, despite major political, religious, cultural, and even geographical transitions.

Turbulent history makes the shrine[s] of al-Husayn's head an intriguing case-study for examining the well-known phenomenon of the durability of sacred places. Peter Brown, the renowned historian of Late Antiquity, explains the methodological problematics concerning the automatic assumption of continuity with a wonderful simile. 'To explain the Christian cult of the martyrs as the continuation of the pagan cult of heroes', he asserts, 'helps as little as to reconstruct the form and function of the late-antique Christian basilica from the few columns and capitals taken from classical buildings that are occasionally incorporated in its arcades'.[11] A few other scholars also point to the methodological pitfalls of stressing 'stasis' and leaving 'ancient survivals' unexplained, or explained away with the all-too-easy suggestion of 'inherent' spirituality and 'intrinsic' sanctity.[12]

Pre-dating all those works, Ignaz Goldziher points to the pre-Islamic antecedents of saint worship in Islam and offers an appealing explanation for the function of its continuity: the preservation of particular ethnic and geographical identities within the universal (or should we say global?) *umma*.[13]

'Localized practices are the strongest support for old traditions', writes Goldziher. He goes on to claim the long historical memory of the people:

> There is the temple of a god to which people have made pilgrimages for many hundreds of years in order to worship and ask for help in need. Popular tradition does not forget the help which they sought and believed they obtained at these places.[14]

Addressing the replacement of a shrine in honour of one god with a shrine in honour of another, the anthropologist Samuli Schielke identifies an act of symbolical and physical triumph. In contrast to Goldziher, he describes the construction of a mosque over a pre-Islamic site of worship as defeating and replacing the preceding cult. In his words, this act is 'an expression of cultural break rather than continuity, in essence'.[15] The historian David Frankfurter, in his insightful introduction to Christianity in late antique Egypt, underscores continuity and integration:

> The installation of a holy site, either by apparition or deliberate missionary innovation, the presence of a holy man or miraculous relic, offers indigenous local culture the chance to assimilate new religious ideas into native idiom, existing social networks, and the experience of the natural environment'.[16]

Put differently, Frankfurter avers – and his thesis very much calls to mind Goldziher's – that indigenous holy sites and local traditions are preserved by being incorporated into the new religious culture, re-consecrated and even revitalised.[17]

Frankfurter's model seems to best explain the fact that sacred places and holy days often enjoyed great longevity in the religious culture of the Middle East. Moreover, medieval Muslim scholars refer to the phenomenon outspokenly, telling of the inclusion of holy sites previously venerated by other creeds into Islam's sacred topography.[18] The challenge of the modern historian and scholar of Islam is to explain this process in each of the different historical settings anew. In order to do so for the case of Mashhad al-Husayn, I have compiled a large corpus of sources that shed light on the history of the shrine. This corpus includes Arabic works of different genres: chronicles, biographical dictionaries, fatwas, travellers' accounts, geographical treatises, homilies, hagiographical works, religious polemics, inscriptions, artifacts, and archaeological remains. Close attention to nuances in the narratives presented in those sources may reveal the intricate process of the construction of new meanings over time, or the coexistence of simultaneous different meanings that the place held for its various visitors.[19]

Part Two is devoted to sanctified stretches of time. It delves into the contested sanctity of Rajab, the seventh month of the Islamic calendar year, and surveys the development of its rites, once again as 'thickly' as possible. Like Part One, it proceeds in a roughly chronological order – from pre-Islamic Arabia, through the formative period of Islam and the early caliphate, the Fatimid and Ayyubid periods, and on to the later stages of the Mamluk state. It chronicles the changing expressions of the veneration of the month in religious thought, practice and literature, based on multiple genres and texts: historical, liturgical, prescriptive, polemical and documentary. Here I attempt to decipher the meaning and abiding relevance of the sacred time of Rajab, as well as the continuous opposition to its commemoration.

In my search for references to Rajab, I returned, as much as possible, to the works of authors who refer to the shrine of al-Husayn and its cult, or at least voice their opinion on sacred places, as well as on sacred times. These include the polymath al-Biruni (d. c. 440/1048), the Imami scholar Ibn Tawus (d. 664/1266), the Sufis al-Ghazzali (d. 555/1111) and al-Jilani (d. 561/1166), the Hanbali jurists Ibn Taymiyya (d. 728/1328) and Ibn Rajab (d. 795/1392–3), the Egyptian historian al-Maqrizi (d. 845/1442) and his Isma'ili counterpart, the Yemeni *dā'ī* Idris 'Imad al-Din al-Qurashi (d. 872/1467). Having their perspective on both case-studies may lend greater coherence to the study of the common theme of the construction of sanctity in medieval Islam.

During the pre-Islamic era, Rajab had constituted one of the four sacred months (*al-ashhur al-ḥurum*) during which the Arabs laid down their arms and engaged in a host of religious devotions. A protracted debate over the permissibility of the continuous veneration of Rajab evolved in the formative period of Islam and has been going on for centuries. Nonetheless, from no later than the tenth century onwards, Sunni and Shi'i authors have compiled manuals that record and recommend a variety of special personal rites for Rajab. Official public acknowledgement of the special status of the month is indicated in sporadic and extremely laconic references in sources pertaining to the Umayyad period (especially in Mecca), and then to the Ikhshids (935–968) in Egypt, and the Hamdanids (905–1004) in Northern Syria and the Jazira. Especially in Cairo, public rites of Rajab developped into extravagant festivities under Fatimid (969–1171) and Mamluk (1250–1517) rule.

While political authorities played a significant role in those enterprises,[20] there were also vibrant initiatives 'from below'. Typically, new rituals assumed the guise of venerable old traditions, yet provoked the recurrent criticism of the ʿulamaʾ. The carnivalesque atmosphere of some of the later festivities certainly defied accepted views of sacred time and incurred fierce opposition,[21] challenging us to try and penetrate the perspectives (in the plural) of the practitioners, rather than adopt that of their censors.

In my Final Comments I hope to demonstrate that juxtaposing the construction of temporal and territorial sanctity indeed enables a fresh look at each category (and especially at the much less researched concept of sacred time in Islam), a more comprehensive understanding of the phenomenon as a whole, and some new insights into the historical development of the religious culture of Muslims. The concluding discussion will focus on the thematic links between Parts One and Two. It will highlight commonalities between perceptions of and practices at sacred places and times, as well as the effect of their conflation.

A few short Excurses supplement the narrative of each part of the book, digressing from the main plotlines in order to elaborate on a number of themes: the foundation of an Islamic lunar calendar, the concept of *istighfār* (seeking pardon); the embellishment of shrines and its symbolic meanings; treatises in praise of Ascalon (*Faḍāʾil ʿAsqalān*) and treatises in praise of Rajab (*Faḍāʾil Rajab* and *Faḍāʾil al-Awqāt*, The Merits of Times); Ibn Taymiyya's polemics agains the sanctification of places; Victor Turner's contribution to the study of medieval pilgrimage; and pilgrimage to Ascalon in late Ottoman and Mandatory Palestine.

A long-term historical investigation of thought on and practice in times and places deemed holy – by putting two controversial case-studies under the microscope and then 'zooming out' for a macroscopic perspective, as it were – is an ambitious undertaking. To begin with, the potential database for such a study is dispersed and vast, even if one wishes only to tap into historical, geographical, devotional, legal and theological literature from the Sunni,

Imami and Isma'ili traditions. Tapping into the theoretical input of more than a hundred years of preoccupation with the sacred in modern academic studies of religion, sociology and anthropology is a likewise daunting task. Encouraged by Peter Burke's *History and Social Theory* (1992) to make selective and eclectic use of this rich scientific legacy while I was working on my PhD, I consulted the great early theoreticians and a few more recent models, which I found inspiring and of explanatory strength for the interpretation of my medieval historical sources, this time too.

Notes

1. Ibn Ṭāwūs, *al-Iqbāl*, vol. 3, p. 174.
2. 'And hold fast, all of you together, to God's rope (*wa-iʿtaṣimū bi-ḥabl Allāh*) and do not separate. And remember God's favour unto you' (Q. 3: 98). *Ḥabl Allāh* is also one of the names of the Qur'an (Mir, 'Names of the Qur'an', p. 512b), and a designation for the caliphs or caliphate (see Crone and Hinds, *God's Caliph*, pp. 39–40. I thank Abigail Krasner Balbale for this reference).
3. Eliade, *Sacred and Profane*.
4. For an intellectual biography, see Kohlberg, *Medieval Muslim Scholar*.
5. Ibn Ṭāwūs, *al-Iqbāl*, vol. 3, pp. 183–5, 218, 236–7.
6. Ibid. pp. 123–4. See also Kohlberg, *Medieval Muslim Scholar*, p. 391. The full text of the invocation (*naṣṣ al-ziyāra al-rajabiyya li-l-imām al-Ḥusayn ʿalayhi al-salām*) is also available on http://ar.wikishia.net/view/ (last accessed 11 May 2019).
7. For a definition of a 'secondary' centre of pilgrimage, see Cohen, 'Pilgrimage centers', p. 37.
8. 'Prototypical case' is the term that Victor Turner uses for sanctity based on sacred scriptures; see Turner and Turner, *Image and Pilgrimage*, pp. 17–18. The hajj is commanded in Q. 2: 125, 5: 2, 97, 22: 27; Ramadan fast is based on Q. 2: 89, 185.
9. Mol, '*Laylat al-Qadr*', p. 83; see also Brunschvig's short piece 'Le culte et le temps' on scholarly debates regarding the appropriate times for performing the core Islamic rites, the significance of observing them on a timely basis and the necessary conditions for postponing those religious obligations.
10. Albeit in a very haphazard manner; see Talmon-Heller, *Islamic Piety*, Appendix I.
11. Brown, *Cult of the Saints*, p. 6.
12. See Bowman, 'Popular Palestinian practices', pp. 70–1.

13. Goldziher, *Muslim Studies*, vol. 2, pp. 255–341.
14. Ibid. p. 303.
15. Schielke, *Perils*, p. 142.
16. Frankfurter, 'Introduction', p. 6.
17. Ibid. pp. 8, 73. For the term 'great tradition', see above, p. 15.
18. See Frenkel, 'Constructing the sacred', and Talmon-Heller, *Islamic Piety*, pp. 188–90.
19. See Rodman, 'Empowering place'.
20. Stephenson, *Ritual*, p. 43.
21. Ibid. p. 49.

1

Etic Concepts and Emic Terms

Space and time are universal categories, and the ways in which religious persons relate to them are often widely shared across cultures.[1] Mircae Eliade begins the first chapter of his influential *The Sacred and the Profane* (1959) by defining some of those ways. 'For religious man', he posits, 'space is not homogenous. He experiences interruptions, breaks in it; some parts of space are qualitatively different from others'. Eliade describes those parts as characterised by a strong 'magnetism', subsequently claiming that identifying the sacred 'is not a matter of theoretical speculation, but of a primary religious experience that precedes all reflection on the world'.[2] He also notes that places considered sacred are protected from defilement by the threat of grave penalties for the violation of their sanctity; they are surrounded 'by a network of restrictions and disabilities which forbid them to be used by men except in particular ways, and in certain cases forbid them to be used at all . . .'[3] William Robertson Smith, who defined holy places and things as set apart by society in order to emphasise their symbolic value, notes that the restrictions imposed on access to the holy place stem from the notion that unclean persons and actions will not be tolerated in the sacred place.[4]

Chapter Two of Eliade's *The Sacred and the Profane* opens with another, parallel claim about discontinuity: 'Time, too, like space, is neither homogenous nor continuous'. He then pronounces a binary division between sacred and profane time: whereas the former is circular and embedded in the liturgical calendar, the profane has 'an ordinary temporal duration in which acts without religious meaning have their setting'.[5] Emile Durkheim, who also stresses the distinction between profane and sacred realms considered superior in dignity and transcendental power,[6] likewise regards the division as a universal phenomenon. In his words, all known religious beliefs present one common characteristic: 'they presuppose a classification of all the things, real and ideal . . . into two classes or opposed groups . . . [:] profane and sacred'. The repertoire of holy things, however, stresses Durkheim, varies from religion to religion.[7]

Another great thinker, the medieval theologian Ibn Taymiyya (d. 728/1328), also contends that every faith-based community distinguishes between sacred and profane in its own way, and those who do not share those distinctions cannot be included in it: 'There is a consensus among scholars that those who render the agreed-upon sacred – profane, or . . . the agreed-upon profane – sacred, are infidel apostates'.[8] Hence, while Durkheim and Ibn Taymiyya wrote from exceedingly different vantage points, they both made a similar observation: shared perceptions of the holy, along with common practices of sanctification, define communities and set them apart from other collectives. This truism makes the study of perceptions of the holy – the mission of this book – so pertinent to the understanding of religious cultures and communities, as well as the historical processes that shape them.

Whereas the 'canonical' works quoted above accentuate the dichotomy between the sacred and profane, current scholarship tends to blur these differences. The new online edition of the classic *Encyclopedia of Religion* (formerly edited by Eliade) clearly manifests this trend. Its mission, as stated in library catalogues, 'is to reflect both changes in academia and in the world since 1987'; for that purpose, many of the 2,750 original entries were heavily updated, and approximately 600 entirely new articles were added. These new articles expand the purview of the sacred to include museums, malls, respites and moments of ecstasy,[9] and attempt to formulate definitions that encompass all of the world's spiritual traditions. While I admittedly find such inclusiveness rather confusing and sometimes counterproductive, a continuum between sacred and prophane and the cohabitation of the elevated and the mundane characterise Islamic conceptions more closely than the classical dichotomous paradigm, as I intend to show.[10]

Reversing Eliade's famous hypothesis of the archetypical shrine as standing at the very heart of the world and constituting the *axis mundi* in the pilgrim's mental map, Victor Turner coined the oxymoron 'the center out there'. With this term Turner accentuated the remoteness of many popular pilgrimage sites from the socio-political centres, and their distinction. Building on Turner's emphasis on the 'popular' characteristics of excentric pilgrimage centres, the sociologist Erik Cohen suggests a continuum between Eliade's 'formal' and Turner's 'popular' centres.[11] On the 'formal' end of the spectrum he pinpoints shrines that typically sit in central locations. Devotees engage there in 'serious, decorous, and lofty religious activities', in accordance with the orthodox precepts of their 'great tradition'.[12] Ludic and folksy elements play a secondary role therein and are even occasionally suppressed by the authorities. At the 'popular' pole, where more peripheral shrines are located, ludic and folksy practices by and large take precedence over somber and sublime devotions; rituals are less formalised, less decorous and conducted in accordance with local 'little tradition'. Cohen, who applied this conceptual framework to the study of contemporary pilgrimage centres in Thailand, developped a list of four indicators with which to determine these sites' location on the continuum.[13]

Parameters by which the degree of 'formality' can be determined in our case – based on Cohen's suggestion, but with some modification – may include the observance of formal Islamic devotions vs the use of relics and ritual objects; sponsorship by the political or religious establishment vs initiatives 'from below'; and the availability (vs absence) of entertainment and commerce at or near the site. The 'excessive' presence of women was often regarded – especially by men of religion, and sometimes also by ruling authorities – to indicate a deviation from proper and 'serious' religious activity. Possibly, these typologies may be helpful not only for the comparative analysis of different stages in the history of a sacred space such as Mashhad al-Husayn, but also for the comparative study of rites around sacred time, the subject matter of Part Two.

In pre-Islamic Arabia, time (*dahr*) was identified with impersonal, destructive, or at least uncertain destiny. According to the Qur'an, the pagan Arabs used to say: 'We live and we die and nothing but time destroys us' (Q. 45: 24). The censure of time (*dhamm al-dahr*) and its image as enemy were recurrent themes in so-called *Jāhilī* (pre-Islamic) Arabic poetry.[14] The following 'divine saying (*ḥadīth qudsī*)' undoubtedly reacts to that attitude, warning: 'The son of Adam should not say, "Curse time," for I am Time. I send the day and the night, and if I wish, I would take them away'.[15]

The Qur'an's vision of space and time is God-centred. Time is God's creation. It is moralized and subject to God's purpose; therefore, it is virtuous. Night and day and the twelve months of the year are all 'appointed times for the [believing] people',[16] and 'All that are in the heavens and the earth entreat Him. Every day He excerciseth (universal) power' (Q. 55: 29).[17] Regarding space, the Qur'an declares: 'To God belong the East and the West; whithersoever you turn, there is the Face of God; God is All-embracing, All-knowing' (Q: 2: 115).

While the Qur'an emphasises that God's presence is not restricted to place and designates each and every day an 'appointed time' for worship, Eliade's observation that neither space nor time are conceived as consisting of uniform units holds just as true for Muslims. Some hours, days, weeks and months were believed to be essentially, qualitatively, different from each other.[18] This too is explicitly stated in the Qur'an. Verse 97: 3, for instance, determines that '*laylat al-qadr* (the Night of Power) is better (*khayr*) than a thousand months'. Al-Ghazzali (d. 555/1111), who lists fifteen blessed nights in the Islamic calendar, compared the plenty that these promise the *murīd* (the mystical wayfarer) to the plenty that merchants encounter at annual fairs.[19]

A wide assortment of Arabic terms is used to signify and describe far-ranging degrees of the holiness of times, places, and objects. Some of these terms are synonymous, whereas others partially overlap. They stem from the following Arabic roots:

- *ḥ-r-m*: impermissible or inviolable, and by extension, sacred. *Ḥarām* – a word loaded with moral, legal, social and political implications[20] – can be interpreted as 'forbidden: unclean' and also as 'forbidden: ultraclean'.[21] Mecca and Medina are known as *al-Ḥaramayn*, the two sacred sanctuaries.[22] The first *Allāhu akbar* ('God is Greatest') pronounced by the Muslim in prayer is called *takbīrat al-iḥrām*, explains Constance Padwick, 'because it shuts off the prayer-time as sacred, and makes unlawful all ordinary right acts, only the acts and words of the set prayer being permitted'.[23]
- *q-d-s*: holy, exalted, or venerated. God and Jerusalem are called *al-Quddūs* and *Bayt al-Maqdis*, respectively.

- *f-ḍ-l*: excellent, virtuous, or of superior qualities. This root dominates the literary genres that sing the praises of the Qur'an, the Prophet, jihad, Mecca, and the like.
- *sh-r-f*: distinguished, noble, elevated. It is used to describe the Ka'ba and the Noble Sanctuary of Jerusalem and to honour the privileged descendants of Muhammad (*al-Ashrāf*).[24]
- *'a-ẓ-m*: glorious, formidable, or great in estimation, rank and dignity; treated with respect. God is commonly called *al-'Aẓīm* – incomparably great.
- *b-r-k*: blessed, hallowed, exalted. *Baraka* denotes blessings, or abundance of good, or the emotive and spiritual force that is bestowed by God[25] and transmitted by the holy.
- *kh-y-r*: good or best.[26] *Khayrāt* (blessings) is synonymous with *baraka*.
- *f-r-d*: set apart, distinguished, or singled out.
- *k-r-m*: venerated and treated with deference. The Qur'an is invariably described as *al-Karīm*.
- *j-l-l*: majestic, exalted or revered.
- *s-r-r*: mysterious. Sufi and Shi'i authors relate it to the 'mystery' or secrets (*sirr*, *asrār*) of the sacred.
- *mawāqīt* [*al-ḥajj*]: a term that captures the geographical and temporal sanctity of the pilgrimage's setting,[27] by jointly referring to the appointed times *and* prescribed places for the rituals.

With the probable exception of the root *ḥ.r.m*, which is usually reserved for those few cases of sanctity on which there exists broad consensus,[28] the usage of most of the terms is far from consistent, even within the same text. For instance, a number of terms are interchangeably used to describe the holiness of the Ka'ba and that of Medina, Jerusalem, any neighbourhood mosque, and the prophets' tombs, despite the vast differences between them on the 'holiness scale'. These differences are reflected in legal compendia: although bloodshed and hunting are forbidden in both Mecca and Medina, only in Mecca donning the *iḥrām* (special attire) is obligatory, and non-Muslims are not allowed.[29] Likewise, interchangeable adjectives derived from the very same roots express the sanctity of the twenty-seventh day of Ramadan (*laylat al-qadr*), Fridays, and the disputed *mawlids* (celebrations of birth/death anniversaries) of Sufi shaykhs. In his above-mentioned compendium, Ibn

Tawus intersperses most of these roots throughout the chapter on Rajab. The introduction to this chapter alone speaks of the month's elevated spiritual power with the terms *taʿẓīm*, *sharaf*, *faḍl*, *jalāl*, *ikrām*, *ḥuramāt*, *barakāt*, *khayrāt* and *asrār*.[30]

The same Arabic roots may also express the notion that ritual performance sanctifies time and place. Maxims such as 'Surely, the land does not make its people holy, but rather its people make it holy (*fa-inna al-arḍ lā tuqaddisu ahlahā lakinna ahlahā yuqaddisūnahā*)'[31] and 'The best hours of the night and day are the hours of prayer (*afḍal sāʿāt al-layl wa-l-nahār awqāt al-ṣalāt*)' give voice to this belief.[32] The theologian and Qurʾanic commentator Abu Mansur al-Maturidi (d. 333/944) suggests that both time and place are consecrated by devotions, alluding to Q. 72: 18: 'and the places of worship are only for God'. He explains that, just as mosques are holy due to the prayers they host, 'it is possible that certain times are more distinguished in virtuousness than others, because the worship performed within a locality is necessarily performed then [that is, also at a certain time]'.[33] Comparing the efficacy of prayer at different sites – for example, claiming that a prayer in Mecca equals 100,000 prayers elsewhere, while a prayer in Medina equals 1,000 prayers elsewhere, and a prayer in Jerusalem is worth 500 prayers elsewhere[34] – is a typical strategy of the *Faḍāʾil* literature written in praise of places and times. As Gustave von Grunebaum notes, this type of comparison was a popular means for ranking the relative sanctity of places.[35]

Notes

1. Denny, 'Islamic ritual', p. 71.
2. Eliade, *Sacred and Profane*, pp. 20, 9–16, 53.
3. For Eliade's articulation of the dangerous sides of the holy, see his *Patterns*, pp. 370–1.
4. Smith, *Lectures*, pp. 147–9. For these taboos in the Arabian context, see Serjeant, '*Ḥaram* and *ḥawtāh*', pp. 45, 55.
5. Ibid. pp. 69–72.
6. Durkheim, *Elementary Forms*, pp. 52–3, 347. See also Zerubavel, *Hidden Rhythms*, p. 118, on taboos that set apart the mutually exclusive categories of sacred and profane.
7. Durkheim, *Elementary Forms*, pp. 36–42.

8. *Wa-l-insān, matā ḥallala al-ḥarām al-mujma' 'alayhi aw ḥarrama al-ḥalāl al-mujma' 'alayhi aw baddala al-shar' al-mujma' 'alayhi, kāna kāfir murtadd bi-ittifāq al-fuqahā'* (Ibn Taymiyya, *Majmū'at al-Fatāwā*, vol. 3, p. 267).
9. Morgan, 'Sacred space', and Swartz, 'Sacred time'.
10. See also the ten degrees of holiness listed in the *Mishna* – beginning with the whole land of Israel, ascending to its walled cities, Jerusalem, the various parts of the Temple on Mt. Moriah and the Holy of Holies at the summit – based on the escalating restrictions on the access of impure persons (*Mishna, Kelim* 1: 6–9). I thank Jackie Feldman for referring me to this text.
11. Cohen, 'Pilgrimage centers'. The article begins with a neat juxtaposition of Eliade and Turner's typologies.
12. The 'great tradition', as famously articulated by the anthropologist Robert Redfield, is that of 'the reflective few . . . cultivated in schools or temples'. He likens the great and little traditions to two currents of thought and action, distinguishable, yet flowing into and out of each other (Redfield, *Peasant Society*, pp. 70–2).
13. Cohen, 'Pilgrimage centers', pp. 33–7.
14. Böwering, 'Time'; Goodman, 'Time in Islam', pp. 138–9, 161.
15. Translated in Denny, 'Islamic ritual', p. 72.
16. Stowasser, *The Day Begins*, pp. 22, 31–3.
17. This is Marmaduke Pickthall's translation of Q. 55: 29. Arberry translates differently: 'Whatsoever is in the heavens and the earth implores Him; every day He is upon some labour'.
18. The modern world, governed by scientific time, is not dissimilar in this sense: different times still have different meanings (see Wishnitzer, *Reading Clocks*, p. 22).
19. Katz, *Birthday*, pp. 143–6.
20. See Marmon, *Eunuchs*, p. 6.
21. Denny, 'Islamic ritual', pp. 69–70.
22. Harry Munt expands on the use of this root in the Qur'an and early Arabic sources; ibid. *Holy City*, pp. 25–8.
23. Padwick, *Muslim Devotions*, p. 34.
24. Ibn Manẓūr, *Lisān al-'Arab*, vol. 4, p. 2241.
25. On *baraka* in medieval Islam and Judaism, see Meri, 'Aspects of *baraka*'.
26. Ibn Manẓūr, *Lisān al-'Arab*, vol. 2, p. 1298.
27. See Gardet, 'Muslim views', pp. 198–9.
28. Ibn Manẓūr (d. 711/1311) lists town, mosque and month as the sacred entities

described as *ḥarām*: *Wa-balad ḥarām wa-masjid ḥarām wa-shahr ḥarām* (Ibid. *Lisān al-ʿArab*, vol. 2, p. 845).

29. Lazarus-Yafeh, 'Mecca and Jerusalem', p. 202; al-Ibrashy, 'Death, life and the barzakh'.
30. Ibn Ṭāwūs, *al-Iqbāl*, pp. 115–16.
31. Munt, *Holy City*, p. 7. This was Saʿmaʿa's provocative respose to the greetings of Caliph Muʿawiya b. Abi Sufyan to an Iraqi delegation to Syria – '*wa-qadamtum al-arḍ al-muqaddasa*' – cited from Ibn al-Faqīh, *Kitāb al-Buldān*, p. 164.
32. Al-Naysābūrī, *Rawḍat al-Wāʿiẓayn*, p. 431.
33. Mol, 'Laylat al-Qadr', pp. 86–7.
34. Mujīr al-Dīn, *al-Uns al-Jalīl*, vol. 1, p. 350.
35. Von Grunebaum, 'Sacred character', pp. 27, 31–2. See Excursus below for lists of compilations in praise of Ascalon and in praise of Rajab.

2

The State of the Art

The veneration of saints and pilgrimage to their shrines – one of the concerns of this book – has been at the centre of a number of works since Goldziher's pioneering study of 1911.[1] Gustave von Grunebaum explored the sacrality of Islamic cities (1962), suggesting a typology of Muslim holy places arranged in hierarchical order: localities whose sanctity stems from the blessing (*baraka*) of a tomb of a prophet or a saint, or the erstwhile presence of descendants of Muhammad or religious sages; a location that is destined to play a role at the end of days; and a place of cosmological import (determined by the order of creation or the site's proximity to heaven). Von Grunebaum emphasises that those sources of sanctity are in no way mutually exclusive and that combinations between them give rise to various cults.[2] We will return to those typologies in our discussion of Ascalon and its surroundings.

Cohen's typology of pilgrimage centres, described above, suggests a useful middle ground between the models of Eliade and Turner. I find it especially helpful for the characterisation of a shrine's different historical phases on the spectrum between 'central' vs 'peripheral', and 'formal' vs 'popular' (with all the problematics that these terms carry), enabling us to avoid unwarranted dichotomies and to be more sensitive to variability.

The 'spatial turn' of the 1990s in geography, anthropology, sociology and the study of religion – and to a lesser extent, in Islamic studies and Middle Eastern history, too – has nurtured endless discussions on place and space as social constructs, rather than simply 'locations'. An awareness that a single place may have multiple meanings for different 'users' based, among other characteristics, on their gender and position in the social hierarchy was articulated by Margaret Rodman (1992).[3] In 2010, Kim Knott identified two major tendencies in the scholarship on religion and space: one focusing on the pilgrim's embodied experience in their place of destiny (including the 'poetics' and aesthetics of the sacred place); the other, focusing on the representation and production of sacred space, as well as practice therein, as expressions of knowledge and power.[4] Many works, my own included, implicitly combine both tendencies (to varying proportions), in an attempt to capture something of the religious experiences (in the plural) of devotees *and* to reveal the socio-economic and political dimensions of the settings of religious sites and festivities.

A list of a few noteworthy titles written in the field of pre-Ottoman Middle Eastern history from these perspectives in recent decades includes works on the visitation of the great cemetery of al-Qarafa in Cairo. Christopher Taylor (1999) has mapped out the topography and textual tradition of the mausolea therein; the articles of Tetsuya Ohtoshi (1993, 2006) offer a historical ethnography of the rites performed there; and May Ibrashy (2014) adds a discussion of the contested perception of the cemetery as a sacred place. Dividing their attention between surveys of the built environment and the analysis of texts, Yehoshua Frenkel (2001), Paul Cobb (2002), Joseph Meri (2002), Nancy Khalek (2011), Zayde Antrim (2012) and Stephennie Mulder (2014), as well as my own work (2007) dwell on the construction of the sanctity of Syria from early Umayyad to late Mamluk times, as on the history and sometimes also architecture of its shrines. While Antrim's main concern is the discourse (or rather, multiple discourses) of place in various Islamic literary genres, part of her book focuses on the production of sacred geography and sacred history. Mulder draws from the disciplines of archaeology, art history and textual analysis, for a detailed and perceptive study of shrines in Syria, bringing to life also the roads leading to them and the rituals that were performed on their precincts. She provides compelling evidence on cross-sectarian patronage of sacred places, especially that of Sunni authorities and pilgrims for monuments connected with the family of the Prophet, which were initially established by Shiʿis. Arezou Azad (2013), Yaron Friedmann (2013) and Harry Munt (2014) have ventured to describe and analyse the special status of the lesser researched cities of Balkh, Kufa and Medina, respectively.[5]

There are significantly fewer works concentrating on time and Islamic liturgical calendars, despite the ancient link between timekeeping and the religious sphere[6] and the fact that practices of Islam are mostly independent of space but firmly tied to time. While the daily prayers may be practised anywhere on the earth, provided that the place is clean according to the shariʿa, the same flexibility does not exist in terms of time. The specific times of the obligatory fasts are likewise strictly observed.[7]

An early study of liturgical calendars is that of al-Biruni (d. c. 440/1048), who dedicated his *al-Āthār al-Bāqiyya ʿan al-Qurūn al-Khāliya* (translated into English as *The Chronology of Ancient Nations*) to the calendars of the Persians, Sogdians, Khwarazmians, Jews, Syrians, Harranians, Greeks, and Arabs (leaving the study of Indian calendars for a later stage of his career). In addition to the scientific aspects of time division, he expounds on the religious festivals that dot the annual cycles of those eight nations, stressing that each nation follows a calendar of its own,[8] thus setting its members apart from others.[9]

Modern researchers have rarely treated Islamic calendars as cultural artifacts and have devoted more attention to the scientific computation of the hijri calendar.[10] An exception to this rule is Rev. Sherrard Burnaby's comparative study of the Jewish and Muslim calendars, written in 1901.[11] Deemed a treatise that 'requires some of the idealism of the classical scholar and of the mathematician' in a book review published in 1902,[12] part of this work indeed tends to cultural aspects, although most of it is obviously the work of Burnaby 'the mathematician'. Over a century was to pass before the publication of another book-length study on this topic, Barbara Stowasser's *The Day Begins at Sunset* (2014). Stowasser devotes a larger part of her book to cultural and religious perspectives, although a significant portion is also devoted to scientific aspects. She does not pay much attention to sacred time. The same can be said for Avner Wishnitzer's *Reading Clocks, Alla Turca: Time and Society in the Late Ottoman Empire* (2015). A sophisticated cultural history of the late Ottoman Empire, *Reading Clocks, Alla Turca* examines the Ottoman subjects' outlook on time and temporal traditions, especially after the introduction of scientific timekeeping methods. Wishnitzer also comments on the multi-layered nature of calendars – that is, on the overlap between astronomical, astrological, seasonal, agricultural, recreational and fiscal cycles.[13] In a similar vein, Yehoshua Frenkel illustrates how, centuries after the formal adoption of a strictly lunar Islamic calendar, daily life and popular religion in the pre-modern Muslim world were still organised around a number of different calendars. Frenkel puts emphasis on the staying power of seasonal agricultural calendars, which were tied to the solar year and its natural rhythm.[14]

Wishnitzer notes that the calculation of auspicious and inauspicious times in the Ottoman Middle East was to a large extent based on the belief that every hour was under the influence of some celestial body, as was determined by the chief astrologer, the *müneccimbaşi*.[15] This is most likely as true of the pre-modern Middle East. We may imagine that much of this wisdom was imparted orally and, therefore, has left few traces. Nonetheless, as noted by Charles Burnett and Tawfik Fahd, texts of classical astrology, known as *Ikhtiyārāt al-Sāʿāt* (Choices of Hours), determined the best times for embarking on certain activities, ranging from when to have intercourse with one's wife, over when to elect a new king, to embarking on a war.[16] I will leave the domain of astrology beyond the scope of this book, however, and deal with the idea of privileged times within the sphere of explicitly religious notions (even though the two can hardly be hermetically separated).

Hava Lazarus-Yafeh and Gustave von Grunebaum examine the disparities between the annual Qurʾanic cycle and its counterparts. Whereas the former is punctuated only by two religious festivals, the other calendars are brimming with the holidays of popular, often-syncretistic local cults that cater to personal and communal needs of merrymaking and congregation.[17] Marion Katz adds a third popular demand which was met by the development of a richer liturgical calendar: the demand for supplementary means of salvation for the guilt-ridden Muslim. She also points to the correlation between the proliferation of special times for celebration and devotion in the later Middle Ages, due to the growing tendency to venerate the Prophet and commemorate important events in his life.[18]

The all-Islamic *mawlid al-nabī* (birthday of the Prophet) and the annual celebrations of the *mawlid*s of a variety of holy figures have garnered wider scholarly interest.[19] Annual non-canonical (or at least contested) rites, such as the celebration of mid-Shaʿban, were treated by academic experts on Islamic law from the perspective of medieval Muslim jurists – that is, as an instance of *bidaʿ* (unwarranted innovation).[20] Such studies tend to focus on the criticism of 'popular religion' and its 'deviation' from the pescriptions of the shariʿa.

From the present study's perspective, the 'orthodox' and 'non-orthodox' belong on the same continuum, of course.

'Special occasions' – as understood, commemorated and occasionally denied by medieval and contemporary Muslim scholars – is one of the topics that Marion Katz discusses in her study of *mawlid al-nabī* and returns to in her study of prayer in Islam.[21] Beyond that, Katz observes that the assumption of time and place being parallel categories prevails in Muslim sources, but only rarely is explicitly addressed. Having reached a similar conclusion, I wish to demonstrate how this assumption was implicitly addressed in the sources, expanding on some of Katz's penetrating insights. But while her work is primarily written from the perspective of the scholar of religious phenomena, I incline towards a more historical outlook.

Such an outlook characterises the work of Paula Sanders, who in 1994 observed:

> . . . although it is commonly said of Islam that it is an 'orthopraxis' rather than an 'orthodox' religion, few scholars have dedicated their energy to studies of Islamic ritual in the pre-modern period. To the extent that such studies have been undertaken, they have tended to focus on the prescriptions found in legal literature . . . [or are written] from the point of view of 'popular religion'.[22]

Sanders herself offers a sophisticated analysis of the religious elements of Cairene ceremonial between the late tenth and late twelfth centuries. Despite the contemporary academic literature's heightened attention to ritual as an integral part of culture and social life, since the publication of Sanders's work modern historiography on Islamic dynasties still has little to say about rituals.

While this book repeatedly addresses rituals that were orchestrated by the state, especially under the Fatimids and Mamluks, it follows Durkheim's emphasis on ritual as common action, empowering the individual and producing the collective emotions and exaltation which make up the experience of the sacred.[23] It is also about the ideas that enlightened those rituals, and the literary genres that articulate them. In this respect, it is much in line with a number of studies on pre-modern Islam that are based on a broad spectrum of prescriptive, narrative, documentary and sometimes also material sources, and that juxtapose religious thought and practice. Relevant examples include Shaun Marmon's *Eunuchs and Sacred Boundaries in Islamic Society* (1995), which explores Islamic ritual, *baraka* and charisma at the tomb of the Prophet in Medina; Michael Cook's all-embracing treatment of the Islamic duty of *al-amr bi-l-maʿrūf wa-l-nahy ʿan al-munkar, Commanding Right and Forbidding Wrong* (2000); Marion Katz's long-term study of the narratives and rites pertaining to *mawlid al-nabī, The Birth of the Prophet Muhammad* (2007); her *Prayer in Islamic Thought and Practice* (2013); Megan Reid's analysis of trends in Islamic asceticism and devotion, *Law and Piety in Medieval Islam* (2014); and my *Islamic Piety in Medieval Syria* (2007), which surveys religious life under the Ayyubids, revolving around mosque, cemetery and shrine.

The genre of *Faḍāʾil al-Awqāt* and comparable compilations of petitionary prayers attributed to Muhammad (such as al-Ghazzali's ninth book of the *Iḥyāʾ*) and the Shiʿi imams have attracted little scholarly interest.[24] *Faḍāʾil al-Awqāt* typically cite hadith (often hadiths considered 'weak' and 'untrustworthy' by medieval experts in the field)[25] in praise of certain days or months. They advocate the performance of various combinations of religious devotions at those times as unproportionally rewarding. The manuals devoted to Rajab recommend individual supplications and public nocturnal prayer assemblies, suggesting the proper words for the related *duʿāʾ*, repentance and pleading for forgiveness. Besides Marion Katz's chapter 'Time and merit in the celebration of the *mawlid*',[26] very little has been written on this topic since Constance Padwick's *Muslim Devotions* (1966).[27] From our point of view, it may also tentatively be regarded – and I am, of course, aware of the gap between prescriptive literature and actual practice – as an ethnography of the practices of Muslims, in times and places they believed to be blessed and virtuous. I would argue that these manuals, which are laden with surprising anecdotes on the appearance, transmission and performance of devotions, still await not only the eyes of scholars of religion, but also of scholars in the fields of gender, folklore and Arabic literature.

Rajab has not received much attention in academic literature, even though Islamic sources of a wide range of genres explain the sacred status of this month or polemicise against it. In the 1970s, Meir Kister devoted a pair of long and erudite articles to traditions concerning the months of Shaʿban and Rajab.[28] Little had been written on this topic before, with the exception of K. Wagtendonk's *Fasting in the Koran* (1968), to which I will return shortly. In later works that focus on Islamic life and devotions, or on public ritual, Rajab tends to be overlooked or mentioned only in passing, a phenomenon clearly indicated by the fact that it very rarely appears in the index.[29]

Mashhad Ra's al-Husayn's history and architecture aroused the interest of the pioneer of Arabic epigraphy, Max van Berchem, and the archaeologists L. H. Vincent and E. J. H. Mackay in the early twentieth century.[30] In recent decades, historians such as Moshe Sharon, Caroline Williams, Daniel De Smet, Khalid Sindawi, Stephennie Mulder, B.Z. Kedar, Itzhak Reiter and myself[31] have returned to the subject. Notwithstanding, I believe that there is still scope for a comprehensive inquiry into the cult at the Husayni shrines, examined against the backdrop of the erratic history of the medieval Middle East and in light of theoretical models of pilgrimage and shrines. This is the objective of Part I of my book.

Notes

1. Goldziher, 'Veneration'.
2. Von Grunebaum, 'The sacred', pp. 26–7, 31.
3. Rodman, 'Empowering place', pp. 640–56, esp. 647; Feldman, 'Contested narratives', p. 112.
4. Knott, 'Religion, space', pp. 29–43, esp. 32–4; Feldman, 'Contested narratives', pp. 107, 110.
5. See the Works Cited at the end.
6. Ethington, 'Placing the past', pp. 465–7.
7. Bağlı, 'Material Culture', pp. 309–10.
8. Al-Birūnī, *Chronology*. On the life and works of this 'greatest authority on Muslim perceptions of Time', see Yano, 'al-Bīrūnī', and Stowasser, *The Day Begins*, pp. 88–138.
9. For a modern articulation of this idea, see Zerubavel, *Hidden Rythms*, pp. 13, 70–81.
10. For example, Dallal, 'Calendar'. Elisheva Carlebach's monograph *Palaces of Time* perceives the Jewish calendar as a dynamic cultural construct. There is no 'Islamic' equivalent, so far.
11. Burnaby, *Elements*, pp. 387–92.
12. M. G., 'Review'.

13. Wishnitzer, *Reading Clocks*, pp. 18–20. Wishnitzer remarks that even in the modern world, governed by scientific time, different times still have different meanings (ibid. p. 22).
14. Frenkel, 'Popular culture'.
15. Wishnitzer, *Reading Clocks*, pp. 20–1.
16. Burnett, 'Astrology'; Fahd, 'Ikhtiyārāt'.
17. Lazarus-Yafeh, *Religious Aspects*, pp. 38–9; von Grunebaum, *Muhammadan Festivals*, p. 53.
18. Katz, *Birth of the Prophet*, pp. 165–6.
19. Kaptein, *Muhammad's Birthday*; Katz, *Birth of the Prophet*; Fuchs, Jong and Knappert, 'Mawlid'; Winter, 'The *Mawlids* in Egypt'; Schielke, *Perils of Joy.*
20. See Kister, 'Shaʿbān'; Rispler, 'The 20th century'; Ukeles, *Innovation or Deviation.*
21. Katz, *Birth of the Prophet*; Katz, *Prayer in Islam.*
22. Sanders, *Ritual*, p. 5.
23. Stephenson, *Ritual*, p. 38–42; Durkheim, *Elementary Forms*, pp. 462–7.
24. Exceptions to this rule are Padwick's *Muslim Devotions*, and McGregor, 'Notes', who makes this observation about the state of the art. See ibid. pp. 202, 206.
25. Malik, *Grey Falcon*, pp. 162–3.
26. Katz, *Birth of the Prophet*, pp. 143–68.
27. See, for example, al-Ḥasakānī, *Faḍā'il Shahr Rajab*, vol. 2, pp. 511–12.
28. Kister, 'Rajab is the month'. See also Kister, 'Radjab'; Kister, 'Shaʿban'.
29. The *Encyclopaedia of Islam* (second edition)'s entry on *mawākib* (processions) exemplifies this point (Sanders et al., 'Mawākib').
30. Van Berchem, 'La chaire'; Vincent and Mackay, *Hébron.*
31. Sharon, *CIAP*; Williams, 'Cult of ʿAlid saints'; De Smet, 'La translation'; Sindāwi, 'The head'; Mulder, *The Shrines*; Talmon-Heller, Kedar and Reiter, 'Vicissitudes'; Talmon-Heller, 'Job'.

PART I

A SACRED PLACE: THE SHRINE OF AL-HUSAYN'S HEAD

Introduction

Then in the distance they could see part of the exterior of the mosque of al-Husayn. In the center was an expansive window decorated with arabesques . . . With joy singing in her breast, she asked: 'Our master al-Husayn?' He confirmed her guess. Her pace quickened for the first time since she left the house. She began to compare what she saw with the picture created by her imagination and based on what she had seen from her home of mosques like Qalawun and Barquq. She found the reality to be less grand than she had imagined. In her imagination she had made its size correspond to the veneration in which she held its holy occupant. This difference between imagination and reality, however, in no way affected the pervasive intoxication of her joy at being there . . . They entered . . . She felt that her body was dissolving into tenderness, affection and love and that she was being transformed into a spirit fluttering in the sky, radiant with the glow of prophetic inspiration. Her eyes swam with tears that helped relieve the agitation of her breast, the warmth of her love and belief, and the flood of her benevolent joy. She proceeded to devour the place with greedy, curious eyes: the walls, ceiling, pillars, carpets, chandeliers, pulpit, and the mihrab niches indicating the direction of Mecca . . . How often had she wished to visit this site . . . Here she was standing within the shrine. Indeed, here she was touching the walls of the tomb itself . . . She stroked the walls and kissed them. (Naguib Mahfouz, *Palace Walk*)[1]

Mahfouz's moving description of an Egyptian housewife's visit to the al-Husayn Shrine in Cairo was written in the mid-1900s. It captures the 'magnetism' of the holy place and the over-whelming emotion and bodily sensations of a believer upon entering it for the first time after years of desire and anticipation.[2] The author skillfully portrays the shrine's impact on Amina, the housewife in *Bayna al-Qaṣrayn*, known in English as *The Cairo Trilogy*. Although a work of fiction, Mahfouz accurately depicts what is known in Cairo as *Masjid al-Imām al-Ḥusayn* or, in colloquial Egyptian, *Jāmiʿ Sīdnā Ḥsein*. Built in the middle ages and restored in the late nineteenth century, the shrine presumably houses the severed head of the Prophet's grandson al-Husayn b. ʿAli. While this relic constitutes one of the most potent symbols of Shiʿi martyrology and its emphasis on self-sacrifice, suffering and salvation, it is intensely venerated by Sunni Muslims as well.[3] As clearly depicted in *Palace Walk*, as well as in anthropological studies of Islam in contemporary Egypt, its mausoleum has retained its position as one of the most important shrines and congregational mosques in Cairo for hundreds of years.[4]

The following chapters focus on the narratives, material structures and rituals of sites that were associated with al-Husayn's severed head in Cairo, Damascus and Ascalon. It is based on a variety of medieval sources and draws from the output of a wide range of contemporary researchers specialising in various branches of Middle Eastern studies, including art, anthropology and religion. Chronologically speaking, we will span the formative period of Islam until the late Mamluk era, with some digressions into earlier and later intervals.

Notes

1. Mahfouz, *Palace Walk*, pp. 168–9.
2. Compare with Edith Turner's definition of pilgrimage: ibid. 'Pilgrimage: An overview', pp. 714–15.
3. Mahmoud Ayoub goes so far as to claim that 'In Islamic history, and especially in Shiʿi piety, the head of al-Husayn played a role closely analogous to that of the cross in early and medieval Christian history' (Ayoub, *Redemptive Suffering*, p. 133).
4. Schielke, *Perils of Joy*, pp. 22, 28, 181.

3

From Karbala to Damascus: A Relic with Multiple Shrines

According to oft-repeated accounts of medieval Muslim historians, the Umayyad army attacked the encampment of the Prophet Muhammad's grandson, al-Husayn ibn ʿAli, and his small entourage at Karbala (in southern Iraq) on the tenth day of Muharram 61/680. By the end of the day, al-Husayn was severely wounded or already dead. The victorious Umayyads then proceeded to cut off his head. Seventy-one other members of the Prophet's family – men, women and children – were killed in the assault. Al-Husayn's attempted revolt against the newly established ruling dynasty was nipped in the bud. While his body was interred on the battle ground, his head was carried off on the point of a spear in a triumphal procession, initiated by Kufa's Umayyad governor ʿUbayd Allah b. Ziyad.[1] The procession exhibited also the heads of the other men killed at Karbala, as well as the survivors: mainly women, and only one of al-Husayn's sons, the young boy ʿAli Zayn al-Abidin, who in the years to come was recognized as the fourth imam, the spiritual leader of the ʿAlids (or proto-Shiʿis). They were paraded through several towns *en route* to Damascus. The inhabitants of Tikrit, Mosul, Qarib al-Daawat, Hims, Baalbek and Damascus are said to have rejoiced at the sight of the defeated insurrectionists, whereas their counterparts in Qinnisrin, Shayzar, Kafr Tab, Saybur and Hamah took offense at the killing and humiliation of the Prophet's kin.[2] Along the way, the decapitated head allegedly performed various wonders. For instance, it recited from the Qurʾan and convinced monks and rabbis to embrace Islam. Blood that dripped from the head in different places affected miracles and consecrated the ground, generating new sacred spaces and cults.[3]

Figure 3.1 Shemr about to murder al-Husayn and sever his head, at Karbala (from the archive of Persian lithographed illustrations, Ulrich Marzolph, Kitzingen).

Figure 3.2 Muʿawiya's troops parading al-Husayn's severed head (from the archive of Persian lithographed illustrations, Ulrich Marzolph, Kitzingen).

When the procession of the defeated kin of the Prophet reached Damascus, al-Husayn's head was brought before the Caliph Yazid. According to several sources, the caliph cruelly revelled at the sight. Other sources claim that he was appropriately remorseful and moved to tears.[4] In his multiple accounts of this episode, the renowned historian al-Tabari (d. 310/923) depicts Yazid as wavering between elation and anguish. On the one hand, he orders his wife to mourn for the Prophet's grandson; on the other hand, he insolently pokes a cane inside al-Husayn's lifeless mouth. An elderly companion of the Prophet who entered the court at that point was horrified by the gruesome scene. 'By God', he cried, 'I have seen the Messenger of God, peace and blessings upon him, kiss those lips!'[5] Al-Biruni (d. c. 440/1048) contends that Yazid knocked out the front teeth from al-Husayn's skull while reciting a poem about vengeance.[6]

The later Syrian scholars ʿAli Ibn ʿAsakir (d. 571/1176), Sibt ibn al-Jawzi (d. 654/1257) and Ibn Taymiyya (d. 728/1283) display the Umayyads in a more favourable light. In Ibn ʿAsakir's version, for example, Yazid was truly sorry over al-Husayn's fate and laid most of the blame on the ruthless governor Ziyad b. ʿUbayd Allah.[7] Sibt ibn al-Jawzi summarises al-Tabari's versions by saying that Yazid rejoiced when the head was brought to him, but then became deeply sorry for his death and for the fate of his women.[8] In the depiction of the Ismaʿili Yemeni historian Idris ʿImad al-Din (d. 872/1467),[9] both Ibn Ziyad and Yazid b. Muʿawiya fool with the head. He also relates 'historical anecdotes (*ruwāt al-akhbār*)' about the further whereabouts of the head. Those include a night vision of one of the guards in charge of the mourners' tent (*suridaq*), which was erected by Yazid to appease the pro-ʿAlid people of Damascus, as it were. The guard saw the prophets Adam, Nuh, Ibrahim, Musa and ʿIsa coming to comfort Muhammad for the brutal death of his grandson, accompanied by angels.[10] Angels appear also in a touching story about al-Husayn's childhood, one of many hagiographical anecdotes that serve as 'precursors' of his future martyrdom and saintly status.[11] Another storyteller records the puzzled reactions of a delegate of the Byzantine emperor and that of a representative of the Head of the Jews (*raʾs al-jālūt*). The Christian is appalled by the mistreatment of the relic, and the Jew is taken back by the utter lack of respect the Muslims show towards the progeny of their Prophet. The lesson is clear: even the Jews and Christians scored better than the Umayyads in honouring the family (*ahl al-bayt*) of their prophets.[12]

According to the Imami Shiʿis, forty days after the massacre at Karbala, on the twentieth day of Safar, the head was returned to Karbala and interred with the body of al-Husayn.[13] Al-Biruni notes that forty men visited the site that very day – a precedent that apparently evolved into a yearly ritual.[14] The number forty is not incidental, of course; as in the Judeo-Christian tradition, so in Islam the number is associated with waiting, mourning and purification.[15] Other reports state that Yazid sent the head to Medina, where the local governor had it buried next to the tomb of al-Husayn's mother, the Prophet's daughter Fatima.[16] Yazid's beautiful and clever nanny (*ḥāḍina*) Rayya claimed that the skull was stored in a Damascus armory. Only a few decades later it was duly interred 'among the graves of the Muslims (*fī maqābir al-Muslimīn*)' in Damascus, by Yazid's heir, Sulayman b. ʿAbd al-Malik (r. 96–9/715–17).[17]

There are two medieval shrines in Damascus commemorating al-Husayn ibn ʿAli, in walking distance from each other.[18] The first – still venerated as Mashhad al-Husayn, as beautifully depicted by Stephennie Mulder[19] – can be found in the north-east corner of the Great Umayyad Mosque, the city's sacred heart. As per the tenth-century geographer Ibn Hawqal, the shrine stands on the very spot where al-Husayn's head was exhibited in 61/680, which happened to be where Yahya b. Zakariya (John the Baptist) had been slain centuries earlier.[20] Prophet Yahya's head was allegedly found in a labelled coffin when the St John Cathedral was transformed into the Umayyad Mosque by caliph al-Walid (r. 705–15). This discovery became part of the mosque's 'foundation story'. Upon completing the grand new building, the head's exact location was marked with a special column featuring a basket-shaped capital.[21] All this happened only seventy-five or so years after the Arabs' conquest of Damascus, when its Muslim population must have been small and the Islamisation of the cityscape was still in its early stages.

Nancy Khalek, who strives to demonstrate how the Muslims of Syria forged their identity within an existing Byzantine material, aesthetic and spiritual landscape, claims that 'in Damascus they instituted a cult centred on corporeal relics, similar to and in relationship with the Christian cult of relics'.[22] For Khalek, the institution of the remains of John the Baptist in the Great Mosque of Damascus was no less than a turning point, which made the veneration of relics and the visitation of tombs a part of Islamic piety. The discovery and appropriation of the head of John by the Muslim conquerors of Damascus demonstrates the continuity of perceptions of sacred space and the adaptability of narratives and cults to new political-religious settings. Moreover, the reconstruction of the sanctity of the place, its physical space and its story played a role in Islamic identity formation, so Khalek. John

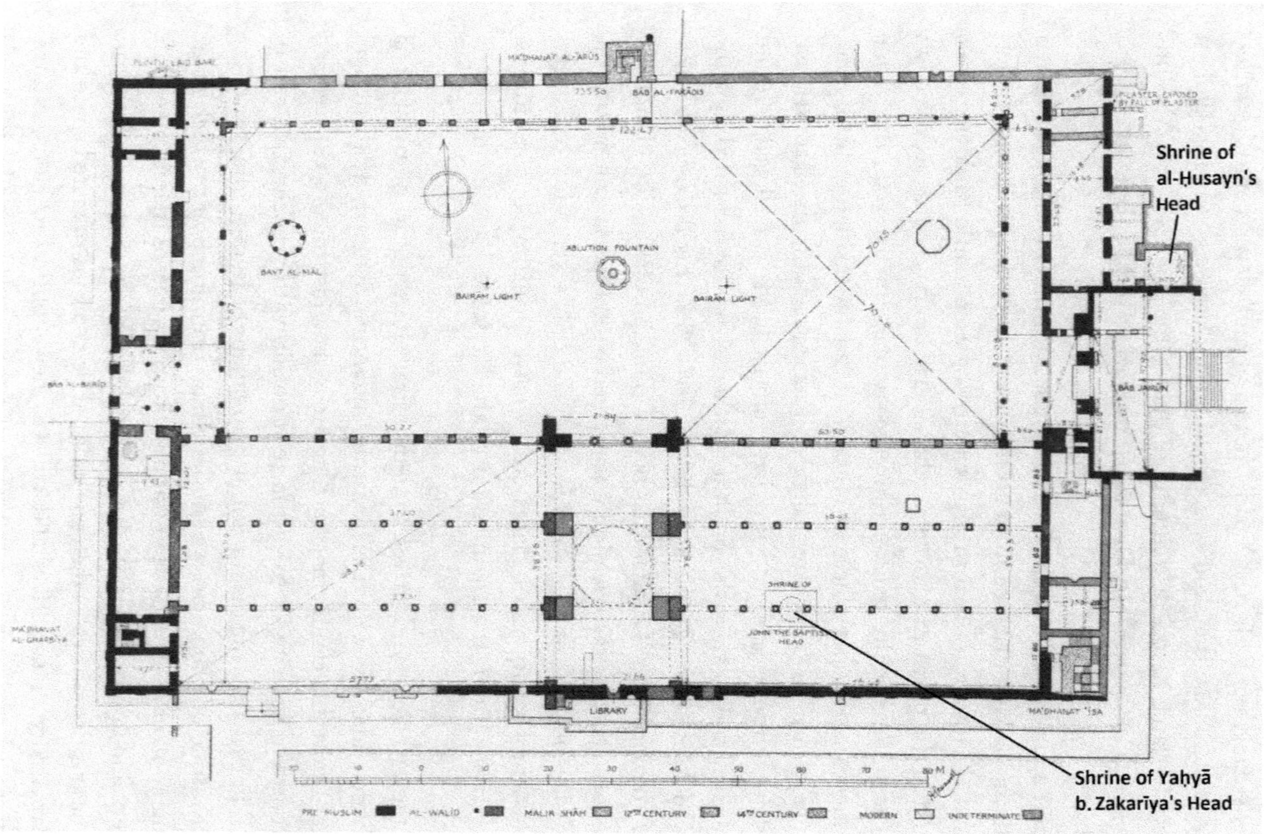

Figure 3.3 The Umayyad Great Mosque of Damascus – floor plan with shrines of Yahya b. Zakariya (John the Baptist) and al-Husayn (after K. A. C. Creswell, *Early Muslim Architecture*, vol. 1, *Umayyads, A.D. 622–750*, Oxford: Clarendon Press 1932, Fig. 57. Courtesy of Special Collections, Fine Arts Library, Harvard University).

became Yahya, an Islamic prophet with an Islamic narrative, based on the Qur'an and the 'stories of the prophets (*qiṣaṣ al-anbiyā'*)'.[23]

The earliest known sources to explicitly identify the Umayyad Mosque as the actual burial place of the head of al-Husayn are the Damascene historian Ibn 'Asakir and the Maghribi traveller Ibn Jubayr (580/1184). In his guidebook on Muslim holy places, *Kitāb al-Ishārāt ilā Ma'rifat al-Ziyārāt*, Ibn al-Harawi (d. 611/1215) was the first to make note of a shrine devoted to al-Husayn near Bab al-Faradis. Only in the mid-1300s, so it seems, was this site also considered the actual tomb. Al-Hawrani's sixteenth-century guidebook tells of pilgrims who visit this shrine in the hopes of attaining blessing (*tabarruk*) and having their needs fulfilled (*iltimās al-ḥawā'ij*).[24]

Cognizant of those conflicting traditions, a few Mamluk-era historians who sought to retrace the path and pinpoint the final destination of the tortured head of al-Husayn pronounce frank exasperation. Al-Dhahabi (d. 748/1348) cites early sources according to whom *al-musawwada* ('the ones in black'), namely the Abbasids, desecrated the grave and removed its contents upon arriving in Damascus. He concludes that 'only God knows

Figure 3.4 The Shrine of Yahya b. Zakariya (John the Baptist), Umayyad Great Mosque of Damascus (photo: James Gordon). https://commons.wikimedia.org/wiki/File:Shrine_of_John_the_Baptist,_Great_Umayyid_Mosque,_Damascus.jpg

Figure 3.5 Gateway to the shrine of Husayn's Head in the Umayyad Mosque (photo: Stephennie Mulder), courtesy of the author.

what has happened to it'.[25] Idris Ibn al-ʿImad also acknowledges that there are several opinions regarding the final burial place of the head. He reiterates the above-mentioned claims that it ended up in Damascus, or in Medina next to the grave of Fatima, or in Raqqa, fallen in the hostile hands of the descendants of the third caliph ʿUthman, with whom Yazid reputedly bargained for the head of the murdered caliph.[26]

At least a dozen sites commemorate the voyage of the head throughout the Middle East. They include places that the martyr's head touched or that his blood stained, and places purportedly marking its actual burial site. They may be found in Raqqa,[27] Aleppo,[28] Balis[29] and Nisibin[30] in Northern Syria; Najaf (near his father ʿAli) in southern Iraq;[31] Mosul in the Jazira region[32]; Ascalon in southern Palestine;[33] Cairo;[34] Damascus, Karbala and Medina.[35] Even distant Merv (modern-day Turkmenistan) was said to have been graced by the head's presence. Kaʿb, a secretary of the powerful Barmaki family of scribes that served the Abbasid caliphs, reports to have seen the relic there in 256/870. It was stored in a labelled basket, at the local governor's residence,

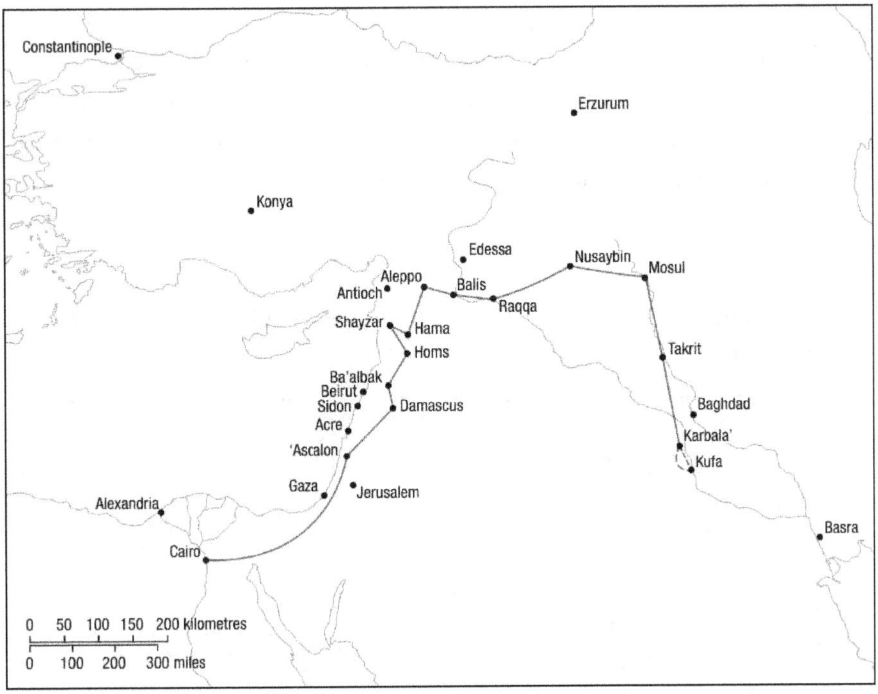

Figure 3.6 Route of al-Husayn's head from Karbala to Damascus and Cairo (Stephennie Mulder, *The Shrines of the ʿAlids in Medieval Syria: Sunnis, Shiʿis, and the Architecture of Coexistence*, Edinburgh: Edinburgh University Press, 2014, p. 256. Courtesy of the author).

smelling of musk. Kaʿb and his host wept and prayed when it was taken out and brought before them.[36]

An entirely different approach to relics can be found in a remarkable line of verse by the Egyptian grammarian Ibn Qatana (640/1242–3): 'Do not look for our *mawlā* (master) al-Husayn in the lands of the east or the west; call them all and turn towards me, [for] his shrine is in my heart'. The preacher and historian Sibt ibn al-Jawzi (d. 654/1257), who quotes this verse from 'one of our shaykhs', voices similar thoughts: 'Wherever the head of al-Husayn or his body may be, he dwells in the hearts and minds'.[37]

Most believers obviously did not adopt such a mystical view, but were interested in the physical location of tombs or relics of prophets and saintly Muslims, as well as the sites that were honoured by their presence.[38] The fact that more than one mausoleum was affiliated with the same figure usually did not deter the faithful from visiting these places. According to James Grehan's witty analysis of saint worship in the Ottoman Levant, 'redundancies were a widely accepted fact'.[39] Still, the debate over the head's true location keeps fueling Sunni-Shiʿi polemics (like many other medieval controversies, which are waged nowadays across myriad websites), as well as the current Salafi campaign against saint and tomb veneration.

Notes

1. For a concise account of these dramatic events, see Afsaruddin, *First Muslims*, pp. 79–81.
2. Van Berchem, *Opera Minora*, p. 639; Sindawi, 'Head', p. 264; Mulder, *Shrines*, pp. 255–7.
3. Ayoub, *Redemptive Suffering*, p. 133; Sindawi, 'Head', pp. 264–73. See also introduction to Ibn Ṭāwūs, *al-Malhūf*, pp. 13–30.
4. Shoshan, *Poetics of Islamic Historiography*, pp. 100–2; Ayyoub, *Redemptive Suffering*, p. 120.
5. Al-Ṭabarī, *History*, pp. 175–6.
6. Al-Bīrūnī, *Chronology*, p. 328. On the human fascination with gruesome trophy skulls and other decapitated heads in far ranging periods and contexts, see Larson, *Severed*, esp. pp. 74–5.
7. Lindsay, 'Caliphal and moral exemplar', p. 263. On the Syrian scholar's efforts to rehabilitate the Umayyads' image, see Borrut and Cobb, *Umayyad Legacies*, pp. 12–13.
8. Sibṭ ibn al-Jawzī, *Tadhkirat al-Khawāṣṣ*, p. 238. See also his long account of al-Husayn's death and its aftermath, where he seems quite sympathetic to the Shiʿi cause. *Tadhkirat al-Khawāṣṣ* was indeed published by several Shiʿi publishers and raised a lively debate on the internet, regarding the author's fidelity to the sunna.
9. On Idris ʿImad al-Din, the nineteenth *dāʿī muṭlaq* (the head of the community; lit. chief summoner) of the Tayyibi community in Yemen, 'unchallenged doyen of Ismaʿili historians of all ages' and author of the only general history of the Ismaʿilis written by an Ismaʿili, see Daftary, *Ismaili History*, pp. 92–9. The chapter was first published as 'Idris ʿImad al-Din and Medieval Ismaili Historiography', pp. 52–8.
10. Idrīs ʿImād al-Dīn, *ʿUyūn al-Akhbār*, vol. 4, pp. 113–26. For another version of this story, see Sindawi, 'Head', p. 269.
11. One day, when the Prophet worried that al-Husayn and his brother Hasan did not return home, the angel Gabriel reassured him that God had charged one

of the angels with safeguarding the two. Muhammad then found the children napping in a sheep enclosure; the guardian-angel had spread his wings, holding one under them and the other over them as cover. See Ayoub 'The excellences', and Giladi, 'History and emotions', p. 34 (based on Ibn Ẓafar, *Anbāʾ Nujabāʾ*, pp. 57–8, and Ibn Ṭāwūs, *al-Malhūf*, pp. 92–5).

12. ʿImād al-Dīn, *ʿUyūn al-Akhbār*, vol. 4, pp. 127–8.
13. Ibn Ṭāwūs, *al-Malhūf*, p. 225. See also Meri, *Cult of Saints*, pp. 192–5, on the veneration of Al-Husayn in the Middle East.
14. See al-Bīrūnī, *Chronology*, p. 328; and Ayoub, 'Arbaʿīn'. On the sacred space of Karbala, see Sindawi, 'Sanctity of Karbala', pp. 33–40. Its great significance for Shiʿis is also reflected in their custom to carry little tablets known as *turba*, *torbat*, or *mohr*, which are made from the clay of Karbala, and to place their foreheads on them during the *sujūd* (prostration) of daily prayers. See Gleave, 'Prayer and prostration', pp. 241–9. For a contemporary explanation of the custom and its origins in Prophetic hadith, see www.al-islam.org/nutshell/laws_practices/7.htm (last accessed 8 May 2019).
15. Schimmel, *Numbers*, pp. 248–9.
16. Ibn Saʿd, *Kitāb al-Ṭabaqāt al-Kabīr*, vol. 7, p. 234.
17. Ibn ʿAsākir, *Taʾrīkh Madīnat Dimashq*, vol. 69, p. 158; al-Dhahabī, *Siyar*, vol. 3, p. 319.
18. Among the first sources to refer to these possible locations is Ibn Hibbān (d. 354/965), *Mashāhīr ʿUlamāʾ al-Amṣār*.
19. Mulder, *Shrines*, pp. 201–6. For an account of the recurrent restorations of the shrine by Sunni and Shiʿi patrons, see ibid. pp. 206–20.
20. A number of Shiʿi traditions link al-Husayn's martyrdom to that of John the Baptist, who is mentioned in Q. 19: 7 under the name Yahya b. Zakariya. For a survey of the parallels between the two, see Sindawi, 'Al-Husain Ibn ʿAli'. Muhammad is supposedly told that, while John the Baptist's death corresponded to the death of 70,000 men, that of al-Husayn corresponded to the death of 70,000 upon 70,000 (Khalek, *Damascus*, p. 132, n. 121).
21. On the veneration of Yahya b. Zakariya in medieval Syria, see Meri, *Cult of Saints*, p. 200. According to thirteenth-century Syrian historians, a(nother) part of Yahya's skull was discovered in Baʿlbak in 435/1043–4 and subsequently transferred to Maqam Ibrahim in Aleppo (see Talmon-Heller, *Islamic Piety*, p. 56).
22. Khalek, *Damascus*, pp. 7–9.
23. Ibid. 85–94, 117–18. See also Cobb, 'Virtual sacrality', pp. 49–50. See p. 10 above, for the both emic and etic notion that shared perceptions of the holy,

along with common practices of sanctification, are significant for defining communities and setting them apart from other collectives.

24. Meri, 'Late medieval', p. 27. Mulder has discovered that later generations believed that al-Husayn's daughter Sayyida Ruqayya is buried in this mausoleum. For Mulder's admirable attempt to make sense of the conflicting reports regarding the location and designation of Damascene shrines, see Mulder, *Shrines*, pp. 188–221. As for Sayyida Ruqayya, she was also commemorated in Cairo, in a large *mashhad* erected in 527/1133; see Williams, 'Cult of ʿAlid saints', pp. 44–7, and the map of Fatimid Cairo below.
25. Al-Dhahabī, *Siyar*, vol. 3, p. 319.
26. Muhammad, *Masājid Miṣr*, pp. 367, 371; Idrīs ʿImād al-Dīn, *ʿUyūn al-Akhbār*, vol. 4, p. 129; vol. 5, p. 738.
27. See Ababsa, 'Shiʿi Mausoleums', for the historical and current Husayni cult in Raqqa.
28. The Aleppan *mashhad* centres around a rock on which some of the martyr's blood was allegedly spilled when his decapitated head was transported from Karbala to Damascus. For an in-depth look at the history and architecture of this site, see Mulder, *Shrines*, pp. 82–9.
29. Known as Mashhad al-Hajar, this shrine is named for another rock on which al-Husayn's head was placed during a stopover in Balis; Mulder, *Shrines*, pp. 55–6.
30. Al-Harawi mentions two sites that commemorate the passage of al-Husayn's head through Nisibin: Mashhhad al-Raʾs and Mashhad al-Nuqta (the Drop [of Blood] Shrine).
31. Soad Maher Mohammad dismisses the authenticity of this identification. In her judgement, the site in Najaf was built by the Ilkhanids in the late thirteenth or fourteenth century and underwent several renovations over the years (Mohammad, *Mashhad al-Imām ʿAlī*, pp. 153–5). According to Ibn Taymiyya, ʿAli is buried in Kufa, and the identification of his grave in Najaf is but an invention of the Buyids (Ibn Taymiyya, *Majmūʿat al-Fatāwā*, vol. 27, p. 246).
32. Meri, *Lonely Wayfarer*, p. 182.
33. Sibṭ ibn al-Jawzī, *Tadhkirat al-Khawāṣṣ*, p. 239.
34. See Meri, *Cult of Saints*, p. 192; Sibṭ ibn al-Jawzī, *Tadhkirat al-Khawāṣṣ*, p. 239.
35. Vaglieri, 'al-Ḥusayn'; Sibṭ ibn al-Jawzī, *Mirʾāt al-Zamān*, vol. 8, pp. 167–71.
36. Al-Muqaddasī, *Aḥsan al-Taqāsīm*, p. 294. Abu Muslim, the architect of the Abbasid revolution, is said to have transferred the head from Damascus to his native Khorasan after the Abbasid victory over the Umayyads in 133/750 (Muḥammad, *Masājid Miṣr*, vol. 1, p. 367. See also Sindawi, 'Head', p. 266).

37. *'fa-huwwa sākin fī-l-qulūb wa-l-ḍamā'ir, qāṭin fī al-asrār wa-l-khawāṭir'* (Sibṭ ibn al-Jawzī, *Tadhkirat al-Khawāṣṣ*, pp. 239–40).
38. Grehan, *Twilight of the Saints*, pp. 107–9; and Talmon-Heller, 'Job', p. 130.
39. See, for example, a relatively long and learned post from May 2006 in a series entitled 'False graves and shrines': http://ar.islamway.net/article/1613 (last accessed 8 May 2019).

4

The Commemoration of al-Husayn in Fatimid Ascalon

The Fatimids, a Shiʿi Ismaʿili dynasty, claimed direct lineage from the Prophet's daughter Fatima and her son al-Husayn. After proclaiming a new caliphate in 297/909 in North Africa and establishing their seat of government in Mansuriyya near Kairouan in 336/948, their dominion was extended to Egypt in 358/969, and then to most of Syria. The Fatimid Empire lasted, with changing borders, for two and a half centuries. Attempting to balance their Ismaʿili mission with the need to find favour with the caliphate's Sunni majority, the regime adopted a 'two-tiered approach'. The head of the Fatimid state served in the double capacities of imam and caliph. He was the infallible and absolutely indispensable religious leader for the Shiʿi minority and a political ruler for all his subjects. And while all subjects were granted religious freedom, the Fatimids continuously developped their esoteric doctrine and spread it among the Ismaʿili elite and beyond the borders of their empire.[1]

The prolific Mamluk-era historian al-Maqrizi (766/1364–845/1449) is responsible for much of our knowledge concerning governance and ritual during the Fatimid period in Egypt. Robert Irwin suggests that al-Maqrizi 'had a passionate and somewhat antiquarian interest in the Fatimids', whom Sunni authors often shunned, because they were the founders of his beloved city, Cairo.[2] In his *Ittiʿāẓ al-Ḥunafāʾ bi-Akhbār al-Aʾimma al-Fāṭimiyyīn al-Khulafāʾ* (Lessons for the Seekers of Truth in the History of the Fatimid Imams and Caliphs), al-Maqrizi focuses almost exclusively on this age. Besides preserving significant portions of otherwise non-extant works by his forerunners – such as Ibn Zulaq (d. 386/996), al-Musabbihi (d. 420/1029),

Ibn al-Muyassar (d. 677/1278–9) and al-Bataʾihi (d. 588/1192) – al-Maqrizi weaves otherwise lost Fatimid documents, letters and sermons into his own narrative.[3]

The empire's inaugural Friday sermon (*khuṭba*) in Egypt, as cited by al-Maqrizi, invoked blessings for the imam-caliph al-Muʿizz, who conquered the Land of the Nile, and on 'his pure forefathers and descendants, the righteous imams'. In the years to come, the Fatimid *khuṭba* would open with a more elaborate, formulaic declaration based on Q. 33: 33, listing Muhammad 'the chosen one', ʿAli the 'approved one', Fatima 'the pure', and al-Hasan and al-Husayn, the two grandsons of the Prophet, 'from whom God has removed all impurity and has sanctified', and 'the rightly-guided imams'. Hence the Fatimids' rule was legitimised by virtue of their descent from the *ahl al-bayt* (lit. the People of the House), also known as *ahl al-kisāʾ* (the people of the cloak or mantle).[4] The Imamis and most Ismaʿili sects regard al-Hasan as imam, but exclude his descendants from the imamate, regarding as such only the offspring of al-Husayn.[5] The Sunnis have adopted a much more encompassing definition of the *ahl al-bayt*, which usually includes all the progeny of Muhammad's four daughters and several branches of his clan. Concomitantly, they do not privilege *ahl al-bayt* in the same way as the Shiʿis do.

While the veneration of the Prophet's family in Egypt predated the Fatimid era, it evidently became a pivotal cult only under their dominion.[6] Throughout their reign, the Fatimids had consistently nurtured devotion to the *ahl al-bayt*. In 402/1012, three tombs in Misr, near the Ibn Tulun Mosque, were recognized as the burial site of the descendants of ʿAli al-Asghar b. Zayn al-ʿAbidin (the grandson of al-Husayn). Soon after, the imam-caliph al-Hakim bi-Amr Allah had a shrine built over the site.[7] During the final decades of Fatimid rule, over ten Cairene shrines were dedicated to the men and women from Muhammad's family.[8] Ibn Jubayr, who visited Cairo in 578/1182, a decade after the demise of the Fatimids, counts nineteen *mausolea* for members of the Prophet's family; fourteen for men and five for women.[9]

Nasir Khusraw, the Ismaʿili traveller and missionary (*dāʿī*) who reached Cairo in the summer of 439/1047, during the days of the long reign of the imam-caliph al-Mustansir, repeatedly designates the caliph as the descendant of the Prince of the Faithful (*amīr al-mu'minīn*) al-Husayn b. ʿAli. In one of his poems he writes:

> The sons of ʿAli are the Imams of truth,
> as famed as their father for their greatness.
> Their father spread justice throughout the land;
> Why should we be surprised that his sons follow their father's wisdom?
> (*Dīvān*, 31: 25–7; 32)[10]

Legal documents also repeat this designation of the Fatimid imams. A marriage contract signed during the reign of al-Mustansir begins with the following testimony:"

> Muhammad is the messenger of God, the pure and trusted envoy; ʿAli is his legate, the commander of the faithful; Fatima is the mistress of the ladies of the world, and his grandsons al-Hasan and al-Husayn are the doors of mercy. The imams who descend from al-Husayn are God's trustees for mankind, the moons of the nights, the suns of the days.[11]

It is against this backdrop that the unearthing of the head of al-Husayn on Fatimid territory in the late eleventh century acquires its significance. The unearthing was claimed by Badr al-Din al-Jamali, a freed military slave of Armenian origin, who was appointed to the powerful office of vizier by the imam-caliph al-Mustansir in 466/1073. Al-Jamali had already proven himself to be an outstanding governor of Damascus and commander-in-chief at Acre. Moreover, he had formed a new large Armenian contingent within the army, which was personally loyal to him. In his new role as vizier, he was expected to restore order and stability following a disastrous period for the Fatimids. To begin with, strife within the military had deteriorated into a full-scale civil war that caused the destruction of great parts of Cairo. In the north the empire lost battles and territory to both the Seljuks and the Artuqids. These setbacks were exacerbated by a severe economic crisis, famine and plague.

Ruthless in his quest for absolute power, al-Jamali managed to save the caliphate despite all its ailments[12] and was duly imparted with a long row of honorifics: 'the most illustrious lord, helper of the Imam, sword of Islam, commander of the armies (*amīr al-juyūsh*), protector of the Qadis of the Muslims and guide of the propagandists of the believers (that is, Ismaʿili *du'ā'*)'. His honorific Isma'ili title did not deter him from abolishing the privileged position of the Isma'ili school of law. He did so in his capacity as 'protector of the qadis', thereby putting all the major schools of law on an equal footing and revealing his reservations regarding Isma'ili exclusivity.[13]

Over the course of his twenty-one years in office Badr al-Din al-Jamali was also an avid builder. He oversaw the restorations at the Ahmad Ibn Tulun Mosque (in 470/1077), the construction of a large shrine known as Mashhad or Masjid al-Juyyushi on the Muqattam Hills of southeastern Cairo (in 478/1085)[14] and the repair of the Sayyida Nafisa Mausoleum (in 482/1089). In addition, he funded several minarets, a marketplace and a new mosque on Rawda Island. Pushing out Cairo's southern and northern walls, he enlarged the city and changed its shape from square to rectangular (in 440/1087). The new areas were surrounded by massive walls and accessed via three fortified gates.[15] Beyond Cairo, Badr al-Din was responsible for the construction of a Friday mosque in Alexandria (479/1086), built from the proceeds of a fine that was exacted on the city's inhabitants for rebelling against him. Furthermore, he initiated the first Islamic-era reconstruction of the Sanctuary of Abraham (also known as the Cave of the Patriarchs) in Hebron.[16]

An inscription that adorns an ornate wooden minbar (pulpit) in the form of eighteen lines of highly sophisticated angular and floriated Kufi

Figure 4.1 Masjid al-Juyushi (Badr al-Din) in Cairo, north-eastern façade, early twentieth century (EA.CA.3400 K. A. C. Creswell, Image © Ashmolean Museum, University of Oxford, courtesy of Fine Arts Library, Harvard College Library).

script ties Badr al-Jamali's name to that of the imam al-Husayn.[17] In the judgement of art historians such as Jonathan Bloom and Yasser Tabbaa, the minbar is a masterpiece of Fatimid-era Syrian craftsmanship and one of the earliest surviving wooden artifacts that fall under this category. Its flanks feature hexagonal ornaments with vegetal arabesque fillets, ornaments that predate all other existing geometric ornament in Syria by about fifty years (see Figs. 4.2 and 4.3).[18] It was commissioned in 484/1091–2, at the height of the vizier's career,[19] and currently stands in the Sanctuary of Abraham in Hebron, although Badr al-Din did not place it there. Its original destination was a shrine mentioned on a slab of marble with the fragment of another inscription of the same year (484/1091–2), which was found among the ruins of Ascalon.[20] The inscription on the minbar warrants our careful attention and detailed analysis. It proudly commemorates the discovery of 'the head of our master (*mawlānā*) the imam the martyr Abu ʿAbd Allah al-Husayn b. ʿAli Ibn Abi Talib', in the *thaghr* (outpost or frontier town) of Ascalon.[21]

The designation of Ascalon as an outpost seems to be significant. Another mid-eleventh-century inscription – either the epigraph of a building, or an official's epitaph – also refers to Ascalon as an outpost.[22] It is the central motif in traditions concerning the merits of settlement in Ascalon, dating back to Umayyad and early Abbasid times. The preacher who delivered the first sermon after the laying of the foundations for Fatimid Cairo at the old mosque of Misr in 358/969 follows suit and lists the defense of frontier towns as one of the imam-caliph's missions:

> O God, grant victory to his [the caliph's] troops, to those he has sent forth to fight the polytheists, to carry out jihad against the heretics, to defend the Muslims and safeguard the frontier towns (*thughūr*) and the *ḥaram*, to eliminate oppression, insinuation and greed, and to spread justice among the people.[23]

In Badr al-Jamali's inscription on the minbar, the discovery of al-Husayn's head in the *thaghr* of Ascalon is presented as a miracle (*muʿjiz*),[24] a sign (*āya*) of heavenly grace for the Fatimid dynasty, 'a cause for delight' for His faithful partisans, a special favour to 'the commander of the armies, the sword of Islam, the succor of the Imam . . . Abu al-Najm Badr al-Mustansiri'. The

Figure 4.2 Badr al-Din's minbar, front view (photo: B. Z. Kedar, courtesy of photographer).

Figure 4.3 Badr al-Din's minbar, side view (photo: B. Z. Kedar, courtesy of photographer).

١) بسم الله الرحمن الرحيم نصر من الله وفتح قريب لعبد الله ووليه معد ابي تميم الإمام ٢) المستنصر بالله امير
المؤمنين صلوات الله عليه وعلى ابائه الطاهرين وابنائه البررة ٣) الاكرمين صلاة باقية الى يوم الدين مما امر
بعمل هذا المنبر فتاه السيد الاجل امير الجيو ٤) ش سيف الاسلام ناصر الإمام كافل قضاة المسلمين وهادي دعاة
المؤمنين ابو النجم بدر المستنصري ٥) عضَّدَ الله به الدين وامتع بطول بقائه امير المؤمنين وادام قدرته واعلى
كلمته للمشهد الشريف بثغر ٦) عسقلان مسجد مولانا امير المؤمنين ابو عبد الله الحسين بن علي بن ابي طالب
صلوات الله عليهما في شهور سنة اربع وثمانين واربعمائة

Figure 4.4 Inscription on Badr al-Din's minbar's gate, transcribed (Moshe Sharon, *Corpus Inscriptionum Arabicarum Palaestinae*, vol. 1, Leiden: Brill, p. 155, courtesy of the author).

patronymic (*nisba*) 'al-Mustansiri' indicates that the caliph was al-Jamali's direct patron.[25] But since the vizier was already more powerful than his master at this juncture, perhaps the imam-caliph's mention constitutes not much more than 'a dating device', as suggested by Irene Bierman in her study of the vizier's building projects.[26]

Following the honorifics, the epigraph warns that the 'evil-doers (*al-ẓālimūn*)' that hid the sacred relic in order to 'obliterate its light' will face the wrath of heaven. In all likelihood, the epithet 'evil-doers' is directed at the Umayyads who were especially abhorred by Shiʿis for killing al-Husayn and maltreating his body.[27] A prevalent metaphor in religious (and political) contexts, light appears to specifically refer in this instance to the divine eternal light radiating from all Shiʿi imams. This same light wondrously shone over the route along which al-Husayn's decapitated head was carried from Karbala to Damascus, as we have seen above.[28]

Further down the epigraph, the religious practices expected to take place at the shrine mosque in honour of the head are enumerated. Prayer of 'those wishing to have their prayers accepted' comes first, then seeking intercession (*shafāʿa*) and finally visitation (*ziyāra*).This short inventory is followed by a list of the assets that Badr al-Jamali endowed for the upkeep of the site. The appointment of custodians and guardians is also mentioned. Badr al-Din presents his motivations for the construction of the shrine as 'pleasing God and seeking his reward' and 'publically manifesting the honour of this imam [al-Husayn] and unfurling his banners'.

Contemporary historians have endeavoured to ascertain the worldly imperatives behind the purported miraculous discovery of the head of al-Husayn in Ascalon and the subsequent establishment of the shrine in its honour. One hypothesis posits that the monument was erected in order to tighten the Fatimid state's hold on one of its last remaining strongholds in Syria, as most of Syria had been captured by the Turkish Seljuqs by then. It also bears noting that Ascalon was a major trade hub on the main route leading from Egypt to the Levant, and alongside Cairo, Tyre, Qus and Alexandria, it was the site of a Fatimid minting facility.[29] Throughout the long reign of Caliph al-Mustansir (427/1036–487/1094), the Fatimids took additional measures to secure their control of Ascalon. Like a handful of other border and coastal cities, Ascalon was buttressed with fortifications, a garrison and a special governor sent directly from Cairo.[30] The governor's letter of appointment from the 1070s, which is preserved in an encyclopedic work on administration written by al-Qalqashandi (d. 820/1418), sheds light on Ascalon's strategic importance to the Fatimids:

> . . . the city of ʿAsqalān, may God the Exalted protect it, was the *thaghr* of Islam, the one and only in Syria, and the *ribāṭ* (stronghold) that whoever is in it gains the highest reward . . . [T]hese are the reasons that the infidels covet it, and we thus pay . . . special attention to it because of its great importance, and choose the best men to nominate [as governors] over it.[31]

The construction of the shrine may have been, then, an attempt to bolster the religious prestige of a strategically and economically important city in order to draw to it pilgrims and visitors.[32] Alternatively, it may be argued that Badr al-Jamali established the *mashhad* for the purpose of strengthening his personal position within the Fatimid ruling elite, rather than that of the Fatimids in the larger geo-politics of the Middle East. While the inscription attributes the shrine's endowment to the imam-caliph al-Mustansir, it states that al-Jamali found the head, buried it in a dignified manner and 'resolved to construct this minbar especially for the venerable martyr'. Furthermore, the vizier's name is accompanied by a long list of honorifics that emphasises his priority and reflects his status. Owing to the acute weakness of al-Mustansir and the old Fatimid elite, by this stage al-Jamali was already the undisputed ruler of Egypt.[33]

To whom did the epigraph speak? It turns to the 'believers', urging them to protect, honour and maintain the pure holy site, the shrine and mosque of ʿAli's son al-Husayn (*al-mashhad al-sharīf . . . masjid mawlānā amīr al-muʾminīn Abī ʿAbd Allāh al-Ḥusayn b. ʿAlī*).[34] But it is uncertain whether the term 'believers' is referring to Ismaʿilis in particular, Shiʿis in general, or the entire *umma* (Muslim community). Visitation of tombs of the *ahl al-bayt* has always been far more important to Shiʿis. Embedded in Imami theology, such visits are an integral part of the stream's rite, and there was hardly any objection to the building of mausolea and tomb-mosques in the Shiʿi camp.[35] Sunni scholars were more ambivalent towards the practice of *ziyāra*, and they did not place the *ahl al-bayt* on a pedestal higher than the Prophet's Companions or other early righteous Muslims *a priori*. What is more, the epigraph cites a popular Shiʿi hadith known as *al-thaqalayn* ('the two precious gifts', meaning the Qurʾan and the *ahl al-bayt*). According to tradition, Muhammad uttered the words of this hadith after designating his cousin and son-in-law ʿAli (al-Husayn's father) as his successor in Ghadir

Khumm, issuing the famous declaration: 'He whose master I am, ʿAli is his master'.[36]

Badr al-Din's decision to begin the inscription with content that mostly appealed to the Fatimid Ismaʿilis and then to employ pan-Islamic language is reminiscent of two later Ayyubid-era inscriptions chiseled onto the portal of a shrine in honour of al-Husayn in Aleppo. Stephennie Mulder, who delved into these Syrian epigraphs, notes that the first extols the twelve martyred Shiʿi imams, reflecting the Shiʿi view of history and its bitter resentment towards the Sunnis whom they blame for the death of their imams. The second, adjacent epigraph praises the four Rightly Guided Caliphs and all the Companions, reflecting the Sunni admiration towards some of the most abhorred figures in the eyes of the Shiʿis! By dint of their spatial orientation and physical arrangement, Mulder reads the two seemingly incompatible inscriptions as a single message calling for conciliation and unity.[37] Jean-Michel Mouton attributes similar intent to the Sunni Burid rulers of Damascus (r. 497/1104–549/1154), claiming that they promoted the cult of the relics of the Prophet in a way that was conducive to rapprochement with the Shiʿi population of the city.[38]

In the final analysis of the inscription on Badr al-Din's minbar, given the epigram's inclusive terminology, the unspecific nature of the rituals mentioned in it and what is known of the vizier's religious affiliation and policy, I would argue that he was creating an 'ecumenical' space, reaching out to both Sunnis and Shiʿis alike. As already demonstrated by Paula Sanders, Yaacov Lev and Daniel De Smet, the late eleventh and early twelfth centuries were a period of de-Ismaʿilisation in the Fatimid state.[39] Sanders explains that the Fatimid administration made a deliberate attempt to create an Islamic *lingua franca* that would relate to a broad range of Muslims. To this end, the regime de-emphasised patently Ismaʿili ideas and encouraged the rise of new popular forms of religious adherence.[40] De Smet regards the proliferation of the cult of saints as a result of this de-Ismaʿilisation of the Fatimid state. He claims that the establishment of the shrine in honour of al-Husayn was not initially dictated by Ismaʿili doctrine.[41] Neither was the institutionalisation of the celebration of the birthdays of the Prophet, ʿAli, Fatima, al-Hasan and al-Husayn, which provided holidays for Cairo's entire population, Shiʿi and Sunni alike. So did the caliphs' birthdays (*mawālid*), which had been celebrated at least since 516/1122, when the *mawlid* of the tenth Fatimid imam-caliph al-Mansur al-Amir bi-Ahkam Allah (known as *al-Āmiri*) was turned into a major event for all subjects.[42]

Due to al-Husayn's pivotal role in the genealogy of the Shiʿi imams in general and of the Fatimids in particular and, notwithstanding, his all-Islamic standing as the grandson of the Prophet, the promotion of his cult was wholly consistent with the Fatimids' specifically Ismaʿili affiliation. It was also in line with their claim to be the rightful heirs to the Prophet for all Muslims.

Owing to the lack of sources concerning the monument's reception by the population of Ascalon and its surroundings, it is impossible to determine whether this enterprise indeed managed to cut across sectarian lines and constituted an early instance of what Mulder refers to as 'architecture of coexistence'. The only extant information about the mosque-shrine in the first decades after its establishment pertains to continuous royal contributions. *Akhbār Miṣr*, a twelfth-century history of Egypt by Ibn al-Maʾmun al-Bataʾihi, recounts the shrine's embellishment in 516/1122, some thirty years after its dedication. The imam-caliph al-Amir bi-Ahkam Allah commissioned one chandelier (*qandīl*) of gold and one of silver for the '*mashhad* in the outpost of Ascalon'. In parallel, another chandelier was fashioned for the mausoleum of the Fatimid imams in Cairo (known as *Turbat al-Aʾimma*, *al-Turba al-Muʿizziyya*, or *Turbat al-Zaʿfrān*). The author's father, al-Maʾmun al-Bataʾihi – who had served as governor of Ascalon and later, until his imprisonment in 519/1125, as the imam-caliph's vizier – personally contributed 2,000 dinars for the crafting of gold and silver chains that were apparently used to hang these lamps from the ceiling.[43]

Notes

1. Lev, *State and Society*, pp. 133, 140–52; Hamdani, *Between Revolution and State*, p. 31.
2. Irwin, 'Mamluk history', pp. 159, 167.
3. Jiwa, *Towards a Shiʿi Empire*, p. 2.
4. Ibid. p. 20.
5. For the disagreements regarding the identity of the first imams, see Walker, *Orations*, pp. 66–8.
6. Hamdani, 'Ismaʿili studies', p. 516; De Smet, 'Les fêtes', pp. 190–3.

7. Leisten, 'Dynastic tombs', p. 478, n. 107, citing al-Maqrīzī, *Khiṭaṭ*, vol. 2, pp. 20, 125; al-Sakhāwī, *Tuḥfat al-Aḥbāb*, pp. 114, 118.
8. Williams, 'The cult: Part I', and ibid. 'The cult: Part II'. De Smet, 'Fêtes', p. 196.
9. Ibn Jubayr, *Riḥla*, pp. 45–56; Lev, *State and Society*, pp. 151–2. Ibn Jubayr's interest in architecture and art, as well as his love of detail, is discussed by Netton in ibid. 'Ibn Jubayr', vol. 2, pp. 86–7.
10. Hunsberger, *Nasir Khusraw*, p. 142.
11. Ragib, 'Un contract', p. 34.
12. Lev, *State and Society*, pp. 44–5.
13. Lev, *Saladin in Egypt*, p. 197; ibid. *State and Society*, pp. 46–7.
14. For more on Mashhad al-Juyyushi, see Williams, 'The cult: Part II', pp. 40, 57, 67–8; Bloom, *Arts of the City*, p. 136. The contents of the epigraph are discussed in Ibn 'Uthmān, *Murshid*, p. 192.
15. Sayyid, *al-Qāhira*, p. 9. See Fig. 17.1.
16. Dadoyan, *Fatimid Armenians*, pp. 126, 144–5; Williams, 'The cult: Part I', p. 9; Bloom, *Arts of the City*, pp. 117–36; Bierman, *Writing Signs*, pp. 105–8.
17. The circumstances behind the minbar's relocation to Hebron will be discussed below.
18. For a detailed account of this minbar and its design, see Contadini, *Fatimid Art*, pp. 111–13 and pls 51–2; Bloom, 'Woodwork in Palestine', p. 135; ibid. *Arts of the City*, pp. 134–6; Golmohammadi, 'Minbar (B.);' Tabbaa, 'Originality and innovation', pp. 192–4.
19. Al-Imad, *The Fatimid Vizierate*, pp. 96–109; Dadoyan, *The Fatimid Armenians*, pp. 107–27; Daftary, *The Ismā'īlīs*, p. 222.
20. Sharon, *CIAP*, vol. 1, pp. 159–61.
21. See Nol, 'Cities, Ribāṭs' for a discussion of *thaghr* and *thughūr*, suggesting that *thaghr* meant fortress rather than frontier.
22. Huster, *Ashkelon 5*, p. 56; Sharon, *CIAP*, addendum to vol. 3, pp. 21–3.
23. Trans. from al-Maqrīzī, *Itti'āẓ*, in Jiwa, *Mediterranean Empire*, p. 82.
24. For other examples of miraculous rediscoveries of forgotten holy sites and relics, see Meri, *Cult of Saints*, pp. 43–7; Talmon-Heller, *Islamic Piety*, pp. 190–8, Frenkel, 'Constructing the sacred'.
25. Lev, *State and Society*, pp. 46–7.
26. Bierman, *Writing Signs*, pp. 105–8.
27. Afsaruddin, *First Muslims*, pp. 77–9.
28. See Mulder, *Shrines*, p. 81.
29. Al-Imad, *Fatimid Vizierate*, p. 44.

30. Ibid. p. 207.
31. Sharon, *CIAP*, vol. 1, p. 134; al-Qalqashandī, *Ṣubḥ al-Aʿshā*, vol. 11, p. 62.
32. Daftary, *Ismāʿīlīs*, pp. 185, 207.
33. Al-Imad, *Fatimid Vizierate*, p. 106.
34. Thomas Leisten analyses these overlapping terms (*mashhad* and *masjid*) in ibid. 'Dynastic tomb', esp. p. 478, n. 107. Ayman Fuʾad points out that mosques with shrines are the creation of the Fatimid era; see ibid. *al-Qāhira*, p. 14.
35. Diem and Schöller, *Living and the Dead*, vol. 1, pp. 29–33; vol. 2, pp. 248–9. See also Haider, *Origins*, pp. 243–7; Newman, *Twelver Shiism*, p. 61.
36. These inscriptions have most recently been published by Moshe Sharon, *CIAP*, vol. 1, pp. 154–9, vol. 5, pp. 28–38. On the pulpit's design, see Tabbaa, 'Originality and innovation;' Williams, 'The cult: Part II', p. 42.
37. Mulder, *Shrines*, pp. 82–99, esp. pp. 97–8. Following in Anne-Marie Eddé's footsteps, Mulder demonstrates that Shiʿism was 'a force to be reckoned with' in Ayyubid Syria; ibid. pp. 268–9.
38. Mouton, 'Reliques', p. 250; see also Pouzet, *Damas*, pp. 254–6.
39. According to Yaacov Lev, Egypt was going through this process from Badr al-Din's military dictatorship in the 1070s up to the Fatimids' demise approximately a hundred years later (Lev, *Saladin*, p. 117).
40. Sanders, 'Rise of Hafizi', pp. 100–1; Sanders, *Ritual*, pp. 74–82. See also De Smet, 'La translation', pp. 35–8.
41. De Smet, 'La translation', p. 43.
42. De Smet, 'Fêtes', pp. 195–6. See also Fuchs and de Jong, 'Mawlid'. Katz does not regard these occasions as festivals of the common people, but mainly of the Shiʿi ruling class. See Part Two for more on this issue.
43. Sayyid, *Nuṣūṣ*, p. 40. According to al-Maqrīzī, a second pair of chandeliers was sent to the al-Husayn Shrine in Karbala; al-Maqrīzī, *Ittiʿāẓ*, vol. 3, p. 85.

5

Excursus: Donations to Mosques and Shrines

Several decades before the donation of the twin chandeliers to the Husayni shrine in Ascalon, the Persian traveller, poet, philosopher and Isma'ili *dā'ī* Nasir Khusraw wrote a detailed description of an 'amazing' chandelier, or polycandelon, that he saw in Fustat sometime between 439/1047 and 442/1050. He outlines a silver lamp-holder with sixteen branches, each of which is 1.5 cubits long, holding seven hundred lamps, originally ordered by the caliph al-Hakim for the old mosque of 'Amr ibn al-'As.[1] Ibn Tuwayr and al-Qalqashandi (who reproduces some of Ibn Tuwayr's text) describe the same object as a 'huge, beautifully structured polycandelon that contained about 1500 lamps (*barraqāt*; glass cups), while its base included around 100 star-shaped lanterns (*qanādīl*)'.[2] This attention to detail is probably not accidental. As we will see in Part Two, lighting mosques and thoroughfares was a central ritual in Fatimid festivities, to the degree that a special term was coined for the nights of the first and fourteenth days of Rajab and Sha'ban: *layālī al-wuqūd* (the nights of kindling lights).[3] Nasir Khusraw also admiringly noted silver chandeliers bearing the Fatimid ruler's name in the Dome of the Rock.[4] In 1060, the sudden fall of one of those chandeliers, an immense *tanūr* which held 500 small glass lamps that hung from the dome's ceiling, was taken as a bad omen. The historian Mujir al-Din recalls that the incident frightened the residents of Jerusalem, who predicted that something terrible was about to happen in the lands of Islam. 'And indeed', he writes (in the fifteenth century), 'that event was the Frankish conquest of Jerusalem'.[5]

A Prophetic saying designates the donation of oil for the illumination of a sacred place such as Jerusalem as a proper substitution for actual prayer there. Moreover, it promises the donor that, as long as the oil he had provided for keeps burning and giving light, the angels will keep praying for him.[6] Al-Samhudi (d. 911/1505), the celebrated historian of Medina, recalls the very first contribution to the Prophet's Mosque: Syrian-made lamps, oil and chains, donated by the companion Tamim al-Dari and his servant Abu al-Barrad. When Muhammad entered the place of worship, he praised the two, exclaiming: 'You have illuminated Islam, as God has enlightened your path'.[7] In the twelfth century, the Prophet's tomb in al-Medina is said to have been illuminated by one gold, two crystal and over forty silver lamps (see Fig. 19.2). Ibn Taymiyya's public condemnation of the donation of gold or silver chandeliers and candlesticks to shrines in the fourteenth century obviously indicates that patrons continued to send such presents.[8]

In the Qur'an and other Islamic sources, light stands for knowledge, wisdom, revelation, inspiration, guidance, faith, scripture and truth.[9] Linking

Figure 5.1 Mosque lamp (Albert Gayet, *L'Art Arabe*, Paris: Librairies Imprimeries Réunies 1891, p. 243, Fig. 122).

the love of beauty and the love of God, al-Ghazzali explicitly mentions light as enjoyable:

> Healthy disposition derives pleasure from looking at lighs, flowers and pretty-coloured, finely painted, harmoniously formed birds, to such an extent that by looking at them man's cares and anxieties are alleviated, not seeking any benefit beyond the looking.[10]

Lights and lamps also have a symbolic dimension, as alluded to in the famous *Āyat al-Nūr*: 'God is the light of the heavens and the earth. His light may be compared to a niche possessing a lamp' (Q. 24: 35).[11] Lamps hanging within carved niches (that is, mihrab images) decorated medieval shrines. According to Mulder's interpretation, this image was meant to communicate to all Muslims an allusion to the divine light of the Light Verse. For Shiʿi Muslims, it was a reference to the imams, who are often described in the Shiʿi tradition as bearers of divine light, or as the 'lights of the faith'.[12]

I will end this arabesque-like survey of medieval lighting devices with a curious anecdote about the chandeliers of al-Aqsa, one that reflects the emblematic role of kindling light in a sacred place, in this case within the framework of religious polemics. It is taken from the travelogue of the Jewish traveller Meshullam of Volterra, who visited Jerusalem in 886/1481. He writes:

> The Moslems go inside [al-Aqsa] only after bathing five times, and they do not approach a woman three days previously. Many Moslem servants in the state of purification are there and they light seven lamps inside. I know, my friends, that there can be no doubt about this, because every year when the Jews go to the Synagogue on the eve of the 9th of Ab [commemorating the destruction of the Temple], all the lamps of the Temple Court [that is, al-Haram al-Sharif] go out on their own accord, and cannot be kindled again, and the Moslems know when it is the 9th of Ab, which they observe somewhat like the Jews because of this.[13]

Besides fancy lamps, candlesticks, devotional books and deluxe copies of the Qur'an, pieces of furniture such as minbars were the most commonplace donations to mosques and mausolea.[14]

Figure 5.2 Madrasa lamp, Cairo, fourteenth century (photo: Avshalom Avital, courtesy of the L. A. Mayer Museum for Islamic Art, Jerusalem).

Let us now take a quick look at minbars. Linda Jones neatly summarises medieval Muslim sources and contemporary research on the function and symbolism of the minbar. Derived from the root *n-b-r* (to be high or lofty) and positioned to the immediate right of the mihrab (prayer niche indicating the direction of Mecca), the pulpit is not merely an oratory tool, as she explains. It symbolises the devotee's ascent and orientation towards God. The specific wood from which pulpits were produced and the number of stairs leading to the preacher's seat were reportedly modeled on those of the pulpit of the Prophet. Likewise, preachers were expected to imitate his bodily gestures when mounting the stairs and addressing the faithful.[15] Although

Muslim tradition suggests that the minbar was introduced either by the Prophet himself or by one of his Companions exclusively for preaching the Friday sermon (*khuṭba*), it was primarily viewed as Muhammad's throne as ruler. For this reason, it was also used by the early caliphs. At that period, there were question marks over whether minbars should be set up exclusively in capital cities, or in the provinces, too. Nevertheless, these pulpits could soon be found throughout the Islamic world, and provincial governors stood on the minbar and delivered sermons in their capacity as the sovereign's local representative.[16]

Later generations continued to see the minbar as a symbol of authority, and the donation of minbars was a combined statement of sovereignty and religious devotion. Al-Basasiri, the Fatimid emir who captured Baghdad from the Sunni Seljuqs in 450/1058 and held it for a couple of months, sought to mark the rise of the new era by constructing a new pulpit in the city's Great Mosque. He declared the pulpit of the former rulers sinister, as 'from it hatred of the family of Muhammad has been proclaimed'.[17] The donation of a minbar by the Fatimid vizier al-Afdal ibn Badr al-Din al-Jamali carried yet another meaning, that of converting a space to Islam. Al-Afdal ordered his minbar for the mosque of the monastery of St Catherine, thereby signifying the completion of the Islamisation of the southern Sinai.[18] As will be discussed below, Saladin's erection of minbars in Hebron and Jerusalem aptly represented both his achievement of sovereignty over those sacred cities and his (re)Islamisation of the space after its reconquest.

Notes

1. Nasir Khusraw, *Book of Travels*, p. 53; Halm, *Fatimids and Traditions*, pp. 54–5. Al-Hakim seems to have abolished the ceremony for part of his reign (Walker, 'Popular Festivals', p. 77).
2. El-Toudy and Abdelhamid, *Selections*, pp. 188–9.
3. See p. 157 below.
4. Lev, *State and Society*, p. 53. For a description and illustrations of such lighting devices, see R. Hillenbrand, 'Uses of light', pp. 106–8.
5. Mujīr al-Dīn, *al-Uns al-Jalīl*, vol. 1, p. 443; quoted in Abouli, 'Saladin's legacy', p. 180. To the best of my judgement, the editor of *al-Uns al-Jalīl* mistakenly translates the hijri date as 1128. Abouali mistakenly places the event in al-Aqsa.

6. Mujīr al-Dīn, *al-Uns al-Jalīl*, vol. 1, p. 354.
7. Shalem, 'Fountains of light', pp. 3, 9, 10, n. 35.
8. See Ibn Taymiyya, *Majmū'at al-Fatāwā*, vol. 27, p. 68. His general attitude towards shrines is discussed below.
9. Graham, 'Light in the Qur'an'.
10. Translated and explained in Hillenbrand, 'Some aspects', pp. 254–5. For additional references on beauty and the sacred, see below.
11. Allan, *The Art*, p. 34; ibid. 'On giving'.
12. Mulder, 'Seeing the light'.
13. Adler, *Jewish Travellers*, p. 190.
14. Blair, *Text and Image*, pp. 242–3.
15. Jones, *Power of Oratory*, pp. 57, 64.
16. Pedersen, 'Minbar (A.)'. In his description of Palestine in the ninth century, Ibn Hawqal counted 'around twenty minbars', namely twenty congregational mosques (Ibn Ḥawqal, *Ṣūrat al-Arḍ*, p. 168).
17. Walker, *Orations*, p. 9; ibid. 'Islamic ritual', p. 124. See also Hillenbrand, *Islamic Perspectives*, pp. 78–9, and Tabbaa, 'Monuments' (on breaking minbars in Baghdad in 504/1111).
18. See Mouton, 'La presence chrétienne', pp. 613–24. According to Mouton's map, the monastery of St Catherine was the only Christian establishment left in the Sinai after the destruction (or abandonment) of eleven churches and two monasteries, as well as the transformation of three churches into mosques. On the minbar set in St Catherine, see also Bloom, *Arts*, p. 164; Ayyad, *Making of Mosque*, pp. 91–6.

6

Why Ascalon? Christian Martyrs and Muslim *Murābiṭūn* (Defenders)

'A long time has passed', the historian Ibn Fadl Allah al-ʿUmari (d. 749/1349) skeptically remarks, 'between the killing of al-Husayn and the construction of the [Fatimid] shrine in Ascalon'. Citing the ninth-century *Akhbār al-Dawla al-ʿAbbāsiyya*, al-ʿUmari appears to back the theory according to which al-Husayn's head was sent to Medina for re-interment next to his brother al-Hasan.[1] Al-ʿUmari's contemporary, the theologian and jurist Ibn Taymiyya, is more outspoken in his dismissal of the authenticity of the head in Ascalon. He insists that, until the establishment of the *mashhad* there, more than 430 (*hijri*) years after the death of al-Husayn, there was no textual or material indication whatsoever – be it on an epigraph, or a pilgrimage account – that the city ever housed the martyr's remains. Therefore, Ibn Taymiyya concludes, it is highly unlikely that al-Husayn's skull was inhumed in Ascalon, of all places.[2]

In the following pages, we will examine the validity of the claim of al-ʿUmari and Ibn Taymiyya via a careful examination of the sources, in an attempt to find an earlier text identifying Ascalon as the hallowed burial place of the head of the martyred al-Husayn. After all, it is plausible that Badr al-Din chose to invest in an already consecrated place. As noted by the anthropologist Michael Sallnow, 'reenergizing sacred sites and reorienting them to new politico-religious centers' is a way to extend political control and consolidate it.[3] However, given the lack of textual evidence for a earlier Husayni shrine, we will be obliged to acknowledge that Badr al-Jamali's *mashhad* is based on an altogether 'invented tradition', as defined by Eric Hobsbawm and Terence Ranger. They coined this oxymoron for a new 'ritual and symbolic complex', on the basis of the rather recent formulation of a myth presented in the honourable garb of antiquity, feeding a sense of continuity with a significant past.[4] Medieval mentalité was, in general, receptive to the miraculous unearthing of relics and the formation of new cults. Despite the reservations of some scholars, it adopted the discovery of al-Husayn's head and perpetuated its veneration for centuries to come.

While Mamluk historians such as al-ʿUmari question the historical continuity of the cult of the martyred al-Husayn in Ascalon, an Ascaloni cult of other martyrs pre-dated Islam. More specifically, the hill upon which the Fatimids built the shrine was once considered the burial place of decapitated Christian martyrs.[5] Their story is told by the bishop and historian Eusebius of Caesarea, who documented Emperor Diocletianus' violent campaign of oppression against the Christians in Palestine. On 14 December 308, the sixth year of the persecutions, he writes, a few Egyptians were interrogated by the gates of Ascalon. Having confessed their Christian faith and admitted that they were on a mission to aid their persecuted co-religionists in Cilicia, the defendants were brought before the governor for sentencing. A few of these Egyptians had their eyes and feet mutilated. Three others who had displayed 'marvelous bravery, enduring various kinds of martyrdom' were condemned to death. Two of them, Primus and Elias, were beheaded by the sword.[6]

Surprising as it may be, the badly damaged lower portion of the renowned Madaba Map – a sixth-century floor mosaic map of the Middle East, found in the town of Madaba in Transjordan – depicts the city of Ascalon (Ἀσκάλω[ν]) in its entirety. Just beyond the north-eastern corner of the town's walls, one can make out the Greek words [Τὸ τῶ]ν Αἰγυ[π]τίων – 'of the Egy[p]tians'.[7] The anonymous pilgrim of Piacenza who visited Ascalon in c. 570 CE mentions such a church. Like other Christian travellers of this era, he was interested in tombs of revered monks and martyrs, apart from biblical sites and monasteries.[8] Over half of the forty-five tombs that he visited while travelling from Jerusalem to Gaza and the Sinai fell under the first category.[9] Ascalon, the said pilgrim writes, is the 'resting-place of the three brothers who were Egyptian martyrs . . . They are usually called "the Egyptians"'.[10]

Was this tradition perpetuated? In all likelihood, the report of the pilgrim from Piacenza is the last existing report of a Christian visitor to the shrine of the three martyrs in *extra muros* Ascalon. Later pilgrims do not mention this site. A case in point is the Frankish Bishop Arculf, who dictated an account of his late-seventh-century Holy Land visit to the Abbot Adomnan of Iona (679–704). In the eight century, Epiphanius the Monk mentions Ascalon, noting that two other saints, Cosmas and Damian, were buried in *intra muros* Ascalon, inside its fortress.[11] The shrine to the Egyptians is also absent from the mosaic maps of Umm al-Rassas and Muʿin, which depict eighth-century Ascalon.[12] During these years, the city was better known for a well that was presumably dug by the Patriarch Abraham (on the basis of Genesis, 26: 22), as a number of Christian and Jewish late antique and medieval sources mention this site.[13]

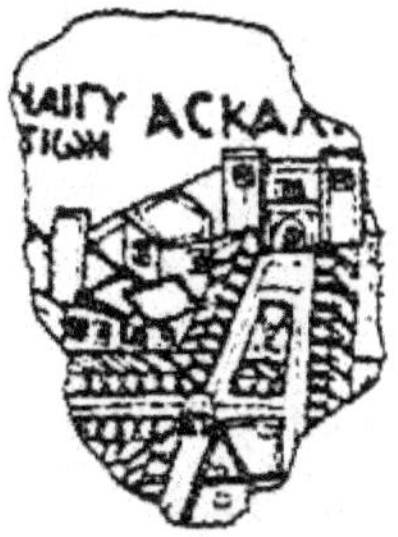

Figure 6.1 Madaba Map – Ascalon (Eugenio Alliata, 'The legends of the Madaba Map', in *The Madaba Map Centenary, 1897–1997*, p. 86. Courtesy of Studium Biblicum Franciscanum, Flagellation Monastery, Via Dolorosa).

What happened, then, to the church that had been established in memory of the beheaded Egyptians of Ascalon? Did the edifice, or perhaps only the local hagiographical tradition, survive into the Muslim era? Was the narrative modified at some point between the seventh and the late eleventh century to accommodate a decapitated Muslim martyr? Given the church's vulnerable location outside the city's walls, it stands to reason that it was abandoned and razed during the Arab conquests or in their aftermath. Alternatively, the shrine may have been destroyed in a raid in the decade of political instability known as the second *fitna* (64/683–74/693), or neglected later on as the Christian population diminished.

Following this politically tumultuous period, the caliphate encouraged Muslims to return to Ascalon by granting land and annual subsidies. Umayyad religious propaganda extolling the *faḍāʾil* (virtues) of Syria's coastal cities built up Ascalon's sanctity. Muslims willing to settle in this town and contribute to its defense were promised heavenly rewards equal to those granted warriors embarking on jihad. One hadith goes so far as to claim that pious *murābiṭūn* (defenders) who spent a day and night in Ascalon were guaranteed the standing of a *shahīd* (martyr), even if they died sixty years later in a land of infidels![14] The fact that the 'lives' of several illustrious early

Muslim sages and mystics include at least a brief sojourn in Ascalon may testify to the efficacy of such propaganda, or may be considered part of it. The city itself was bestowed the honorary titles *ʿarūs al-Shām* ('the bride of Syria'), *iḥdā al-ʿarūsayn* ('one of the two brides', the other being Gaza), and *dhurwat al-Shām* (the 'summit' of Syria).[15] In a number of traditions that evidently circulated during the Umayyad period (and were subsequently classified by hadith authorities as utter fabrication), the Prophet specifically refers to Ascalon. He mentions its cemetery as the burial place of martyrs, of whom 70,000 will enter Paradise on the Day of Resurrection. As noted above, the tombs of prophets and saints and a role in eschatological events were typical sources of sanctity for Islamic cities according to von Grunebaum's typology. The third source he lists – some sort of cosmological distinction – is absent from early traditions praising the virtues of Ascalon, as is any reference to al-Husayn or his head.[16]

What do we know about Islamic rule in Ascalon up to the eleventh century? As recorded in an inscription dated Muharram 155/December 771–2, the Abbasids initiated the construction of a mosque and minaret in Ascalon.[17] Following a local rebellion, the city was raided and sacked in 162/797. One of Ascalon's churches (three of which have been excavated) was destroyed in 311/924, perhaps during the short-lived Qarmati occupation. The church was soon rebuilt with the permission of the Abbasid Caliph al-Muqtadir. Three years later, the Church of the Virgin (also known as 'the Green Church') was burnt down by Muslims. Prohibited from rebuilding the church this time, the local bishop left the city, thereby probably ending the line of bishops in Ascalon and marking another signpost in the Islamisation of the city.[18]

In his brief yet enthusiastic entry on Ascalon in the 990s, the geographer al-Muqaddasi describes a well-fortified town with a mosque in the cloth market. He makes no mention of any sacred tombs.[19] The same can be said for Nasir Khusraw, an avid pilgrim of such places, who visited Ascalon in 438/1047. He does report of a splendid bazaar, a Friday mosque and a huge stone arch, the vestige of another mosque.[20] None of these sources clarify the fate of the ancient church of the Egyptians. That site's foundational relic, a martyr's skull, perhaps remained (both literally and figuratively) underground, where it awaited the arrival of later settlers or rulers who would (both literally and figuratively) exhume it and give it a new identity – this time Muslim. Drawing on other examples of the 'rebirth' of a shrine, it seems possible that a faintly remembered pre-Islamic narrative of cruelly decapitated martyrs of faith lingered on in the collective memory of the people of Ascalon, even though the commemorative shrine of those martyrs had long disappeared from the landscape. In the eleventh century, the Isma'ili Fatimids brought to life the site of that lost shrine with a new Islamic-Shi'i narrative. They founded a new mausoleum and established new rites therein: Islamic congregation and prayer, as well as the visitation of the martyred al-Husayn.

All this is but a conjecture, the tentative conclusion of the unsuccessful quest for a source earlier than Badr al-Jamali's epigraph of 484/1091–2, which points to an affiliation of Husayn's head with Ascalon. So far, all the sources likewise claiming that Ascalon constituted the Umayyad- or early-Abbasid-era burial place of the head of al-Husayn, which I have been able to find, post-date the inscription. The earliest of those sources is a little-known history of the Abbasid dynasty, written by Muhammad Ibn al-'Imrani (d. c. 580/1184–85). The book's introductory chapter summarises the era of the Prophet, the Rightly Guided Caliphs and the Umayyads. Within this framework, the author surveys the aftermath of the battle at Karbala.[21] He relates the chilling account of 'an old man from Kufa', who presents al-Husayn's death and beheading as the first in a series of killings that plagued the Umayyad dynasty and the house of Ziyad Ibn 'Ubayd Allah ever since.[22] Following the decapitation of al-Husayn, Ziyad launched a gruesome procession that brought the skull to Caliph Yazid who was then busy laying siege to Byzantine Antioche. Along the way, a miraculous pillar of light arose from the martyr's head to the sky, a marvel that impelled no less than 700 Christian monks to embrace the Islamic faith and convert their abbey into a mosque.[23] Unfortunately for modern scholars interested in Islamisation, Ibn al-'Imrani does not reveal the location of this wondrous mass conversion. He does mention that the sight of the head softened Yazid's heart. Overcome with remorse and anguish, the caliph washes the skull in rose water and wraps it in delicate shrouds. A group of men from Ascalon, who happened to witness this turn of events, asked Yazid for permission to bury the head in their city. The caliph duly granted this wish. A shrine, Mashhad al-Ra's, was built for the relic in Ascalon, and according to Ibn al-'Imrani, it 'draws visitors from all over to this day and age'.[24] Thus, Badr al-Jamali's quite recent invented tradition had become 'naturalised' in Ibn al-ʿImrani's chronicle, backed by a coherent historical narrative.

Ibn al-ʿImrani's contemporary, the historian Ibn al-Azraq al-Fariqi (d. 571/1176), offers a competing narrative. He suggests that Yazid's son, Caliph Muʿawiyah II, wanted to rid himself of the potentially dangerous remains of al-Husayn. To this end, he charged a 'group (*ṭāʾifa*)' with finding a suitable, remote location in which to dispose of the head. They chose Ascalon. Al-Fariqi explains that Muʿawiya also saw to the reburial of more than twenty other heads of al-Husayn's martyred companions at that time. The place he chose was to the north of the walls of Damascus, in what was known in the twelfth century as the Mosque of al-Qasb. On a personal note, he adds that this had been his favourite mosque during the three years he had spent in Damascus, 'a blessed place; not one who came to pray, or vow or invoke God there on a Friday night, did not get his need fulfilled'. Regarding the head of al-Husayn, al-Fariqi relates that it stayed in Ascalon until 549/1153–4, when the Fatimid caliph of Egypt realised that the Franks were about to conquer the city. The caliph then set out to Ascalon, to bring the sacred head to Cairo with his own hands. And, indeed, only three days later Ascalon was lost to the Franks. Al-Fariqi ends his account with the information that the Fatimids spent a great sum of money on the construction of a new shrine in honour of the head in Cairo and furnished it with splendid vessels of gold and silver, carpets and drapery that were transferred from the head's previous abode in Ascalon.[25]

Based on a rumour he probably heard in his hometown of Damascus, Sibt ibn al-Jawzi disseminated a new version. According to 'some people', he writes, 'in the days of the Egyptians' – that is, when the Fatimids ruled Syria – the head was taken (stolen?) from its shrine at Bab al-Faradis in Damascus and brought to Ascalon, where it was housed in a monument especially built for this purpose. When the Franks threatened to conquer the town, the relic was transferred to Cairo.[26] Sibt Ibn al-Jawzi's contemporary, the Egyptian historian Ibn al-Muyassar, like Ibn al-ʿImrani and Ibn al-Fariqi, seems to believe that the head was interred in Ascalon before the construction of the Fatimid *mashhad* towards the end of the eleventh century. Ibn al-Muyassar's version deviates only slightly from the one told in Badr al-Din inscription, except that it dates the foundation of the shrine (or its completion) to the time of Badr al-Din's son, Shahnshah al-Afdal.[27] This sounds quite plausible: as chief commander of the Fatimid military, al-Afdal visited Ascalon in 491/1098, soon after re-securing the state's control over Jerusalem. While savouring this victory over the Seljuks, he came upon the 'rundown [or decimated] burial site of al-Husayn's head (*makān dāris fīhi ra'ʾs al-Ḥusayn*)' and decided to construct a monumental shrine for the prized relic. When the building was ready, so communicates Ibn al-Fariqi, al-Afdal carried the perfumed head to its new abode with his own two hands. It bears noting that al-Maqrizi repeats this story almost verbatim. A near coeval of al-Maqrizi, the Ismaʿili historian Idris Ibn al-ʿImad, also claims that the Fatimids took the head from Damascus to their new capital Cairo (*al-Qāhira al-Muʿizziyya*, as the city was initially called), via a several-decades-long stop in Ascalon. Upon reaching its final destination, the relic was enshrined in a grand monument that became a pilgrimage site.[28]

Neither of the chroniclers, however, seems to have been aware of the dated inscription that was commissioned by the shrine's founder, Badr al-Jamali.[29] The survey of their narratives does not yield any evidence that pre-dates al-Jamali's inscription from the late eleventh century, according to which the head was laid to rest or commemorated in Ascalon. Texts that make this claim are either informed by creative anachronisms or based on hindsight. Notwithstanding, they demonstrate that several decades after its establishment the site was successfully incorporated into the map of Islamic sacred 'storied' places, deserving of visitation.

Notes

1. '*Wa-l-mudda baʿīd bayna maqtal al-Ḥusayn wa-mabnā mashhad ʿAsqalān*' (al-ʿUmarī, *Masālik al-Abṣār*, vol. 1, p. 281). Such reference to al-Husayn's head is absent from *Akhbār al-Dawla al-ʿAbbāsiyya*, ed. ʿAbd al-ʿAzīz al-Dūrī and ʿAbd al-Jabbār al-Mūṭlibī (1971), but perhaps al-ʿUmari had another version at his disposal. On al-ʿUmari and his work, see Richards, *Egypt and Syria*, pp. 3–9.
2. Ibn Taymiyya, *Majmūʿat al-Fatāwā*, vol. 27, pp. 240–1.
3. Sallnow, *Pilgrims*, pp. 97–8; cited in Frankfurter, *Pilgrimage*, p. 14.
4. Hobsbawm and Ranger, *Invention of Tradition*, pp. 1–14.
5. See Talmon-Heller, Kedar and Reiter, 'Vicissitudes', pp. 16–17.
6. Cureton, *History of the Martyrs*, p. 34.

7. Vincent and Mackay, *Hébron*, pp. 237–40; Avi-Yonah, *Madaba Mosaic*, p. 70; and, more recently, Alliata, 'The legends', p. 86.
8. Mayerson, 'Urbanization in Palestina', p. 241. See also Safrai, 'Is the map', p. 435.
9. Limor, *Holy Land Travels*, pp. 213, 238. In older scholarship he was refered to as Antoninus Placentinus.
10. Trans. in Wilkinson, *Jerusalem Pilgrims*, p. 85.
11. Ibid. p. 119. It also bears noting that the tenth-century Georgian-Palestinian Calendarium of saint-days mentions three Egyptian martyrs: Arès, Promos and Élie. Curiously enough, they were commemorated on a different day and in a different place than their above-mentioned compatriots: on 12 June in the village of Métoba in the vicinity of Jerusalem. See *Le Calendrier Palestino-Géorgien du Sinaiticus (Xe siècle)*, p. 248. I thank Milka and Rehav Rubin for this information.
12. Piccirrillo, 'Ascalon in mosaics', pp. 166–71.
13. See Masarwa, 'Transforming the Mediterranean', pp. 23–5. Later Muslim travellers also refer to it; see below.
14. The idea of *ribāṭ* is predicated on Qur'anic verses such as 8: 6 and 3: 200, and on the hadith. For the history of Palestine's coastal frontier and its glorification in Islamic traditions, see Goitein, 'The sanctity of Jerusalem', pp. 135–48; Elad, 'Coastal cities', pp. 146–67; Livne-Kafri, 'Jerusalem', pp. 77–8.
15. Ephrat, *Spiritual Wayfarers*, pp. 19–21. For a survey of the fortifications themselves, see Masarwa, 'Transforming the Mediterranean', pp. 160–7.
16. Bashear, 'Apocalyptic', pp. 197–8. In the Islamic tradition, the number seventy and its multiplications typically stand for plenty, rather than conveying an exact count (Schimmel, *Numbers*, p. 268). For its many recurrences in prayer formulas, see Part Two.
17. Sharon, *CIAP*, vol. 1, p. 132.
18. Schick, *Christian Communities*, pp. 95, 251–3; Peers, 'The church', p. 74. Local Jews are said to have actively participated in the church's demolition.
19. Al-Muqaddasī, *Aḥsan al-Taqāsīm*, p. 174; trans. in Collins, *Best Divisions*, p. 158. On the Jewish merchants of Ascalon, see Yagur, 'Between Cairo and Jerusalem', esp. pp. 58–61.
20. Nasir Khusraw, *Book of Travels*, p. 38. He does mention the tomb of Abu Hurayra near Tiberias, which he refrained from visiting even though he had wanted to do so, having been told that Shiʿi children pelt visitors with stones there (ibid. p. 19).

21. Ibn al-ʿImrānī, *al-Inbāʾ*, p. 9 (Shukrī ʿArrāf refers to this work in his *Ṭabaqāt al-Anbiyāʾ*, vol. 2, pp. 267–9). According to Qasim al-Samarrai (the editor of *al- Inbāʾ*s 1971 edition), Ibn al-ʿImrānī weaves folktales that 'added a considerable dose of spice to the bland reports of [earlier] historians like Tabari'. Tabari's text, however, is likewise not devoid of hagiographic elements (which are indeed part and parcel of pre-modern historiography); it also depicts a pillar of light emanating from al-Husayn's head and a white bird fluttering around it.
22. Ibn al-ʿImrānī, *al-Inbāʾ*, p. 55.
23. For more on the motif of light in the al-Husayn legend, see Valiegri, 'Al-Ḥusayn'.
24. Ibn al-ʿImrānī, *al-Inbāʾ*, p. 54.
25. Al-Fāriqī, *Taʾrīkh*, pp. 33–4.
26. Sibṭ ibn al-Jawzī, *Mirʾāt al-Zamān*, vol. 8, p. 169.
27. Al-Afdal was nominated by Badr al-Jamali's officers as vizier upon his father's death, thereby establishing the precedent of a hereditary vizierate in the Fatimid state.
28. Idrīs ʿImād al-Dīn, *ʿUyūn al-Akhbār*, vol. 4, 129; ibid. vol. 5, pp. 738–9.
29. Ibn al-Muyassar, *Akhbār Miṣr*, p. 38; al-Maqrīzī, *Ittiʿāẓ*, vol. 3, p. 22.

7

Excursus: Medieval Pilgrimage – Victor Turner's Input

Probably best known for introducing the term *communitas* to the scholarship on pilgrimage and rites of passage,[1] Victor Turner has made other valuable contributions to the research of sacred space. Although the paucity of source material on most medieval Muslim sites prevents us from fully applying Turner's insights to the subject at hand, his thought-provoking work at the very least promises to expose these limitations and still present constructive questions.

While conducting fieldwork in Mexico, in a region with many Catholic shrines and annual celebrations, Turner found it useful to expand his research horizons beyond any single place to networks of holy sites and to engage with the topography of rituals practised therein. He went on to map out the 'catchment area' from which pilgrims of each shrine were drawn and the attendant liturgical calendar, according to which they arrived at the various sites. In addition, Turner determined the spread, as well as overlap, of religious celebrations throughout the region. This research not only produced maps and diagrams, but also an imaginative analysis of the nexus between the local, regional and national; between nearby and far-off destinations; and between centre and periphery. Some of the most important destinations of pilgrimage, Turner concludes, are geographically peripheral. In other words, pilgrims do not necessarily flock to the 'centre', which Mircae Eliade has dubbed the *axis mundi*. And while shrines at the centre represent the authority of the dominant religious system, the peripheral shrine – whether more accessible for local pilgrims, or to the contrary, demanding the risky crossing of a stretch of wilderness – is often imbued with more power and 'magnetism'.[2]

As aluded to earlier, there are no extant sources that may indicate Mashhad Ra's al-Husayn's catchment area in the first decades following its establishment. Therefore, we are unable to determine whether the new building served primarily as Friday mosque for Ascalon's residents, or as a monument that attracted visitors from outside the city. And if so, whether those visitors arrived from the rural hinterland of Ascalon, the further towns of Gaza and Ramla, or perhaps the even more distant Jerusalem and Cairo. The conjecture that Mashhad Ra's al-Husayn was a pilgrimage destination seems plausible. Turner observes that even residents of capital cities that boast universally recognized sacred places embark on journeys to remote peripheral shrines.[3] My impression is that Muslims typically chose local sacred sites for a *ziyāra*, due to the significant role of local saints in the religious lives of their immediate surroundings, or as an expression of local patriotism, or simply in order to eliminate long-distance travel and its hardships.[4]

As far as can be seen, Badr al-Jamali was targeting a mixed crowd of Muslims (see the discussion on p. 52, above). But do we know anything about the composition of the town's inhabitants in the late eleventh and early twelfth century? In addition to the above-mentioned Nasir Khusraw, two itinerant scholars passed through the region during these years. Qadi al-Qudat ʿAbd al-Jabbar al-Hamadhani (d. 415/1024) visited the town several decades before the opening of Mashhad Ra's al-Husayn. Abu Bakr Ibn al-ʿArabi of Seville spent six months there in 485/1092 – that is, shortly after the establishment of the shrine – 'without being sated'. Polemicising against the Shiʿis, al-Hamadhani notes their existence and active proselytisation (*daʿwa*) in Ramla, Acre, Tyre and Ascalon.[5] Although only indirectly, Ibn al-ʿArabi also sheds light on the various denominations inhabiting the city. He refers to Ascalon very favourably, as 'a sea of learning (*adab*) whose waves range high and engulf, and whose water channels gush freely'.[6] He must have found Sunni, perhaps even Maliki teachers and brethren there, to make his stay so remarkable, as elsewhere in his work he complains that the Palestinian coast was full of 'deviant' Ismaʿilis and Imami Shiʿis. He even reports that his life was in danger while staying in Acre, due to a theological argument he had with several Ismaʿilis.[7] Despite passing through Ascalon the very year of the edifice's construction, Ibn al-ʿArabi makes no mention of the head of al-Husayn or the shrine.

To sum up the experimentation with Turner's inspiring ideas on the basis of sporadic medieval excerpts, I would argue that it helps to formulate questions and prompts the search for more data in new sources. It also cautions against the application of tempting theories that cannot be properly sustained by historical evidence.

Notes

1. Victor Turner, *Ritual Process,* ch. 4. For criticism of this concept, see Eade and Sallnow, 'Introduction'.
2. Victor Turner, *Dramas*, esp. pp. 178–9, 209–28. See also Erik Cohen's typology, as discussed above on p. 11.
3. Conspicuous examples include the Muslim pilgrimage from Jerusalem to Nabi Musa, the Jewish pilgrimage to Meron and the visitation to Nabi Samuel on the part of many Jerusalem residents of different faiths, even though the central sacred places of al-Aqsa and the Wailing Wall were accessible to Muslims and Jews respectively!
4. On the local veneration of Muslim saints, see also Taylor, *Vicinity*, p. 83; Talmon-Heller; 'Graves'; Grehan, *Twilight.*
5. Gil, *History of Palestine*, p. 312; al-Hamadhānī, *Tathbīt*, vol. 2, p. 595.
6. See the English translation in Drory, 'Some observations', p. 108. Ibn al-ʿArabi studied with al-Ghazzali and al-Turtushi, all of whom spent time in Jerusalem.
7. Drory, 'Some observations', pp. 121–4; Friedman, *Shīʿīs*, pp. 48–52.

8

From Ascalon to Cairo: The Duplication of Sacred Space

Ascalon was the last city to fall to the Crusaders, who after seizing Jerusalem in July 1099 captured the remainder of Palestine one city at a time. Ascalon's resilience may have stemmed from the massive walls that the Fatimids had built around it, especially during the vizierate of al-Ma'mun al-Bata'ihi. The latter also commissioned shipyards for improving the Egyptian fleet and its ability to protect the empire's coastal regions. The thirteenth-century geographer Ibn Shaddad seems to undermine the effect of this project on Ascalon, explaining that the Franks could not capture the city for such a long time simply because of the lack of a harbour in which their ships could dock.[1] Still, the later al-Qalqashandi (d. 820/1418) praises the Fatimids for the protection of their coastal borders and their concern with jihad; he lists Ascalon as one of the six cities that had been assigned fleets of nearly a hundred military ships and regiments of more than 5,000 registered well-paid warriors.[2] Other contributing factors to Ascalon's late conquest by the Franks may have been the ethos of the *ribāṭ* and *thughūr* (that is, the religious merit of defending Islamic fortresses and garrison towns), which had been fostered in Ascalon for centuries; the frequent changing of the city's guards; and perhaps even – who knows? – its patron saint, al-Husayn ibn ʿAli.

In any event, as the gateway to Egypt, Ascalon was of considerable strategic importance to the Fatimids, and they held on to the city in the face of recurrent attacks on the part of the Latins.[3] The latter were also well aware of the advantages of controlling the town, even though it lacked a proper port. Moreover, Ascalon's population had swelled with retreating soldiers and refugees, Muslim and Jewish, fleeing from places threatened or already captured by the Franks. According to William of Tyre, the Crusader historian, all these newcomers, even the children, were added to the military payroll with the objective of encouraging them to stay and defend the city.[4] A Genizah letter, written shortly after the conquests of 1099, mentions that Jews from Fustat and Ascalon had raised money to 'redeem the Scrolls of the Torah and . . . ransom the people of God who are in [Latin] captivity' (in this order!). Over 200 salvaged codices of the Hebrew bible, eight Torah scrolls and a hundred other volumes from the conquered town of Jerusalem arrived in Ascalon thanks to this fundraising.[5]

Only in the summer of 548/1153, after half a century of frequent clashes and countless raids by both sides culminating in a Frankish siege of seven months, the Muslim defenders of Ascalon finally surrendered.[6] King Baldwin III allowed the population to leave with its belongings. With the defeat at Ascalon, the Fatimids had lost all their Syrian possessions. It is against this backdrop that Ibn ʿAsakir, the eminent Syrian historian, compiled *Faḍl ʿAsqalān* – a non-extant work singing the praises of Ascalon, with which he exhorted Muslims to retake the city.[7] Thirty-five years later, Muslim troops indeed did so.

In the meantime, al-Husayn's head was withdrawn to the safety of Cairo. Ibn al-Azraq al-Fariqi, the author of the earliest surviving report on the transferal of the relic to Cairo together with the furniture and drapery of the mausoleum, credits the governor and qadi of Ascalon for its timely evacuation.[8] The later Ibn Iyas notes that 'the Muslims feared for the head of al-Husayn from the Franks', and therefore the caliph ordered its transfer to Cairo.[9] In light of several conspicuous incidents in which the Franks had desecrated Muslim holy sites – among them the looting and destruction of Mashhad al-Muhassin, a shrine commemorating al-Husayn's purported stillborn child on the outskirts of Aleppo in 518/1124[10] – there was reason to believe that the shrine in Ascalon would endure a similar fate.[11]

Characteristic of relic *translatio* stories, the skull's passage from Ascalon to Cairo was associated with wonders. Aside from showing signs of fresh blood[12] and smelling of musk – a typical marker of sanctity, immortality and divine presence[13] – the exhumed skull magically protected the servant who had carried it to Egypt. Citing Qadi Muhyi al-Din b. ʿAbd al-Zahir

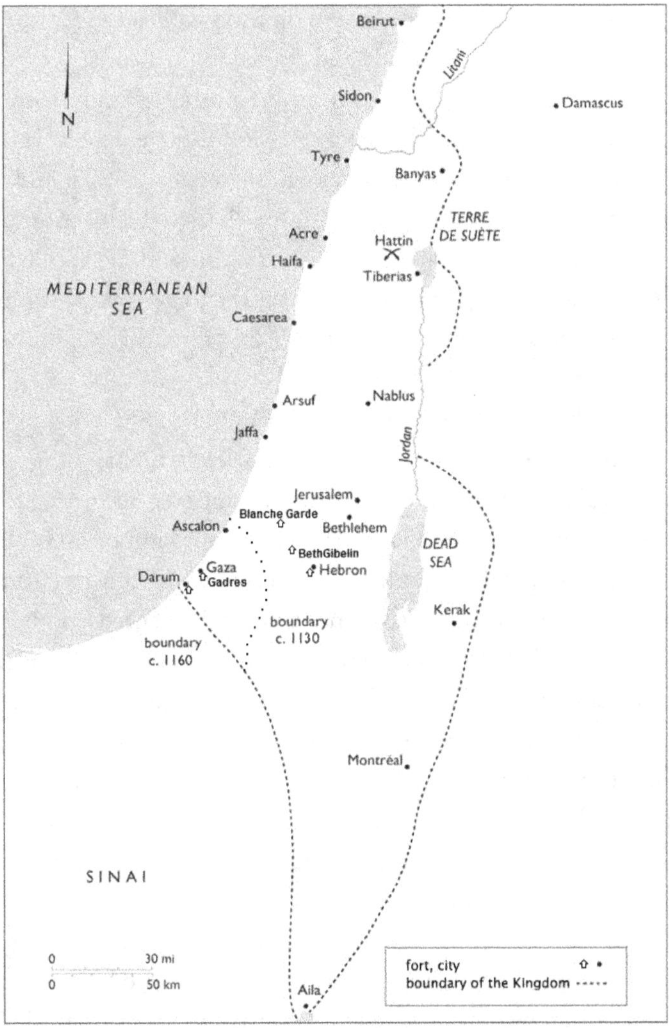

Figure 8.1 Map of the Latin Kingdom of Jerusalem, 524/1130 and 555/1160.

(d. 692/1293), Shihab al-Din al-Qalqashandi relates that Saladin, who had seized control of the palace in Cairo after the death of the last Fatimid caliph in 567/1171, intended to punish that servant for some untold offense. The sultan chose the notorious torture method of fastening *khanāfis* (beetles or centipedes) to the man's shaven head, so that the insects would drill into his skull, causing a slow and painful death. However, the alleged offender suffered no harm. Taken before the puzzled Saladin, he explained how he had carried the sacred head of al-Husayn on his own head to Cairo years ago, thereby earning the saint's gratitude and protection. In consequence, Saladin set the man free and 'showed him favour'.[14] Another version of this episode is even more hostile towards the sultan, as it contravenes his Sunni iconic image as an ideal ruler and compassionate human being.[15] First and foremost, this account notes that Saladin was trying to divulge the location of a secret chamber of treasures in the Fatimid palace. To this end, he applied the same means of torture as in the previous story. Yet, once again the saint interceded on behalf of the relic bearer. In this version, however, there is nothing about the sultan's subsequent repentance.[16]

ʿAbd al-Wahhab al-Shaʿrani (898/1492–973/1565) adds a few more realistic, although not necessarily historical details concerning the relic's transference, which I have not found in earlier sources. According to this Sufi writer, Saladin had to pay the Franks the handsome sum of 30,000 dinars in order to release the precious skull. Upon receiving it, the ex-Fatimid vizier placed it in a silk bag on a musk- and ambergris-scented ebony platform. Thereafter, Saladin led a military escort that delivered the head from the north-eastern suburbs of Cairo (al-Qaṭāʾiʿ) to the royal palace. Along the way, the skull performed wonders that convinced even skeptical ʿulamaʾ of its authenticity.[17] A mystic rather than a historian,[18] al-Shaʿrani may well have been describing how the ceremony should have been executed from his perspective, rather than what actually transpired. Interestingly, there is no trace of Sunni-Shiʿi animosity in his description.

Two stopovers between Ascalon and Cairo, where the head was set down in order to allow the porters some rest, appear in an earlier account by the more skeptic al-Harawi (d. 611/1215). Over time, the shrines of al-Zanbur and al-Tibr were erected on what came to be known as those 'two blessed spots'.[19] Roughly 250 years later, Ibn Shahin (d. 873/1468) opens his short chapter on Egyptian holy places with the hypothesis that these two monuments mark the final resting places of al-Husayn's skull and of his brother al-Hasan.[20] In Yaacov Lev's estimation, the Mosque of al-Tibr was actually built in the mid-tenth century (namely, before the Fatimids) as a mausoleum for the head of Ibrahim b. ʿAbd Allah (d. 145/763), a Shiʿi who rebelled against al-Mansur, the second Abbasid caliph. As in the case of the Umayyad Mosque in Damascus, historiography and popular lore fed off each other to create the foundational story of the Mosque of al-Tibr. Not only did the monument preserve the age-old sanctity and *baraka* of the site, but it also perpetuated the root cause of its consecration: the severed head of a martyr. What had changed over time was the affiliation of that head.

Returning to our head, we may speculate that in 1153, insomuch as Ascalon's defenders and inhabitants had been reluctant to leave behind al-Husayn's skull as they withdrew from the vanquished city, the Fatimid administration must have been eager to bring this remnant of the dynasty's illustrious forefather to their seat of government in Cairo. The significance of the relic is evident from accounts of the struggle over where to house it in the capital. Al-Qalqashandi, who mentions Mashhad Ra'ʾs al-Husayn in his description of the Fatimid Eastern Palace, depicts this struggle. He contends that a mausoleum had been prepared in advance for the relic, by Vizier al-Salih ibn Talaʾiʿ b. Ruzziq who intended to enshrine the head in a newly built congregational mosque outside the city walls, opposite the southern gate (Bab al-Zuwayla).[21] However, the men of the court of al-Faʾiz (r. 549/1154–555/1160), the adolescent imam-caliph, demanded that it be housed in a *mashhad* on the palace grounds, near the tombs of other direct ancestors of the Fatimids. Undoubtedly cognizant of the need to bolster the legitimacy of a mere child who rose to power in the aftermath of a recent coup, his courtiers sought to emphasise his ties to *ahl al-bayt* and the distant ʿAlid past.[22] Al-Faʾiz's entourage ultimately prevailed, and the head was interred within the palace confines (see Fig. 17.1 for a map of Fatimid Cairo).

A casket (*tābūt*), which had been made especially for al-Husayn's head, was found in the mosque named after him during restoration work in 1939. It is a fine example of twelfth-century Islamic woodwork. Decorated on three sides, half of its surface is filled with a Qurʾanic inscription composed in Naskhi and Kufi scripts. The other design elements consist of hexagons, stars and rich vegetal arabesques. The signature of the artist, the Aleppan carpenter ʿUbayd Ibn Maʿali who also renewed the cenotaph of the great jurist al-Shafiʿi in 1178, attests to the fact that he was proud of this work.[23] In Caroline Williams's estimation, the casket was produced while the head was in transit from Ascalon, in approximately 550/1155. The Qurʾanic verses that adorn it were carefully selected to convey the Shiʿi doctrine of redemption, as they refer to *ahl al-bayt*, intercession, purity, light, *walāya* (fidelity (to

Figure 8.2 Wooden casket of the head, c. 550/1154 (John A. and Caroline Williams Archive, courtesy of Aga Khan Documentation Center at MIT).

the imams)) and self-sacrifice. Moreover, ample use was made of the number seven, which represents the seven imams and the seven pillars of the Isma'ili doctrine[24] and holds a prominent place in Isma'ili cosmology, spiritual hierarchy and topography of the human body and soul.[25]

The relocation of al-Husayn's head calls to mind the earlier removal from Ifriqiya (Qayrawan) to Cairo of the Fatimid forefathers' coffins (*tawābīt*) in 362/973. This had been the initiative of al-Mu'izz li-Din Allah (341/953–365/975), the first Fatimid caliph to reign over Egypt. After traversing the North African desert, the three coffins were triumphantly displayed to the public in the newly established capital. Thereafter, the remains were buried in the Fatimids' Eastern Palace, in what came to be known as Turbat al-A'imma (the mausoleum of the imams).[26] The Isma'ili historian Idris Ibn al-'Imad draws a correlation between the two episodes:

> It is said that he [al-Mu'izz bi-Allah] carried the coffins of al-Mahdi bi-Allah, al-Qa'im bi-Amr Allah, and al-Mansur bi-Allah to Cairo and buried their noble bodies there. It is also said that the coffins of the [three] hidden imams (*al-a'imma al-mastūrīn*)[27] were brought there. And we have already mentioned that the Fatimid imams [*a'immat al-ẓuhr*, lit. 'the revealed imams'] brought the head of the imam al-Husayn to Cairo and buried it there.[28]

The caliph's custom of visiting this mausoleum upon returning to the palace on Fridays and holidays[29] seems to betray an unusual preoccupation with ancestral tombs and lineage. In 386/996, Caliph al-ʿAziz took the coffins with him on his campaign against the Hamdanid rulers of Aleppo. His firm belief in the talismanic power of relics notwithstanding, al-ʿAziz never made it to the battle field; he fell ill and died on the road to northern Syria.[30] His son and immediate heir, al-Hakim bi-Amr Allah (r. 386/996–411/1021), displayed a similar obsession with familial relics and was prepared to take some extreme measures in order to possess them. A case in point was his decision to plunder the house of Jaʿfar al-Sadiq, the sixth Shiʿi imam (and the last to be recognized by both the Imamiyya and the Ismaʿiliyya), in Medina. As per the lengthier versions of this story, al-Hakim sent a certain *dāʿī* (proselytiser) to the house which had been sealed for nearly 250 years. The agent burst in and expropriated al-Sadiq's prayer mat,[31] bed, sword, *muṣḥaf* (codex) of the Qurʾan and lists of ʿAlid notables (*rusūm al-ashrāf*). Justifying this act of pillage, al-Hakim declared that he had the strongest claim to the imam's estate.[32] In addition, he planned an even more ambitious, not to say outrageous, project: transferring the remains of Muhammad and the first two caliphs to Cairo. He was stopped in the nick of time.[33]

The relocation of al-Husayn's skull a century and a half later may be viewed as yet another Fatimid initiative to obtain ancestral relics and create sacred space for attendant rites, with the objective of bolstering the dynasty's credentials as the rightful heir to the Prophet. As noted earlier, the head was laid to rest in a special shrine adjacent to the mausoleum housing tombs of the Fatimid imam-caliphs in the Great Eastern Palace, yet separate from them, at the outset of the reign of al-Faʾiz.[34]

The sources on the reception of this new monument in the Great Eastern Palace are significantly richer than those on the shrine in the peripheral city of Ascalon. It served as a major venue for the public observance of the two most important days on the Shiʿi calendar: al-ʿAshura (the tenth day of Muharram) and Ghadir Khumm (the eighteenth day of Dhu al-Hijja), conflating holy space with sacred time.[35] More often than not, religion and politics were inseparably mixed on these occasions. According to holiday protocol, the Fatimid imam-caliph would arrive at the Husayni shrine for receiving 'the salute and homage (*li-l-khidma wa-l-salām ʿalayhi*)'. The chief qadi would then utter the formula 'Peace be upon the Commander of the Faithful, and God's mercy and blessing'. In closing, he would kiss the imam's foot.[36]

Drawing on Ibn al-Muyassar, al-Maqrizi surveys other rituals that were performed at this *mashhad* until the Fatimid Empire's demise. For instance, anyone entering the imam-caliph's service would first go to the shrine, kneel and kiss the ground in front of the tomb.[37] On al-ʿAshura Day, devotees tearfully lamented al-Husayn's untimely death and cursed his killers.[38] The love for al-Husayn and the hatred towards his enemies were nurtured in Shiʿi hadith collections that cite the Prophet explicitly commanding those feelings and promising various rewards for compliance.[39] At times, tensions and conflicts between participants of various denominations and between rulers and ruled – rather than the spirit of 'communitas', as suggested by Eade and Sallnow in their critique of Turner's phenomenology – may have prevailed at the shrine.[40] Such an occurrence may have propelled the imam-caliph al-Amir in 516/1122–3 to issue a decree that banned public recitations of the tragedy of al-Husayn (*qirāʾat masraʿ al-Ḥusayn*) in order to avoid disturbances.[41]

Ibn Tuwayr (d. 617/1220), a Sunni, describes the first time that the Day of al-ʿAshura rites were performed at the shrine of the head of al-Husayn, instead of at the al-Azhar Mosque. Having served in the administration of both the last Fatimids and the first Ayyubids in Egypt,[42] he was indeed a veteran observer of Egyptian court ceremony. In his comprehensive account of the inauguration of the ʿAshura rites, Ibn Tuwayr depicts the chief qadi and the notaries (*al-shuhūd*) making their way to the shrine in the early morning hours, donning clothes of mourning. They were joined by other men of religion and government officials at the *mashhad*, where professional reciters of the Qurʾan and poets chanted solemn dirges for three hours in a row. At the end of the mourning session at the shrine, according to Ibn Tuwayr's descriptions, the dignitaries returned to the palace for a solemn meatless 'meal of sorrow (*simāṭ al-ḥuzn*)'. Great quantities of food were prepared, so that there was enough to be shared with 'the people' after the dignitaries had had their fill. Throughout the morning hours, Cairo's shops remained closed and mourners (*nawwāḥ*) walked the streets.[43]

The recital of poetry about al-Husayn (and other Shiʿi imams)[44] was considered meritorious and always accompanied pilgrimage to the tomb of al-Husayn at Karbala. Ibn Qawlawayh – the author of the first extant collection of Shiʿi traditions regarding *ziyāra* to the tomb of the Prophet, the shrines of the imams and those of other members of *ahl al-bayt* – devotes an entire chapter to 'The merits of whoever recites a poem about al-Husayn, weeps, and induces weeping'.[45] Some of the poems depict delegations of angels visiting the tomb (the angels Gabriel and Michael supposedly visit it every night!), greeting the pilgrims, escorting and protecting them, and most importantly interceding on their behalf, so that all their sins are forgiven.[46]

Paula Sanders delves into the official Fatimid court ceremonies on ʿId al-Ghadir, analysing the evolution of the day's rituals in light of political developments. Shiʿis believe that Ghadir Khumm is when Muhammad expressly designated ʿAli as his heir on the eighteenth day of Dhu al-Hijja 10/632, upon their return from what was to be the Prophet's last hajj.[47] In the second half of the twelfth-century – after the schism in the Fatimid dynasty and the ascension of the imam-caliph al-Hafiz (r. 524/1130–544/1149)[48] – the formal rituals of ʿId al-Ghadir in Cairo were held at the Husayni shrine. What had earlier been a mass celebration with a broad, inter-denominational appeal[49] was converted into an unmistakably sectarian, Ismaʿili-Hafizi festival. At this stage, the ceremonies were stripped of their popular elements. They consisted of a sermon (*khuṭba*), the reading of Muhammad's announcement designating ʿAli his successor, and two *rakʿa*s (cycles) of prayer at the shrine. Finally, an extravagant procession in honour of the imam-caliph took place within the royal compound.[50]

If in late-eleventh-century Ascalon Badr al-Din endeavoured to create a shrine with an all-Muslim appeal – inclusive of all believers who come to pay their respects to the Prophet's grandson, pray in a sacred place by a sacred relic and ask for saintly intercession (*shafāʿa*) and blessing (*baraka*) – the shrine's mid-twelfth-century Cairene counterpart was geared toward Ismaʿilis. As the dynasty struggled to survive, it sought to rally behind exclusive symbols and holy places of its own. Within a few years, however, the Sunnis would reassert their hegemony over Egypt, ushering in a new chapter in the history of the shrine.

Notes

1. Sharon, *CIAP*, vol. 1, p. 130–4.
2. El-Toudy and Abedlhamid, *Selections*, pp. 222–3.

3. For a detailed history of this conflict, see Prawer, 'Ascalon'.
4. Sharon, *CIAP*, vol. 1, pp. 134–5.
5. Goitein, *Mediterranean Society*, vol. 5, pp. 373, 376.
6. For details, see Hoch, 'The Crusaders' strategy'.
7. Elisséeff, 'Ibn ʿAsākir', p. 714. See also Lindsay, 'Caliphal and moral', p. 257; Stewart, '*Maqāmāt*', p. 226. For a list of *Faḍāʾil ʿAsqalān*, see the excursus on p. 85. See also Anabseh, 'The sanctity'.
8. Al-Fāriqī, *Taʾrīkh*, p. 211. The note on the removal of other objects besides the relic is curious, since according to other informants the minbar was left behind and only several decades later transported to Hebron, where it still stands till today (see below, pp. 103–4).
9. Ibn Iyās, *Badāʾiʿ*, vol. 1/1, p. 227.
10. Mulder, *Shrines*, p. 74.
11. Another relic that was relocated in anticipation of Frankish occupation and desecration is *Muṣḥaf ʿUthmān*, a special copy of the Qurʾan. See Mouton, *Damas*, p. 258, and Talmon-Heller, 'Scriptures as holy objects', pp. 233–5.
12. Al-Maqrīzī, *al-Khiṭaṭ*, vol. 2, p. 408.
13. See Ergin, 'Fragrance of the Divine', p. 72; Hedrick and Ergin, 'Shared Culture'.
14. Ibn ʿAbd al-Ẓāhir, *al-Rawḍa*, pp. 30–1; al-Qalqashandī, *Ṣubḥ al-Aʿshā*, vol. 3, p. 396. Carrying the head is said to have had wondrous, albeit symbolic consequences also for the camel that took it from Damascus to Medina in the days of Yazid (as in al-Waqidi's version regarding the burial of the head): its meat became too bitter to eat. See Sibṭ ibn al-Jawzī, *Tadhkirat al-Khawāṣṣ*, p. 240.
15. Eddé, *Saladin*, pp. 486–509.
16. Al-Maqrīzī, *al-Khiṭaṭ*, vol. 2, pp. 408–9; also see Sindawi, 'Head', p. 269 and n. 41.
17. Al-Shaʿrānī, *al-Ṭabaqāt al-Kubrā*, vol. 1, p. 21. For these wonders, see al-Qalqashandī, *Ṣubḥ al-Aʿshā*, vol. 3, pp. 395–6; al-Maqrīzī, al-*Khiṭaṭ*, vol. 2, pp. 408–10; Sindawi, 'Head', p. 269, n. 41.
18. Winter, *Society and Religion*, pp. 72–5.
19. Meri, *Lonely Wayfarer*, p. 96. On al-Harawi's critical attitude, see below, p. 94. Lev offers a different narrative in ibid. *State and Society*, p. 150; ibid. *Saladin*, p. 122.
20. Ibn Shāhīn, *Kashf al-Mamālīk*, p. 98. In 1105/1693, the Sufi shaykh al-Nabulsi visited a domed shrine known as Raʾs al-Hasan wa-l-Husayn near Hamah. Although noting that this identification is certainly unfounded (*amr lā yakhlū*

min mayn wa-lā mayn), he recited the *Fātiḥa* and an invocation at the site (al-Nābulsī, *al-Ḥaqīqa*, p. 163).

21. Al-Qalqashandī, *Ṣubḥ al-Aʿshā*, vol. 3, pp. 395–6.
22. Sanders, 'Ḥâfiẓî historiography', p. 101.
23. His brother Salman was one of the four craftsmen that produced Nur al-Din's famous minbar; Yeomans, *Art and Architecture*, p. 115. As the historical record demonstrates, artisans had no inhibitions about working for both Sunni and Shiʿi patrons.
24. Williams, 'Qurʾanic inscriptions', pp. 3–14; Bloom, *Arts*, pp. 166–7; Tabbaa, *Transformation*, pp. 96, 185, n. 48. The casket is presently kept in the Museum of Islamic Art in Cairo.
25. Schimmel, *Numbers*, pp. 149–50; Ebstein, *Mysticism and Philosophy*, pp. 192–4.
26. Leisten, 'Dynastic tomb', p. 473; al-Maqrīzī, *al-Khiṭaṭ*, vol. 2, p. 351. Alternative names have been noted above, p. 52.
27. According to Ismaʿili lore, those imams bridge the time-gap between Muhammad b. Ismaʿil (d. c. 179/795), the seventh imam of the Ismaʿilis, who went into hiding, and the emergence of the Ismaʿili imams as the Fatimid caliphs in 296/909.
28. Idris ʿImād al-Dīn, *ʿUyūn al-Akhbār*, vol. 5, p. 738.
29. Jiwa, *Mediterranean Empire*, p. 104; al-Maqrīzī, *Khiṭaṭ*, vol. 2, p. 352.
30. Canard, 'al-ʿAzīz biʾllāh', p. 825.
31. The prayer mat was apparently used by later caliphs to embellish the *muṣallā* (outdoor prayer space) on festival days. See Ibn ʿAbd al-Ẓāhir, *al-Rawḍa*, p. 40; al-Sayyid, *Nuṣūṣ Ibn al-Maʾmūn*, p. 86. See also Walker, *Orations*, p. 40.
32. ʿIzz al-Dīn Ibn al-Athīr, *al-Kāmil fī al-Taʾrīkh*, vol. 8, p. 59; Ibn Taghrī Birdī, *al-Nujūm*, vol. 4, p. 222. Walker, 'Purloined symbols', pp. 368–9.
33. For an in-depth look at this nearly-successful undertaking, see the Andalusi geographer Abū ʿUbayd al-Bakrī (d. 487/1094), *al-Masālik*, pp. 609–10; Lev, *State and Society*, p. 150. On the Abbasid search for relics, see al-Hibri, 'The Abbasids'.
34. De Smet, 'Translation', pp. 37–41; Sanders, 'Ḥâfiẓî historiography', p. 100. By 555/1160, Vizier al-Salih finished building what he hoped would be his own mausoleum. See Dadoyan, *Armenian*, p. 172; Williams, 'The cult: Part II', p. 53.
35. Ibn Qawlawayhi's *Kāmil al-Ziyārāt* (fourth/tenth century), a compilation largely devoted to the visitation of the grave of al-Husayn in Karbala, lists several preferred dates for a visit there: Yawm ʿArafa, Niṣf (mid) Shaʿban and the month of Rajab. For the latter, see Part Two.

36. Leisten, 'Dynastic tomb', pp. 475–9; Sanders, *Ritual*, pp. 18–19.
37. Muhammad, *Masājid Miṣr*, p. 369.
38. Al-Maqrīzī, *al-Khiṭaṭ*, vol. 2, p. 408. According to Daftary, ceremonies marking al-Husayn's martyrdom in Karbala were inaugurated already during the reign of the first Fatimid caliph; ibid. *The Ismāʿīlīs*, pp. 207, 185. De Smet surmises that Yawm al-ʿAshura became an official holiday around 515/1121; ibid. 'Les fêtes', pp. 190–3. For more on the Fatimid ʿAshura, see Lev, *State and Society*, p. 146.
39. See, for example, twelve such hadiths in Ibn Qawlawayhi, *Kāmil al-Ziyārāt*, pp. 112–17.
40. Eade and Sallnow, *Contesting the Sacred*, pp. 5, 18.
41. Lev, *State and Society*, pp. 145–6; Stewart, 'Popular Shiʿism', p. 55.
42. Sayyid, introduction to al-Maqrīzī, *al-Khiṭaṭ*, vol. 2, pp. *31–3.
43. Ibn Ṭuwayr, *Nuzhat al-Muqlatayn*, pp. 223–4; al-Maqrīzī, *al-Khiṭaṭ*, vol. 2, p. 420.
44. See Asani, 'Devotional practices', pp. 165–7.
45. Sindawi, 'Visit', p. 240; Ibn Qawlawayh, *Kāmil al-Ziyārāt*, pp. 208–11.
46. Sindawi, 'Visit', p. 252; Ibn Qawlawayh, *Kāmil al-Ziyārāt*, pp. 223–6, 231–6.
47. On Twelver and Ismaʿili narratives and commemoration of this event, see Sanders, *Ritual*, pp. 121–6.
48. Following the assassinations of Caliph al-Amir (495/1101–524/1130) and Vizier Kutayfat, and the disappearance of al-Tayyib, the infant heir, the throne was assumed by al-Hafiz, the deceased ruler's cousin (Sanders, *Ritual*, p. 4). For detailed accounts of those events, see Daftary, *The Ismāʿīlīs*, pp. 256–323; ibid. *Short History*, pp. 106–14, 185–93.
49. Paula Sanders, *Ritual*, p. 129.
50. Ibid. pp. 131–4, 202, n. 49.

9

Excursus: Arabic Treatises in Praise of Ascalon

A Preliminary List of Ninth- to Fifteenth-century Works

- Abū al-Ḥasan ʿAlī b. Muḥammad al-Madāʾinī (d. 225/839–40), *Fatḥ ʿAsqalān* (The Conquest of Ascalon).[1]
- Abū Muḥammad al-Ḥasan Ibn Ādam al-ʿAsqalānī (d. 325/937?), *Juzʾ fīhi Faḍl ʿAsqalān* (A Chapter in Praise of Ascalon).[2]
- ʿAlī b. al-Ḥasan Ibn ʿAsākir (d. 571/1176), *Faḍāʾil ʿAsqalān* (The Merits of Ascalon).[3]
- Taqī al-Dīn ʿUthmān b. ʿAbd al-Raḥmān Ibn al-Ṣalāḥ al-Shahrazūrī (d. 643/1245), *al-Aḥādīth fī Faḍl al-Iskandariyya wa-ʿAsqalān* (Hadith on the Merit of Alexandria and Ascalon). Ms. 1389 in Berlin Stadtbibliotek (20 folios).[4]
- Anonymous, *Faḍāʾil al-Shām wa-Faḍāʾil Mudunihā wa-Bayt al-Maqdis wa-ʿAsqalān wa-Ghazza wa-l-Ramla wa-Arīḥā wa-Nāblus wa-Baysān wa-Dimashq wa-Ḥumṣ wa-dhikr al-anbiyāʾ al-mashhūrīn fīhā wa-dhikr al-ṣaḥāba al-madfūnīn fīhā* (The Merits of Syria and its Towns Jerusalem, Ascalon, Gaza, Ramla, Jericho, Nablus, Beth-Sheʾan, Damascus and Homs, with the mention of its known Prophets and the Companion that were buried in the Land). Ms. Tubingen no. 26 (24 folios), copied in Damascus in 741/1340–1.[5]
- [A chapter of] Shams al-Dīn Muḥammad al-Asyūṭī (d. 880/1475–6), *Itḥāf al-Akhiṣṣā bi-Faḍāʾil al-Masjid al-Aqṣā* (Presenting the Choice Merits of the al-Aqsa Mosque).[6]

Notes

1. Bahādur, *Muʿjam mā ullifa*, p. 21.
2. Mentioned by Ibn Ḥajar in his *al-Muʿjam al-Mufahras*, p. 182.
3. Mentioned by al-Dhahabī in his *Taʾrīkh al-Islām*, vol. 48, p. 75. Ibn ʿAsakir also compiled a work in praise of Rajab (see below).
4. Bahādur, *Muʿjam mā ullifa*, p. 67.
5. Dated to the seventh/twelfth century. See Ibrāhīm, *Faḍāʾil*, pp. 166–7, 283–93.
6. For details of the published edition, see the Works Cited.

10

The Shrine in Cairo under the Sunni Ayyubids and Mamluks

Upon overthrowing the Fatimid imamate in 567/1171, Saladin reestablished Sunni dominion over Cairo. A host of changes were introduced: the name of the Fatimid imam-caliph was eliminated from Friday sermons; the preachers who delivered the *khuṭba* once again donned the black garb of the Abbasids; the Shiʿi formula for the call to prayer was replaced by the Sunni version and the names of the first three Rightly Guided Caliphs, whom the Shiʿis loathed, were re-introduced into the liturgy. Patently Ismaʿili decorations, such as heavy silver plates inscribed with the names of the imam-caliphs that typically hung above the mihrab, were removed from mosque walls. The institution most closely associated with the Fatimids, al-Azhar, lost much of its prestige, as it ceased to function as a Friday mosque and Ismaʿili missionary centre. The Fatimid palaces were gradually replaced with a Sufi *khānqāh*, commercial space and artisan workshops.[1] Ismaʿili judges gave way to Sunni judges, Ismaʿili *daʿwa* sessions were discontinued, and madrasas for teaching Islamic law according to the four Sunni schools were established. The Ayyubids built twenty-three madrasas in Cairo and Fustat alone.

The Husayni shrine remained popular and continued to attract local devotees, as well as pilgrims from afar. Such continuity should not surprise us. In her survey of forty medieval shrines in Greater Syria and Egypt, many of which commemorate ʿAlid figures, Stephennie Mulder has found that nearly all of them were venerated and maintained by both Shiʿis and Sunnis alike, at different times and simultaneously. The Sunni rulers who initiated the construction and reconstruction of ʿAlid monuments and saw to their upkeep must have found these undertakings religiously plausible and politically advantageous. Some of them may have endeavoured to assert Sunni 'rights' at *ahl al-bayt* shrines, others to co-opt local Shiʿis and promote rapprochement or, at least, coexistence with the other denomination.[2] Saladin's conduct in Aleppo may have been a case in point. Upon taking the city, which was known for its considerable Shiʿi population, he visited the local Shrine of the Rock (which was also dedicated to the head of al-Husayn)[3] and contributed 10,000 dirhams towards its upkeep. His son al-Malik al-Zahir, ruler of Aleppo (1186–1217), was also a generous benefactor of this monument.[4] In all likelihood, the Shrine of the Rock drew both Sunni and Shiʿi crowds, who did not necessarily agree over the saint's role, or the meaning and purpose of pilgrimage to his shrine. Despite being a saintly figure for Sunni and Shiʿi Muslims alike, only the Shiʿis confer al-Husayn's suffering and martyrdom with a far-reaching cosmological and redemptive function.

Ibn Jubayr, a self-proclaimed adversary of Shiʿism, visited Mashhad Raʾs al-Husayn in Cairo during the spring of 578/1182. In fact, it is the first site mentioned in the relevant chapter of his travelogue, 'A Note on Misr and Cairo and Some of their Wonderful Monuments'. Although he deems the shrine 'beyond description and beyond the powers of the mind to comprehend', he does describe it, of course: as an ornately decorated monument built around a silver coffin which holds the relic.[5] He was also impressed by the piety of its visitors, who crowded the main hall, circumambulated the relic, touched the cloth mantle on the coffin, wept, and fervently prayed by the head. To borrow the words of Ian Netton concerning Ibn Jubayr's description of Mecca and Medina and the ceremonies which he witnessed there, his narrative is 'infused with reverent joy',[6] conveying an 'addictive use of superlatives', so typical of the *adab* (etiquette) of the tourist. Still, I believe that unwittingly, perhaps, Ibn Jubayr offers some valuable insights into the religious experience at holy places in general and at the shrine of Husayn's head in particular. To begin with, he perceives the sacred as beautiful and beauty not only as pleasurable, but also as spiritually uplifting.[7] For him, the site's impact was obviously enhanced by its architecture, liturgy and sacred objects. Last but not least, he posits that the *baraka* of the place was generated by the gathering of devout men and the aggregation of their prayers there,

Figure 10.1 Restored cenotaph at the Masjid al-Husayn, Cairo, illuminated by lanterns (photo: Russel Harris, courtesy of Aga Khan Documentation Center at MIT).

and he expresses a wish to be included among the beneficiaries of the saint's *baraka*. In more 'academic' terms, Ibn Jubayr seems to be saying that ritual performance consecrates the place and lends it power.[8]

While Ibn Jubayr probably only visited the *mashhad* once during his three-week stay in Cairo, his contemporary, the Cairene mystic shaykh Abu al-Hasan ʿAli, was a regular. According to the guidebook of Ibn ʿUthman (d. 615/1218), the shaykh's tombstone in al-Qarafa Cemetery even reads that 'He was known for his frequent and regular visitation of al-Husayn (*ʿurifa bi-ziyārat al-Ḥusayn, wa-kāna muḥāfiẓ ʿalā ziyāratihi*)'.[9] Abu al-Hasan also surfaces in a later guidebook, written by Ibn al-Zayyat (d. 814/1412), who professes to have researched the graveyard's true deceased occupants and its most beneficial spots for prayer.[10] According to Ibn al-Zayyat, the Shaykh had claimed that whenever he came to the shrine he would greet al-Husayn with the words 'Peace be upon you, O grandson of the Prophet',[11] to which the saint always responded with a greeting.

Greeting the dead was widespread among pilgrims to al-Qarafa, as demonstrated by Tetsuya Ohtoshi. The practice was based on the notion that the dead are able to perceive the visitor's arrival, greetings and words and to recognize the situation of the living.[12] On one occasion, however, Abu al-Hasan left the shrine disappointed and saddened for not having heard the saint's greeting in answer to his. Shortly thereafter al-Husayn appeared to him in a dream and explained why he had not replied: he had been in the middle of a conversation with his grandfather![13]

The recurrent appellation of al-Husayn by his grandfather, the Prophet, in the anecdote related above seems to indicate the Sunni affiliation of both visitor and narrator. The visit of Qadi al-Mahfuzi, a non-Sunni traveller, seems to confirm that the shrine indeed became a pilgrimage site and that the faithful had no doubt as to the relic's authenticity. We have no information about this qadi, except that his visit was recorded in a book that found its way to Yemen during the tenure of the sixth Tayyibi leader, the *dāʿī muṭlaq* ʿAli b. Hanzala al-Mahfuzi (d. 626/1229).[14]

The presence, and possibly even dominance, of mystics in and around Mashhad Raʾs al-Husayn stood out in the late Mamluk and Ottoman eras.[15] Under the early Ayyubids, however, a study circle of jurists (*ḥalqat tadrīs wa-fuqahāʾ*) regularly met at the shrine. It was headed by Bahaʾ al-Din al-Dimashqi, who sat at the *qibla* wall, facing the coffin. This amalgam between the seemingly unrelated functions of a mausoleum and a madrasa was to become quite popular in the Islamic world. For instance, a host of madrasas were established with plans to bury the founder on the premises, so that he would benefit from the *baraka* of study and recitation by their graveside.[16] Some *madrasas* also served as reliquaries. A prominent example is the Dar al-Hadith al-Ashrafiyya in Damascus, built by the Ayyubid Sultan al-Malik al-Ashraf (d. 635/1237), as home to a reputed sandal of the Prophet. The combination between the cult of Muhammad as a saint and the 'academic' instruction of his lore evidently made perfect sense to al-Malik al-Ashraf and his contemporaries.[17] Another institution that disseminated both *ʿilm* (learning) and *baraka* was the Mamluk Madrasa al-Jawhariyya of Cairo. This institution, as presented by Jonathan Berkey, boasted a magical pearl and a talismanic bowl that were renowned for their healing powers.[18] In Saladin's time, however, the primary reason for establishing a *madrasa* – all the more so within the erstwhile Fatimid palace – was to restore Sunni hegemony and to institutionalise Sunni learning.[19]

In roughly 634/1236, a *madrasa* with a brick minaret was attached to the Cairene shrine of al-Husayn's head.[20] A fire (rumoured to have been set by Jews) almost consumed the building in 640/1242–3, had not the emir Jamal al-Din b. Yaghmur, deputy of Sultan al-Malik al-Salih in Cairo, extinguished the conflagration with his own hands. His devotion to al-Husayn earned him some rhymed praise, composed and recited in his honour by a local lyricist. Subsequently, it was written down for posterity by the historian Ibn ʿAbd al-Zahir and copied by later authors into their chronicles.[21] After the overthrow of the Ayyubid dynasty in 658/1260, the shrine continued to thrive under the Sunni Mamluks. Around 689/1290, the Maghribi traveller Muhammad al-ʿAbdari describes Turbat al-Husayn as the greatest of Cairo's many visitation sites (*mazārāt*). Despite his vehemently anti-Shiʿi bent, he concedes that it was probably one of the Fatimid sultans who brought the relic to Egypt.[22]

By ʿAbdari's time, the veneration of al-Husayn in Cairo had obviously lost any specifically Shiʿi meaning and character. But was there a consensus that the relic held in the shrine was indeed al-Husayn's head? Most visitors to the *mashhad*, be they Sunni or Shiʿi, probably did not brood over the relic's history or authenticity. Notwithstanding, there were scholarly and popular strategies that retained the revered status of sites with question marks over the 'true' occupants of their tombs, even in cases of acknowledged uncertainties regarding the actual identity of tombs.[23] Al-Harawi, for example, was well aware of the uncertain authenticity of many traditions about the graves of Companions and Followers, which often left no trace on the ground. Of such places he writes in his guide to the Muslim pilgrim: 'its [physical] remains are gone; [only] stories persist (*dhahabat āthāruhā wa-baqiyyat akhbāruhā*)'. Hence, what matters is the sincere intention and genuine belief of the visitor (*ṣidq niyyatihi wa-ṣiḥḥat ʿaqīdatihi*).[24]

An atypical and unpopular stand on this issue was upheld by Ibn Taymiyya. In answer to the question whether *duʿāʾ* (invocation) is recommended at the following places – the Dar al-Hadith al-Ashrafiyya, by the so-called sandal of the Prophet; the tombs of the Companions in Damascus, which are adjacent to the sanctuary of the sandal (or footprint) of Musa; ʿIsa's cradle in Jerusalem; Aleppo's Maqam Ibrahim; and the Cairene Mashhad

Figure 10.2 Masjid al-Husayn with elevated view of Ayyubid minaret and gate (photo: Matjaz Kacicnik, courtesy of Aga Khan Trust for Culture).

Ra'ʾs al-Husayn – he denies the authenticity of all those relics and tombs and the advantage of invocation at those places. Moreover, he negates the permissibility of travel (*ziyāra*) for the purpose of performing religious devotions there.[25]

The historians al-Nuwayri (d. 733/1333) and Ibn Kathir (d. 774/1373) reached a similar conclusion regarding the *mashhad*. Ibn Kathir, a disciple of Ibn Taymiyya, writes that the Fatimids 'brought a head and placed it at the site of the above-mentioned mosque and said: this is the head of al-Husayn. And the rumour got around and people came to believe it'.[26] According to al-Nuwayri, it stands to reason that Yazid sent the remains of his defeated enemy to Shiʿi communities in order to demoralise them. However, so he claims, back then neither Syria nor Egypt were inhabited by Shiʿis![27] Ibn Taymiyya's student Ibrahim b. Ahmad al-Ghayani (known as *khādim al-shaykh*, 'the shaykh's servant') admits with sorrow that Mashhad Raʾs al-Husayn was the most popular shrine in Cairo. He complains that all possible innovations and misguided deeds (*bidaʿ wa-ḍalāl*) are performed there. Not least the taking of sacred oaths, while it should be known that the proper place for oaths, so he lectures, is between the minbar and the mihrab of a mosque, and not by graves or relics.[28] Ibn Taymiyya had also written on this subject, cautioning that 'an oath taken near something that is not prescribed for Muslims to venerate does not become intensified, as it does not become intensified at shrines (*mashāhid wa-maqāmāt*)'.[29] As in many other matters, his opinion hardly influenced popular practice. Centuries later, a Christian ethnologist who had spent some time in the Levant observed that of all oaths, easily made and easily violated (so he estimates) by local peasants, an oath made in the name of one's local sanctuary is most seriously taken and truly binding.[30]

In 740/1339–40, during the reign of the Mamluk Sultan Muhammad ibn Qalawun, the Cairene *mashhad* was again badly damaged in a fire. It was repaired soon thereafter. The next renovations of which I found record took place much later, in 1175/1761–2, commissioned by the Ottoman emir ʿAbd al-Rahman Katkhuda, and then again in 1873, just five years before the reconstruction of the Husayni shrine in Ascalon (see the building in Figs. 11.1 and 11.2).[31] During the latter building project, the compound acquired its still extant Turkish-style minarets. The only remnants from the medieval building of the *mashhad* to be seen are the Fatimid lower part of the southern gateway and a minaret that has survived from the Ayyubid period (see Fig. 10.2). More recently, a great silver *mashrabiyya* (lattice screen) was installed over the coffin by the Bohra Dawudiyya – a small Isma'ili sect which since 1970 has engaged in the funding of a controversial restoration of Fatimid-era monuments in Cairo (see Fig. 10.1).[32] The Bohra Dawudiyya are also responsible for placing a marble dais, a symbolic open mosque, that stands today in place of the shrine in Ascalon (see Fig. 12.3).[33]

It may be of interest that medieval Alexandria also boasted a relic in the form of a severed head: the skull of Mark the Evangelist, who is considered to have been the founder of the Egyptian Coptic Church and its first patriarch. According to Coptic tradition, as told by Georg Christ in his *Trading Conflicts* (2012), medieval Venetian merchants had tried to steal the relic, but miraculously the wind did not allow their ship to leave the port, until they gave up their plot and left the head behind. Trying again in 828/1419, Venetians in Alexandria purchased the relic from a local merchant. The enraged Copts, obviously unwilling to rely on another miracle, filed a petition to the Mamluk sultan and pleaded that the head should not be shipped away. Centuries later, in 1968, following the rapprochement between the Roman-Catholic and Coptic churches, the Venetian patriarch sent a small bone of St Mark from the reliquary of San Marco to Alexandria. Due to domestic politics, however, it was not united with the skull in Alexandria, but rather placed in a newly erected cathedral in honour of St Mark in Cairo.[34]

Notes

1. Lev, *Saladin*, pp. 85–6, 112, 124–40; Hofer, *Popularization of Sufism*, pp. 38–41. Only in 665/1267 was the *khuṭba* resumed in al-Azhar (Sayyid, *al-Qāhira*, pp. 19–20).
2. Mulder, *Shrines*, esp. pp. 7–8, 261–2; Talmon-Heller, *Islamic Piety*, pp. 196–8.
3. See above, p. 38.
4. Mulder, *Shrines*, pp. 87–9.
5. He was similarly struck by the beauty of al-Rabwa, the supposed refuge of Mary/Maryam and Jesus/Isa in Damascus (Ibn Jubayr, *Riḥla*, pp. 45, 276; trans. Broadhurst, *Travels*, pp. 36–7, 287). See also Talmon-Heller, 'Graves', p. 603.
6. Netton, 'Penitent pilgrim', p. 87.

7. For a discussion of the Arabic medieval discourse on beauty, see Behrens-Abouseif, *Beauty*, pp. 6–7, 171, 184–5. Al-Ghazzali's perception of the beauty of God's creation and divine beauty is expounded in Hillenbrand, 'Some aspects,' pp. 249–60. See also pp. 57, 88, below.
8. As articulated in Knott, 'Religion, space', p. 34.
9. Ibn ʿUthmān, *Murshid*, p. 438; Taylor, *Vicinity*, p. 164.
10. See Taylor, *Vicinity*, pp. 230–4.
11. This is the only formula of greeting upon entering Mashhad Raʾs al-Husayn that I have found. For formulas that were used by visitors to the saints of al-Qarafa, see Ibn ʿUthmān, *Murshid*.
12. Ohtoshi, 'Manners, customs', pp. 24–5.
13. Ibn al-Zayyāt, *al-Kawākib al-Sayyāra*, p. 65; trans. in Taylor, *Vicinity*, p. 164.
14. ʿImād al-Dīn, *ʿUyūn al-Akhbār*, vol. 4, p. 130.
15. According to ʿAbd al-Rahman al-Jabarti (1754–1822), Sufi fraternities (and especially the Rifaʿiyya) used the shrine for processions, *mawlid* celebrations, religious indoctrination, official visits and even as venue for distributing charity during the Ottoman period. For a few of many examples, see ibid. *ʿAjāʾib*, vol. 3, pp. 195, 257; vol. 4, pp. 11, 64, 174, 192.
16. Berkey notes that in the later Mamluk period the connection between institutions of learning and places of burial was so natural that the terms madrasa and *turba* could be conflated (Berkey, *Transmission*, p. 144).
17. For a full account of this story, see Talmon-Heller, *Islamic Piety*, pp. 203–5.
18. Berkey, 'Tradition, innovation', pp. 38–9.
19. See Lev, *Saladin*, pp. 112, 124–6.
20. Jonathan Bloom, *Minaret*, p. 215; Behrens-Abouseif, *Minarets*, p. 66.
21. Ibn ʿAbd al-Ẓāhir, *al-Rawḍa*, pp. 31–2; al-Maqrīzī, *al-Khiṭaṭ*, vol. 2, p. 410; Ibn Khallikān, *Wafayāt*, vol. 7, p. 206.
22. Al-ʿAbdarī, *al-Riḥla al-Maghribiyya*, p. 149. Later, he spent several days in Jerusalem and visited 'the holy border city of Ascalon' (ibid. p. 231). See the description of his visit below.
23. Grehan, *Twilight of the Saints*, pp. 107–15. The reservations of some Mamluk historians will be discussed further below.
24. Meri, *Lonely Wayfarer*, pp. 4–5 (text and trans.).
25. Ibn Taymiyya, *Majmūʿat al-Fatāwā*, vol. 27, p. 55. For a detailed presentation of his views on this matter, see the excursus below, pp. 112–16.
26. Ibn Kathīr, *al-Bidāya wa-l-Nihāya*, vol. 8, p. 222.
27. Al-Nuwayrī, *Nihāyat al-Arab*, vol. 20, pp. 478–81.

28. Al-Ghayyānī, *Nāḥiya*, pp. 17–18.
29. Memon, *Ibn Taymīya's Struggle*, p. 318.
30. Ganneau, 'Arabs in Palestine', p. 327.
31. Al-Tibbāʿ, *Itḥāf al-Aʿizza*, vol. 2, p. 400.
32. Williams, *Islamic Monuments*, pp. 216–17; Sanders, 'Bohra architecture', pp. 159–65; ibid. *Creating Medieval Cairo*, pp. 115–16, 127, Fig. XX.
33. Members of the Bohra Dawudiyya have also been undertaking pilgrimage to Ascalon in recent years. For more on these developments, see Talmon-Heller, Kedar and Reiter, 'Vicissitudes', pp. 209–14; Friedman, *Shiʿis in Palestine*, pp. 197–201.
34. Christ, *Trading Conflicts*, pp. 155–65.

11

Excursus: al-Husayn and Saladin in Palestinian Lore

Twentieth-century Palestinian historians and publicists attribute to Saladin not only the liberation of Muslim land from the yoke of the Shiʿi Fatimids and the Christian Crusaders, as well as the return of its mosques and pulpits to their true purpose, but also the establishment of rites which would protect its borders against further intrusions. Despite an apparent lack of evidence grounded in medieval texts,[1] Palestinian histories and ethnographies – such as those written by ʿUmar Salih al-Barghuthi and Khalid Tutakh (1923), ʿArif al-ʿArif (1943), Mahmud Saliha (1999) and Salim Tamari (2009) – either surmise, or proclaim as historical fact, that Saladin was the founder of at least five (and up to ten) shrines in the territory he had liberated. He is also considered the architect of their attendant annual festivals (*mawāsim*). By rendering strategic locations into pilgrimage destinations, so these writers posit, Saladin rallied enthusiastic young men to these vulnerable places, especially around Eastertime, for the sake of deterring Christian pilgrims from harassing Muslims and, if necessary, resorting to jihad. The visitation of Maqam al-Husayn[2] and Wadi al-Naml over the course of a two-and-a-half-days-long *mawsim* in mid-April, on the last Thursday of the Greek-Orthodox Lent, is sometimes listed among those festivals. Fixing the date of the *mawsim* according to the Christian rather than the hijri calendar was typical of such popular celebration, as it ensured its recurrence in the same season every year.[3]

In the 1930s and 1940s the *mawāsim* evolved into hotbeds of Palestinian patriotism and nationalism. At that time, the festival would begin on a Wednesday, with the imam of the Friday mosque of the near-by town of

Majdal raising a banner in honour of al-Husayn. He led the way to Maqam al-Husayn, sitting atop a horse, followed by a long procession of men, women and children in their best clothes. They were accompanied by members of Sufi orders and derwishes, musicians and marching scouts. At some point they all gathered around the *maqām* to listen to sermons delivered by preachers assembled from other parts of Palestine; to participate in Sufi *dhikr* and dance dabka; sing and recite patriotic tunes, love lyrics and local folk songs; chant anti-British and anti-Zionist slogans; and cheer politicians who repeatedly glorified Saladin for the liberation of the land. The flag of 'Arab Palestine' was hoisted next to the banner of 'Sayyidna Husayn'.[4]

Palestinian folklore, which commemorates the deeds of Saladin and his men at multiple sites, preserved the memory of his battles over Ascalon in a small shrine adjacent to that of Raʾs al-Husayn, named after a certain Shaykh al-Mawsili. According to a local tale recorded in 1875 by Nuʿman al-Qasatli, the Arab scribe of the PEF delegation for the Survey of Western Palestine,[5] when Saladin was battling for Ascalon against the armies of the Crusaders, Muhammad al-Mawsili and two of his brothers miraculously arrived from

Figure 11.1 The Shrine of Seyid Hussein, April 1943, from the northeast (Library of Congress, Prints & Photographs Division, Matson [Eric G. and Edith] Photograph Collection, reproduction number: LC-DIG-matpc-21687).

Figure 11.2 Courtyard of the Shrine, April 1943 (Library of Congress Prints & Photographs Division, Matson [Eric G. and Edith] Photograph Collection, reproduction number: LC-DIG-matpc-21686).

Figure 11.3 Symbolic open mosque commemorating the shrine of al-Husayn, planned and donated by the Bohra Dawudiyya of Gujarat, Ascalon, 2000 (photo: B. Z. Kedar; courtesy of the photographer).

Mosul, where they had been plowing their fields, to join the Muslim forces. All three were killed and subsequently buried by Saladin, who personally erected the *maqām* in their honour. Fourteen thousand(!) additional warriors were purportedly laid to rest beneath this monument.[6] ʿAref al-ʿAref (1892–1973) adds that the popular name for Wadi al-Naml – Wadi al-Damm, the Valley of Blood – hints at the large number of Muslim casualties of 'the bloody historical battle for Ascalon between the Crusaders and Saladin'.[7]

Badr al-Din al-Jamali, the Fatimid patron of the shrine and the instigator of the cult of al-Husayn in Ascalon, left no trace in Palestinian collective memory. The heroic and devoutly Sunni Saladin was obviously 'favoured' over the vizier of the Fatimid-Ismaʿili caliph in local lore, and his figure even outshone that of al-Husayn on 'his' *mawsim*.[8]

Notes

1. For speculations on the evolvement of this myth, see Talmon-Heller, 'Job (Ayyūb)'.
2. '*Maqām*' is used more often than the term *mashhad* by these authors, and to the same effect.
3. See the excursus below.
4. Barghūthī and Ṭūṭaḥ, *Taʾrīkh Filasṭīn*, pp. 199–201; al-ʿArif, *al-Mūjaz*, pp. 324–6; Ṣāliḥa, *al-Majdal*, pp. 210–11. For a divergent view of the *mawāsim*'s role in the consolidation of Palestinian nationalism, see Tamari, *Mountain*, p. 33.
5. Al-Qasatli claims to have heard this story from the participants of the *mawsim* of 1875; see Talmon-Heller, 'Job (Ayyūb)', pp. 131, 134.
6. Al-Qasāṭlī, *al-Rawḍa al-Nuʿmāniyya*, p. 185. Forty of those martyrs were commemorated in the nearby village of Naʿaliyya.
7. Al-ʿAref, *al-Mūjaz*, pp. 49–50.
8. See Khalidi, *Palestinian Identity*, p. 31; Aubin-Boltanski, 'Ṣalāh al-Dīn', pp. 91–107; Eddé, *Saladin*, p. 493.

12

The Shrine in Ascalon under the Ayyubids and Mamluks

Al-Harawi, the author of a pilgrim's guide to Muslim sacred places (*Kitāb al-Ishārāt ilā Maʿrifat al-Ziyārāt*), visited Ascalon in 570/1174. He writes that the frontier town (*thaghr*) of Ascalon was renowned for Abraham's well, a strong fort and a shrine for al-Husayn's head, which the Muslims had delivered to Cairo in 549/1154.[1] For readers wondering how a Muslim could have entered the Latin-ruled town, it bears to cite another twelfth-century traveller, Ibn Jubayr. The latter notes that each side promised the other a secured status upon payment of a tax, and he concludes: 'the soldiers engage themselves in their war, while the people are at peace . . .'[2] Movement between Frankish and Muslim territory was prevalent. And yet, the roads throughout the land, and especially in the vicinity of Ascalon, were teeming with warriors and brigands from both sides.[3]

Al-Harawi dreams, both figuratively and literally, of the return of Ascalon to Muslim hands. He notes that he spent a night in the city's 'shrine of Abraham'. By this he must have meant Mashhad al-Husayn, where an apparition of Muhammad promised him that Ascalon 'will be for Islam, and a sign unto mankind'. Upon awakening, al-Harawi shared his dream with others by scribbling a graffiti message on the southern wall of the shrine, which – he was happy to note – was seen by soldiers and passers-by when the city had indeed returned to Muslim hands. As for the dream, it is worth noting that dreams induced by staying at a holy place were a known and seriously regarded occurence, probably from times immemorial until today, as contemporary anthropologists make note of this phenomenon as well. Some sites were, and still are especially visited in the hopes of triggering such a vision.[4]

Al-Harawi's choice to spend the night in the shrine, however, may have been induced also by his confidence that no one would dare harm him in such a sacred place. A taboo on violating the sanctity of shrines and upsetting their patron-saint by theft or vandalism in 'their' abode, although not mentioned in the medieval sources I know, is repeatedly observed in ethnographies of Palestine from the late Ottoman period until today. Clermont Ganneau, for example, reports wryly in 1881 that he had spent a night in a rural Palestinian shrine 'on the bare but holy floor', certain that he was safe.[5]

Leaning on al-Harawi's report, it seems that, despite the concerns of the Fatimids who had experienced the Frankish siege and the evacuation of the town by its Muslim inhabitants,[6] the building of the *mashhad* was not harmed during the thirty-three years of Frankish rule. Most likely, it was used by them.

In 583/1187, a month after Saladin's epic victory over the Frankish army at the Horns of Hattin, Muslim forces were sent to capture Ascalon. They encountered a well-fortified town[7] that had been emptied of its knights: they had left to join the battle at Hattin and never came back. Given the meagre hope for reinforcements, the Latin defenders surrendered after a mere fourteen days under siege. Ascalon's inhabitants were allowed to leave with their belongings to either Jerusalem or Tripoli, which were still under Crusader rule; a hundred families, most likely Eastern Christians, chose to remain. With Ascalon out of the way, the Ayyubids overran the other Frankish forts and settlements in the south and turned their sights on the main prize: Jerusalem.

Roughly four years later, Ascalon became a bone of contention in the protracted negotiations between Saladin and the leader of the Third Crusade, King Richard the Lionheart, who had taken the city in Dhu al-Hijja 587/ January 1192 and rebuilt its walls.[8] In September of that year, the two parties finally hammered out an agreement. As reported by Saladin's biographer, Baha' al-Din Ibn Shaddad, the Muslims came to the realisation 'that Ascalon should be demolished and that our men and theirs should cooperate in its demolition lest he [Richard] take it over [again] with its defenses intact', thereby leaving the roads to Jerusalem and Egypt vulnerable to Crusader attacks. Having agreed to the defensive tactic of razing the city rather than risking its conquest by Richard the Lionheart and his men, Saladin reluctantly dispatched sappers and stone-masons to raze the city's walls and supervise the

Franks' withdrawal.[9] A close associate of Saladin, his secretary ʿImad al-Din al-Isfahani, did not conceal his criticism: 'If care had been taken to restore [the city from the Franks] from the day it was taken and held, its strength would not have been blunted, and we should not have tired of loving it'.[10] Al-Maqrizi describes the undertaking at length:

> [Saladin] divided the towers among the emirs for demolition, and great was the lamentation and weeping among the inhabitants . . . at its razing. For it was one of the most beautifully constructed towns, and strongly fortified in its walls, and most delightful to dwell in [*sic*]. Destruction and burning did not cease until the month of Shaʿban had ended [21 September].

The Egyptian historian adds the following curiosity:

> The illustrious Qadi Abu-'l Hasan ʿAli ibn Yahya al-Katib [who was present at the demolition] related to me . . . 'I saw this inscription: The construction of this tower was ordered by our illustrious master, the Emir of the Armies Badr al-Jamali, and executed by his servant and lieutenant Khutluj, in Shaʿban. I marveled at the coincidence that it should be built in Shaʿban by a Khutluj and destroyed in Shaʿban by a Khutluj!'[11]

The decorated minbar of Mashhad Raʾs al-Husayn was sent to a safe haven in Hebron. This time around, the Muslims' caution was warranted, as Ascalon was to undergo another four deliberate demolitions. The first was executed by Richard the Lionheart in 588/1192. Pursuant to the Jaffa-Tel ʿAjul Treaty with Saladin, he was obligated to level whatever had been repaired in Ascalon since the earlier destruction.[12] Saladin's brother al-Malik al-ʿAdil initiated the next round in 594/1198. Nearly fifty years later, the Ayyubid Sultan al-Salih Najm al-Din Ayyub dismantled the fortifications that the Latins had managed to build anew after retaking the city in 637/1239, thereby leaving it a veritable ghost town. The final round was carried out by the Mamluk Sultan Baybars in 668/1270. He toppled whatever was left standing and filled the anchorage with rubble.[13] Al-Maqrizi concludes:

> Thus was destroyed a city which had no like, a frontier station without equal, and a structure which time will not replace. All this stemmed from the kings' inability to repel the Franks on the battle grounds, thus compelling them to demolish the cities and efface their trace.[14]

Figure 12.1 Ruins of Ascalon in 1875, view from east wall (from Lieut. Kitchener's Photographs, vol. 1, *Survey of Western Palestine* P3981-P4039, Archive Store Room, courtesy of the Palestine Exploration Fund).

Al-Maqrizi's comments reveal the continuous use of the appellation *thaghr* (frontier town), with all its religious connotations, for Ascalon and his correct understanding of the Ayyubid and Mamluk scorched-earth strategy as dictated by military weakness.

Saladin incorporated Badr al-Jamali's *minbar* into the Cave of the Patriarchs (*al-Ḥaram al-Ibrāhīmī*, or *al-Khalīlī*) in Hebron. Following his conquest of this city in 583/1187,[15] the compound – which the Franks had turned into the St Abraham Cathedral Church and the seat of the local lordship at the turn of the twelfth century – underwent renovations and was converted back into a mosque.[16] The installation of al-Jamali's pulpit in that mosque aptly communicated Saladin's triumphs over the Fatimids and later over the Franks. What is more, even after Richard the Lionheart's arrival and the military successes of the Third Crusade, the Muslim control of Hebron seemed secure. The minbar's new abode was quite prestigious, too, as indicated by the fact that some of the pilgrims setting out to Mecca via Jerusalem used to add a *ziyāra* to Hebron to their itinerary.[17] After the Franks had purportedly stumbled upon the remains of the Patriarchs in a cave beneath the sanctuary in the summer of 513/1119,[18] the town's status had markedly risen in the eyes of non-Christians as well. It would have been interesting to compare the solemn ceremony marking the discovery and reburial of the Patriarchs' remains on the part of the Latin canons of the cathedral to the reinternment of al-Husayn's head in Ascalon some two decades earlier, but unfortunately the description of the Fatimid ceremony are extremely terse, beyond emphasising the respectful handling of the head. The eventual fate of the relics perhaps speaks to the different attitudes regarding such items: the 'Christian' relics of Hebron were divided among important pilgrims who then proceeded to deliver them to churches throughout Europe.[19] The 'Muslim' relic seems to have been transferred to Cairo in its entirety, as we have seen in Chapter 8, and was not taken apart later either.

It bears noting that Badr al-Jamali's minbar was not the only one that Saladin had transferred to prominent mosques in territories seized from the Franks. A better-known case is the splendid pulpit that Nur al-Din Zangi (d. 577/1174), Saladin's predecessor as the head of the counter-crusade, commissioned from an Aleppan artisan in 564/1168. It was decorated with a long inscription, proclaiming (or rather foreseeing) the victory of Islam and the defeat of the infidels. A few months after the re-taking of Jerusalem, in the summer of 583/1187, Saladin bestowed Nur al-Din's pulpit to the al-Aqsa Mosque. In his description of the mosque's re-consecration for Muslim worship, al-Katib al-Isfahani, Saladin's secretary, celebrates the installation of the minbar in rhymed prose. Strikingly, he likens the minbar, waiting in Aleppo for the time of its installation in Jerusalem, to 'a sword in the scabbard of protection'.[20]

As we have seen, the *mashad* in Ascalon remained on the itinerary of Muslim travellers. The geographer Zakariya b. Yahya al-Qazwini (d. 682/1283) claims that people from all over the Islamic world come to pledge vows at the gravestone and seek the *baraka* (blessing) of the saint. Perhaps its loss to the Franks and then the fact that the Muslims regained control of the region enhanced the Muslim veneration of the place.[21] While mentioning the city's destruction in 587/1191, he writes of the building as though it were still intact, describing it as 'a large shrine with marble columns'.[22] The traveller Muhammad al-ʿAbdari (d. c. 700/1300) passed through Ascalon in 689/1290, after his visit to Cairo (see above). He laments the sheer magnitude of Ascalon's ruin at some length and specifically mentions the Ascaloni Mosque of ʿUmar, of which only some walls and marble pillars remain. Thereafter, he describes the Husayni shrine, which he calls Mazarat Raʾs al-Husayn, as a great tall mosque with a big cistern. He informs his readers that it was built by one of the Fatimids, who had his name inscribed above the entrance. Like most Sunni authors, he pejoratively calls the Fatimids 'Banu ʿUbayd',[23] thereby denying their association with Fatima and belittling them. The identical impressions of the much better-known globetrotter Ibn Battuta (d. 1368–9 or 1377) were undoubtedly copied from Muhammad al-ʿAbdari's travelogue.[24]

Ibn Battuta refrained from reproducing the more personal experiences of his forerunner, who admits to have felt ill at ease once darkness fell over the deserted town and to have returned to civilisation in a hurry. Earlier that same day, al-ʿAbdari had visited a large cemetery in nearby Wadi al-Naml (Valley of Ants). A local custodian, who claimed to be on the Mamluk payroll, showed him many of the graveyard's tombs, explaining that they belong to saints and martyrs.[25] Like the earlier traveller al-Harawi, who describes the road leading to Ascalon,[26] al-ʿAbdari does not fail to comment that according to the Qurʾan Solomon convened men, *jinni* and birds in Wadi al-Naml. Upon his arrival there, the king was amused to overhear an ant issue the following warning: 'O Ants, enter your dwelling-places, lest Solomon and his armies crush you, unperceiving' (Q. 27: 18).

Some early commentators regard the Qurʾanic story as an allegory. Others, 'map the book onto landscape'[27] and locate the valley in Palestine, Syria or Taʾif (Arabia), thereby producing – to use Jonathan Z. Smith's terms – 'a reification of scriptural myth within a visible, walkable landscape'.[28] Looking at the same phenomenon from the perspective of the anthropologist of pilgrimage and tourism, we may say that mapping the book onto the landscape, or rather attaching a Qurʾanic reference to a concrete place, produces a 'storied place' and gives meaning to its visitation.[29] Al-Harawi and al-ʿAbdari naturally avoid such theorisation. According to their brief description of the cemetery of Wadi al-Naml, early Muslim saints (*awliyāʾ wa-tābiʿūn*) whose place of burial is unknown are commemorated therein.[30]

As for Mashhad Ra'ʾs al-Husayn, the Mamluk-era chronicler Ibn Fadl Allah al-ʿUmari (d. 749/1349) also testifies that it stood erect in an otherwise ruined city. Moreover, he claims that it was repurposed as a mausoleum for the head of al-Malik al-Kamil Muhammad b. Ghazi, the last Ayyubid ruler of Mayyafariqin (south-eastern Anatolia), who was killed and decapitated by the Mongols in 658/1260.[31] In contrast, the geographer ʿIzz al-Din Ibn Shaddad (d. 683/1285) relates that al-Kamil's head was brought to Damascus by the Mongol Khan Hülegü, who had killed the Ayyubid prince with his own two hands. It was hung at Bab al-Faradis, where Yahya b. Zakariya (John the Baptist) and al-Husayn's heads had been displayed centuries earlier. At long last, al-Kamil Muhammad's head was also interred at the Umayyad Mosque,[32] as noted by the later historian al-Safadi (d. 764/1363), who also identifies the burial site in Damascus as the shrine of al-Husayn's head. Both al-ʿUmari and al-Safadi cite from an elegy that was composed in honour of al-Kamil, designating the martyr as a *ghāzī* (holy warrior) and companion of al-Husayn in the Garden of Eden![33] Doubts concerning their authenticity notwithstanding, the two narratives reflect how the collective memory about sacred places preserves, or conflates, important elements of earlier traditions, producing creative collages. In any event, the shrines in Cairo, Damascus and Ascalon all continued to bear the name of the best known and most revered decapitated martyr, al-Husayn b. ʿAli.

Another traveller who visited Ascalon is the Andalusi Khalid al-Balawi, who reports to have seen the city's ruins in 738/1337. Ascalon, so his travelogue reads, had been 'incomparably blessed (*qalīlat al-naẓīr fi-l-ḥusn*)' in the past and was very disappointing in the present. Joseph Drory, who translated al-Balawi's florid prose, maintains that his accounts are both credible and valuable. He summarises the traveller's impressions of the city thus: 'Balawi finds only a desolate, dilapidated and deserted town, which time has eaten, yet even drunk its charms . . . there remained only useless relics (*aṭlāl bāliya*) and empty, derelict alleyways'.[34]

Muhammad Shams al-Din al-Asyuti, likewise writing in the fourteenth century about the sanctity of Syria and its holy places, devotes several paragraphs to Ascalon in his *Itḥāf al-Akhiṣṣa bi-Faḍāʾil al-Masjid al-Aqṣā*. After having established the 'special pre-eminence and peculiar privileges of Palestine', a land upon which 'God looks down twice a day', [35] al-Asyuti argues against the lingering belief in the merits of Ascalon. He dismisses as outright fabrications the traditions that adorn the city with the titles 'one of the brides [of Syria] (*iḥdā al-ʿarūsayn*)' or 'the bride of Paradise (*ʿarūs al-janna*)'; traditions that bestow it an eschatological role, such as predictions whereby 70,000 martyrs will rise from the dead in the town's graveyards and intercede on behalf of the *umma* on their way to Paradise; and accounts of the Prophet praying in an Ascalon cemetery and promising rewards to those who take up residence in the city. He writes, demonstrating a critical attitude and an understanding of the linkage between religion and politics: 'Some scholars explained that the reason for the spread of such traditions is that Ascalon used to be a dangerous frontier town and a place of *ribāṭ*, which the enemy has attacked time and again, causing many Muslims to sacrifice their lives there'. In the second half of the fourteenth century, however, it is more meritorious to perform *ribāṭ* elsewhere, says al-Asyuti, 'for an attack [on Ascalon] by the foe is unlikely to occur these days'.[36] Neither al-Balawi nor al-Asyuti mention the *mashhad* in honour of al-Husayn, and we are left to wonder whether this omission indicates that the building had been abandoned by its Mamluk guardian and fallen into disrepair some time between c. 689/1290 and 738/1337.

In Mujir al-Din's *History of Jerusalem and Hebron*, the very first book dedicated to the history of Palestine (written in the late fifteenth or early sixteenth century), we do find yet another mention of a large shrine, 'built by one of the Fatimid caliphs of Egypt in the vicinity of Ascalon, on a site which they had claimed was the place of the head of al-Ḥusayn b. ʿAli'.[37] Mujir al-Din obviously dismisses the authenticity of this claim in his *History of Islam* (*al-Taʾrīkh al-Muʿtabar*), in the section about al-Husayn's death and the difference of opinions regarding the burial place of his head. He writes: 'It has been said that the caliphs of Egypt took a head from Ascalon to Egypt, buried it there, and built over it a shrine known as Mashhad al-Husayn'.[38] As for the building, it seems as though Mujir al-Din is speaking of a still standing edifice.

Centuries later, some time between 1916 and 1943, the Palestinian historian of Gazza ʿUthman Mustafa al-Tabbaʿ (1882–1950) visited the site. He describes a large two-story building with a mosque, adjacent rooms and a spacious courtyard, dedicated to al-Husayn. He also informs us that the reconstructed shrine was built in 1887 by the Ottoman governor (*mutaṣarrif*) Ra'uf Basha. The latter had nominated a native of the nearby village of al-Jura as keeper (*khādim*) and *mu'adhdhin* for the mosque. Al-Tabba' adds that the man's genealogy allegedly goes all the way back to al-Husayn! He ends the passage with a poem he had seen inside the shrine, perhaps on one of its walls. Undated as it is, I dare conjecture that this poem reflected a conviction nearly a thousand years old.

> Al-Husayn's head rests in this place . . . of the progeny of the Chaste [Fatima], grandson of the Chosen [the Prophet Muhammad], son of the Imam 'Ali of the righteous first Muslims (*al-salaf*) . . . How many of his guests have found what they had sought, and returned home content and enriched . . . How many sick people had hoped to be cured through him and returned well . . .[39]

Notes

1. Meri, *Lonely Wayfarer*, pp. 82–3.
2. Ibn Jubayr, *Travels*, p. 301. See also Netton, 'Ibn Jubayr', vol. 2, p. 84.
3. Prawer, 'Ascalon', p. 194. For an anecdote about an attack on a Muslim merchant carrying silk and silver from Aleppo to Fatimid Ascalon, see Talmon-Heller, 'The cited tales', pp. 130–1.
4. For more on these sorts of visions in medieval Islam, see Sirriyeh, 'Dreams', pp. 119–20; for Ibn Taymiyya's critical stand towards this phenomenon, see below. On the phenomenon from the standpoint of an anthropologist working in present-day Israel, see Bilu, 'Charismatic dreams', p. 298.
5. Ganneau, 'Arabs in Palestine', pp. 325–7.
6. Jews and Eastern Christians apparently remained in Crusader Ascalon. See Yagur, 'Between Cairo and Jerusalem', p. 23, and ch. 2.
7. For details of the Frankish fortification of Ascalon in 1153–87, 1192 and 1239–47, see Pringle, *Secular Buildings*, p. 21. For a nineteenth-century description of the city's picturesque ruins turned into orchards by neighbouring Palestinian peasants, see Conder, *Tent Work*, pp. 281–2.
8. For a dramatic rendering of the confrontation between these two mythic figures, both on the field of battle and at the negotiating table, see Tuchman, *Bible and Sword*, ch. 4.
9. Ibn Shaddad, *Rare and Excellent*, pp. 230–2.
10. Translation in Eddé, *Saladin*, p. 164.

11. Broadhurst, *History*, pp. 93–4.
12. See Prawer, 'Ascalon', pp. 209–12.
13. Levanoni, ''Askalān'; Sharon, *CIAP*, vol. 1, p. 141; Eddé, *Saladin*, pp. 262–70.
14. Broadhurst, *History*, pp. 124–5. The nearby town of Majdal became the region's new administrative centre, and a communal mosque was established there in 699/1300 (Huster, *Ashkelon*, pp. 5, 61, 122).
15. According to most sources, Hebron fell to Saladin immediately after Ascalon; Sharon, *CIAP*, vol. 5, p. 14. Mujīr al-Dīn al-Ḥanbalī reports about the transfer of the minbar; ibid. *al-Uns al-Jalīl*, vol. 1, pp. 60–1. See also Gil, *History of Palestine*, p. 194.
16. The churches of Ramla, Gaza and Tarsus, the Frankish Cathedral of Tripoli and the Cathedral of St John the Baptist in Beirut were likewise converted into mosques after the Muslim re-conquest (Hillenbrand, *Islamic Perspectives*, pp. 374–5).
17. Meri, *Cult*, p. 162; Talmon-Heller, *Islamic Piety*, p. 202.
18. For a detailed account of that discovery, see Kedar, 'Holy Men', pp. 5–11.
19. Pringle, *The Churches*, vol. 1, pp. 225–8.
20. See Talmon-Heller, 'Islamic preaching', p. 62.
21. That was Ibn Shaddad's estimation regarding Mashhad Ruhin in Northern Syria. The overall direct influence of the Latin crusades and conquest on the Islamic sanctification of the land is hard to measure, of course. For my discussion of this issue, see Talmon-Heller, 'Graves'.
22. Al-Qazwīnī, *Āthār al-Bilād*, p. 222.
23. Al-ʿAbdarī, *Riḥla*, pp. 231–2.
24. *Riḥlat Ibn Baṭṭūṭa*, p. 80. Amikam Elad has reservations concerning Ibn Battuta's credibility and doubts whether he visited Ascalon at all: It is hard to believe that he went all the way from Gaza to Jerusalem, and then back south to Ascalon. See Elad, 'The description', pp. 256–72.
25. Al-ʿAbdarī, *Riḥla*, p. 232.
26. Meri, *Lonely Wayfarer*, pp. 80–1.
27. David Frankfurter uses this expression in his introduction; see ibid. *Pilgrimage and Holy Space*, p. 46.
28. Smith, *To Take Place*, p. 92.
29. Feldman, 'Contested narratives', p. 110.
30. Meri, *Lonely Wayfarer*, pp. 82, 150.
31. On Mayyafariqin, see Al-ʿUmarī, *Masālik al-Abṣār*, vol. 1, p. 282; on al-Kamil, see Humphreys, *From Saladin*, pp. 335–77.

32. Translated in Mulder, *Shrines*, p. 195. An inscription at the shrine also notes the location of the Ayyubid caliph's head, but oddly dates its burial to 888/1483.
33. Al-Ṣafadī, *al-Wāfī*, vol. 4, p. 216.
34. Drory, 'Balawi's impressions', pp. 381–91, esp. p. 390.
35. Al-Asyūṭī, *Itḥāf al-Akhiṣṣa*, vol. 2, pp. 169–72.
36. *li-istibʿād nuzūl al-ʿaduww bihā hādhihi al-ayyām* (al-Asyūṭī, *Faḍāʾil al-Shām*, p. 169).
37. Mujīr al-Dīn, *al-Uns al-Jalīl*, vol. 1, p. 380, vol. 2, p. 74.
38. Ibid. vol. 1, p. 300.
39. Al-Ṭabbāʿ, *Itḥāf al-Aʾimma*, vol. 2, pp. 397–401. For more details on this stage in the site's history, see also Talmon-Heller, 'Job (Ayyūb)'.

13

Excursus: Ibn Taymiyya on the Veneration of the Head of al-Husayn

Ibn Taymiyya (661/1263–728/1328) dedicated over a hundred fatwas, treatises and other genres of writing to polemics against tomb veneration and the sanctification of places. He thought the construction of shrines an offence and did not tire of cautioning that travel (*safar*) for the purpose of worship in shrines is utterly devoid of religious merit, save for pilgrimage to Mecca.[1] As we have seen, Ibn Taymiyya's fierce opposition to these practices was hardly the majority view. He encountered stiff resistance not only among rank-and-file Muslims, but also from religious scholars and rulers. While many Ayyubid and early-Mamluk-period ʿulamaʾ criticised the flock for improper behaviour at cemeteries and mausolea, they did not object to the visitation of graves *per se*, as did he. In fact, many of them partook in *ziyāra*s themselves and believed that certain aspects of this practice were permitted, even beneficial.[2]

In making his case, Ibn Taymiyya draws on a wide range of arguments. He often cites the prophetic hadith whereby God will spill his wrath on the Jews and Christians for turning the graves of their prophets into places of prayer.[3] He stresses that

> the establishment of mosques over [as well as praying beside] tombs is non-Islamic, forbidden by the words of the Prophet and the consensus of the scholars . . . It is an imitation of the ways of the polytheists . . . and constitutes the veneration of the created (*al-makhlūq*) rather than the creator.[4]

No less frequently Ibn Taymiyya accuses the Shiʿis, whom he regards as 'the worst people among those who follow the [correct] direction of prayer', of corrupting Islam and implanting the *bidʿa* (unwarranted innovation) of tomb worship among the faithful.[5] Ibn Taymiyya dates the spread of this misguided practice to sometime during the Abbasid caliphate's decline. His *terminus a quo* for its emergence is the fourth generation of Muslims, as he is certain that when Islam was in its prime, during the era of the first three generations, nobody engaged in saint veneration nor erected *mashhads*. This dovetails neatly with Ibn Taymiyya's oft-repeated appraisal that the first three generations of Islam, the *salaf*, are superior and constitute authoritative sources for posterity.[6] In his estimation, the visitation of shrines and tombs became commonplace under the loathed Shiʿi Fatimids, Buyids and Qarmatis, who whitewashed the practice by spreading false hadith.[7]

Ibn Taymiyya dedicates several essays to refuting the sanctity of the Husayni shrines in Ascalon and Cairo. In his *al-Qāʿida fī Ziyārat Bayt al-Maqdis* (The Foundation of the Visitation of Jerusalem/the Holy Land) of 716/1316, he asserts that

> travel to Ascalon these days is not prescribed by the shariʿa, neither as a religious duty (*wājib*) nor as a commendable act (*mustaḥabb*). There was merit in settlement in Ascalon, or travel to it, when it was one of the frontier towns of the Muslims (*thughūr*) and those who were engaged in defending it in the path of God (*al-murābiṭūn fī sabīl Allāh*) had occupied it.[8]

By the early fourth/tenth century, he argues, the circumstances had changed, as Muslims no longer had to defend themselves against the Byzantine enemy. Thereafter, much to Ibn Taymiyya's regret, the caliphate lost the Syrian coast. First, 'the treacherous Shiʿis and hypocrites (*al-rāfiḍa wa-l-munāfiqūn*)' gained power and ruled over Egypt, the Maghrib and Syria; then most of Syria fell to the Crusaders.[9] As a result, the frontier shifted from the Mediterranean Coast to towns near Aleppo.[10] 'Nowadays', he concludes, 'a deserted place' like Ascalon can no longer be deemed a frontier town, and there is no merit in traveling to it.[11]

To my understanding, this sensitivity to historical context strikingly led Ibn Taymiyya to regard the sanctity of place to be a temporal and relative phenomenon that is contingent upon historical developments, such as changing borders and population flows. According to this reasoning, land cannot be permanently sacred, nor can it accord sanctity to its inhabitants. The merits of a place depend on the worship of God there. Hence a location that stimulates obedience, faith and good works (he uses the terms *ṭāʿa*, *ḥasanāt*, *maṣāliḥ*, *īmān* and *ʿamal ṣāliḥ*) – either because conditions are favourable, or, to the contrary, because conditions demand a special effort on the side of the believer (as in the *thughūr*) – enjoys extra merit. One should choose his abode (*iqāma*) with the intention to maximise his piety, he advises.[12]

Ibn Taymiyya does not hesitate to debunk the authenticity of Ascalon's and Cairo's Husayni shrines. Noting the absence of early sources, both textual and material, according to which the martyr's head was interred in Ascalon, he emphasises the unlikelihood that later authorities were better informed than their predecessors, who 'had [indeed] collected the reports on al-Husayn and his killing'.[13] He even doubts that al-Husayn's head was ever sent to Damascus from Karbala. Like the ninth-century traditionist and historian al-Bukhari, he believes that it was taken to Medina and interred in the al-Baqiʿ Cemetery near the graves of his brother al-Hasan and his mother Fatima.[14] Furthermore, he argues that transferring the relic to Ascalon, of all places, ran counter the Umayyads' political interests. Had Yazid wanted to erase al-Husayn's memory, he would not have sent his head to a city like Ascalon, the abode of so many pious *murābiṭūn*.[15]

Consequently, if the shrine in Ascalon never hosted the head in the first place, then certainly its replacement – that is, the mausoleum in Cairo – is a sham as well.[16] He also explains that, under the Fatimids (whom he refers to by the pejorative epithets Qaramita, *zanādiqa*, *munāfiqūn*, *ahl al-juhl*, *al-mubtadiʿūn*, and so on), it was ill-advised to speak up and reveal the truth. As a result, false Ismaʿili propaganda became so deeply entrenched in society that even the return of Sunni hegemony with the establishment of Zangid and Ayyubid rule could not uproot the lie.[17] Finally, Ibn Taymiyya goes so far as to suggest that the head in question may have belonged to some Christian![18] And although it is unlikely that he was aware of the beheaded Egyptian Christian martyrs of Late Antique Ascalon, his remark calls to mind that ancient 'layer' of the site.[19]

Ridiculing the veneration at Mashhad Raʾs al-Husayn, Ibn Taymiyya quotes 'some Christians' who rejoice at the foolishness of ignorant Muslims and compare the Christian pair of Jesus and Mary to al-Husayn and Nafisa. Nafisa bint Hasan b. Zayd (d. 208/824–5) was ʿAli's great-granddaughter and Jaʿfar al-Sadiq's daughter-in-law, and probably the first ʿAlid to be buried in

Egypt. Her mausoleum in Cairo was restored and enlarged by Badr al-Jamali in the summer of 482/1089, shortly before the establishment of Mashhad Raʾs al-Husayn in Ascalon, and subsequently became a popular pilgrimage destination.[20] As expected, Ibn Taymiyya did not hide his negative view of this cult, either.[21] His disciple Khadim al-Shaykh al-Ghayani describes a specific encounter between Ibn Taymiyya and three monks from Upper Egypt, who claimed that Jesus and Mary were worthier than al-Husayn and Nafisa. In response, Ibn Taymiyya explained the unbending monotheism of Islam, thereby, so al-Ghayani, leaving his interlocutors speechless.[22]

Ibn Taymiyya recurrently claimed that the identification of numerous venerated tombs of prophets, Companions and Muhammad's kin was based on unreliable sources, including stories (*ḥikāyāt*) of dreams, marvels, the scent of perfume and other purported 'signs'.[23] He ridicules Muslims who, mimicking the Jews and Christians, build monuments in places where they or others have dreamt that Muhammad once prayed. Even worse in his mind are the contrived stories about the Prophets' footprints and the like.[24] Arguing against popular notions, he claims that there is a consensus among ʿulamaʾ that the apparition of a prophet or saint at a certain spot does not render the place a pilgrimage destination.[25] Having said all that, Ibn Taymiyya explicitly denies the importance of the correct identification of Raʾs al-Husayn, or, for that matter, any relic or tomb. He emphasises that there is absolutely no *sharʿī* obligation to determine the burial sites of the prophets, even more so of the *ahl al-bayt*. One can believe in, evoke the memory of and pray for (but certainly not to) these figures in the absence of such knowledge.[26]

Yaqut al-Hamawi (d. 626/1229) claimed otherwise. He states that all men are in fact in need of this knowledge, hence justifying the composition of his famous geographical lexicon *Muʿjam al-Buldān* in religious terms. He especially mentions the '*mawāqīt*[27] of pilgrims and visitors, the domiciles of the Companions and Followers, the tomb-shrines of saints and the pious'. In support of his claim he cites the Qur'anic verse 'Journey through the land and behold' (Q. 6: 11), followed by a saying attributed to Prophet ʿIsa: 'The world is a place of visitation and an abode of transition. Be you then travellers in it and take warning from what remains of the traces of the early ones'.[28]

Ibn Taymiyya, however, believes that according to the shariʿa the only prescribed prayer venues are mosques and sites along the pilgrimage route to

Mecca (*mashāʿir al-ḥajj*). Deliberate travel to graves and other alleged holy places for the sake of visitation (*ziyāra*), prayer, or invocation is reprehensible to his mind.[29] It is the effort that the devotee invests in supplication, rather than its location, that determines its acceptance by God. All things being equal, praying by a cross, so Ibn Taymiyya argues, would have exactly the same outcome as prayer at one of these allegedly sacred places![30] Here, Ibn Taymiyya is in full agreement with the earlier Maliki critic of 'innovations' (*bidaʿ*), al-Turtushi, who deals with the question whether it is more meritorious to perform an act such as prayer in a certain place, at a certain time and in a certain way. Al-Turtushi claims that all mosques are equal, and one should not deliberately go to pray in a specific mosque, not even al-Qubaʾ (in spite of its association with the Prophet), or Jerusalem, the only exceptions being the mosques of Mecca and Medina.[31]

And yet, finally, Ibn Taymiyya does not deny the sanctity of place and time altogether, or in all of his writing. He also states, quite conventionally, that 'the more meritorious (*afḍal*) a place or time, the better [rewarded] are good works and the stronger [more severely punished] is sinning therein (*kānat al-ṭāʿa fīhi afḍal wa-l-maʿāṣī ashadd*)'.[32] His contention regarding the difference between the sanctification of place and time, however, is quite original:

> Hallowing a location which religious law does not keep holy is worse than hallowing a time which the Shariʿa has not hallowed . . . because the unlawful worship of mortal beings by religious acts, more than an act of venerating a certain time, comes closer to idol-worship . . . [33] the greatest place of worship is the [Meccan] Sanctuary, and it is a graver offence to defile the sanctity of a location in space, than a location in time. This is why it is forbidden to seek grounds of game and grazing in the sacred place [Q. 5: 96] though in the sacred month one may search for these (everywhere) . . . the prohibition of slaying within the Sacred City (Mecca) is permanent, while this does not hold true for the sacred month.[34]

Notes

1. For a book-length study of Ibn Taymiyya's views on these issues, see Olesen, *Culte des Saints*. See also Talmon-Heller, 'Historiography'.
2. Talmon-Heller, 'Graves', pp. 601–20, esp. p. 611.

3. Ibn Taymiyya, *Majmūʿat al-Fatāwā*, vol. 27, p. 56. For Ibn Taymiyya's anti-Christian polemics exposing Christian errors and demonstrating that Muslims have been led down this misguided path, see Thomas, 'Apologetic and polemic', pp. 255–9.
4. Ibn Taymiyya, *Majmūʿat al-Fatāwā*, vol. 27, pp. 216–17.
5. Mourad and Lindsay, *Intensification*, pp. 107–9. On Ibn Taymiyya's fierce polemic against the Shiʿis and his participation in military operations against the Shiʿis, see al-Jamil, 'Ibn Taymiyya', pp. 229–46, esp. pp. 232–5.
6. Rapoport and Ahmad, *Ibn Taymiyya*, pp. 10–13.
7. Ibn Taymiyya, *Majmūʿat al-Fatāwā*, vol. 27, p. 78. Ibn Taymiyya's chronology is not far-fetched. According to Najm Haider, Imami scholars (such as Ibn Qawlawayh, Shaykh al-Mufid and al-Kulayni) began to extol the merits of pilgrimage, especially to the Husayni shrine in Karbala, during the tenth century; ibid. *The Origins*, pp. 243–7. See also Newman, *Twelver Shiism*, p. 61; Sindawi, 'Visit to the tomb', pp. 231, 248.
8. Ibn Taymiyya, *al-Qāʿida*, p. 15. He deals at length with the legal definition of travel (*safar*) for the sake of visiting the tombs of prophets and righteous men (Ibn Taymiyya, *Majmūʿat al-Fatāwā*, vol. 27, pp. 98–107).
9. Ibn Taymiyya, *Majmūʿat al-Fatāwā*, vol. 27, p. 54. On the pejorative term *rāfiḍa*, see Mourad and Lindsay, *The Intensification*, pp. 108–11. On Ibn Taymiyya's disparaging attitude towards the Fatimids, see ibid. p. 29.
10. Ibn Taymiyya, *Majmūʿat al-Fatāwā*, vol. 27, pp. 136–7.
11. Ibid. p. 34. On the lingering prestige of *ribāṭ* in the coastal towns of Syria-Palestine long after those towns lost their strategic significance (which Ibn Tamiyya aims to destroy), see Ephrat, *Spiritual Wayfarers*, p. 80; ibid. 'The Shaykh', pp. 13–15.
12. Olesen, *Culte*, pp. 206–7; Ibn Taymiyya, *Majmūʿat al-Fatāwā*, vol. 27, pp. 39–40, 15, 44–5, 82–3.
13. Ibn Taymiyya, *Majmūʿat al-Fatāwā*, vol. 27, pp. 241, 245.
14. Ibid. pp. 207–8. Elsewhere he writes that al-Husayn's head was interred at the al-Baqiʿ Cemetery in Medina (Olesen, *Culte*, p. 45; Ibn Taymiyya, *Majmūʿat al-Fatāwā*, vol. 27, p. 79). He expressly prohibits pilgrimage (*safar*) to this graveyard or to al-Qubba, a mosque on the city's outskirts, unless one happens to be in the area (Olesen, *Culte*, p. 43).
15. For the views of Ibn Taymiyya's contemporaries, see pp. 61, 22 above.
16. Ibn Taymiyya, *Majmūʿat al-Fatāwā*, vol. 27, pp. 215, 218.
17. *fa-zaraʿūʾ fihim min akhlāq al-zanādiqa . . . mā lam yumkin an yanqaliʿa illā baʿd*

ḥīn . . . kāna al-nifāq wa-l-bid'a fihā kathīr mastūr (Ibn Taymiyya, *Majmū'at al-Fatāwā*, vol. 27, p. 256). For more on the debate regarding the Fatimids' lasting impact on Egypt, see Part Two.

18. Ibn Taymiyya, *Majmū'at al-Fatāwā*, vol. 27, p. 242.
19. See above, p. 62.
20. See Williams, 'The cult: Part II', pp. 40, 57, 67–8; Bloom, *Arts*, p. 136; El-Toudy and Abdelhamid, *Selections*, p. 39, n. 206. Ibn al-'Uthman (d. 615/1218) devotes a lengthy entry to Sayyida Nafisa in his guide to visitors to the cemetery of al-Qarafa (Ibn 'Uthmān, *Murshid al-Zuwwār*, pp. 159–92). See also Kassam and Blomfield, 'Remembering Fatima', pp. 218–19.
21. See Ibn Taymiyya, *Majmū'at al-Fatāwā*, vol. 27, p. 217; Memon, *Ibn Taymīya's Struggle*, p. 295.
22. Shams and al-'Imrān, *Sīrat Shaykh al-Islām*, pp. 89–90.
23. See, for example, Ibn Taymiyya, *Majmū'at al-Fatāwā*, vol. 27, pp. 38, 96–7, 235, 241.
24. Ibid. p. 78.
25. Memon, *Taymiyā's Struggle*, p. 257.
26. Ibn Taymiyya, *Majmū'at al-Fatāwā*, p. 198. Compare with Ibn Taymiyya's objection to commemoration in time, based on the similar claim that knowing the exact date of a significant event in the history of Islam (for example, *laylat al-isrā'*) is not called for, and neither is its annual celebration (see Part Two).
27. See p. 13 above.
28. Jwaideh, *Introductory Chapters*, pp. 2, 4.
29. Taylor, *In the Vicinity*, pp. 169–73. Ibn Taymiyya expands on the legal definition of *safar* (travel) with the objective of visiting tombs of prophets and righteous men; see Ibn Taymiyya, *Majmū'at al-Fatāwā*, vol. 27, pp. 7, 8, 14, 22, 78–80, 184, 188, 204.
30. Ibn Taymiyya, *Majmū'at al-Fatāwā*, vol. 27, p. 100.
31. Maribel Fierro suggests that the omission of Jerusalem from Turtushi's short list of legitimate destinations was related to the fact that the city was under the rule of the Crusaders in his time. See ibid. 'al-Turtushi and the Fatimids', pp. 132–3.
32. Ibn Taymiyya, *al-Mustadrak*, vol. 3, p. 106–7.
33. Memon, *Ibn Taymīya's Struggle*, pp. 15, 258.
34. Ibid. p. 144.

14

Summary

A shrine in the peripheral town of Ascalon, on the Mediterranean coast of Palestine, has for the past millennium marked the burial place of the head of al-Husayn b. ʿAli, the martyr of Karbala. It was venerated by Ismaʿili, Imami and Sunni Muslims, despite disagreements over the itinerary and whereabouts of al-Husayn's severed head, al-Husayn's role and the meaning of his martyrdom, and the very sanctification of tombs and relics.

The narrative claiming the head's burial or reburial in Ascalon is outlined in a long inscription from 484/1091, commissioned by the Fatimid vizier Badr al-Din al-Jamali. Whether mainly intended to promote the vizier's own reputation, strenghthen the Fatimids' hold on the Syrian littoral, bolster Ismaʿilism, or advance an ecumenical religious program revolving around the beloved grandson of the Prophet Muhammad, the 'discovery' of a relic of the son of Fatima – the purported ancestor of the Fatimids – served the dynasty's claim to spiritual leadership and imperial rule. The (re-)burial of the head entailed the construction of a grand new mosque-shrine in *extra muros* Ascalon.[1] It was designed to host both formal Friday prayers and *ziyāras* by admirers of al-Husayn. Whether it was actually at the time regarded as an institution that represents the hegemonic religious system and its formal 'great tradition' (*à la* Mircea Eliade and Robert Redfield), or as a place rooted in the local lore of the periphery and an outgrowth of its popular tradition (*à la* Victor Turner), or somewhere on the continuum between the two (*à la* Erik Cohen), is impossible to say.[2]

Notwithstanding the lack of evidence as to the prior existence of a Husayni mausoleum or cult in Ascalon, the reception of Badr al-Jamali's 'invented tradition' may be tied to the fact that the shrine was built on what was already hallowed ground in several respects. First, Ascalon was known as a *thaghr* (garrison town) from the era of the great conquests. Residing in the city for the sake of defending Muslim territory was a prestigious and rewarding religious undertaking known as *murābaṭa* under the Umayyads and early Abbasids. Second, the new *mashhad* stood on the site of a fourth-century Byzantine sanctuary similarly dedicated to beheaded saints. Although that sanctuary was probably dismantled long before the construction of the Fatimid mausoleum, local memory might have retained the notion that it was a sanctified place associated with martyrdom. The new Islamic-Ismaʿili narrative about the place exhibited some continuities with its past.

Beyond the local circumstances, the promotion of the cult of al-Husayn was apparently linked to the Fatimid-era veneration of the *ahl al-bayt*, of which al-Husayn was a key consensual figure. Contemporary historians are divided over whether this campaign had been initiated from 'above' or 'below'. Catherine Cubitt's conclusions regarding the cult of early Anglo-Saxon martyrs[3] may be relevant to our case as well: the Fatimids' establishment of a shrine for the Husayni relic can *mutatis mutandis* also be defined as 'royal sponsorship of a murdered royal saint'. Even if mainly undertaken for the sake of enhancing the dynasty's prestige, the cult of al-Husayn revolved around a genuinely popular hero who was widely perceived as the innocent victim of an unjust tyrant and who suffered an exceedingly gruesome death.

Once established, the belief in the power of the site in Ascalon endured, despite the head's transfer from that location, as well as the city's abandonment and large-scale destruction during the Third Crusade and its aftermath. Truly remote and peripheral and devoid of its relic and minbar, the empty Husayni *mashhad* still retained some standing as a pilgrimage site. At this phase of its history it attracted visitors that were willing to brave 'a stretch of wilderness'[4] in pursuit of a spiritual or mystical experience, or rugged adventure, conforming to Turner's model of pilgrimage to the 'center out there'. As time marched on, it stands to reason that most of the site's pilgrims had only a faint notion of its history. Nonetheless, they were happy to pay their respects to a saintly Muslim at the site of his (erstwhile) burial.

In the Ayyubid period, a swath of land adjacent to the ruined city, Wadi al-Naml (Valley of the Ants), was known for its sacred history based on the 'emplacement' of the incident depicted in *Sūrat al-Naml* (Q. 27: 18) at the site. The local cemetery was identified as the graveyard of the martyrs of the

Great Conquests and the theatre of Saladin's wars. Notwithstanding, Ascalon still enjoyed the reputation of a garrison town (*thaghr*) that was defended and sanctified by the most pious *murābiṭ*s of the Umayyad and Early Abbasid periods. At the end of the 1200s, a Mamluk endowment paid for a custodian to take care of the sacred place and its visitors.[5] The shrines seem to have been standing at least until the early sixteenth century and probably deteriorated thereafter.

The evacuated relic was placed in a Cairene shrine in 549/1154. It was located at the very heart of the Fatimid ritual centre and seat of government, near the mausoleum of the Fatimid imams, signifying that they were indeed the progeny of the noble martyr. At that stage, the official rites that were performed by the head's casket were of an unmistakably sectarian, Isma'ili shade.[6] They included the initiation ceremonies for the Fatimid administration's newly appointed officials,[7] the salutation of the imam-caliph[8] and the ceremonial commemorations of the two most important days on the Shi'i calendar, Yawm al-'Ashura and Yawm Ghadir Khumm. Among the distinguishing features of these highly formal and solemn occasions were the professional reading of the Qur'an, recital of poetry and lamentations, and the distribution of food by the imam-caliph and his representatives.[9] Ghadir Khumm was naturally celebrated with expressions of thanksgiving and joy, whereas the commemoration of Husayn's sacrifice and death was informed by sorrow, mourning and rage. Both sets of emotions were undoubtedly intensified by the presence of the sacred relic on site, the dense congregation and the manifold repetition of rites.

With the reassertion of Sunni hegemony under the Ayyubids, Mashhad Ra's al-Husayn, like other Cairene institutions, was divested of all patently Shi'i elements. It ceased hosting official events and no longer constituted a significant source of political legitimisation. Metaphorically speaking, it became a 'peripheral' or excentric site, although it remained in the same geographical location in the heart of Cairo. During the Ayyubid and Mamluk eras, the cult of al-Husayn (and other 'Alids) became more of a private matter. Muslim travellers from afar came to admire the building whose beauty was reported to be quite inspiring. Local devotees, including madrasa students and mystics, regularly came to engage in prayer, recite special invocations, circumambulate the tomb, or study Islamic law by its side. Visitors wept, touched and kissed the railing. Some took solemn oaths; others held wondrous dialogues with the patron-saint of the shrine.

The fact that the place drew both Sunnis and Shiʿis does not necessarily mean that the two groups held a common set of beliefs regarding the saint's role or the meaning of visitation (*ziyāra*) to his shrine. Al-Husayn was depicted as a martyred hero and saintly figure by the entire Muslim world, but only for the Shiʿa did he play a key part in the genealogy and legitimisation of spiritual-political leadership. While pilgrimage to the tombs of the *ahl al-bayt* were core features of Shiʿi Islam from at least the ninth century on, Sunni medieval scholars did not privilege Muhammad's family members over the Companions or other early righteous Muslims, and they were more ambivalent towards the practice of *ziyāra*.

Prominent Sunni scholars denied Mashhad Raʾs al-Husayn's authenticity and sanctity. Ibn Taymiyya (d. 728/1328), al-Nuwayri (d. 733/1333), al-ʿUmari (d. 749/1349), Ibn Kathir (d. 774/1373) and Mujir al-Din (d. 928/1522), who wrote between the fourteenth and sixteenth centuries, argued that the martyr's head never reached Ascalon; hence, it could not have been moved to Cairo and reburied there. Conversely, contemporaneous travellers, chroniclers, preachers and Sufis – such as Ibn al-Azraq al-Fariqi (d. 571/1176), Muhammad Ibn al-ʿImrani (d. c. 580/1184–5), Ibn Jubayr (d. 614/1217), Sibt ibn al-Jawzi (d. 654/1256), Ibn al-Muyassar (d. 677/1278–9), al-Maqrizi (d. 845/1442), Idris ʿImad al-Din (d. 872/1467) and ʿAbd al-Wahhab al-Shaʿrani (d. 973/1565) – recognized the relic as al-Husayn's severed head. Although their narratives vary, all of them found it plausible that it was indeed buried in Ascalon, and they considered the site's visitation a beneficial endeavour. Historical truth regarding such matters was apparently insignificant to the Sufis who performed *dhikr* in the shrine of Cairo, or to mystics and wanderers who visited out-of-the-way Husayni venues such as Ascalon. Al-Harawi in the late twelfth century and ʿAbd al-Ghani al-Nabulsi in the seventeenth century articulated this approach while describing their stops at such places.[10]

The denial of the sanctity of Mashhad Raʾs al-Husayn by scholars such as the Maliki jurist al-Turtushi and the Hanbali theologian and mufti Ibn Taymiyya was based on their principled opposition to the consecration and visitation of places other than the canonical pilgrimage sites in Mecca, Medina and Jerusalem, as well as their opposition to the lingering *faḍāʾil* (praise) of Ascalon.[11] They claimed that God rewards the efforts involved in supplication irrespective of the prayer's location, and the merits of places depend on the worship of God therein. We will return to the idea that the performance of religious rites promotes sanctity in Part Two.

Notes

1. Cohen addresses such a case in ibid. 'Pilgrimage', p. 43.
2. For a neat juxtaposition of Eliade and Turner's typologies, see Cohen, 'Pilgrimage centers'.
3. Cubitt, 'Sites and sanctity'.
4. See Cohen, 'Pilgrimage centers'.
5. See above, p. 121.
6. Sanders, *Ritual*, pp. 131–4, 202, n. 49.
7. Muḥammad, *Masājid Miṣr*, p. 369.
8. Ibn Ṭuwayr, *Nuzhat al-Muqlatayn*, pp. 223–4.
9. See above, p. 81.
10. See above, pp. 76, 82–3.
11. See Talmon-Heller, 'Historiography', pp. 8–9.

PART II

A SACRED TIME: THE MONTH OF RAJAB

Introduction

'The number of months with God is twelve in accordance with God's decree on the day he created the heavens and the earth', declares verse 9: 36 of the Qur'an, subjugating time to its Lord, and adds: 'four of them are sacred (*ḥurum*)'. While Ramadan is explicitly designated in the Qur'an as the sacred month of the fast and an unspecified sacred month or 'well-known months' (Q. 2: 197) as the time of the hajj, the other sacred months remain unnamed.[1] The Prophet's 'farewell sermon (*khuṭbat al-wadāʿ*)', which Muhammad purportedly delivered from atop his she-camel on his last hajj, reveals the names of those months. Filling in the lacuna in the Qur'an, the Prophet explains: 'The year is made up of twelve months, four of them are sacred, three of which are sequential – Dhu al-Qaʿda, Dhu al-Hijja and Muharram, and Rajab Mudar between Jumada and Shaʿban'.[2]

Over the ages, Muslim jurists and Qur'an exegetes have wrestled with the meaning of and relation between these passages. They all acknowledge that the pagan Arabs considered as sacred Dhu al-Qaʿda, Dhu al-Hijja, Muharram and Rajab (the eleventh, twelfth, first and seventh months), and that they marked their special status by abstention from warfare and the performance of various religious devotions.

With the transition to Islam and the abolishment of many customs of the *Jāhiliyya*, a new purely lunar, rather than lunisolar calendar was established,[3] and two new annual festivals were instituted. Several years after the Prophet's death the year-count was also re-set: year one of the hijri era was declared by the caliph ʿUmar ibn al-Khattab to have begun on 1 Muharram (16 July) of 622 CE. Despite those dramatic transitions, at least some pre-Islamic notions concerning time's division into units, the differentiation between sacred and profane time, and the means for distinguishing between these realms were preserved.

The standing of the four holy months, Rajab included, was called into question under Islam, demonstrating that the classification into sacred and profane is specific to every faith-based community and an important means for distinguishing between them.[4] Against the claim that the sacred months were God's chosen favourite time (*ikhtāra Allāhu al-zamān, wa-aḥabbuhu ilā Allāh al-ashhur al-ḥurum*) and Islam only heightened their pre-Islamic merit and veneration (*kānat al-jāhiliyya tuʿaẓẓimuhu fi jāhiliyyatihā wa-mā zādahu al-Islām illā faḍl wa-taʿẓīm*),[5] it was argued that the consecration of Rajab was one of the 'bygone remnants of the beliefs of the age of ignorance (*ghabirāt min baqāyā ʿuqūd al-jāhiliyya*)' which Muhammad repealed and abrogated.[6] Centuries later, Ibn Dihya reminds us that the pagan Arabs worshipped their gods on those months, and Ibn Rajab explains that they sanctified those months for the sake of the safety of the pilgrims going to and from the *jāhilī* hajj and *ʿumra*.[7] A few sages ingeniously avoided the problematics of perpetuating the customs of the pagan Arabs by claiming that the veneration of Rajab actually derives from the law (shariʿa) of Abraham, which was revived by the Prophet Muhammad, rather than from pre-Islamic Arabian custom.[8] Or that it was timeless, as in the following graphic image: 'Rajab is of the sacred months, its days are written on the seventh gate of heaven'.[9]

In the vast corpus of hadiths, Kaʿb al-Ahbar and other Companions include Rajab also in another set of sacred months – the seventh, eighth and ninth – claiming that these months were God's 'favourite' times.[10] Shaʿban, the ninth month, appears in a Prophetic hadith as a month straddled by the two significant months of Rajab and Ramadan; it was consoled for its lesser prestige when God ordered the reading of the Qurʾan during Shaʿban. Thus it was made it into *shahr al-qurrāʾ* (the month of the Qurʾan reciters).[11] It was also designated as the month of the Prophet, as per the probably most cited Prophetic saying on the three months: 'Rajab is the month of God, Shaʿban is my month, and Ramadan is the month of my people'. Or in the following variation: 'Verily, Rajab and Shaʿban are my [the Prophet's] months, and Ramadan is the month of God'.[12]

Clearly, as the years passed, Rajab was increasingly considered part of this set of three (rather than four) sacred months. An unusual hadith that was included in an eleventh-century compilation in praise of Rajab – which is unequivocally repudiated by the editor of the modern edition of the work as fake (*mawḍū'*), due to its transmission by a 'notorious liar' – seems to attest to the confusion surrounding this issue at the time. It asserts:

> These four sacred months, there is something [special] about the tenth of each one of them . . . the tenth of Muharram is the day of al-'Ashura, and the tenth of Dhu al-Hijja is Yawm al-Nahr (the day of ritual slaughter, that is, 'Id al-Adha). On the tenth of Rajab God erases what he wants [of sins] and determines [guilt]. As for the tenth of Dhu al-Qa'da – I have forgotten.[13]

What seems to have been forgotten is the root cause of the sanctity of the four months that were named in the Farewell Sermon and, thereafter, the notion that they are sacred. Although I did not find any sources that pinpoint or explain the reason behind this 'switch' from four to three sacred months, both sets of sacred time reiterate the continuity of the pre-Islamic significance of months as the meaningful unit of religious time in Arabia,[14] and both include the month of Rajab.

Ultimately, the idea of divine mercy and retribution, which is so central to the monotheistic faiths, shaped Islam's position on the holy months, distinguishing it from earlier conceptions. The companion Ibn 'Abbas (d. 68/687) offers the Muslim faithful this advice in his commentary on Q. 9: 36: '"So wrong not yourselves in them (*fa-lā taẓlimū' fīhinna anfusakum*)," during all [twelve] months, but especially during the particular four months that He has made sacred . . . sinning on them is graver, and good works and their recompense are excessive'.[15] Similarly, the companion Abu Qatada (d. circa 40/660) is quoted as saying: 'There is greater recompense for good works performed during the sacred months, and wrongdoing is weightier'.[16]

Muslim scholars translated the idea that the weight of sins and good deeds, as well as their consequences, are amplified over the course of Rajab and the other sacred months (*ja'ala al-dhanb fīhinna a'ẓam, wa-ja'ala al-'amal al-ṣāliḥ wa-l-ajr a'ẓam*),[17] into meticulous calculations of the extravagant rewards for each and every ritual performed during this month, as we shall see below. Consequently, the variety of devotions for Rajab that turn up in medieval Muslim texts is indeed staggering. Some are recommended for any occasion throughout the entire month; others are designated for specific days and nights, often in commemoration of 'important events (*ḥawādith ʿaẓīma*)' in the lives of the prophets. These events comprise the deliverance of Noah (the prophet Nuh) from the ark or flood;[18] the birth of Abraham and Jesus; Muhammad's conception or birth;[19] the beginning of his prophetic mission (that is, the first revelation of the Qurʾan);[20] his night journey;[21] and the change of the prayer direction (*qibla*) from Jerusalem to Mecca.[22] The Shiʿis added several other dates to this list: ʿAli's birthday; his marriage to the Prophet's daughter Fatima;[23] the day when Muhammad was informed that his cousin ʿAli was his intended heir (*waṣī*);[24] and the death of ʿAli's archenemy Muʿawiyya b. Abi Sufyan (the first Umayyad caliph).[25] The visit of all the rivers of the world to the Zamzam Well in Mecca is also expected to occur during Rajab – in eschatological times, of course.[26]

All the dates mentioned above originate in extra-Qurʾanic traditions; the Qurʾan pays no attention to fixing historical events in time.[27] Al-Biruni, the great Islamic scholar of the eleventh century, is more blunt, saying that 'all this rests only on the authority of popular story-tellers, who do not draw upon learned [Islamic sources] nor upon the agreements between *ahl al-kitab* (that is, Jews and Christians)'.[28] Still, despite disagreements regarding the proper dates of almost every occasion deserving of commemoration, as well as some opposition to the very idea of such commemoration, most scholars, not to mention the rank and file, found the merging of sacred history and sacred time natural. Hence they willingly marked the anniversary of significant events such as the Prophet's night journey with annual rites and festivities.

This part of the book traces the evolution of Rajab's attendant rites between the seventh and fifteenth centuries. As in Part One, we will proceed in a chronological manner, addressing agreements and differences in opinion, continuities and changes, central and excentric rituals, sponsorship from above and initiatives from below. While such an arrangement may appear to be straightforward, I have struggled with the well-known yet unresolved methodological questions regarding the provenance of multi-layered texts, especially compilations of hadith recycling early material in later periods. As articulated by Tarif Khalidi, 'Traditions are untidy and the elements that enter into their make-up themselves belong to the debris of earlier traditions. Unlike an event, a tradition is not "born" but emanates in slow stages from a cultural background'.[29] Needless to say, the resolution of these issues on either the macro- or micro-level is beyond the scope of this work. Moreover, the object of our study is also a non-linear maze of opinions and rituals that defy simple stratigraphy, much less an orderly, sequential, or thematic presentation. For this reason, dating is often impossible and perhaps not of the essence. As in our study on sacred space, here too we will encounter the recurrence of similar narratives in varying historical contexts and try to account for repetitions, continuities, transformations and innovations. Again, we will attempt to approach the religious experience of the worshipper and to decipher the power relations behind the production and representation of the sacred.[30]

Notes

1. For traditional and modern attempts to grapple with such ambiguities and contradictions, see Knysh, 'Months'.
2. Ibn Saʿd, *al-Ṭabaqāt al-Kabīr*, vol. 2, p. 167. Ibn Rajab cites it from the *al-Ṣaḥīḥayn*, the canonical collections of hadith; ibid. *Laṭāʾif*, p. 217.
3. See the excursus on the Islamic calendar.
4. See the quotes of Durkheim and Ibn Taymiyya on this matter, p. 10 above.
5. See, for example, in al-Khallāl, *Faḍāʾil*, p. 59.
6. Al-Ṭurṭūshī, *Kitāb al-Ḥawādith*, p. 130. For references to other hadiths that deny the continuation of the sanctity of Rajab, see also Kister, 'Rajab is the month', p. 193; al-Jīlānī, *al-Ghunya*, vol. 2, p. 729, n. 63; ʿAwda, '*Risālat al-Adab*', p. 133. Al-Jilani and Ibn al-Qariʾ propagated the perpetuation of the sanctity of Rajab.
7. Ibn Diḥya, *Adāʾ mā wajab*, pp. 30, 36; Ibn Rajab, *Laṭāʾif*, p. 222.
8. See Ibn Rajab, *Laṭāʾif*, p. 222; ʿAwda, '*Risālat al-Adab*', p. 129; Ibn al-ʿImād, *Risālat al-Bayān*, MS. 1190, fol. 17; MS. 39/909, fol. 8. Compare with the 'Islamisation' of the pre-Islamic pilgrimage to Mecca by the attribution of its rites to Abraham in Lazarus-Yafeh, *Some Religious Aspects*, p. 26. A similar debate raged over the disputed status of Medina's *ḥaram*. See Munt, *Holy City*, pp. 77–93.
9. Al-Jīlānī, *al-Ghunya*, vol. 2, pp. 750.

10. Ibn Rajab, *Laṭāʾif*, p. 222; Frenkel, 'Popular culture', pp. 6–7; Knysh, 'Months', p. 409.
11. Kister, 'Shaʿbān is my month', pp. 18–19. Many of the Shaʿban traditions greatly resemble those about Rajab. See ibid. pp. 15–37.
12. This hadith is attributed to Muhammad: al-Jīlānī, *al-Ghunya*, vol. 2, p. 731; al-Naysābūrī, *Rawḍat al-Wāʿiẓayn*, p. 435.
13. Al-Khallāl, *Faḍāʾil*, p. 67. See the discussion of the tenth day of Rajab on pp. 129, 140, 149.
14. See Goitein, 'Ramaḍān', pp. 92–4. On Shaʿban, see Kister, 'Shaʿbān', pp. 26–34.
15. Al-Bayhaqī, *Kitāb Faḍāʾil al-Awqāt*, p. 81. Some commentators read the warning of Q. 9: 36 as pertaining to all months, denying the distinction of Rajab (Ibn Rajab, *Laṭāʾif*, p. 222).
16. Al-Baghawī, *Tafsīr*, on Q. 9: 36.
17. Ibn Rajab, *Laṭāʾif*, p. 222.
18. According to a couple of sources, God purified the land from heresy and evil once Noah had boarded the ark, and all the ark's passengers fasted during Rajab in gratitude for their salvation; al-Jīlānī, *al-Ghunya*, vol. 2, p. 726; Kister, 'Radjab', p. 375. For the 'hidden story' of Noah and the ark, which serves as a blueprint for the Ismaʿili *daʿwa*, see Hollenberg, *Beyond the Qurʾan*, pp. 69–70.
19. Kister, 'Rajab is the month of God', pp. 197, 200. With respect to the wonders of that particular night, see Katz, *Birth of the Prophet*, pp. 29–31. For alternative dating of the birth of the Prophet, see ibid. p. 3.
20. Kohlberg, *Medieval Scholar*, p. 285; al-Khallāl, *Faḍāʾil*, p. 76; Ibn Ṭāwūs, *al-Iqbāl*, vol. 3, p. 169; al-Jīlānī, *al-Ghunya*, vol. 2, p. 748; Kister, 'Rajab is the month', p. 197.
21. According to al-Biruni, the beginning of the Prophet's mission and the night journey occurred on the twenty-sixth and twenty-seventh day of Rajab, respectively (al-Bīrūnī, *Chronology*, p. 329). The earlier Abu Ishaq Ibrahim al-Harbi (third/ninth century) argued for Rabiʿ al-Awwal (see Abū Shāma, *al-Bāʿith*, p. 232; Ibn Rajab, *Laṭāʾif*, p. 233).
22. Ibn Ṭāwūs, *al-Iqbāl*, vol. 3, p. 254. Muslim sources offer at least six dates for the change of the *qibla*, which supposedly happened at an early stage of the Medinan period of Muhammad's prophecy; Kimber, 'Qibla'.
23. Ibn Ṭāwūs, *al-Iqbāl*, vol. 3, p. 245.
24. Ibn al-ʿImād, *Risālat al-Bayān*, MS 1990, fol. 15. The actual designation purportedly took place on the eighteenth day of Dhu al-Hijja 10/632 at Ghadir Khumm. See p. 81, above.

25. On the 'confluence' of events of sacred history in the Islamic tradition, see Reid, 'al-ʿAshūrāʾ'. Ibn Rajab, among others, repudiated all these dates (Ibn Rajab, *Laṭāʾif*, p. 233).
26. Kister, 'Rajab is the month', p. 198. See also Mol, '*Laylat al-Qadr*', pp. 92, n. 62, 94.
27. See Böwering, 'Time'.
28. Bīrūnī, *Chronology*, pp. 326–7 (speaking specifically of the amalgamation of 'great events' on the tenth day of Muharram).
29. For Tarif Khalidi's discussion of the nature of hadith and its complexities, see ibid. *Arabic Historical Thought*, pp. 19–28; Khalek, *Damascus*, p. 3.
30. Using, *mutatis mutandi*, Kim Knott's categories for the study of religion and space; see pp. 17–18 above.

15

Rajab in Pre-Islamic Arabia and in Early Islam

In his succinct and definitely favourable description of the ethics of the people of Muhammad's tribe, the Quraysh, before the rise of Islam, the historian and geographer al-Yaʿqubi (d. 284/897) writes that they disapproved of immoral acts, severance of kinship bonds and mutual wrongdoing and that they punished crimes. As for their religious customs, they 'made pilgrimage to the House, performed the rites [of the hajj], were hospitable to guests, and venerated the sacred months'.[1] He names Rajab as one of the sacred months celebrated by the people of Quraysh.

The multiple, allegedly ancient appelations of Rajab listed in Islamic sources probably reflect some of the pre-Islamic convictions regarding the sanctity of the month. Those include the epithets *al-aṣabb* ('the pouring [of mercy]'), *al-rajm* ('the stoning [of Satans]'), *al-muʿallā* ('the elevated'), *al-aṣamm* ('the deaf [and silent]', namely devoid of the sound of weapons), *Rajab Mudar* (the month of the Mudar, one of the leading Quraysh clans), and *shahr al-ʿatīra* ('the month of the sacrificial slaughter').[2] Muslim scholars of the twelfth century list up to eighteen different appellations for Rajab. For obviously polemical purposes, Ibn Dihya al-Kalbi (d. 633/1235) stresses that they are all derived from the misguided convictions of pagan Arabs, especially from the tribes of Mudar.[3] He attributes to them the idea that wrongdoing is graver if occurs on sacred grounds, preaching that sin is grave whenever it is performed.[4] Another of their misconceptions, notes ʿAbd al-Qadir al-Jilani (d. 561/1166), was that it is permitted, as well as effective, to wish for your enemy's misfortune (*al-duʿāʾ ʿalā al-ẓulma*) during the month of Rajab.[5]

Truce

Al-Biruni explains that '*irjabū*" commands abstinence from fighting and warlike expeditions.[6] Bloodshed was strictly forbidden in pre-Islamic Arabia during the holy months. The ancient prohibitions on hunting, fighting and sexual relations 'while in a sacral state' are documented, among others, in an early south Arabian text and in a Greek text.[7] The strength of the taboo on manslaughter in Rajab is reflected in the striking claim that in the *Jāhiliyya* an Arab would even refrain from avenging his father's death if he happened to encounter the killer during that month.[8] Al-Ya'qubi remarks that back then people knew that throughout Rajab their lives and property would be safe on the fairgrounds and that 'one did not need to pay protection money',[9] pointing to the practical advantages of the restrictions imposed by sacrality, and the severe punishment expected for its violation.

The early Muslims seem to have held on to this taboo, although the Qur'anic injunctions on this matter are open to several interpretations. On one hand, it says: 'Travel freely in the land four months' (Q. 9: 2) and 'wrong not yourselves in them' (Q. 9: 36), which seem to indicate that Islam enjoins truce during the holy months. The restrictive injunction 'Then, when the sacred months have passed, slay the idolaters wherever you find them' (Q. 9: 5) points to the continuation of the pre-Islamic tradition. So does the call upon the faithful to take vengeance on the idolaters who provocatively persecute Muslims and wage war against them precisely during sacred times – as in the verses stating 'The holy month for the holy month; holy things demand retaliation' (Q. 2: 194). On the other hand, permission to unrestricted warfare is given and explained as follows:

> They question you [O Muhammad] with regard to warfare during the sacred month. Say, warfare therein is a great transgression, but to turn men from the path of God, to disbelieve in Him, to [deny entry] into the Sacred House, and expel its people from it are more heinous in God's eyes (Q. 2: 217).

The majority opinion among medieval scholars seems to be that these passages repealed the ban on warfare during certain months, allowing Muslims to retaliate against aggression whenever it occurs. Verse Q. 9: 29 lifts the remaining restrictions, so that waging war becomes permissible year-round and pre-Islamic prohibitions and taboos become null and void. Competing views on this generally hinge also on the interpretation of the actions of Muhammad and his Companions, more specifically on the conflicting dating of Muhammad's raids against his enemies. Some transmitters, such as ʿAtaʾ b. Abi Rabah (d. 106/724–5), swore in God's name that Muhammad never sanctioned fighting in either Mecca or during the sacred months, except in self-defense, and that attacking on those months is opposed to the perfectly valid Qurʾanic commandment 'So wrong not yourselves in them [that is, during the sacred months]' (Q. 9: 36). Others contend that the Prophet actually led military campaigns on the first days of the erstwhile sacred month of Dhu al-Qaʿda, and therefore it was allowed.[10] In contrast, the Hanbali jurist Ibn Qayyim al-Jawziyya (d. 751/1350) argues that the view sanctioning unrestricted warfare is based on a miscalculation of one of the Companions. In the faraway days of the clashes between the Muslims and their pagan enemies, that Companion struck a convoy of Quraysh on the premise that it was the last day of Jumada al-Akhir (the sixth month), unaware of the fact that it actually was the first day of Rajab, when fighting is off-limits. Having explained away this incident, Ibn Qayyim al-Jawziyya declared that there is no record of the Prophet or the Companions attacking infidels during the sacred months, and no evidence that the injunction against warfare had been repealed in early Islam.[11] Be that as it may, according to the findings of Hideyuki Ioh, based on multiple sources portraying the formative period of Islam, the prohibition against warfare during the sacred months had gradually lost its force after the murder of the third caliph, ʿUthman b. ʿAffan, in 35/656.[12]

ʿ*Umra* (Minor Pilgrimage) and Ritual Slaughter

Before the rise of Islam, when Rajab was indeed characterised by cease-fire, Meccan Arabs and Bedouins from the Hijaz would go on the ʿ*umra* (minor pilgrimage) to the sanctuary of Mecca during Rajab. In all likelihood, the devotions included circumambulating the Kaʿba (*ṭawāf*),[13] invocations of the deities (especially for the fertility of livestock)[14] and the sacrifice of the herd's firstlings (*al-ʿatīra* or *al-faraʿ*). To the best of our knowledge, such offerings were also given at other sanctuaries in Arabia during this period, where it was also customary to dedicate every hundredth animal to the visited sanctuary. The consecrated beast was declared *ḥaram* (forbidden, or inviolable) and allowed to roam freely.[15] According to some Muslim authors, herd owners with at least one hundred heads used to hunt down a gazelle and sacrifice it instead of the consecrated firstling.[16] Mocking this pre-Islamic custom, Ibn Dihya (d. 633/1235) claims that the pagan Arabs preferred to sacrifice an animal they had hunted down in place of the more valuable sheep they had originally vowed to slaughter in Rajab.[17] An iconic anecdote whereby the renowned pre-Islamic Arab poet Hatim al-Ta'i would slaughter ten camels on each day of Rajab and openhandedly distribute the meat to passers-by suggests otherwise, however – if it is of any historical value.[18]

Residents of the Arabian Peninsula customarily travelled to fairs (*sūqs*) during Rajab. For instance, the pre-Islamic fair of Ṣuḥār (Sohar, Oman) was held from the tenth to the fifteenth day of Rajab, and the fair of Dabā (present day Dibba), some 100km to the north of Sohar, took place on the last day of the month.[19] The fair of Hubasha, the site of some pagan shrines in western Arabia (a six- or eight-day walk to the south of Mecca), opened annually on the first day of Rajab and lasted for eight days. It was allegedly visited by Muhammad while he was an employee of Khadija, the Meccan merchant whom he later married.[20] Al-Fakihi, a ninth-century historian of Arabia, notes that the Rajab fair of Hubasha was the last of the pre-Islamic fairs to survive. It was destroyed in Rajab 197/813 by the emir of Mecca and Medina, Dawud b. ʿIsa b. Musa, in retaliation for the murder of the Abbasid governor he had sent to Hubasha, upon the advice of Meccan jurists. The site was abandonned thereafter, and according to medieval historians this was the end of the Rajab fairs in Arabia.[21] Travel to Mecca for the Rajab *ʿumra* (minor pilgrimage), however, continued throughout the centuries.

Did the Prophet go on *ʿumra* during Rajab, according to the Arab sources? ʿA'isha has expressly negated the presumption by saying that the Prophet never performed an *ʿumra* in the month of Rajab.[22] And yet, in the fourteenth century Shaykh ʿAli ibn Ibrahim al-ʿAttar (d. 724/1324) reports as following:

> One of the things that I have heard about the people of Mecca – may God increase its honour – is that they perform the *ʿumra* frequently during Rajab. This is something for which I know of no [*sharʿī*] basis; all I know is

> that it was reported in the hadith that the Messenger of God said: an *ʿumra* in Ramadan is equivalent to the hajj.[23]

Meir Kister has collected a number of accounts about the perpetuation of Rajab rituals in Mecca and their further evolution during the early Islamic period.[24] According to one of these sources, the first Umayyad caliph, Muʿawiya b. Abi Sufyan (d. 660/680), would send scents to perfume the Kaʿba during Rajab (that is, at the time of the *ʿumra*) and Dhu al-Hijja (for the hajj). Other tidbits of evidence indicate that under the Umayyads and early Abbasids Meccans continued to observe special devotions in and around the Kaʿba over the course of Rajab and that ruling officials supported those practices. Khalid b. ʿAbdallah al-Qasri (d. 126/743), who served as governor of Mecca, is said to have lit the lamps along the route between the hills of al-Safa and al-Marwa, not only during the hajj, but throughout the month of Rajab as well. ʿAbdallah b. Muhammad, who governed Mecca under the Umayyad caliph Sulayman b. ʿAbd al-Malik a hundred years later, used to illuminate the first night of Rajab.[25]

The *ʿumra* to the sanctuary of Mecca is probably the best example of a rite that 'survived' the transition from *Jāhiliyya* to Islam, albeit transformed, other than the hajj itself.[26] The sacrifice of the *ʿatīra* or *faraʿ*, also known as *al-rājiba* or *al-rajabiyya*, did not disappear either. Was the ritual slaughter (*dhabḥ*) in Rajab sanctioned by early Islamic sources? Some sayings attributed to the Prophet, the caliph ʿUmar and the traditionist ʿAbdallah b. ʿUmar indeed recommend its continuous performance, but other sayings condemn it,[27] declaring unequivocally that these sacrifices in honour of pagan deities are outside the pale of Islam (*lā faraʿ wa-lā ʿatīra fi-l-Islām*).[28] And yet, the *Ṣaḥīḥ* of al-Bukhari (d. 256/870), the *Musnad* of Ibn Hanbal (d. 241/855) and other canonical compilations of hadith include the somewhat surprising recommendation to sacrifice a ewe on every day of Rajab in every household (*ʿalā ahl kull bayt an yadhbaḥa shāt fī kull Rajab wa-fī kull aḍḥā shāt*). While this hadith apparently places the sacrifices of Rajab on an equal footing with the obligatory offering of ʿId al-Adha,[29] al-Shafiʿi explains that the former was only volitional. Several centuries later, Ibn Hajar al-ʿAsqalani (d. 852/1449) claims that the Prophet did not abolish it in principle, but that he negated the idea of making this sacrifice especially in Rajab, saying: 'Offer sacrifices, no matter which month is it . . .'[30] If these contrasting testimonies can teach us anything, I believe that they demonstrate that the pre-Islamic practices of sacred times were not readily abandonned.

Fasting

Muslims who observed a lengthy fast during Rajab in the early Islamic period were accused of confusing the month with Ramadan, or of imitating pagan customs. Abu Bakr, the first caliph, who was known for his close ties with Muhammad, allegedly smashed the clay pots that members of his household filled with water in preparation for the fast and asked them: 'Do you [really] want to liken it [Rajab] to Ramadan?'[31] Another anecdote depicts ʿUmar, the zealous second caliph, as outraged by this custom. He smacks the hands of fasters and scolds them, saying that 'this month was venerated by the people of the *Jāhiliyya*'.[32] A hadith citing ʿAʾisha, the Prophet's widow, makes the same case in a more subtle fashion by spelling out the Prophet's pattern of fasting. ʿAʾisha claims that Muhammad used to fast for three days every month of the year and that after his arrival in Medina she never saw him complete an entire month's fast, save in Ramadan.[33]

Wagtendonk cites hadiths along these lines, for the purpose of backing his highly speculative idea whereby Ramadan – a month that had not been celebrated in pre-Islamic Arabia at all – was originally intended to replace pre-Islamic Rajab as the Islamic holy month. He avers that there is a profound difference between pre-Islamic fasting during Rajab and the Islamic fast of Ramadan. Whereas the former was an expression of gratitude for the seasonal blessings of spring, Ramadan – detached from the seasonal cycle – is observed in honour of God's revelation of the Qurʾan.[34] Whether practitioners indeed made such a distinction is questionable in my mind. In any event, Arabs clearly fasted during both Ramadan *and* Rajab after the transition to Islam, and non-Arab converts to Islam adopted this custom, despite hadiths maintaining that the obligatory fast of Ramadan abrogates all other fasts.

As per a tenth-century compilation of Shiʿi hadith, Jaʿfar al-Sadiq (d. 148/765), the sixth imam, recommended at least three days of fasting in Rajab, preferably at the beginning, middle, and end of the month. Moreover, he promised wonderful rewards to Muslims fasting during Rajab, not least the escort of thousands of angels to 'apartments in Paradise under which rivers shall flow'.[35] A conversation that allegedly took place between al-Sadiq and a disciple named ʿAli b. Salim, who came to visit him on Rajab, perhaps indicates that fasting during this month was not a common practice at the time, however. The imam asks his guest whether he had already fasted on any part of the month, 'which has been preferred and greatly sanctified by God', and prompts him to do so over its remaining days.[36] In another Shiʿi account of this meeting, by al-Fattāl al-Naysābūrī (d. 508/1114–5), the imam stresses the great rewards for fasting towards the end of Rajab.[37]

The fact, that most of the chapter on Rajab in *The Merits of the Three Months* (*Faḍāʾil al-Ashhur al-Thalātha*) by Ibn Babawayh (d. 381/991) is devoted to listing the exceedingly lush material and spiritual rewards for fasting anywhere between one and thirty days during this month, perhaps also demonstrates that tenth-century Shiʿi scholars were still trying to encourage this practice. Ibn Babawayh's chapter is replete with colourful descriptions of the thrones, crowns and castles wrought of gold and ebony and precious stones, as well as the luxurious fabrics awaiting the devout fasters of Rajab in Paradise. He also promises reassuring escorts of angels, locked gates, wide ditches and gallons of water, to protect the fasters against the torments of the grave and hellfire.[38]

A number of hadith transmitters stress that people who fast during Rajab are entitled to *shafāʿa* (intercession) for legions of relatives whose sins will be wiped out and who will enter Paradise on the Day of Judgement.[39] Remittance of sin is advocated, time and again, as the central merit of Rajab, as God has singled out the month with pardon (*Allāh khaṣṣa Rajab bi-l-maghfira*). According to one etymology, the three consonants that make up the word 'Rajab' stand for *raḥmat Allāh* (God's mercy), *jawd Allāh* (God's generosity), and *birr Allāh* (God's kindness), implying that these divine traits are provided in abundance throughout the month.[40] A corollary of this belief is that during Rajab prayers are more likely to be answered and that 'the pens [of heaven] are busy testifying, jotting down acts of obedience and erasing sins'.[41] According to a hadith transmitted by Qays b. ʿAbbad (d. c. 85/705), this writing and erasure, which is mentioned in Q. 13: 39, takes place on the tenth day of Rajab.[42]

In sum, some traditions imply belief in the greater expiatory power (or 'ritual efficacy') of fasting and other devotions if performed on holy days rather than on regular days.[43] Other traditions stress the increased availability of intercession during such times, especially that of the angels.[44]

The above-mentioned Ibn Babawayh says: 'whoever fasts in the middle of the month earns intercession as for [all of the large tribes of] Rabiʿa and Mudar (*shafāʿa fi mithl Rabīʿa wa-Muḍar*)'. Those that fast at the end of the month are anointed 'kings of Paradise' (*mulūk al-janna*) – a status that enables them to intercede on behalf of their parents, children, brothers, aunts and uncles, acquaintances and neighbours, even if they all warrant hellfire. The most detailed tradition incrementally raises the merits of fasting during Rajab one day at a time. Finally, fasting on all thirty days of the month is said to be rewarded with a full pardon of one's sins, extensive intercessory powers, heavenly bliss and immeasurable wealth in Paradise.[45] Better yet, Muhammad is said to guarantee comprehensive protection from hellfire (that is, seventy ditches, each as wide as the expanse between the heavens and earth!)[46] to those who fast in good faith during *any* part of Rajab.

For menstruating women or people too weak for extended fasts, the alternative of donating a loaf of bread to the poor on each day of Rajab is suggested.[47] 'Feeding the poor (*ṭaʿām al-masākīn*; as in Q. 5: 95)' was a substitute for a number of unfulfilled religious obligations beside missed fast-days, such as Friday prayers, or improperly-executed hajj rituals.[48] In addition to its social function, it was considered a sign of repentance and an efficient means for 'purifying' one's wealth and expiating one's sins.[49] Those unable to both fast and afford such expenditures are advised to recite the daily praise (*tasbīḥ*) of the Lord a hundred times: 'Praise exalted God, praise Him who alone is worthy of praise, praise the most powerful and noble, praise Him who wears glory, which is rightfully His'.[50] A hundred, in this case, probably stands for very many, countless. Such recurrent repetition is advised also regarding other supererogatory petitionary prayers (*duʿāʾ*), some of which are mentioned below,[51] perhaps not only to indicate total devotion, but also to produce a hypnotic affect, typical of Sufi *dhikr* ceremonies.

Prayers and Supplications

While marking Rajab with customs such as truce, ritual slaughter and perhaps also fasting was in all likelihood a carry-over from Pre-Islamic Arabia, prayer was Islamic in form and content. The first new Rajab devotion post-dating the advent of Islam was possibly an annual prayer gathering reportedly held in Janad (Yemen) towards the end of Muhammad's life. The ceremony is mentioned in a Mamluk bibliographical dictionary within the framework of an anecdote about the Banu Aswad. This Arab tribe had converted to Islam under the influence of the missionary companion Muʿadh b. Jabal, who introduced them to the Qurʾan. Later on, some Jews attended one of their weekly Friday sermons in Janad. After Muʿadh skillfully answered a question about the keys to heaven (*mafātīḥ al-janna*), the Jews decided to convert to Islam. From that point forward, great crowds used to flock to al-Janad Mosque on the first Friday of Rajab to commemorate this event every year with a communal prayer (to which the author refers as *al-ṣalāt al-mashhūra*, the well-known prayer), 'and they would witness blessings such as rainfall'.[52]

Seclusion in mosques (*iʿtikāf*) appears to have been an early Rajab practice in some locales. Shurayh ibn al-Harith al-Kindi, who was nominated judge in Kufa by the caliph ʿUmar ibn al-Khattab, dealt with the case of a pious woman who had vowed to spend the entire month of Rajab in the local mosque, at some unspecified time during his nearly sixty years in office. He suggested that she perform an alternative voluntary devotion (*nask*), perhaps in order to appease her husband: fast each day throughout the month and feed a pauper (*maskīn*) after breaking the fast each night. Shurayh al-Kindi admits that this judgement of his was based on his personal opinion (*raʾy*), rather than on the Qurʾan or on precedent (*sunna māḍiya*), revealing the novelty of the dilemma.[53] The historicity, or at least plausibility of the case seems to be indicated by another short reference in the sources: a decree attributed to Ziyad ibn Abihi (d. 53/673), the governor of Iraq during the early Umayyad period, forbidding women to perform *iʿtikāf* during Rajab.[54] Regardless of whether al-Kindi's ruling was related to that decree or based on a fictional anecdote, it demonstrates an understanding of the desire for a significant spiritual experience during the holy month.

A lively account of an early ritual for the absolution from sins during Rajab turns up in the manual *al-Ghunya li-Ṭālibī Ṭarīq al-Ḥaqq* (Sufficient Provisions for the Seekers of the Path of Truth) by the Hanbali mystic ʿAbd al-Qadir al-Jilani (d. 561/1166). It is a complete guide on all aspects of Islam, to which I already referred above, with instructions for the Sufi novice, comparable to al-Ghazzali's *Iḥyāʾ ʿUlūm al-Dīn*.[55] In the concluding chapter of the section on Rajab, readers are advised that during this month 'supplication (*du'ā'*) is answered, minor demeanors are taken lightly [that is, overlooked], and the punishment for iniquity is doubled'. Thereafter, al-Jilani retells a story of 'Ali (who is presented as the narrator) and his son al-Husayn. While performing the *ṭawwāf* (circumambulation around the *Ka'ba*), the two overheard a man uttering a supplication that they had never heard before. They approached him to inquire about this prayer. He confesses to have been known as the most frivolous among the Arabs (*mashhūr fī-l-'Arab bi-l-lahū wa-l-ṭarab*) in his youth, having transgressed continuously, even during Rajab and Sha'ban. He then tells 'Ali and al-Husayn that his father had received the words of the supplication from the Prophet in a dream. Proclaiming the supplication 'a jewel from the jewels of the divine', the likes of which he had only once heard during the time of 'Umar ibn al-Khattab, 'Ali encouraged the man to preserve it and continue to perform it.[56]

The fourth Shi'i imam, 'Ali Zayn al-'Abidin (d. c. 92/710) – also known as *al-Sajjād* (the one who constantly prostrates) – is said to have authored and performed another special supplication for the month of Rajab. The text of this prayer is included in the fifth recension of *al-Ṣaḥīfa al-Sajjādiyya*,[57] a collection of petitionary prayers that Constance Padwick has dubbed a 'Shi'ite breviary'. As evidenced by Padwick's translation of an excerpt from the invocation (*du'ā'*) for Rajab, it constitutes a touching plea for mercy that was inspired by the 'all too human dread of death and the loneliness of the tomb'.[58] The full text appears in a 1411/1990 edition of the *Ṣaḥīfa*, with another short story told by Tawus b. Kaysan al-Yamani (d. 106/725):

> I was passing by the Ka'ba during the month of Rajab, and I saw a man bowing and prostrating himself in prayer. I realised that it was 'Ali b. al-Husayn [that is, 'Ali Zayn al-'Abidin, the son who survived Karbala] and I said to myself: this is a devout man from the Prophet's family; by God, I should adopt this *du'ā'* too. So I observed him carefully . . . 'Ali raised his palms to the heavens and said: My Lord, my Lord, these hands, [which are] stretched towards you, are filled with sin, but my eyes, [which are also] turned towards you, are full of hope . . . Had I not known that there is no escaping you, I would have been the first to run . . . My Lord, if my torment could add anything to your glory, I would have sought to patiently bear it, but I know that neither the

> compliance of the pious adds to your glory nor the disobedience of the sinners detracts from it . . . I am the worst of slaves, and you are the best of Lords. I beg forgiveness, I beg forgiveness [repeated a hundred times].

Tawus reports that he was moved to copious weeping by ʿAli's supplication and body gestures. He adds that during the following Rajab he witnessed ʿAli praying in the same manner, this time in the mosque of Kufa.[59] Obviously, the performance of such invocations was not tied to the sacred precincts of the Meccan sanctuary and could be performed in any mosque or space. This characteristic of rituals of sacred time gives them a significant 'advantage' over rituals of sacred place, although – as we have seen – the blessings of places could be duplicated, 'multiplied', or transported in various circumstances.

Zayn al-ʿAbidin's grandson, Imam al-Sadiq, is said to have transmitted or personally authored a supplication containing God's great name, which is bound to be answered if offered anywhere on the fifteenth day of Rajab. Ibn Babawayh, the above-mentioned Shiʿi compiler of Imami hadith, relates the genesis of this prayer in a touching story about Fatima Umm Dawud (also known as Umm Khalid al-Barbariyya), who was al-Sadiq's erstwhile wet nurse and the mother of the great-grandson of the second Imam, al-Hasan. Her son Dawud, who had apparently been imprisoned by the Abbasid caliph al-Mansur, was taken from Medina to Iraq, in shackles,[60] and she lost contact with him. Al-Sadiq suggested that Fatima recite his supplication, as it is bound to open the gates of heaven, engage the angels and secure an answer from God, if performed during the upcoming greatly blessed month of Rajab. He instructed her to fast during the three 'white days (*al-ayyām al-bayḍ* or *ayyām al-bīḍ*)', namely from the thirteenth to the fifteenth day of the month. On the noon of the last day, she should perform an ablution, wear clean clothes and fixatedly perform in a spotless and perfumed house eight *rakʿa*s, reciting certain verses during each one. When Rajab arrived, Fatima diligently followed al-Sadiq's instructions, and her son was miraculously set free. Dawud himself reports that, just before returning home on the fifteenth day of Rajab, he had a dream of his mother immersed in prayer and surrounded by angels.[61]

This last scene corresponds to the recommendation to synchronise prayer on earth with the prayer of the angels up high, captured in a Prophetic hadith: 'Observe the dawn prayer, then stop praying when the sun is rising until it is fully up . . . Then pray, for the prayer is witnessed and attended by angels'.[62] The participation of angels is mentioned in the Qur'an with regards to the Night of Power (*laylat al-Qadr*), confering the idea that sacred time was celebrated in the domain of the angels, or perhaps consecrated by them: 'The angels and the spirit descend therein, by permission of their Lord, with all decrees' (Q. 97: 4).

The mystic Abu Talib al-Makki (d. 386/996) mentions the first, the fifteenth and the twenty-seventh night of Rajab as especially auspicious nights for praying.[63] The merits of prayer on the fifteenth are also listed in the *Kitāb ʿAmal Rajab* (or *ʿAmal Rajab wa-Shaʿbān wa-Ramaḍān*) by the Imami author Abu ʿAbd Allah b. ʿAyyash al-Jawhari (d. 401/1010–11).[64]

The first mention of a public, rather than private celebration of Rajab in Egypt, as far as I am aware of,[65] is a brief note about prayer assemblies that were held on the Fridays of Rajab, Shaʿban and Ramadan. The venue was the old Friday mosque of Misr (Fustat) in the middle of the fourth/tenth century, in the presence of the ruler of Egypt, Ibn Tughj al-Ikhshid. We are not told whether he initiated or funded those assemblies. Based on the chronicler's comment that the old mosque was not Ibn Tughj's habitual place for Friday prayer,[66] it stands to reason that he joined only on special occasions, and Rajab was considered as such.

Four sermons for Rajab (*Rajabiyyāt*) – attributed to ʿAbd al-Rahim b. Muhammad Ibn Nubata al-Fariqi (d. 374/985),[67] best known for preaching jihad against Byzantium at the court of Sayf al-Dawla al-Hamadhani in Aleppo[68] – also indicate that the special status of Rajab was acknowledged in public in the tenth century. The *Rajabiyyāt* offer a closer look at how the merits of the month were understood and propagated at the time in northern Syria and the Jazira, and perhaps also beyond the Hamdanid domains.

Sermons

Ibn Nubata's *Rajabiyyāt* are part of a homiliary arranged in calendrical order: four sermons for each month (five for Shaʿban), with additional orations for the two festivals and several other occasions. The first Rajab sermon opens with gratitude to the Lord for favouring Rajab 'the month of God, *al-aṣamm* [the deaf], *al-aṣabb* [the pouring] . . .[69] the first of the months of merits . . . in the era of the *Jāhiliyya* and in the time of Islam', and obligating Muslims to glorify it. The preacher then urges his audience to seize the moment and take advantage of the propitious time by engaging in pious deeds such as fasting, acting graciously, feeding the poor, getting up at night for devotions, repenting and seeking forgiveness. Mocking the typical believer who at the outset of Rajab solemnly promises that he will repent during Shaʿban, and at the beginning of Shaʿban swears to repent during Ramadan and so forth until his days are over, Ibn Nubata prods the faithful not to wait for the morrow. He concludes this sermon with the hadith promising Muslims who fast three days in Rajab a taste of the wondrous Rajab River, which flows through Paradise, 'whiter than milk and sweeter than honey'.[70]

Ibn Nubata's oration for the second Friday of the month is by and large an admonition against lax prayer. He provocatively asks his audience: 'What is it with you? Why are you lazy regarding the prescribed time for prayer? Have you no fear of God, or have you not heard the Prophet say: "Prayer alone distinguishes the Muslim from the infidel?"' Ibn Nubata urges every believer not only to pray, but to actively call out those who neglect their prayers. His only explicit mention of Rajab in this sermon surfaces in the hadith that concludes with the following: 'Supplication during Rajab is bound to be answered; O God, bestow upon us your mercy and guidance'.[71] In the third oration, Ibn Nubata returns to the theme of the month's special status as a time during which a repentant can attain forgiveness. Upon thanking God once more for the unique merits of Rajab, the sermon ends with a hadith promising those fasting on the Thursdays, Fridays and Saturdays of the month the equivalent reward of 900 years of worship![72] Needless to say, this equation should be understood as 'hortatory exaggeration rather than rigorous theological statement', and Ibn Nubata's audience must have understood it as a form of artistic expression, rather than a rigid lesson.[73]

Whoever came for the fourth sermon of the Rajab cycle heard verses extolling God for His creation, His preference of 'the community of Muhammad (*ummat Muḥammad*)' over all the other nations and the grace of Prophet's night journey. Ibn Nubata did not explicitly claim that the *miʿrāj* took place during Rajab, but he thanks the Prophet for successfully pleading on the *umma*'s behalf during this month, to have the number of daily prayers set at five rather than fifty. This is an obvious allusion to a well-known tradition about the Night Journey.

The next sermon opens with a reminder of the sanctity of Rajab, via the well-known prophetic hadith:

> Rajab is the month of God; God has favoured it over all other months just as He has preferred me over the rest of mankind. Shaʿban is my month; God has favoured it over all other months just as He has preferred me (Muhammad) over the rest of the prophets. Ramadan is the month of my nation; God has favoured it over all other months, just as He has preferred the Muslims over the rest of the nations.[74]

Clearly, by the mid-tenth century Rajab and the ensuing months of Ramadan and Shaʿban – rather than the pre-Islamic triad of Dhu al-Qaʿda, Dhu al-Hijja and Muharram – constituted a sacred time that merited special devotions, domestic and communal. And yet, its standing remained the object of scholarly debate.

Notes

1. Al-Yaʿqūbī, *Works*, vol. 2, p. 576.
2. Kister, 'Radjab'. Some of the names refer to seasonal practices that involve the cultivation of date palms; al-Jīlānī, *al-Ghunya*, vol. 2, pp. 722–3.
3. Ibn Diḥya, *Adāʾ mā wajab*, pp. 30–44; al-Jīlānī, *al-Ghunya*, vol. 2, pp. 724–7.
4. Ibn Diḥya, *Adāʾ mā wajab*, p. 31.
5. Al-Jīlānī, *al-Ghunya*, vol. 2, pp. 725.
6. Al-Bīrūnī, *Chronology*, p. 321.
7. Munt, 'Pilgrimage', pp. 21, 23, 27.
8. Al-Jīlānī, *al-Ghunya*, vol. 2, p. 726; al-Ḥasakānī, *Faḍāʾil Shahr Rajab,* vol. 2, p. 495.
9. Al-Yaʿqūbī, *Works*, trans. Gordon et al., vol. 2, p. 593. Compare with the security provided by shrines, as on p. 102 above.
10. See, for example, al-Baghawī, *Tafsīr*, vol. 4, p. 45; al-Baghdādī, *al-Nāsikh wa-l-Mansūkh*, pp. 184–5; Ibn Diḥya, *Adāʾ mā wajab*, p. 72.
11. Ibn Qayyim al-Jawziyya, *al-Ḍawʾ*.
12. Ioh, 'The calendar', pp. 489–90.
13. Paret and Chaumont, 'ʿUmra'.
14. For examples of invocations that were allegedly uttered by different tribes upon setting out for Mecca, see al-Yaʿqūbī, *Works*, pp. 378–9. All of these prayers open with the exclamation *labbayka* ('Here we are!').

15. Wagtendonk, *Fasting*, pp. 30, 35–6, 115.
16. Restö, ''Atīra.'
17. Ibn Diḥya, *Adāʾ mā wajab*, p. 39.
18. Al-Iṣfahānī, *Kitāb al-Aghānī*, vol. 17, p. 262. I would like to thank Haviva Yishay for bringing this reference to my attention. For more on the Prophet's recommendation to distribute meat on Rajab, see Kister, 'Radjab', p. 374.
19. Al-Bīrūnī, *Chronology*, p. 324.
20. Ioh, 'The calendar', p. 478. Yaqut mentions Hubasha (pronounced also as Habasha) as 'the site of one of the fairs of the Arabs in the *Jāhiliyya*', in the framework of an anecdote that explains his primary motive for writing the geographical lexicon *Muʿjam al-Buldān*: nobody around him seemed to know where this place was, even though the Prophet had visited it. See the annotated English translation of Yaqut's introduction (*muqaddima*) in Jwaideh, *Introductory Chapters*, p. 9.
21. Al-Azraqī, *Akhbār Makka*, vol. 1, pp. 191–2.
22. Al-Nawawī, *Sharḥ Ṣaḥīḥ Muslim*, vol. 8, p. 485.
23. Al-Albānī, *Musājala ʿIlmiyya*, p. 56.
24. For reports on large crowds gathering in Mecca in the Umayyad period, see Kister, 'Rajab is the month', p. 220.
25. Walker, 'Popular festivals', p. 79; Ibn al-Fākihī, *Akhbār Makka*, vol. 3, p. 240. The latter's successor apparently discontinued this practice altogether.
26. On the 'Islamisation' of the pre-Islamic pilgrimage to Mecca, see Lazarus-Yafeh, 'Religious dialectics', pp. 17–37.
27. Kister, 'Radjab', p. 374; ibid. 'Rajab is the month', pp. 192–6.
28. Ibn Ḥanbal, *Musnad*, 7255, 7737, 9290, 10361.
29. Ibn Diḥya, *Adāʾ mā wajab*, p. 39.
30. Kister, 'Rajab is the month', pp. 193–5.
31. Ibn Taymiyya, *Majmūʿat al-Fatāwā*, vol. 25, pp. 290–2.
32. Kister, 'Radjab', pp. 374–5; Ibn Diḥya, *Adāʾ mā wajab*, pp. 57, 63. For a list of Companions and Followers that used to fast during Rajab, see Ibn Rajab, *Laṭāʾif*, p. 229.
33. Kister, 'Shaʿbān', pp. 17, 37. ʿAʾisha is also cited as arguing against another remainder of pre-Islamic baseless beliefs ('*min iʿtiqād al-Jāhiliyya*', or '*min āthār al-Jāhiliyya*'): that marriage and marital relations should be avoided during the month of Shawwal (Ibn al-ʿAṭṭār, *Tuḥfat al-Ṭālibīn*, p. 228).
34. Wagtendonk, *Fasting*, pp. 119–21. On fasting as a token of gratitude for God's benefactions (*shukr al-niʿma*), see Katz, *Birth of the Prophet*, pp. 63–7.

35. Kister, 'Rajab is the month', p. 204.
36. Ibn Bābawayh, *Faḍāʾil al-Ashhur*, p. 18.
37. Al-Naysābūrī, *Rawḍat al-Wāʿiẓayn*, p. 396.
38. Ibid. pp. 435–40.
39. On the mediation of ordinary people for one another, see Marmon, 'Quality of mercy', pp. 126–9.
40. Al-Jīlānī, *al-Ghunya*, vol. 2, p. 723.
41. Ḍiyāʾ al-Dīn Ibn al-Athīr, *al-Mathal al-Sāʾir*, vol. 2, p. 150.
42. Ibn Rajab, *Laṭāʾif*, p. 223. In the context of the Qurʾanic passage the phrase 'God blots out, and He establishes whatsoever he will' seems to refer to sacred scriptures, but the hadith that mentions the tenth day of Rajab (and some Qurʾan commentaries) obviously allude to the book which records every person's standing and will be presented on the day of resurrection to determine one's fate (mentioned in Q. 84: 7–9). See Raven, 'Reward and punishment'.
43. Berg, 'Ṣawm'. For a perceptive discussion on medieval Islamic and modern scholarly understandings of the expiatory power (or 'ritual efficacy') of devotions like fasting and pilgrimage to Mecca, as well as the theological problematics of this idea, see Katz, 'The *Hajj*', esp. pp. 102–9.
44. See Mol, '*Laylat al-Qadr*', p. 86; Memon, *Ibn Taymīya's Struggle*, p. 135.
45. Ibn Bābawayh, *Faḍāʾil al-Ashhur*, pp. 17–31, 38–9. The same idea is reiterated in his *Thawāb al-Aʿmāl*; see Kohlberg, *Medieval Scholar*, p. 372.
46. Elsewhere, the safe distance from hellfire is described as 'equivalent to that which a crow flies in its lifetime'. See Kister, 'Rajab is the month', p. 214.
47. The opposite – that is, fasting rather than almsgiving – is recommended by Islamic scholars, either when the expiator is too poor to give anything away, or too rich to feel the pinch on his or her pocket. See Fierro, 'Caliphal legitimacy, pp. 55–60; Lev, 'Charity', p. 482. See also the excursus about *istighfār*.
48. Singer, *Charity*, p. 73; Reid, *Law and Piety*, pp. 74–5; Talmon-Heller, 'Charity and repentance'.
49. Lev, 'Charity', p. 240.
50. Ibn Bābawayh, *Faḍāʾil al-Ashhur*, pp. 29–31; al-Naysābūrī, *Rawḍat al-Wāʿiẓayn*, pp. 435–9.
51. See below, pp. 144, 168, 179, 180, 198.
52. Lecker, 'Judaism among Kinda', p. 639; al-Jundī (d. 732/1332), *al-Sulūk*, vol. 1, p. 82. For Ibn al-Mujāwir's take on the mosque, see ibid. *Ṣifat Bilād al-Yaman,* vol. 2, pp. 165–6.

53. Ibn Ḥayyān (d. 306/918), *Akhbār al-Quḍāt*, vol. 2, pp. 325, 360; al-Būṣīrī (d. 840/1436), *Itḥāf al-Khayra*, vol. 3, p. 128.
54. Kister, 'Rajab is the month', p. 220.
55. Malik, *Grey Falcon*, p. 5.
56. Al-Jīlānī, *al-Ghunya*, vol. 2, pp. 756–61. On al-Jilani's continuing popularity in the twentieth century, see Padwick, *Devotions*, p. XVII.
57. Chittick, *Psalms*. For the history of the text and its recensions, see ibid. pp. xv–xix. In Chittick's estimation, 'whether or not historians accept the text as completely authentic will not change the actual influence which Zayn al-ʿAbidin and the *Ṣaḥīfa* have exercised upon Islam over the centuries' (ibid. p. xx).
58. Padwick, *Devotions*, pp. xv, 277.
59. Al-Abtaḥī, *al-Saḥīfa al-Sajjādiyya*, pp. 201–3. For ʿAli's shorter prayer for the first day of Rajab, see ibid. p. 200. See also http://www.duas.org/sajjadiya/sajjadiya.htm.
60. Legendary as the story sounds, partisans of the ʿAlids were indeed persecuted at the time. See Crow, 'Imam Jaʿfar', pp. 59–61. On al-Sadiq's significant role as transmitter of Shiʿi hadith, law and doctrine, see ibid. pp. 63–77.
61. Ibn Bābawayh, *Faḍā'il al-Ashhur*, pp. 32–7. A longer version of the prayer can be found in Ibn Ṭāwūs, *al-Iqbāl*, vol. 3, pp. 240–53.
62. Muslim, *Ṣaḥīḥ*, vol. 2, p. 396.
63. Al-Makkī, *Qūt al-Qulūb*, pp. 135–7.
64. See the reference to this work in Kohlberg, *Medieval Scholar*, pp. 107–8.
65. Al-Maghribī, *Kitāb al-Mughrib*, p. 35.
66. Ibid. p. 16.
67. Jones, *Power of Oratory*, p. 69.
68. Canard, 'Ibn Nubāta'; Frank, 'The Arabs in Anatolia', p. 151.
69. See above, p. 134.
70. Ibn Nubāta, *Dīwān Khuṭab*, pp. 44–5. For a Spanish translation and introduction, see Attou, *Los Sermones*, pp. 1–6, 57, 133–9.
71. Ibn Nubāta, *Dīwān Khuṭab*, pp. 46–7.
72. Ibid. pp. 47–8.
73. Katz, 'Hajj', p. 106.
74. Ibn Nubāta, *Dīwān Khuṭab*, pp. 48–51. For other sayings that characterise all three months in catchy rhymes (for instance, '*Rajab shahr al-tawba, Shaʿbān shahr al-maḥabba, Ramaḍān shahr al-qurba*'), see al-Jīlānī, *al-Ghunya*, vol. 2, p. 737.

16

Excursus: The Founding of an Islamic Lunar Calendar

Listing the four sacred months in his final sermon (*khuṭbat al-wadāʿ*), the Prophet explains: 'Four of the months are sacred [*ḥurum*], three of which are sequential – Dhu al-Qaʿda, Dhu al-Hijja, and Muharram, and Rajab Mudar [which falls] between Jumada and Shaʿban'. Some interpreters regarded this seemingly extraneous detail concerning Rajab's alignment as a reference to the abolishment of the pre-Islamic practice of intercalation (*ibṭālan li-l-nasīʾ alladhī kānat al-ʿArab yafʿalūhu fī al-Jāhiliyya*).

According to the Qurʾan, intercalation was one of the pagan Arabs' misdeeds:

> The month postponed (*al-nasīʾ*) is an increase of unbelief (*ziyāda fī al-kufr*) whereby the unbelievers go astray; one year they make it profane (*yuḥillūnahu*), and hallow it (*yuḥrimūnahu*) another, to agree with the number that God has hallowed, and so profane what God has hallowed (Q. 9: 37).

According to Muslim exegetes, the verse accuses the pagans of Arabia of adding a month, the *nasīʾ*, roughly once every three years, so as to postpone the beginning of the sacred months and delay 'God's peace' for their own convenience. As a result, they also observed the hajj on the wrong days,[1] rendering the sacred profane and the profane sacred.

Al-Biruni, who wrote a comparative essay on calendars in the first half of the eleventh century, postulates that the Arabs learned intercalation (*kabs*) from Jewish people in the area, '200 years before the hijra'– that is, in the fifth century CE.[2] Other medieval Muslim scholars stressed that the abolition of the leap year restored the divinely prescribed 'natural order' and ensured the timely observation of sacred rites.[3] Ibn Taymiyya claims that the abrogation of intercalation restored the correct 'Abrahamic' calendar. He especially refers to the securing of the proper timing of the hajj – which even Abu Bakr erroneously performed during Dhu al-Qaʿda (rather than on Dhu al-Hijja) in the ninth year of the hijra – for years to come.[4]

Ibn Taymiyya points to the moon as a divinely appointed indicator of the months and years, citing the Qurʾan: 'It is He who made the sun a shining light and the moon a derived light and determined for it phases, that you may know the number of years and account [of time]' (Q. 10: 5). Another verse that Ibn Taymiyya quotes in this context is the following: 'They will question you concerning the new moons [*al-ahilla*]. Say: "They are appointed times for the people and the pilgrimage"' (Q. 2: 189). In Ibn Taymiyya's estimation, such passages demonstrate that the beginning of the month or year must be confirmed by an actual sighting of the new moon. Expounding on the merits of the lunar calendar, he avers that the testimony of an eyewitness is the most reliable form of evidence of a new moon's arrival. Unlike mathematical calculations, it is simple and accessible to one and all. Moreover, such evidence cannot be tampered with by men of religion, as was indeed the case, so he adds, in some religious communities. Ibn Taymiyya also suggests that the People of the Book have deviated from the lunar calendar owing to their distortion of Sacred Scriptures (*taḥrīf*) and the corruptive influence of Sabian philosophers.[5]

From the etic perspective of a comparative religion scholar, Hava Lazarus-Yafeh presents the repeal of intercalation and the establishment of a calendar detached from the natural cycle as an attempt to break away from the pagan past and usher in a new strictly monotheistic era.[6] Frederick Denny describes the Islamic ritual year as 'denying any intrinsic value to seedtime and to harvest, to breeding and lambing, to cool summer retreats to Taʾif or to London . . . blessing it all with its lordly progress in a regular round of visits'.[7] A more sociological interpretation of this historical reform is suggested by Hideyuki Ioh, who explains that Muhammad changed the traditional pilgrimage and trading system in Arabia by introducing the lunar calendar. Grounded on a circuit of fairs going clockwise around the Arab Peninsula, the pre-Islamic setup was coordinated with the most favourable seasons for sailing the Red Sea and for inland travel. Since the maintenance of order among the pre-Islamic tribes depended on this pilgrimage cycle, the adoption of the purely lunar calendar triggered vast societal changes, which facilitated the establishment of the new Islamic order.[8]

By adapting a calendar of their own, Muslims also carved out a separate identity *vis-à-vis* the other monotheistic religions.[9] The Ismaʿilis, who also use a lunar calendar, separated themselves from other Muslims by not determining the beginning of a month based on the sighting of the new crescent. Instead, they rely on astronomical calculations. As a result, they end the fast of Ramadan, for example, thirty days after its beginning, regardless of the moon and the rest of the Muslims.[10]

Notes

1. Al-Jīlānī, *al-Ghunya*, vol. 2, p. 725; Ibn Rajab, *Laṭāʾif*, p. 221. See also Knysh, 'Months', p. 412.
2. Al-Bīrūnī, *Āthār*, p. 62, trans. in ibid. *Chronology*, p. 73. For a comprehensive history of the Arabs' transition from a lunar to a lunisolar calendar (in 412 CE) and back to the lunar calendar (in 632 CE), based on al-Biruni, see Burnaby, *Elements*, pp. 367–9.
3. Bonner, 'Time has come', pp. 16–22. See also Stowasser, *The Day Begins*, pp. 14–15, 20–1, 35.
4. Ibn Taymiyya, *Majmūʿat al-Fatāwā*, vol. 1, p. 144; vol. 7, p. 291; vol. 19, p. 155; vol. 25, pp. 79–80 (quoting al-Baghawi's *Tafsīr*).
5. *Daqāʾiq al-Tafsīr*, vol. 3, pp. 213–15. Lazarus-Yafeh discusses *taḥrīf* in her *Intertwined Worlds*, pp. 19–35. On Ibn Taymiyya's understanding of the Sabians, see ibid. *al-Fatwā al-Ḥamawiyya*, pp. 246–51.
6. Lazarus-Yafeh, *Religious Aspects*, pp. 21, 38–42.
7. Denny, 'Islamic ritual', p. 72.
8. Ioh, 'The calendar', pp. 473, 477, 480, 513.
9. Ibn Rajab, *Laṭāʾif*, p. 217; Knysh, 'Months'.
10. Bloom, 'Ceremonial and sacred space', p. 101.

17

Rajab Under Fatimid Rule

With the transition to the Fatimid period, we encounter a relative wealth of material on various aspects of religious life and public rituals. Most of it, however, is filtered through later Mamluk pens. Some fragments of the works by the era's historians and its primary documents have survived the destruction of Fatimid libraries and the vicissitudes of time and were incorporated into later compilations.[1] As we have already seen, this literature is further enhanced by the period's travelogues, memoirs, poems and sermons.

Throughout the last decades of the tenth century, the Fatimid Empire and its newly built capital enjoyed great prosperity and cultural vigour. The rule of a living Shiʿi imam, an exceptional occurrence in the history of the downtrodden Shiʿis, generated significant innovations in thought, literature and especially ritual. The royal court was active and quite imaginative with respect to the commemoration of various religious events: pan-Islamic rites such as *ʿĪd al-Nahr* (Festival of Sacrifice), *ʿĪd al-Fiṭr* (Breaking of the Fast) and the beginning of the New Year; new Shiʿi-Ismaʿili festivals; and, last but not least, age-old Egyptian Nile rites.[2] On account of the differences in how Ismaʿilis and Sunnis determined the new month, as explained in the excursus above, the pan-Islamic holidays of each stream did not necessarily fall on the same day. However, the royal court found creative solutions that enabled everyone to jointly celebrate the festivals, even the breaking of the fast, without violating any of the two religio-legal codes or the Fatimid etiquette of conduct in the presence of the imam-caliph.

In her *Ritual, Politics and the City in Fatimid Cairo* (1994), undoubtedly the most important contribution to research on Fatimid political culture, Paula Sanders studies Fatimid protocol in detail and offers a sophisticated analysis of the dynasty's rites. The supremacy of the imam-caliph in the Isma'ili system assigned him the religious role of God's infallible representative on earth, as well as the political leadership of a wealthy empire. It was manifested, among others, by the central location and vast dimensions of his palace compound, which occupied nearly a fifth of Cairo's total area. The ruler's eminence received expression also in the spatial organisation of the official ceremonies that were held both within and beyond the palace walls. Sanders demonstrates that the Fatimid court initiated a dynamic ritual framework whose symbolic and polemical language conveyed multiple meanings. Ingeniously tailored to several different audiences, the events occasionally marked (and sometimes obscured) the boundaries separating Isma'ilis and non-Isma'ilis, ruler and ruled.[3] As illustrated in the next chapter, the splendid 'bilingual' rites of state that were developped for Rajab epitomise this multiplicity.

The Official Rites of Rajab

The Fatimids commemorated the sanctity of the three consecutive months of Rajab, Sha'ban and Ramadan on an unprecedented scale.[4] Proceeding in chronological order, our survey of the development of the Fatimid rites of Rajab (based on information gleaned from extant medieval sources) begins in the reign of al-Mu'izz li-Din Allah (341/953–365/975), the first imam-caliph in Egypt. In his time, special royal kitchens were busy producing holiday sweets from the first day of the month until mid-Sha'ban. The Shi'i historian Ibn Abi Tayy (d. 630/1233) lists seven types of sweets that came out of these kitchens and were generously distributed among the elite and the common people (*al-khāṣṣ wa-l-'āmm*): *al-khushkanānj wa-l-khalwā' wa-l-basandūd wa-l-fānīd wa-l-ka'k wa-l-tamr wa-l-bundūq*.[5] As the later Sunni al-Qalqashandi notes, magnanimity was a permanent feature of the Fatimid regime: 'regarding how [the Fatimids] ruled their subjects and persuaded the hearts of their opponents, they were generous . . . They met everyone with the hospitality he deserves and reciprocated gifts with multiples of their values'.[6]

The second imam-caliph in Egypt, al-'Aziz (365/975–386/996), was 'famously fond of public events and processions'.[7] During his reign, the fifteenth day of Rajab was marked by an assembly of members of the ruling elite at the Great Mosque of al-Azhar, over which the chief qadi presided.

Al-Azhar was the first Fatimid mosque in Cairo, a venue intended for Isma'ili services, orations and ceremonies; it was rarely visited by members of other groups. On the night of the fifteenth, it was lavishly lit up – as befitting the meaning of its name ('luminous' or 'radiant') and scented with incense burners.[8] Reciters specialising in the Qur'an, poetry and dirges performed their

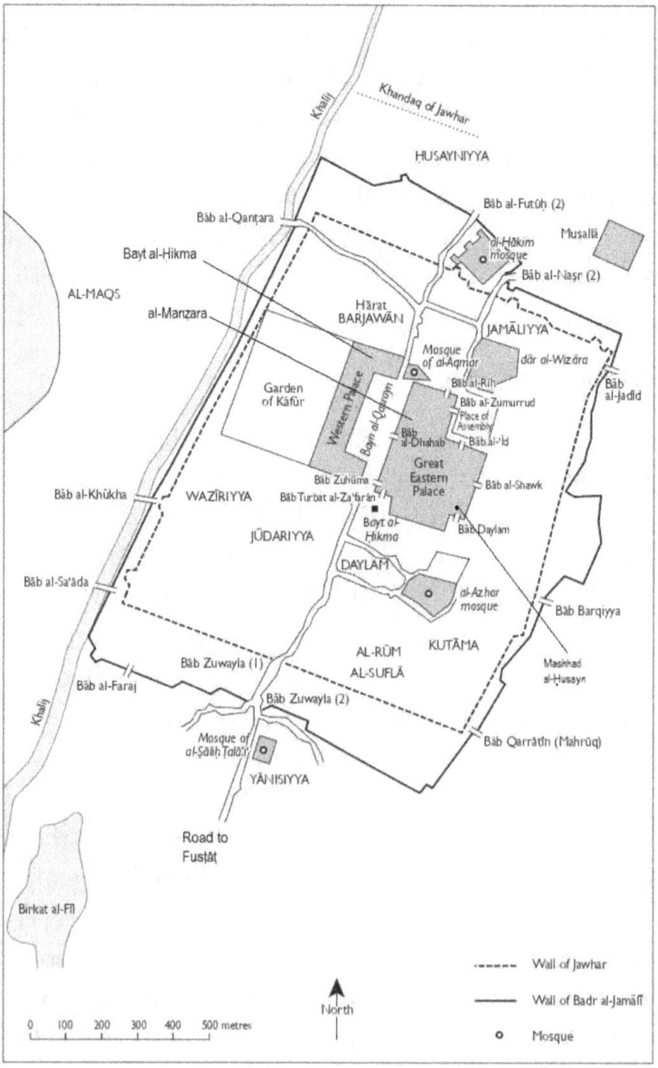

Figure 17.1 Map of Fatimid Cairo (al-Qāhira) (Michael Brett, *The Fatimid Empire*, Edinburgh: Edinburgh University Press, 2017, with minor modifications, courtesy of the author).

art.[9] Throughout the months of Rajab, Sha'ban and Ramadan, when *i'tikāf* (spending time in mosques) was thought to be most commendable, food was distributed in al-Azhar.[10]

Following a twenty-year moratorium put into effect by Caliph al-Hakim bi-Amr Allah, these customs were renewed and made much more inclusive under his successor al-Zahir (411/1021–427/1036). On the first and fifteenth nights of Rajab, the state funded the illumination of all six communal mosques in Cairo and its shrines (*mashāhid*), as well as some of the prayer houses in Sunni Fustat. By al-Zahir's time, these occasions were widely known as *layālī al-wuqūd* ('the nights of kindling lights'). In the pitifully meager extant portions of his work on the Fatimids, the historian al-Musabbihi (d. 420/1029) recalls that the night of mid-Rajab 415/1024 was a remarkable event. In addition to the beautiful illumination of the mosques, he notes the presence of the caliph, his personal servants, ladies of the court (*al-sayyidāt*)[11] and throngs of commoners.[12]

Al-Zahir watched the celebrations from an imperial belvedere (*manẓara*) overlooking al-Azhar Mosque.[13] The high point of the ceremony was when the imam-caliph opened one of the belvedere's windows and revealed his head and face to the crowd, with the flame of an enormous candle. This was quite a rare gesture, for the Fatimid imam was usually kept out of view; interactions with him were limited and extremely ritualised. At any rate, he did not speak to the crowd. Instead, one of his eunuchs leaned out of an adjacent window, extended his head and right hand, and solemnly announced: 'The Commander of the Faithful returns your greetings'.[14] Thereafter, the preacher (*khaṭīb*) of al-Anwar Mosque (later known as the Mosque of al-Hakim) delivered a sermon in which he reminded the audience of the month's virtues, closing with a prayer for the caliph. The preachers of al-Azhar Mosque then delivered orations of their own. Qur'an recitation was performed between the sermons. Consequently, the judge, the notaries, the three preachers and most of the crowd proceeded to the vizier's residence, where shorter sermons were given. The party then moved on to Fustat (also known as Misr), escorted by the governor of Cairo. The final prayer of the night was held in the old 'Amr ibn al-'As Mosque. There also occurred a similar procession on the night of the fourteenth, which included an additional stop at al-Qarafa Cemetery.[15]

Caliphal audiences (*julūs*) were held on the nights of the first and the fifteenth of Rajab, and on the same two nights of Shaʿbān.[16] If one may infer from the experience of the *dāʿī* al-Muʾayyad fi al-Din al-Shirazi (d. 470/1077), seeing the imam-caliph in person made a great impression on his followers. Al-Shirazi had his first personal audience with al-Mustansir (r. 427/1036–487/1094) after two years of anticipation, in 439/1048. He writes:

> My eyes had barely fallen on him when awe took hold of me and reverence overcame me as if I was standing in front of the Messenger of God [Muhammad] and the Commander of the Faithful [ʿAli] . . . facing their faces. I tried . . . to make my tongue intercede with him . . . I found it bound . . . not rising to speech and not finding the way to words . . . then I rose, took his noble hand and kissed it.[17]

At the time of this first encounter, both al-Shirazi and the imam-caliph were young men. Although the former probably became disillusioned with the caliph later on in life, as he witnessed the erosion of al-Mustansir's authority and his humiliating marginalisation,[18] he remained devoted to al-Mustansir until his death thirty years later (the caliph outlived him).[19] Over time, he was elevated to the post of al-Mustansir's chief propagandist (*dāʿī al-duʿāt*) and became responsible for the court-sponsored 'sessions of wisdom (*majālis al-ḥikma*)'.

No less than eight hundred of the sermons that he composed for these assemblies – all of which were supposedly approved by the imam-caliph himself – have survived in a collection titled *al-Majālis al-Muʾayyadiyya*.[20] These sessions were held every Thursday at the Fatimid palace for the initiated – that is, for members of the Ismaʿili elite, who had already taken the oath of allegiance to the imam and paid certain dues to the state. The sermons, which dealt with ethics, theology, philosophy, eschatology and allegorical interpretations of the Qurʾan and hadith, were often tied to a political event or religious festivity, such as the Day of Ghadir, the Day of al-Tarwiya, the hajj, Shaʿban, Ramadan, al-ʿAshura and Rajab.[21] Orations were repeated – most likely in a popularised, non-esoteric version – on Fridays or Mondays at al-Azhar Mosque.[22]

The lion's share of al-Shirazi's twenty-fifth sermon was devoted to the merits of Rajab. It begins with greetings upon the Messenger of God, Muhammad (referred to by the patently Shiʿi honorific *ḥujja*, meaning 'proof of God'), his *waṣī* (legate) ʿAli and the imams of his progeny, who 'guide the believers to the truth'. This is followed by expressions of gratitude to the Lord for having singled out the month of Rajab and having promised to augment the rewards for good deeds performed throughout this month. Then come warnings: al-Shirazi cautions that transgressions during Rajab will be duly punished, and he calls on believers to engage in fasting, prayer, repentance (*tawba*, *ināba*, and *rujūʿ*) and submission during Rajab, for the sake of drawing closer to God and securing divine recompense. To drive these points home, al-Shirazi presents the stories of the Prophets Adam and Noah (Nuh) in the Qurʾan and the historical traditions, referring to their external and inner meanings (*al-ẓāhir wa-l-bāṭin*). According to Ismaʿili lore, Adam and Nuh were the first of six speaker-prophets (*nāṭiq*s) who successively promulgated religious laws to the rank and file, and transmitted their inner meaning to the initiated.[23] In summation, as customary on such occasions, al-Shirazi blesses the *shīʿa*, the faction that enjoys the guidance of the *imams*.[24] Three other sermons in *al-Majālis al-Muʾayyadiyya* also remind the audience of Rajab's merits and blessings, and urge the believers to signify the month by engaging in good works and seeking proximity to the imams (*al-aʿmāl al-ṣāliḥa wa-l-taqarrub ilā al-aʾimma*).[25]

After the death of al-Shirazi, in an effort to downplay the role of the imam-caliph al-Mustansir and reduce his prominence, the vizier Badr al-Din al-Jamali (d. 515/1121), whom we have encountered in Part One as the initiator of Mashhad Raʾs al-Husayn, abolished the caliphal processions and outdoor prayers at the *muṣallā*.[26] Ironically, the changes he had initiated in Cairo – by then a living city with a mixed population, rather than an exclusively Ismaʿili bastion – created optimal topographic conditions for impressive royal processions to span the metropolis. The grand thoroughfare linking the northern and southern edges of the esplanade of Bayn al-Qasrayn (between the eastern and western palaces) became part of a major artery, linking Cairo with Misr (Fustat).[27]

Ibn al-Maʾmun al-Bataʾihi, who lived in Cairo in the twelfth century,[28] portrays the rites that were held there on the first day of Rajab 512/1118. He mentions the handsome gratuities handed out to the city's scholars as well as

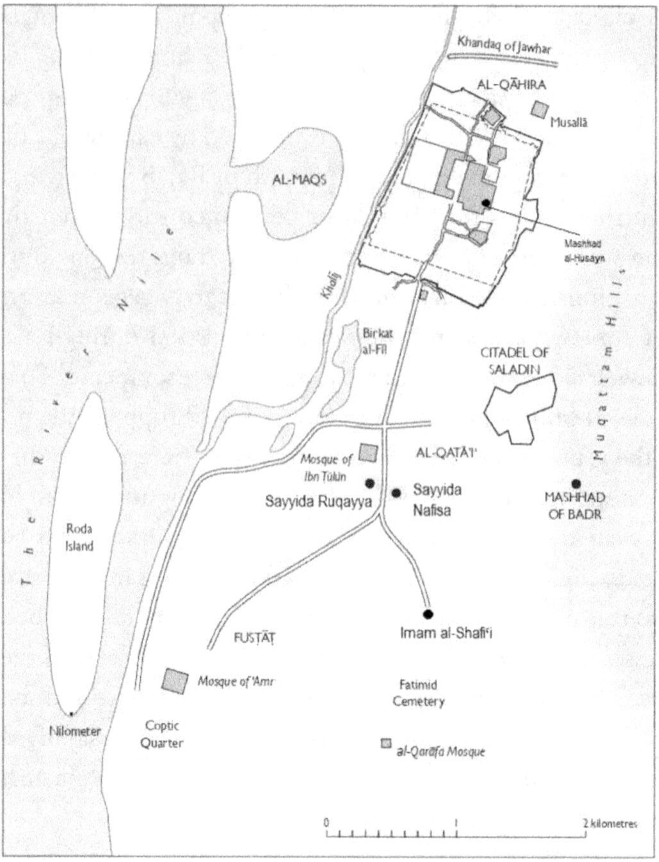

Figure 17.2 Map of Greater Cairo in the twelfth century (Brett, *Fatimid Empire*, with minor modifications, courtesy of the author).

the donations to the poor from the neighbourhood of al-Qarafa. Poets who recited their lyrics on this day at 'the splendid palace' of Vizier al-Afdal b. Badr al-Din were generously compensated for their performance.[29] Poetry played an important role on such occasions. At least from the time of the above-mentioned al-Shirazi, it converged with the Isma'ili *da'wa*, accentuating theological motifs and praise for the imam whose glorification was considered a religiously meritorious practice.[30]

The banquet on the first day of Rajab 516/1122 was a special celebration, as it marked both the full restoration to power of the caliph al-Amir bi-Ahkam Allah[31] and the much-awaited end of a protracted famine. Depicted as remarkably joyous and open-handed on that celebration, al-Amir is quoted as saying: 'I have restored my country to its glory; the days have received their share, now remain the nights'. Soon after, he renewed the processions that Badr al-Jamali had terminated, along with the festivities (*mawāsim*) on the four nights of kindling lights (*layālī al-wuqūd*), the first and fifteenth nights of Rajab and Sha'ban. To this end, the caliph allotted fifty golden dinars for candles and ordered the qadi and his officials to personally distribute on horseback oil for the illumination of the Friday and regular mosques. The head (*mutawallī*) of the treasury distributed sweets.[32] The court had provided beforehand for the preparation of special confections for all fifty-nine nights of these two months. Mounds of spices, nuts (even expensive pistachios), sesame seeds and dates were supplied to the royal kitchens for this purpose. A third of these goods were delivered to the vizier's residence and another third to military headquarters, while the rest was apparently intended for the caliph's palace.[33] According to al-Maqrizi, owing to al-Amir's part in the extortion of onerous taxes, the imam-caliph was advised to fast, rather than feast, during the holy months of Rajab and Sha'ban. Lev surmises that al-Maqrizi related this episode for the sake of mocking the Fatimids and their concept of the imams' infallibility.[34]

Al-Amir's vizier Ibn al-Ma'mun was an eyewitness to the Rajab rituals at a mosque opposite Bab al-Khukha, one of the southwestern gates of the Fatimid wall. He was deeply impressed by the seriousness of the prayers, the distribution of charity and other acts of piety.[35] In his annals of the subsequent year, 517/1123, Ibn al-Ma'mun lists dozens of institutions that received an abundance of quality oil for the four nights: nine Friday mosques in the greater Cairo area, shrines like Mashhad al-Sayyida Nafisa[36] and regular mosques. Sharing his personal experience, he specifically mentions attending Friday noon prayers at the old congregational mosque in Fustat on the second day of Rajab. After being shown there a *muṣḥaf* (codex of the Qur'an) allegedly hand-written by 'Ali b. Abi Talib,[37] he was so moved that he instantly donated a large sum of money for the manuscript's embellishment with gold and had his name written on it. Ibn al-Ma'mun was also generous towards the poor and the custodians of all the holy sites that he visited.[38]

On the fifteenth day of Rajab, while the qadi and his entourage repeated their circuit, the soldiers (*ahl al-rubuṭ*)[39] also received provisions. Tables laden with cakes and an assortment of other sweets were set up in the courtyards of the great mosques. In at least one instance, the tables were plundered by the poor just as the qadi and his party sat down to enjoy the feast.[40] Rather than wait patiently for the qadi's party to have their fill and then enjoy the leftovers, expressing gratitude and loyalty to the imam-caliph, as was expected from the poor according to Fatimid etiquette (and academic theories about gifts and social hierarchies),[41] the crowd rebelled. We may assume that there were other similar cases, especially in the frequent years of famine that plagued eleventh-century Egypt. Perhaps ritual is bound to fail sometimes in periods of social crisis, and the breakdown of norms is to be expected when people need food rather than the communication of symbolic meaning.

In times of plenty, presiding over banquets not only portrayed the imam-caliph as a generous Muslim, but also symbolised his position atop the successful Fatimid religio-political order and his standing as the head of an elaborate system of patronage. This message was clearly conveyed on ʿId al-Fitr (Festival of Breaking the Fast). Following the sacrificial slaughter, the imam-caliph parceled out meat to state officials (*arbāb al-rusūm*), and they distributed their portions further to their own constituents.[42] As Paula Sanders observes in her analysis of ʿId al-Fitr 515/1121, banquets were also intensely political affairs. They provided an opportunity to convey implicit political statements by which competing interests and hostile opponents were either mollified or permanently silenced. A food offering from the caliph's hands constituted a guarantee of *amān* (security) and symbolised the status of those who were lucky to be in the ruler's favour.[43] For all those reasons, the Fatimids spent extravagant sums on meals for army officers, state officials and other members of the ruling class and on food for the needy.

In all likelihood, the distribution of coins in the Fatimid cash economy would have been more efficient than dishing out food and certainly would have preserved, in accordance with Islamic ideals, the anonymity of donor and recipient. Yet, the royal court seems to have preferred the distribution of food, as nostalgically described by the poet ʿUmara al-Yamani (d. 569/1174) shortly after the demise of the Fatimids and Saladin's takeover of Egypt: 'pure torrents of generosity . . . great were the trays offered your guests, borne upon shoulders or on wheels'.[44] This strategy perhaps engendered a measure of intimacy between the otherwise inapproachable imam-caliph and his subjects.

Food was handed over more noticeably and in a larger variety of forms than coins, thus establishing both the palace's generosity and the recipients' social rank in a more spectacular fashion. For Isma'ilis – who believed that their imam was the door to salvation in this world and the next 'the foundation of faith and deed . . . , the guiding light, like lanterns in the darkest night' – receiving food from his hands, even if only indirectly, must have held great significance.

Not only food was considered a potent means for transferring *baraka* from the charismatic ruler to his subjects. Robes of honour (*khila'*) that had previously been worn by the imam-caliph himself for ceremonial public occasions were likewise thought to be infused with his *baraka* and therefore constituted the most desired gift for which esteemed officials and guests of the state could hope.[45] The timing of the bestowal of robes and food – that is, the holidays and sacred months – intensified the blessings and heightened their effect all the more so.

Ibn Tuwayr, a senior official in the later Fatimid governments, describes elaborate, expensive ceremonies.[46] In his time, preparations for the first day of Rajab already began during the second half of the month of Jumada al-Akhira (the sixth month, also known as Jumada al-Thani), when five dozen candles, weighing six Egyptian *qinṭār* a piece, were transported from royal warehouses to the starting line of the procession at the chief qadi's residence.[47] When Rajab finally arrived, throngs of people made their way from Fustat to Cairo. As soon as the evening prayer was finished, the masses stood in anticipation of the 'riding of the judge'. The spectacular procession featured the caliph, who was surrounded by robed gatekeepers, chamberlains and servants bearing the huge candles. As the procession advanced, *mu'adhdhin*s invoked blessings for the imam-caliph and vizier, while Qur'an reciters chanted. All the senior officials escorting the imam-caliph were arranged at a prescribed distance from him, as per their rank within the top echelons of government, in correspondence with their position at the above-mentioned 'sessions of wisdom'.[48] However, given the abundance of men, women and children that joined the procession, Ibn Tuwayr comments that 'no one could tell the chiefs from the subjects (*bi-ḥaythu lā yu'rafu al-ra'īs min al-mar'ūs*)'.[49] In other words, the rite was skillfully choreographed to convey multiple messages: it reinforced the socio-political order of the Fatimid state and the strict hierarchy within the royal court on the one hand,[50] while on the other hand it loosened the boundaries between the Ismaʿili elite and the non-Ismaʿili subjects. The participation of women and children undoubtedly added to its 'informality'.

For commoners, the formal festivities of Rajab were combined with informal gatherings in cemeteries and markets. Delectable statuettes (*tamāthīl*) made from sweet dough and ground pistachio nuts were produced exclusively for this season, perhaps imitating the produce of the royal kitchens and transforming the popular Confectioners' Market (*Sūq al-Ḥalawiyyīn*) near the city's southern gate into 'one of the most beautiful things to see, with all those statuettes of horses, lions, cats, and the like made of sugar . . . [which] everyone, from the nobleman to the miserable, had to buy for his children and family'.[51] Those unable to afford the Rajab sweets could at least enjoy the sight of the wonderful sculptures paraded throughout Cairo at the end of Ramadan.[52]

ʿ*Umra* and Ziyāra

Nasir Khusraw arrived in Cairo in 439/1047 and was impressed by the imam-caliph al-Mustansir in a way that resembles al-Shirazi's memoirs.[53] One of the many examples of the imam-caliph's power and magnanimity that Nasir Khusraw offers in his travelogue are the steps that al-Mustansir took to ensure a punctual hajj, as well as his lavish funding of the Mecca-bound caravans. He explains:

> It is customary for a representative of the imam-caliph to appear in the mosques in the middle of the month of Rajab and proclaim the following: 'O company of Muslims! The pilgrimage season is at hand, and the sultan, as usual, has undertaken the outfitting of soldiers, horses, camels, and provisions'.

According to Nasir Khusraw, this proclamation was repeated during Ramadan and again in the middle of Dhu al-Qaʿda, when the caravan set out for Mecca for the hajj. He was still in Cairo in Rajab 440/1049, when the caliph's speaker regretfully announced the cancellation of that year's convoy due to the famine ravaging the Hijaz. Considering that traversing the 1600-kilometre-long route took some thirty-five days in the eleventh century, the imam-caliph's precaution seems to have been very reasonable.

Nonetheless, he duly sent an official delegation bearing a new cloth cover (*kiswa*) for the Kaʿba via the Red Sea.

The dressing (or 'veiling') of the Kaʿba was an ancient practice, pre-dating Islamic worship in Mecca. Muʿawiyya (r. 40/661–60/680), the fifth caliph of the Islamic state, is said to have established the tradition of the caliph providing the *kiswa*.[54] The annual delivery of a black *kiswa* from Egypt dates to the tenth century CE, if not earlier. The Fatimids replaced the black *kiswa* (black was the colour of the Abbasids) with a white one, likewise adorned with bands of gold-thread embroidery of Qurʾanic verses and pious phrases.[55]

Nasir Khusraw volunteered to accompany the *kiswa* in 440/1049. After fifteen days at sea and another fortnight over land, he and the other delegates spent only six days in the hunger-stricken city. Nasir Khusraw joined the Rajab caravan the following year as well, this time reporting of the atrocities evoked by the famine.[56] He reached Mecca again on the last day of Jumada al-Thani 442/1050 and spent the entire month of Rajab in the holy city. By then conditions must have improved, for he encountered many pilgrims from the Hijaz and the Yemen performing the *ʿumra*, enjoying 'a great season, like the Ramadan feast and the pilgrimage time'.

Nasir Khusraw notes that throughout the days of Rajab the door to the Kaʿba was opened at sunrise, while over the rest of the year, Ramadan included, it was open only a few times a week, if at all. He then offers a detailed account of the door-opening ceremony. The key-bearer, the elderly head of the Banu Shayba clan, was accompanied by five to six men who held back the entrance's heavy brocade covering as he approached the lock.[57] When the door was opened, the pilgrims, who had restlessly crammed around the key-bearer, raised their hands and prayed in unison, so loudly that their voices were heard across the entire city. Before anyone was allowed inside, the old man entered himself, performed the customary two *rakʿas* and delivered a sermon to the crowd.[58] Going over this protocol, Nasir Khusraw conveys – perhaps unintentionally – the powerful effect of the convergence of sacred time and sacred place, aptly symbolised by the image of the open doors of the Kaʿba throughout the days of Rajab.

While travel to Mecca could be undertaken only by the few, a visit (*ziyāra*) to a nearby holy site on holy days was feasible for the many. Hence, crowds of Cairenes headed to the cemetery of al-Qarafa where, according to a report about Rajab 402/1012 cited by al-Maqrizi, people made merry 'as they usually did'.[59] 'Ulama' typically undermined the religious devotions of commoners, but a number of caliphal edicts and ordinances are indicative of the popularity of the events and also of their destabilising potential. A decree published in Rajab 414/1023 called for the cessation of 'reprehensible deeds' during 'the noble blessed months (*al-ashhur al-shuraf al-mubāraka*)'. Pursuant to another edict, women were prohibited from visiting cemeteries after dark. There was also a ban on gatherings in al-Giza, al-Jazira and al-Qarafa, as well as on playing in public musical instruments other than the flute during these months.[60]

The prohibition on women's visits to cemeteries was a recurrent one, repeated time and again. Women may have been specifically targeted so as to prevent the two sexes from intermingling, or because their mere presence 'coloured' get-togethers as dubious from the point of view of formal Islam, or perhaps simply because they constituted the majority of nocturnal visitors at these sites. Marion Katz offers several explanations for cemeteries' allure to women, apart from the rather standard claims that the liminal space of the graveyard enabled women to sidestep the control of male authority, especially at night. Katz speculates that these outings were an opportunity to cultivate family networks and ties, and to gain extra merit in addition to that promised by the act of visitation, through distributing food to the poor, who were regular callers in such places.[61] We will deal with women's devotions and charitable giving during Rajab again in the next chapter, which is devoted to the thirteenth to fifteenth centuries.

Prayers and Supplications

A new Rajab tradition – *ṣalāt al-raghā'ib*, the Prayer for Great Rewards,[62] which was to attract quite a following – had its inauguration in late-eleventh-century Jerusalem, according to the testimony of a rather hostile eyewitness, Abu Bakr al-Turtushi (d. 520/1126). Al-Turtushi, an Andalusi Maliki scholar who lived in Jerusalem for three years during the 1090s, provides a brief account of the event, on the tail end of a vivid description of a supererogatory prayer intended for mid-Sha'ban.[63] He claims that the latter had emerged several decades earlier.

Quoting an eyewitness by the name of Abu Muhammad al-Maqdisi, he writes that until 448/1056–7 . . .

> We never had this Prayer for Great Rewards, which is [currently] observed during Rajab and Shaʿban in Jerusalem. Then, a man from Nablus known as Ibn Abi al-Hamraʾ, a fine reciter (*ḥasan al-tilāwa*), came to us, to Jerusalem. He stood up and prayed in the al-Aqsa Mosque, on the night of mid-Shaʿban. One by one, devotees joined in, and before long, a sizable group was praying in unison. When he came again the next year, many people prayed with him and filled the mosque, and the prayer spread from al-Aqsa . . . to the homes of the people. In the end, it became an established [part of the liturgy] as though it were a *sunna* [and remains so] to this very day . . . As for the prayer of Rajab, it was instituted here in Jerusalem only after 480 [1087]. We had not seen it or heard of it prior to that year.[64]

Al-Turtushi's compilation reveals his antipathy towards *bidaʿ* (religious innovations) in general and his opposition to the veneration of Rajab, which he calls 'bygone remnants of the beliefs of the Age of Ignorance (*innamā hiyya ghabirāt min baqāyā ʿuqūd al-jāhiliyya*)' in particular.[65] He depicts the man who allegedly introduced the new prayer assembly as a stranger devoid of religious authority. Similarly, he labels the people that assembled behind him an 'ignorant crowd', thereby implying that the prayer's wide acceptance does not indicate its religious validity. His understanding corroborates also with the assessment of modern scholars of ritual, who suggest that repetition implied that a custom was an ancient and venerable one and disguised 'its original character as accident' (*à la* Jonathan Z. Smith).[66] The new rite was dressed in the 'respectable garb of antiquity' (as articulated by Eric Hobsbawm and Terence Ranger) also in late hadith compilations that linked it to the Prophet.

While al-Turtushi's account of the very moment of the 'invention of tradition' may be regarded as a literary device aimed at devaluing the prayer, it seems to have been grounded on actual occurrences in eleventh-century Jerusalem. In any event, this account was repeated as historical by a host of other medieval Muslim authors. Al-Ghazzali (d. 555/1111), who spent a few months in Jerusalem in 488/1095, confirms the reports about the successful implementation of the new prayer, which he calls 'the Rajab prayer (*ṣalāt Rajab*)'. He mentions it in his encyclopaedic work *Iḥyāʾ ʿUlūm al-Dīn* (The

Revival of the Religious Sciences), saying that in Rajab he had 'seen the people of Jerusalem eagerly performing it *en masse* (*bi-ijmā'ihim*), refusing to forgo it'. Al-Ghazzali defines the custom 'a recommended (*mustaḥabba*) prayer', in line with his oft-stated faith in the efficacy of prayer, all the more so when performed by a group (*jamā'a*). Nonetheless, he admits that only a 'single line of authority has handed this worship down', thereby actually admitting the doubtful authenticity of the Prophetic hadith supporting it. He goes on to offer a detailed account of the ritual: a prayer replete with repetitions, based on the formulaic numbers of three, seven, twelve, seventy and seven hundred.[67]

Each of these numbers, as Anne-Marie Schimmel explains, has a metaphysical meaning in multiple religious traditions, including Islam, as reflected also in its folklore, high literature, architecture and music.[68] The efficacy of prayer was thought to be enhanced by the use of these symbolic numbers, but perhaps mere repetition, strenuous as it was, had a reassuring or perhaps even empowering on the devotee:

> The person who fasts on the first Thursday of Rajab then performs twelve *rak'as* (prayer cycles) between the evening and night prayers, inserting the *taslima* (salutation) between each pair of *rak'as*, with each *rak'a* including one recitation of the *fātiḥa*, three repetitions of 'We have indeed revealed this on *laylat al-qadr*' [sura 97, al-Qadr], and twelve repetitions of 'Say: He is God, the One and Only' [sura 112].[69] After completing his prayer, he prays for me [that is, the Prophet] seventy times, saying 'O God! Pray for Muhammad the unschooled Prophet and for his family', whereupon he does a full prostration and says seventy times while in the prostrate position 'Most majestic and holy, Lord of the angels and the spirit (*Sabūḥ*, *Quddūs*, *Rabb al-malā'ika wa-l-rūḥ*).[70] Thereafter, he raises his head and says seventy times 'O Lord! Forgive and take pity, overlook that which You know, for You are the most powerful and kind'.[71] He prostrates himself a second time and repeats what he said in the first prostration, and finally, remaining in the prostrated position, asks for his personal needs. They will [indeed] be granted . . . God forgives all the sins of the person who performs this prayer, even if they were like the foam on the sea, numerous as sand, weighty as mountains, or akin to the leaves of trees. When the Hour comes, he will be allowed to intercede for 700 members of his family, who warrant the fire.[72]

A slightly longer version of this tradition is cited in the *Kitāb al-Mawḍūʿāt* (Book of Fabricated Hadith) by Ibn al-Jawzi (d. 597/1201). He identifies the fabricator of this particular hadith as ʿAli b. ʿAbd Allah b. Jahdam Abu al-Hasan (d. 407/1016–17 or 414/1023), the shaykh of the Sufis in Mecca and author of *Bahjat al-Asrār* (Splendour of the Secrets).[73]

The sudden appearance and immediate success of the new prayer, as evidenced by al-Turtushi and al-Ghazzali, demand closer scrutiny through the lens of both the historian conversant with the late-eleventh-century Levant and the scholar of religion, who is sensitive to the structure, function and meaning of religious rites. Why did this supplication take off in late-eleventh-century Jerusalem? To begin with, the Fatimid court's pronounced veneration of Rajab (described in detail above) may have reverberated also in provincial Jerusalem. Furthermore, Fatimid building projects in Jerusalem's Haram, some of which were carried out after the earthquakes of 405/1015 and 424/1033, also must have inspired the local development of new rituals. Within several decades, the sacred esplanade was dotted with prayer niches commemorating Muhammad's night journey, honouring angels and prophets, and signifying the Islamic belief in the resurrection and judgement.

Some of those signposts are mentioned in the first extant travel guide for Muslim pilgrims to Jerusalem: a seven-folio treatise included in a compilation titled *Faḍāʾil Bayt al-Maqdis wa-l-Khalīl wa-Faḍāʾil al-Shām* (The Merits of Jerusalem, Hebron and Syria) by Abu al-Maʿali al-Musharraf b. al-Murajja. Written in the 430s/1040s, the guidebook recommends supererogatory prayers and other rituals for each of the sites on its route.[74] Several of the traditions mentioned therein put an emphasis on seeking penance and reward at specific locations, allegedly refered to in the Qurʾan.[75] A case in point is the Gate of Mercy (*Bāb al-Raḥma*), mentioned in Q. 57: 13 and 7: 46, as a 'wall with a door in it; inside will be mercy, and outside it punishment (or doom)'. Another site that the travel-guide deems to be conducive to prayer and repentance is the south-western Gate of Pardon (*Bāb Ḥiṭṭa*), where God ordered the reluctant Children of Israel to enter, prostrate and say '*ḥiṭṭa*', promising to forgive their transgressions thereby (Q. 2: 58).[76]

Ibn Abi Hamra of Nablus, the man who allegedly taught *ṣalāt al-raghāʾib* in al-Aqsa, was one of very many visitors to late-eleventh-century Jerusalem.

The notion that one could substitute for the hajj with repeated visits to Jerusalem and the performance of the *taʿrīf* (the ceremony performed on Jabal ʿArafat during the hajj) there, albeit highly contested, drew Muslims from distant countries to Jerusalem.[77] The pious custom of donning the special clothes for the pilgrimage to Mecca in Jerusalem was another cause of its 'magnetism'. In all likelihood, some of these pilgrims were in a state of heightened religious fervour and thus easily attracted to peculiar gatherings and spontaneous innovative expressions of piety. Lastly, I would argue that the confluence between the sacred space of Jerusalem and the sacred time of Rajab was an ideal backdrop for the cultivation of new forms of religious devotion, all the more so to the performance of *istighfār* in public assemblies.[78]

Supplications for private prayer on Rajab were compiled in twelfth-century Baghdad by the Hanbali-Sufi ʿAbd al-Qadir al-Jilani. For the first night of the month he recommends one of two supplications that, so he claims, were used by the very first Muslims. He attributes the first supplication to ʿAli b. Abi Talib, who allegedly performed it that night, after the regular evening prayer. The text begins with an invocation of the Prophet and his family, by virtue of whose *ʿiṣma* (infallibility) the devotee hopes to be protected from evil, keep away from sin and avoid punishment. Humbling himself before God, the supplicatory begs for forgiveness. He prays for his spiritual wellbeing, and for his family and all Muslims. Another prayer for this occasion was supposedly taught, at the same early stage of Islam, to the Prophet Muhammad by the Angel Gabriel. With the arrival of the new moon of Rajab, Muhammad transmitted the devotion to his companion Salman al-Farisi and promised him:

> There will be no believer, male or female, who prays thirty *rakʿa*s over the course of this month, recites the *fātiḥa* (sura 1) and *qul huwwa Allāhu aḥad* (sura 112) three times during each *rakʿa*, and *qul yā ayyuhā al-kāfirūn* (sura 109, The Disbelievers) three times during each *rakʿa*, whose sins will not be erased by God.

At Salman's request, the Prophet added detailed instructions for attendant bodily gestures and commendation. Lastly, he advised him to end his prayer with a personal supplication, for on this occasion it is bound to be answered;

his reward will be tantamount to that of a person who fasted the entire month of Rajab. At this stage, al-Jilani discloses that Salman was moved to tears of gratitude.[79]

Fasting

Most advocates of *ṣalāt al-raghāʾib* recommend fasting before its performance – that is, throughout the first Thursday of Rajab. Drawing on a hadith, ʿAbd al-Qadir al-Jilani (d. 561/1166) highlights the merits of Thursdays and those of the month at hand:

> God's Messenger (may God bless him and give him peace) once said: If someone performs two [voluntary] cycles of ritual prayer (*rakʿatayn*) on a Thursday, at some point between the noon and afternoon prayers – reciting the *Fātiḥa* and the verse of the throne (*āyat al-kursī*, Q. 2: 257) a hundred times in the first cycle, and the *Fātiḥa* and *Sūrat al-Ikhlāṣ* a hundred times in the second cycle – and invokes God's blessing upon me [Muhammad] one hundred times, God will grant him the spiritual reward of someone who has fasted in the months of Rajab, Shaʿban, and Ramadan.[80]

While some scholars worry that sanctifying Rajab and especially fasting during that month may undermine the sanctity of Ramadan, al-Jilani upholds the sanctity of the three months of Rajab, Shaʿban and Ramadan. In a series of rhymed aphorisms, he seems to imply spiritual progression between Rajab (the seventh month) and Ramadan (the ninth). For example: 'Rajab is the month of repentance, Shaʿban is the month of love [of God], Ramadan is the month of proximity [to God] (*Rajab shahr al-tawba, Shaʿbān shahr al-maḥabba, Ramaḍān shahr al-qurba*)'.[81]

According to one of many etymologies, the name Rajab derives from *al-tarjīb* – the practice whereby the angels raise their voice in gratitude and praise God (*al-malāʾika yurajjibūna aṣwātahum fīhi bi-l-tasbīḥ wa-l-taḥmīd wa-l-taqdīs li-Allāh*). They intercede on behalf of those who fast during this month, with the objective of wiping away their sins.[82] In a detailed 'table', al-Jilani calculates all the other imaginative material and spiritual rewards that have been promised to 'all the fasters of Rajab'.

A few examples should suffice to give a sense of al-Jilani's text and its many earlier and later counterparts. One day of fasting, he writes, may secure a dwelling in Paradise, while three days should merit the believer a wide ditch to keep the hellfire at bay. Five days may save one from the torments of the grave. Six days would allow the deceased to exit the grave with his face as bright as a full moon. Eight days of fasting will open the same number of gates to Paradise before him. If a Muslim observes ten days of fast, he will acquire beds to rest on along the *al-Ṣirāṭ* bridge leading to Paradise. Three more days (that is, thirteen days of fasting) will earn him a table packed with food by God's throne. Nineteen days of fasting will merit a palace (*qaṣr*) in Paradise, opposite those of Abraham and Adam, with whom he will be able to exchange greetings. Finally, those who fast throughout the entire month will receive the greatest wonder (*karāma*), which al-Jilani describes in Sufi terms: 'Contemplation of [or figuratively 'seeing'] the beautiful face of God (*al-naẓar ilā wajh Allāh taʿāla al-jamīl*) and the company of the prophets, the righteous, the martyrs, and 70,000 angels!'[83] Having advocated the performance of special devotions on Thursday elsewhere in his manual,[84] al-Jilani was obviously undisturbed by the incongruence of his math; he and his readers knew that those were figurative poetic exaggerations. Nonetheless, in a way mitigating this overindulgence with rewards for fasting, al-Jilani devotes a section of his chapter on fasting (*Fī Ādāb al-Ṣiyām*) to preaching proper pious behaviour and sincerity of intention,[85] in the absence of which fasting is no more than meaningless abstention from food and drink.[86] At the end of his lengthy chapter in praise of Rajab fasts, the preacher claims that fasting and almsgiving form the most fruitful combination of good deeds.[87]

Ostensibly quoting the Prophet, al-Jilani suggests two regimens for those who are only capable of or willing to fast three out of thirty days: any Thursday, Friday and Saturday of Rajab; or the first, middle, and last days of the month. In any event, he warns his readers:

> Do not neglect the first Friday night of Rajab, a night the angels call 'the night of great rewards (*laylat al-raghāʾib*)'. That is so because by the time a third of the night has expired, not one angel remains in the heavens or the earth, as they have all gathered by and around the Kaʿba. And God looks at them all and says: 'My Angels, ask for whatever you want from Me'. And they say: 'Our wish is for You to forgive all the fasters of Rajab'. And God replies: 'I have already done it'.[88]

Al-Jilani also delves into the merits of fasting on the three 'white days (*ayyām al-bīḍ*)' by drawing on two imaginative versions of the story of Adam's fall, the first of which was told by ʿAli b. Abi Talib, as it were:

> When God dropped Adam from Paradise down to earth, he was scorched by the sun and his skin became black. Gabriel asked him: 'Would you not like to be white again?' Adam said: 'Yes'. So he told him to fast on the 13th, 14th and 15th of the month. Adam fasted on the 13th, and one third of his body became white again; on the next day, another third; and after the third day, his entire body was white anew. That is why those days are known as *ayyām al-bīḍ*.

According to Ibn Qudama al-Maqdisi (d. 620/1223) – who in his youth had studied with al-Jilani in Baghdad, but then became an expert on law rather than an expert on hadith or a Sufi – there are two reasons behind the name 'white days'. It depicts the natural phenomenon of the bright full moon, which whitens the sky on these nights, and it commemorates an event of sacred history: God absolved Adam from sin and 'whitened his sheet' during this span.[89] We will return to Ibn Qudama in the next chapter, in the section that describes fasting under the Ayyubids and Mamluks.

Notes

1. See Halm, *Fatimids and their Traditions*, pp. xii–xiv.
2. Lev, *State and Society*, pp. 140–8. The Fatimids' introduction of public celebrations during Shiʿi festivals and their efforts to contain Sunni resentment are discussed in the first chapter. For an account of the riches and marvels that were on display during such highly ritualised celebrations, see Walker, *Orations*, pp. 40–1.
3. Sanders, *Ritual*, pp. 16–17, 41; ibid. 'From court ceremonial', pp. 314–17. On the dual meaning of sermons intended for multiple audiences, see Jiwa, *Mediterranean Empire*, pp. 18–19; Daftary, *Short History*, p. 65; and Walker, *Orations*, pp. 58–9.
4. For possible earlier antecedents, see p. 145 above.
5. Al-Maqrīzī, *al-Khiṭaṭ*, vol. 2, p. 405. Paulina Lewicka offers mouth-watering recipes for these sweets in ibid. *Food and Foodways*, pp. 308–9. For more on Ibn Abi Tayy, see Lev, *Saladin*, pp. 41–2.
6. El-Toudy and Abedlhamid, *Selections*, p. 224.

7. Walker, *Orations*, pp. 26–7.
8. See Ergin, 'Fragrance of the Divine' and Hedrick and Ergin, 'A Shared Culture', for an exposition of Islamic censing practices, the perfuming of sacred spaces in the Mediterranean cultures, and the art of incence burners.
9. Al-Maqrīzī, *al-Khiṭaṭ*, vol. 2, p. 523. On *qurrā'* and poets in the service of the Fatimid court, see El-Toudy and Abedlhamid, *Selections*, pp. 158, 179.
10. Lev, *State and Society*, pp. 144–5. For *i'tikāf* in Rajab in an earlier period, see p. 150.
11. Delia Cortese and Simonetta Calderini examine the participation of women in the Fatimid court's religious and secular ceremonies; see their *Women and the Fatimids*, pp. 93–6.
12. Al-Maqrīzī, *al-Mawā'iẓ*, vol. 2, pp. 522–8; trans. in Walker, 'Egyptian Popular Festivals', pp. 76–82; al-Musabbiḥī, *Akhbār Miṣr*, vol. 1, pp. 48, 53. Scholars have demonstrated that the extravagant lighting of bonfires on certain nights pre-dated the Fatimids. Walker, 'Egyptian Popular Festivals', p. 84; Katz, *Birth of the Prophet*, p. 220. See also the excursus above, on mosque lamps.
13. Al-Maqrīzī, *al-Mawā'iẓ*, vol. 2, p. 522; El-Toudy and Abedlhamid, *Selections*, p. 187.
14. Sanders, 'Marāsim'; ibid. *Ritual*, pp. 34–5. On the belvederes of the Fatimid caliphs, see Walker, 'Egyptian Popular Festivals', p. 77.
15. El-Toudy and Abedlhamid, *Selections*, pp. 188–9.
16. Based on al-Qalqashandi's list of ceremonies under the Fatimids (as summarised by Paula Sanders).
17. Qutbuddin, *al-Mu'ayyad al-Shīrāzī*, p. 61.
18. Alexandrin, *Walāya*, p. 5.
19. Qutbuddin, *al-Mu'ayyad al-Shīrāzī*, pp. 99–100.
20. A partially overlapping collection, *al-Majālis al-Mustanṣiriyya*, also preserves the work of the chief qadi 'Abd al-Hakim al-Maliji (in office 450/1058–452/1069). Tahera Qutbuddin contends that al-Mu'ayyad did not write *al-Majālis al-Mustanṣiriyya* (p. 367), while Stern does not determine the authorship. See also Klemm, *Memoirs*, p. 114; Elizabeth Alexandrin presents the *Majālis al-Mustanṣiriyya* as 'one other prominent collection of lectures from the time period' (ibid. *Walāyah*, pp. 84–5). This affiliation certainly suffices for our purposes.
21. Thomson, *Politics and Power*, pp. 151, 153; Qutbuddin, *al-Shīrāzī*, pp. 85–7; Klemm, *Memoirs*, p. 73; Alexandrin, *Walāyah*, pp. 79–109.
22. For information on the *majālis al-ḥikma* that were held in Cairo, see Halm, 'The Isma'ili oath', pp. 91–115; Halm, *The Fatimids*, pp. 46–49; Walker, *Orations*.

23. Halm, *Fatimids and Traditions*, p. 50. On Nuh, see p. 130 above.
24. Ḥusayn, *al-Majālis al-Mustanṣiriyya*, pp. 112–15.
25. *Al-Majālis al-Mu᾽ayyadiyya*, pp. 13–14. The Sunni formula would have encouraged seeking the proximity of God, of course.
26. Sanders, *Ritual*, pp. 67–9. Al-Jamali's relationship with the caliph was discussed above, p. 52.
27. Lev, *State and Society*, pp. 44–5.
28. Ibn al-Ma᾽mun is considered the best source on Fatimid rituals and ceremonial. Excerpts and renderings from his four-volume work have survived thanks to al-Maqrizi. These snippets were compiled by Ayman Fu᾽ad Sayyid in *Nuṣūṣ*, p. v.
29. Ibid. pp. 101–2. See Bauden, 'Maqriziana XII'.
30. See Qutbuddin, *al-Mu᾽ayyad al-Shīrāzī*, pp. 8–11. On Fatimid poets, see El-Toudy and Abedlhamid, *Selections*, p. 179, n. 1221.
31. Sanders, *Ritual*, p. 68. According to Ayman Sayyid, there is no existing evidence of the performance of nocturnal rituals (*iḥyā᾽ al-layālī*) on these occasions between 440/1048 and 516/1122; see Ibn Ṭuwayr, *Nuzhat al-Muqlatayn*, p. 220, n. 2.
32. Sayyid, *Nuṣūṣ*, pp. 36, 93.
33. Al-Maqrīzī, *Itti῾āẓ*, vol. 3, p. 82; ibid. *al-Khiṭaṭ*, vol. 2, p. 405.
34. Al-Maqrīzī, *Itti῾āẓ*, vol. 3, pp. 125–7.
35. El-Toudy and Abedlhamid, *Selections,* p. 74 n. 481; Sayyid, *Nuṣūṣ*, pp. 36, 63, 93.
36. See Chapter 1.
37. Ibn Abī Dawūd (d. 316/828), the author of *Kitāb al-Maṣāḥif*, argues that 'Ali did not have a *muṣḥaf* (ibid. p. 170, n. 3); yet, the website www.bible-quran.com/oldest-quran-tashkent-sana/ lists nine copies titled 'Muṣḥaf ῾Alī' and held in different collections. See also Leehmuis, 'Codices of the Qur'an', p. 348.
38. Sayyid, *Nuṣūṣ*, pp. 40, 64.
39. *Rubuṭ* or *ribāṭ*s here probably does not mean a Sufi institution, but rather literally the fortified residence of soldiers. See Hofer, *Popularization*, p. 60.
40. Sayyid, *Nuṣūṣ*, pp. 63–4, 69, 104.
41. As noted by sociologists, philanthropy is linked to practices of patronage. It exhibits power and rank, maintains and even increases the benefactor's honour and social standing, and is due to be reciprocated at some point with loyalty or other presents. Those ideas are articulated in Marcel Mauss, *Essai sur le don*,

and the many studies that it inspired. For Islamic contexts, see Singer, *Charity*, pp. 22, 223; Lev, *Charity*, p. 130.

42. Sanders, *Ritual*, p. 66. For a description of the splendid banquets held by the court on festivals, see El-Toudy and Abedlhamid, *Selections*, pp. 230–1.
43. Sanders, *Ritual*, pp. 54, 69–70.
44. Ibid. pp. 136–7.
45. Hunsberger, *Nasir Khusraw*, p. 147.
46. Walker, 'Egyptian Popular Festivals', p. 77.
47. According to Nasir Khusraw, an Egyptian *qinṭār* was equivalent to 100 *raṭls*, or around 45kg (see Nasir Khusraw, *Book of Travels*, p. 53). If this sounds legendary, the museum on al-Haram al-Sharif in Jerusalem holds two ancient beeswax candles, several meters long, and so heavy that several men would be needed to lift and carry one (Hillenbrand, 'The uses of light', p. 106).
48. Bierman, *Writing Signs*, p. 96.
49. Ibn Ṭuwayr, *Nuzhat al-Muqlatayn*, pp. 220–3; trans. in Walker, 'Egyptian Popular Festivals', p. 82.
50. For an explanation of the hierarchy within the imam-caliph's legion of 'men of the sword' and 'men of the pen' in Cairo, see El-Toudy and Abedlhamid, *Selections*, pp. 148–74, 227. For more on the political dimension of such events, see Stephenson, *Ritual*, p. 43.
51. Al-Maqrīzī, *al-Khiṭaṭ*, vol. 2, p. 100, cited in Lewicka, *Food*, p. 311.
52. See ibid. p. 312; Sayyid, *Nuṣūṣ*, p. 96.
53. See his poem above, p. 44.
54. Dauphin, Ben Jeddou and Castex, 'To Mecca', p. 24. For the pre-Islamic and contemporary production and delivery of the *kiswa* see Shalem, 'Clothing the sacred house', pp. 178–80.
55. Hunsberger, *Nasir Khusraw*, pp. 148, 186; Bierman, *Writing Signs*, pp. 103–4.
56. Nasir Khusraw, *Book of Travels*, pp. 58–60; Hunsberger, *Nasir Khusraw*, pp. 178–81, 186.
57. The lock was also an object that was sent to Mecca by rulers, as a token of their piety and concern for the sanctuary's security. See Shalem, 'Clothing the sacred house', p. 180.
58. Nasir Khusraw, *Book of Travels*, pp. 79–80; Hunsberger, *Nasir Khusraw*, pp. 186–7.
59. Walker, 'Egyptian Popular Festivals', p. 79. For an in-depth look at visitation to al-Qarafa, see al-Ibrashy, 'Cairo's Qarafa'. On pleasure seeking in al-Qarafa, see Ohtoshi, 'Manners, customs', esp. pp. 22–3.

60. Al-Musabbiḥī, *Akhbār Miṣr*, vol. 1, pp. 14–15; Lev, *State and Society*, p. 144.
61. Katz, *Women*, pp. 142, 145. See also Elbendary, *Crowds and Sultans*, p. 173; Talmon-Heller, *Islamic Piety*, pp. 173, 183, 195, 208–9.
62. For the etymology of the term *al-raghā'ib*, as understood by medieval scholars, see Abū Shāma, *al-Bā'ith*, pp. 138–9.
63. Hiyari, 'Crusader Jerusalem', p. 120. See Fierro, 'Al-Turtushi and the Fatimids'. The prayer may have surfaced during the Seljuq interlude (465/1073–491/1098), and yet we deal with this episode in the Fatimid chapter, on the grounds that the rather short period of Seljuq rule probably did not significantly affect religious life, despite marking a transition from Shi'i to Sunni rule. In any case, we have little information to indicate otherwise. For a brief survey of the Seljuq occupation, see Hiyari, 'Crusader Jerusalem', pp. 135–7.
64. Al-Ṭurṭūshī, *Kitāb al-Ḥawādith*, pp. 266–7.
65. Ibid. p. 130.
66. Grimes, *Ritual Studies*, pp. 312–15; Smith, *To Take Place*, p. 54.
67. Al-Ghazālī, *Invocations*, pp. 9–11; *Worship in Islam*, p. 210. See also Katz, *Prayer*, p. 160.
68. Schimmel, *Numbers*, pp. VI, 18, 67–8, 146–9,199–202, 263–4.
69. Prayers for *laylat al-qadr* also include repetitions of suras *al-Fātiḥa* (sura 1) and *al-Ikhlāṣ* (sura 112), as well as multiple supplications for *istighfār* (Mol, '*Laylat al-Qadr*', p. 86, n. 43).
70. This formula is examined in Padwick, *Devotions*, p. 66.
71. Even Muhammad, considered to be infallible and immune to sinning by Muslim theologians, is said to have asked for forgiveness seventy times every day (Schimmel, *Numbers*, p. 264).
72. Al-Ghazzālī, *Iḥyā'*, vol. 1, p. 268; translated in ibid. *Worship in Islam*, p. 210. For al-Ghazzali's thoughts on sin and repentance, see Stern, 'Notes on the theology', pp. 85–6.
73. Ibn al-Jawzī, *Kitāb al-Mawḍū'āt*, vol. 2, pp. 436–7; and ibid. *Kitāb al-Muntaẓam*, vol. 15, p. 161. See also al-Dhahabī, *Ta'rīkh al-Islām*, vol. 32, p. 349. The text is also available on websites such as www.duas.org/rajab_1st_thu.htm.
74. Ibn al-Murajjā, *Faḍā'il*. For an introduction to this genre, see, for example, Elad, 'Historical value'; Livne-Kafri, 'Muslim traditions'.
75. For a short discussion of 'mapping the book onto landscape', see p. 106.
76. Kaplony, *Ḥaram*, pp. 607–9. For the experience of Ibn al-'Arabi (whose visit to Ascalon was mentioned above) at that place, see Drory, 'Some observations', p. 115. For Ibn al-Murajja's above-cited description in translation, see Kaplony,

Ḥaram, pp. 71–2, 99, 703. Other sites with these qualities, according to Ibn al-Murajja, are the Dome of the Chain (*Qubbat al-Silsila*), the Gate of Israfil, and the place where David realised that God had accepted his repentance (Q. 38: 24).

77. Goitein and Garabar, 'al-Ḳuds'; Duri, 'Jerusalem', pp. 116–19. For a survey of pilgrimage of Jews, Christians and Muslims to Jerusalem at that time, see Talmon-Heller and Frenkel, 'Religious innovation'.
78. Padwick, *Devotions*, pp. 200–1.
79. Al-Jīlānī, *al-Ghunya*, vol. 2, pp. 742–5.
80. Ibid.; English translation from: www.scribd.com/document/273976273/Shaikh-Abd-Al-Qadir-Al-Jilani-Al-ghunya-Li-talibi-Tariq-Al-haqq
81. Al-Jīlānī, *al-Ghunya*, vol. 2, p. 737.
82. Ibid. p. 723.
83. *wa-murāfaqat al-nabiyyīn wa-l-ṣiddīqīn wa-l-shuhadāʾ wa-l-ṣāliḥīn* (al-Jīlānī, *al-Ghunya*, vol. 2, pp. 728–34).
84. Thursday was seen as particularly favourable for jihad, too. The Mamluk historian Ibn ʿAbd al-Ẓāhir, who brings several examples of successful campaigns of Babybars, notes that it is preferable to begin expeditions on Thursday following the example of the Prophet, 'as actions are presented to God only on Thursday.' See Anne Troadec, 'Baybars', 125.
85. Al-Jīlānī, *al-Ghunya*, vol. 2, pp. 750–6.
86. Katz, *Birth of the Prophet*, pp. 114–15.
87. Al-Jīlānī, *al-Ghunya*, vol. 2, p. 734.
88. Ibid. p. 746.
89. Ibn Qudāma, *al-Mughnī*, vol. 4, pp. 445–7.

18

Excursus: *Istighfār* (Seeking Divine Forgiveness)

For the discussion of *istighfār* (seeking divine forgiveness), it is worth turning our attention to Constance Padwick's *Muslim Devotions* (1961), a work that draws on her intimate acquaintance with hundreds of popular manuals she collected over the course of her nearly forty-year sojourn as a Christian missionary in different parts of the Islamic world. Padwick reads these prayers with the sympathetic eye of a deeply spiritual person and analyses them with the expertise of a scholar well-versed in Arabic, Islam and religious studies.[1] Particularly relevant is her beautifully written chapter 'Worship of Penitence', on the central role of *istighfār* in Islamic prayer rites and popular piety.

The chapter begins with a quotation of the Prophet, speaking about himself: 'God is my witness that I seek His forgiveness and turn to Him more than seventy times a day'. Allegedly, Muhammad used the simple formula 'My Lord forgive me, My Lord forgive me' between the two prostrations of every daily prayer.[2] In ʿAli Zayn al-ʿAbidin's above-cited prayer,[3] God is likewise repeatedly begged to forgive. Although Muslims believe that all prophets and imams are free of sin, they see no contradiction between this dogma and man's – any man's – expression of his servanthood, inadequacy and need for God's forgiveness.[4]

Padwick explains that the Islamic belief in the expiatory power of 'holy words' is grounded in the verse 'O believers, fear God and speak words that hit the mark *(qawl sadīd)*, and He will set right your deeds and forgive you your sins' (Q. 33: 70–71).[5] Leaning on the above-mentioned prayer manuals, Padwick lists a few more reasons that Muslims refer to when they place their faith in *istighfār*: the Lord's greatness, His track record of bestowing favour (both arbitrary and in return for penance) and His merciful nature. The latter is reflected in eight of His ninety-nine names: *al-Raḥmān*, *al-Raḥīm*, *al-Tawwāb*, *al-Ghafir*, *al-Ghaffār*, *al-Ghafūr*, *al-ʿAfuww*, and *al-Raʾūf*. God's greatness is evoked no less than a hundred times in a Shiʿi prayer manual, which instructs the devotee to prostrate and cry out: 'If I am the worst of bond-servants, Thou art the best of Lords! Pardon! Pardon!'[6]

The prospects for forgiveness are thought to be substantially improved if the appeal to God is augmented by the intercession of the Prophet or angels 'who bear the throne and all who are around about it . . . and ask forgiveness for those who believe [saying]: "Our Lord, who embraces all things in mercy and knowledge, forgive those who repent and follow"' (Q. 40: 7).[7] The promise of a 'double' *shafāʿa* – the intercession of the angels and the Prophet on behalf of the worshipper, who can then help intercede on behalf of others – must have made the ritual especially attractive to those seeking forgiveness.

Praying together with fellow Muslims was thought to reinforce the individual's plea for forgiveness. This idea is articulated in hadiths that pertain to the *ṣalāt al-janāʾiz* (Funeral Prayer): 'If a community of Muslims a hundred strong [or, in other versions: 'three rows of Muslims'] perform the *ṣalāt* over a Muslim and all pray for his sins to be forgiven, this prayer will surely be granted'.[8] The chances for absolution are even greater during those times of the year when God is particularly merciful – for instance, during Rajab, 'the month of repentance (*shahr al-tawba*)'.[9] *Istighfār* also headlines an integrated set of rituals suggested for *laylat al-qadr*. After performing ablutions and giving alms, the repentant should say: 'God, You are forgiving, You love forgiveness, therefore forgive me'. This formula is to be followed by several renditions of suras 1 (*al-Fātiḥa*) and 112 (*al-Ikhlāṣ*). To conclude, the phrase 'I ask God's forgiveness and I seek repentance with Him (*astaghfiru Allāh wa-atūbu ilayhi*)' should be repeated seventy or a hundred times, numbers that probably stand for 'countless'.[10]

Citing a juicy anecdote from a pocket-sized popular manual published around 1900, Padwick sheds light on the power of *istighfār* in Muslim eyes, or at least on means of propagating this idea. The protagonist of the story is one ʿAbd Allah b. al-Sultan, a notorious sinner with a weakness for wine and pleasures of the flesh, whose lifespan apparently coincided with that of the Prophet. His transgressions notwithstanding, he used to recite a plea for forgiveness each night during Rajab. To everyone's surprise, after that man had died, the Prophet reported that he witnessed a crowd of angels and a thousand houris (fair virgins of Paradise) packed around al-Sultan and competing over the right to give him a drink from the reservoir of Paradise. The Prophet and his Companions were astonished that such an unrestrained transgressor could have been forgiven and honoured in such a way. Upon conferring with the man's widow, they ascertained that the only devotion he had ever performed was indeed *istighfār* during Rajab![11]

Notes

1. See Schimmel, 'Review'. On Constance Padwick's unusual life story, see Cragg, 'Constance E. Padwick'.
2. Padwick, *Devotions*, p. 198.
3. See above, p. 143.
4. Chittick, *Psalms*, p. XXXII.
5. Padwick, *Devotions*, pp. 199, 201.
6. Ibid. p. 4.
7. Ibid. pp. 200–7.
8. Wensinck, Gimaret and Schimmel, 'Shafāʿa'.
9. Al-Jīlānī, *Al-Ghunya*, vol. 2, p. 737.
10. Mol, 'Laylat al-Qadr', p. 86.
11. Bābā, *al-Majmūʿa al-Mubāraka*, pp. 11–14; trans. in Padwick, *Devotions*, pp. 200–1. Please be warned that a fatwa issued against attributing any authenticity to Bābā's compilation of hadiths was published by Shaykh al-Azhar in *al-Manār*, on 26 Rajab 1344/9 February 1926.

19

Rajab under the Ayyubids and Mamluks

Saladin's dethronement of the Fatimid imam-caliph and his occupation of power in Egypt in 567/1171 were declared a historic Sunni victory over the Shiʿa. It was followed by a quick and heavy-handed abolishment of Ismaʿili customs and celebrations (see Chapter One), entailing a rupture in Egyptian court culture and religious life. In the words of the later al-Qalqashandi, 'when the Ayyubid overcame the Fatimid and succeeded them in ruling Egypt, it altered much of the state regulation and changed most of its features'.[1] Still, Ibn Taymiyya, writing more than a century after the demise of the Fatimids, laments what he regards as the lingering effect of Shiʿism in Egypt (see p. 113, above). Yaacov Lev and Devin Stewart similarly argue that Shiʿi customs and Fatimid traditions were preserved by the masses, implying that the Fatimids had left a lasting mark on local culture after all.[2] Marion Katz also suggests that continuities can be discerned in post-Fatimid popular, possibly Sufi forms of devotion.[3]

Having consolidated the empire by wresting control over Fatimid Egypt, establishing rule over most of Syria and the Jazira, and eliminating the Latin Kingdom of Jerusalem, Saladin bequeathed it to seventeen of his sons, brothers and nephews. Upon his death in 589/1193, these successors became princes in a confederation made up of autonomous principalities of varied size and importance. In the process, Cairo lost some of its prestige as the exclusive ruling centre, although the sultan residing in Cairo usually had some control over his kin.[4] In contrast to the imam-caliphs of the late Fatimid period, who concealed themselves from their subjects behind the walls of their elegant abodes, legions of attendants and highly formalised ceremonial procedures, Ayyubid princes had much less of a royal establishment and *cursus honorum*.[5] They lacked any inherent religious authority, although some of them were quite accomplished in religious studies, and they had no pretensions to royal charisma or *baraka*. While the Fatimid court fulfilled a conspicuous role in promoting the special status of Rajab, I have found no evidence of the involvement of the Ayyubid (or earlier Zangid) court in the organisation or funding of festivities during that month. Throughout the decades of Zangid and Ayyubid rule in Syria, Egypt and the Hijaz, Rajab seems to have been mostly venerated informally.

The Mamluks, who took over Egypt in 648/1250 and Syria in 659/1260, created a relatively stable centralised polity ruled out of Cairo. They saw themselves as devout Muslims who protected the faith against both outside enemies (such as the Mongols and Crusaders) and internal threats (such as heterodoxy and Shiʿism). Members of the ruling class extended their patronage over hundreds of religious institutions in capital cities and provincial towns alike, constructing and refurbishing mosques, madrasas, hadith colleges, Qurʾanic schools, Sufi lodges, shrines and mausolea. ʿUlamaʾ and Sufis maintained significant ties with the senior ranks of government and concomitantly reached out to the masses.[6] Some Mamluk rulers assumed a role in the launching of formal public rituals, including some new rites of Rajab. But we shall begin with developments that were initiated in scholarly or Sufi circles, or by rank-and-file Muslims 'from below'.

Prayers and Supplications

If the holdings catalogue of the Ashrafiyya Library of thirteenth-century Damascus and the collection of a fifteenth-century Damascene copyist and book-collector give us any indication of the demand for books in Ayyubid and Mamluk Syria, anthologies of invocations were quite popular. In these two collections, prayer manuals constitute nearly a fourth of all the books on the transmitted sciences – a category that, according to Konrad Hirschler's classification, includes hadith, *fiqh*, Qurʾanic studies, Sufism, sermons, history and biography.[7]

Supererogatory prayer assemblies, especially night vigils, seem to have been in high demand at the time. Public assemblies for the *ṣalāt al-raghāʾib* (prayer of great rewards) on the night following the first Thursday of Rajab, which many observed as a fast day, were held in various localities throughout the Middle East during the Ayyubid and Mamluk centuries.[8] Muslims

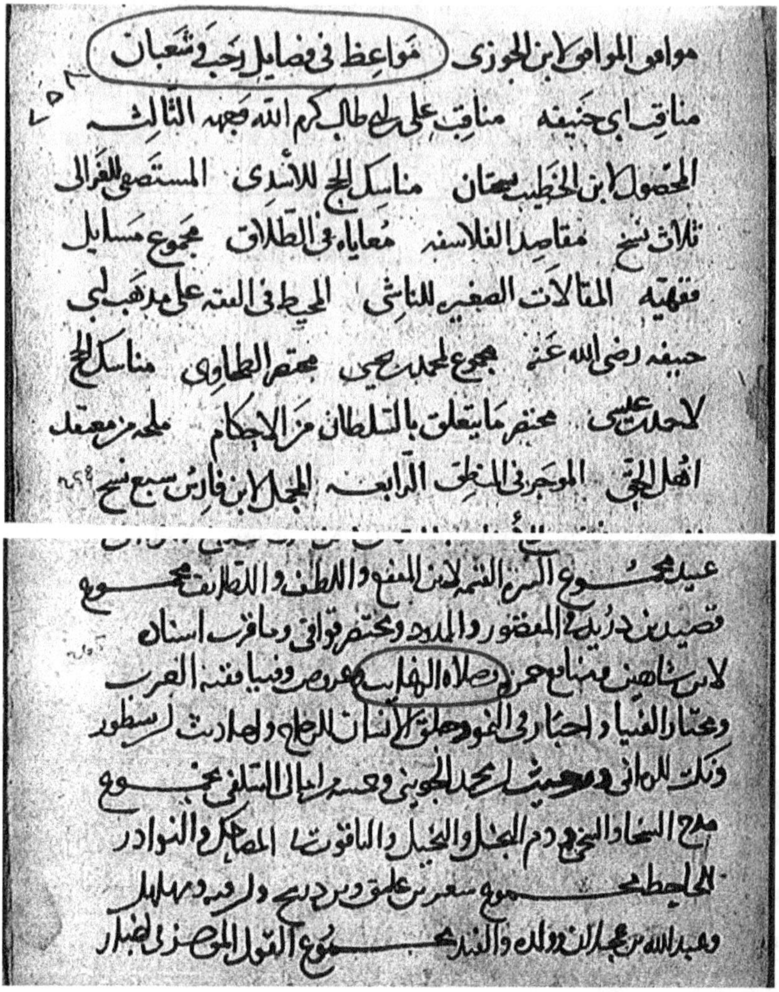

Figure 19.1 List of manuscripts from the Ashrafiyya Library catalogue (670s/1270s), fols. 258a and 265a; titles of *Mawāʿiẓ fī Faḍāʾil Rajab wa-Shaʿbān* and *Ṣalāt al-Raghāʾib* encircled (© Istanbul, Süleymaniye Yazma Eser Kütüphanesi, Fatih 5433, reproduced from Konrad Hirschler, *Culture in Late-Medieval Syria: The Ibn ʿAbd al-Hādī Library of Damascus*, Edinburgh: Edinburgh University Press 2019, plates 30, 44, courtesy of the author).

eagerly performed the demanding rituals, invoking the active participation of angels in the rites of praise and their benevolent intervention in pleading with God to remit their sins. Abu Shama (d. 665/1267), who adamantly opposed this rite, explains its popularity in a polemical vein:

> Once the night of *ṣalāt al-raghā'ib* became well known as meritorious by the ignoramuses on account of that fictitious hadith[9] . . . people became preoccupied with fasting, lighting torches and prayer [on that night]. Some of them began to exaggerate their devotion [to the point of] worshipping all night long, in the hopes of obtaining the highest merit.

According to Abu Shama, the crowd was made up primarily of commoners, 'and those who do not diligently perform their [regular] religious obligations, let alone the prescribed supererogatory prayers *(al-rawātib)*, let alone nocturnal worship'.[10] The grammarian Diya' al-Din Ibn al-Athir (d. 637/1239) also criticises this practice. In Damascus, he observes, the mosques are packed on the eve of the first Friday of Rajab and on mid-Sha'ban. Most of the attendees are people 'just passing through the mosque at night to meet friends for obscene and immoral behavior', rather than 'those who kneel and prostrate or remember and praise the Lord'. Yet, and one cannot miss the ironic undertone, they come to perform the *ṣalāt al-raghā'ib.*[11] Voicing a similar view, the Baghdadi Ibn al-Jawzi (d. 597/1201), a jurist and immensely popular preacher affiliated with the Hanbali school, disparagingly notes that 'this [prayer] is considered to be most great and beautiful by the masses, and even those who do not attend the [regular] congregational prayers show up for the service'.[12] 'Abd al-Ghani al-Maqdisi (d. 600/1203), a fellow Hanbali, does not address *ṣalāt al-raghā'ib* directly, but he argues against preferring certain nights for supererogatory prayer. In a chapter devoted to times for supplication in his *Kitāb al-targhīb fī al-du'ā'*, he answers the question 'which night is best?' – posed, as it were, to the angel Jibril. He cites some twenty hadiths claiming that God answers prayer on every night, and all licit times are equal. For example: 'The Prophet said: God descends to the lowest sky on every night, saying: I answer those who beseech me (*man alladhī yad'ūnī*), I forgive those who ask my forgiveness, I provide for those who ask my support . . .'[13]

As the *ṣalāt al-raghā'ib* penetrated madrasas and learned circles,[14] the scholarly opposition to this rite intensified and inspired a number of polemical treatises and fatwas. Within this framework, the *shar'ī* justifications for consecrating Rajab, singling out a number of its days and nights and performing the prayer under review were called into question. Most scholars argued that it was an invented tradition based on a dubious, 'weak', or 'fabricated' hadith.

Notwithstanding, they would argue that the rite was incorrectly performed.[15] The thirteenth-century Damascene Shafiʿi scholars ʿIzz al-Din ibn ʿAbd al-Salam al-Sulami, al-Nawawi, Ibn al-Athir and Abu Shama, along with their fourteenth-century counterparts ʿAli b. Ibrahim Ibn al-ʿAttar, al-Yafiʿi and Taqi al-Din al-Subki, criticised it. They deplored its public performance and specific timing, furthermore criticising minute features of the ritual. They also frowned at the expense of lighting mosques at night, cast doubt on the participants' motivation and sincerity, and reproached the crowd's behaviour. They particularly worried that the prayer may erroneously be considered a *sunna* if seen to be observed in public by members of their own class, while in fact it was a 'reprehensible innovation (*bidʿa munkara* or *makrūha*)'.[16]

After having been appointed as preacher (*khaṭīb*) at the Umayyad Great Mosque of Damascus, the Shafiʿi jurist ʿIzz al-Din al-Sulami launched his campaign for the revivification of the Sunna and eradication of *bidaʿ* with a sermon and a pair of treatises against the *ṣalāt al-raghāʾib*. In addition, al-Sulami issued a fatwa banning the rite and urged the Ayyubid ruler al-Malik al-Salih Ismaʿil to formally abolish it.[17] Somewhat earlier, in 632/1235, Sultan al-Malik al-Kamil had taken steps to outlaw the prayer in Egypt, under pressure from the Andalusi scholar Abu Khattab Ibn Dihya al-Kalbi (d. 633/1235), who was resolutely and persistently against the veneration of Rajab. He even dedicated a book on this topic – *Adā mā wajab fi Bayān Waḍʿ al-Waḍḍāʿīn fi Rajab* (Composing the Necessary Verification about Rajab) – to the sultan, his erstwhile pupil and later patron.[18] The historian al-Subki, who reports about this episode decades later, adds approvingly: 'Blessed (*ṭūbā*) are those who assume responsibility over some of the affairs of the Muslims and support the suppression of *bidʿa*s and the revival of *sunna*s!'[19]

Al-Subki must have known that such injunctions were short-lived, if at all effective. The fact that al-Sulami lost his position within a few months after criticising the concessions of al-Malik al-Salih Ismaʿil, the ruler of Damascus, to the Franks may also have been connected to his unpopular stand on the rites of Rajab.[20] In fact, as explicitly mentioned in twelfth- to fourteenth-century sources, communal gatherings for the prayer on the eve of the first Friday of Rajab had become accepted practice (*ʿalā ʿādat al-nās*) in Baghdad,[21] as well as in Mecca, Medina, Cairo, Harran, the Hijaz and

Yemen. The prayer may have spread even further, for Abu Zakariyya al-Nawawi (d. 676/1277) laments that the rite was embraced by 'multitudes of practitioners in many lands'.[22]

How should we account for the remarkable success of this rite of Rajab? Ibn al-Jawzi contends that 'in the hopes of establishing their leadership (*riyāsat al-taqaddum*), ignorant imams of mosques have made . . . the Prayer of Great Rewards and the like into a net for catching commoners (*shabaka li-majma' al-'awwām*)'.[23] Ibn Dihya mentions a certain preacher who admits to have done so quite intentionally, in order to 'rouse the hearts of the common people (*li-turaqqiqu bihi qulūb al-'awwām*)'. He also blames popular preachers (*wu''āẓ*) and storytellers (*quṣṣāṣ*) for spreading false hadiths about Rajab.[24] Abu Shama, whose treatise against innovations *Kitāb al-Bā'ith 'alā Inkār al-Bida' wa-l-Ḥawādith* includes the longest and most comprehensive account of the *ṣalāt al-raghā'ib*'s reception and the controversy it stirred, believes that some of those imams led the crowd in prayer only reluctantly, against their better judgement. Summing up a conversation he had with an imam who had been forced to learn the protocol of this rite from a 'simpleton' in his community, Abu Shama exclaims: 'How many imams have said to me that they lead this prayer only to retain the hearts of commoners, guarding their position in the mosque, fearing that it might be taken away from them!'[25] Thereafter, he commends one 'Abd al-Qadir al-Ruhawi of Harran for withstanding the pressure from his flock and refusing to lead the prayer. During a visit to his friend Shaykh al-Shatibi (d. 590/1194) in Cairo, however, Abu Shama overheard the prayer at the Madrasa al-Fadiliyya. While lamenting the intrusion of the *bid'a* into the madrasa, he inadvertently concedes that opinions and practices within the scholarly elite diverged on this matter, even within the stronghold of orthodox Sunni learning.[26]

In Damascus, the *ṣalāt al-raghā'ib* was performed at the madrasa of al-Zaki Hibbat Allah b. Rawaha, during Ibn al-Salah al-Shahrazuri's tenure there.[27] This mufti and hadith expert openly dissented from the generally hostile attitude towards the prayer in scholarly circles, and his argumentation resembled that of al-Ghazzali. Al-Shahrazuri considers it a 'favourable innovation (*bid'a ḥasana*)', yet without claiming that the 'great rewards' hadith is authentic. Instead, his lenient attitude rests on the general desirability of supererogatory devotions. More specifically, he supported it 'on account of it being a prayer and a popular act of worship (*ʿibāda*)' observed 'on a noble and undoubtedly meritorious night'.[28]

In Baghdad, the Imami scholar Ibn Tawus (d. 664/1266) supported it whole-heartedly, claiming to have read in the books of earlier Shiʿi scholars' descriptions of *ṣalāt al-raghāʾib* as performed in both the upper sphere by angels and the lower sphere by humans. He does not name those sources. The version of the text for recitation during *ṣalāt al-raghāʾib* which he reproduces is almost identical to that of the Sunni mystic al-Ghazzali. Ibn Tawus' list of rewards for completing the fast and the prayer is slightly longer, however. It ends on the following note:

> Upon his [that is, a Muslim's] burial in his grave, God sends him the reward for [observing] this prayer in the most beautiful [human] form, which contains a wonderful face and a sweet tongue. It says: 'My beloved, rejoice! You are saved from every hardship [in the afterlife]'. The deceased asks: 'Who are you? I never saw anyone more beautiful than you, or with a better scent'. The reward says: 'My beloved, I am the reward for that prayer you recited in that mosque, in that town, in that month, in that year. I come today to give your recompense, to keep you company and shed your loneliness. When the trumpet of judgement sounds, I will cast shade over your head for the Day of Judgement, and you will never be deprived of good by your Lord'.[29]

The later Egyptian Maliki scholar Ibn al-Hajj al-ʿAbdari (d. 737/1336) discusses *ṣalāt al-raghāʾib* in his *Kitāb al-Madkhal*, in a chapter devoted to festivals that have no *sharʿī* justification in his opinion. Although harshly criticising a wide array of customs as unwarranted innovations (*bidaʿ*), he somewhat unexpectedly condones this prayer so long as it is not observed in public. That said, al-ʿAbdari does take issue with a few minor details, such as the repetition of a chapter from the Qurʾan in a single *rakʿa* on the first night of Rajab. 'No one in the past did that', he emphasises, 'and all goodness springs from following [the lead of the first generations]'.[30]

Ibn al-ʿAttar (d. 724/1324) preached against *ṣalāt al-raghāʾib* much more vehemently, citing his venerated shaykh al-Nawawi:

> It is a shameful and abominable *bidʿa*, one of the reprehensible acts (*munkarāt*); it should be abandoned and shunned, and those who practice

> it should be reprimanded. And the ruler, may God accord him with success, should stop the people from performing it, for he is the shepherd, and every shepherd is responsible for his flock. The ʿulamaʾ have composed books to condemn it and to expose the ignorance of those who perform it . . .[31]
>
> Making it a public annual rite (*mawsim*), and kindling more lights than usual, is an innovation that contradicts the sunna. Additionally, the disruption in the mosques that this entails is forbidden . . . With respect to expenditures and intentions, it is like any other night and should not be treated otherwise . . . The hadiths transmitted about gracing it with a prayer are all fabricated according to the standards of reliable transmission.[32]

In fourteenth-century Arabia, at least according to the description of al-Yafiʿi (d. 738/1367), the *ṣalāt al-raghāʾib* was performed 'by learned scholars and excellent saintly men, and it has taken over the two holy cities [that is, Mecca and Medina]'.[33] Al-Yafiʿi may have been referring, among others, to Siraj al-Din al-Shafiʿi (d. 726/1326), a qadi and preacher who used to lead the prayer at the Prophet's Mosque in an enclosure known as al-Rawda al-Nabawiyya – a favourite spot for supererogatory prayers.[34] The Egyptian historian al-Sakhawi (d. 902/1497) notes that many Sufis participated in the ritual. He emphasises that he himself opposed this custom, based on the hadith that advises against singling out the night before Friday for vigils (*qiyām*).[35]

The night following the first Thursday of Rajab is but one of beneficent dates and times for supererogatory prayer advocated by the prolific Imami scholar Ibn Tawus in several of his works. In his *al-Iqbāl bi-l-Aʿmāl al-Ḥasana*, a comprehensive anthology of invocations and special prayers that he attributes to prophets, imams and other saintly figures,[36] he advises the reader: prepare yourself for Rajab with your mind and heart (*bi-ʿaqlika wa-qalbika*). He also hints that regarding Rajab there exist secrets (*asrār*) to be comprehended along with devotions (*ʿibādāt*) to be performed.[37]

What follows is dozens of references to the merits of each day of Rajab, suggestions for apposite good deeds and promises of lavish rewards for the performance of each devotion. Altogether, Ibn Tawus offers a dazzling array of special prayers and invocations – for certain days and nights, or for the entire month – as well as fasts, visits to shrines, charitable donations and

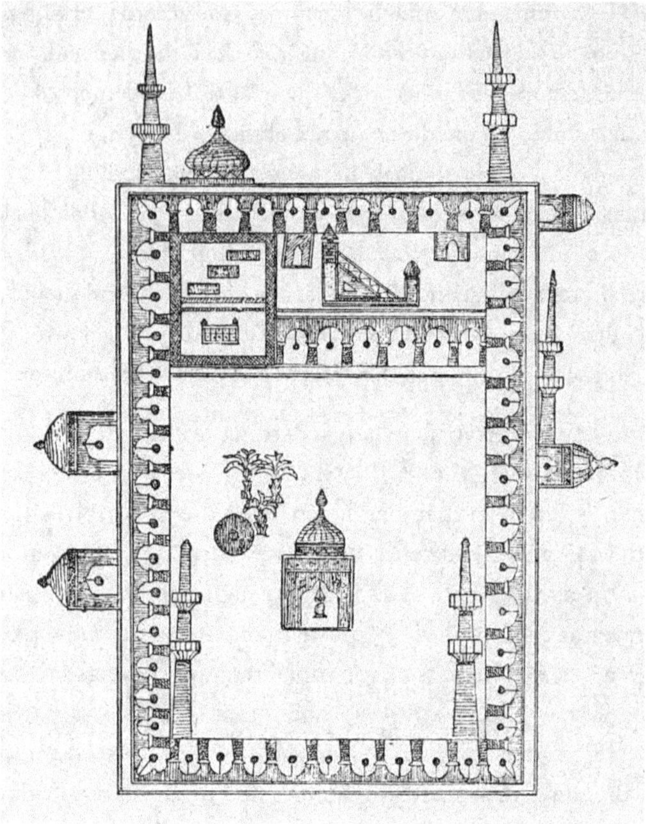

Figure 19.2 Fourteenth-century miniature of the Mosque of Medina with the Prophet's minbar, 'Fatima's palm tree' and dozens of lamps (Gayet, *L'Art Arabe*, Fig. 6, p. 22).

acts of repentance or contrition. He recommends, for instance, saying *Sūrat al-Ikhlāṣ* (112) thousands of times, perhaps in line with the following aphorism that hinges upon triads:[38]

> This community (or nation; *umma*) was given three months that no other community has: Rajab, Sha'ban, and Ramadan; and three nights that no other community has: the thirteenth, fourteenth and fifteenth of each month; and three suras that no other community has: *Yāsīn* [36], *Tabarraka* [*al-Mulk*, 67], and *Qul: 'Huwwa Allāh aḥad'* [*al-Ikhlāṣ*, 112]. Whoever brings together all these sets of three assembles the best that this community has been given.[39]

The importance that Ibn Tawus ascribed to days of commemoration, supererogatory prayers and visits to the graves of imams, according to Etan Kohlberg who dedicated a book to the study of his intellectual world, was emblematic of the 'popular elements' in his thought.[40] In a similar vein, the contemporary Lebanese Shiʿi scholar Shaykh al-Husayn al-Khashn assumes that Ibn Tawus' sources for *ṣalāt al-raghāʾib* were 'popular' (based on the fact that he does not mention any earlier authority by name) and heavily influenced by Sunnis. But while Sunni enthusiasm for the innovated prayer waned in the late Middle Ages, al-Khashn admits with sorrow that the Shiʿis have endorsed this *bidʿa* wholeheartedly and continue to perform it until this very day. Whereas our medieval authors also use 'popular' (derivatives of the root *ʿa-m-m*) in contradistinction to 'highbrow', [41] I would like to argue that tomb visitation, the embracement of strenuous supererogatory communal rituals and other extra-Qurʾanic festivities were popular in the literal sense of the word. They formed part and parcel of a religious culture that was shared in the medieval Middle East by many of the learned and the unlettered alike.[42] And although some learned scholars indeed considered *ṣalāt al-raghāʾib* a deviation from the authentic practice of early Muslims, it was undeniably composed of elements that typically marked sacred time in mainstream *sharʿī* Islam.[43]

The *Ṣalāt Umm Dāwūd*, which was purportedly composed by Jaʿfar al-Sadiq in the eighth century (see above), was designated for mid-Rajab. A query on optional devotions, addressed to the Hanbali mufti Ibn Taymiyya (d. 728/1328), as well as a fifteenth-century commentary by the Ismaʿili *dāʿī* Idris ʿImad al-Din bear witness to this supplication's enduring appeal for Sunnis and Shiʿis in the Mamluk period. Although Ibn Taymiyya does not directly refer to the prayer in his ruling, he apparently disapproves of it, as he explicitly states in his fatwa that there is no *sharʿī* justification for the veneration (*taʿẓīm*) of either the fifteenth or the twenty-seventh of the month.[44]

Idris ʿImad al-Din unequivocally approves of the veneration of Rajab, regarding the fifteenth of the month as especially blessed. A third of his treatise on Rajab is devoted to supplication, with special attention to *duʿāʾ al-istiftāḥ*, the opening supplication of the regular prayer, by which one announces their monotheistic faith and loyalty to God alone. He posits that it is bound to be answered if recited on that day.[45] He also encourages Muslims to observe the rites that Imam Jaʿfar al-Sadiq is reported to have specifically taught Umm Dawud for this day.[46] He explains that the eight *rakʿas* of this supplication are in honour of the eight Ismaʿili imams, counting from ʿAli and down to the Mahdi.[47] The bath on the fifteenth day of Rajab before sunset, according to Idris ʿImad al-Din's allegorical reading, symbolises the purification of the soul, and the full moon of that night symbolises the *daʿwa*'s perfection.[48]

The Night of Ascension

'The proliferation of "special times" of popular celebration and devotion in the Islamic calendar was paralleled by a tendency to commemorate the most important events of the Prophet's life', suggests Marion Katz. She primarily refers to the birth of Muhammad and his night journey and ascention (*al-isrā wa-l-miʿrāj*).[49]

The correct dating of the *isrāʾ* and *miʿrāj* was highly contested for centuries. While some Muslim scholars claim that the date is to remain unknown, others suggested dates, with the two leading possibilities being the seventeenth day of Rabiʿ al-Awwal (the third month of the Islamic calendar) and the twenty-seventh day of Rajab of 621 CE.[50] It is hard to say when the latter date became the preferred time for the celebration of the event. Ibn Nubata (third/tenth century) refers to the Prophet's night journey in his above-mentioned Rajab sermons (*al-rajabiyyāt*), but refrains from explicitly stating that its commemoration took place on a specific day of the month. Likewise, there is no mention of religious rites commemorating this date in Bahaʾ al-Din's account of the historical events that took place on 27 Rajab 583/2 October 1187, the day of Saladin's renowned victory over the Crusaders in Jerusalem.

The city's Frankish inhabitants, who had been under siege since 15 Rajab, capitulated on that day. Bahaʾ al-Din does not even entertain the possibility that the Muslims manipulated the timing of the surrender to enhance its effect. He writes:

> Observe this remarkable coincidence, how God facilitated its [that is, Jerusalem's] restoration to the hands of the Muslims on the anniversary of their Prophet's night journey. This is a sign that God has accepted this proffered obedience. It was a great victory witnessed by a vast crowd of men of religion, Sufis, and mystics.[51]

Although, as every student of history is taught, arguing *e silencio* is insufficiently convincing, one would have expected him to refer to the celebrations of the date, had they taken place on the day of Saladin's victory.

The night of the *isrāʾ* is the theme of one of four sessions of exhortation (*majālis al-waʿẓ*) that took place during Rajab in Baghdad, led by the prolific author, popular preacher and Hanbali jurist Ibn al-Jawzi (d. 597/1201). In the framework of this sermon – the other three sermons for Rajab in this collection were written for the beginning, middle and end of the month – he tells the story of the night journey in detail. He uses the opportunity to discuss the theological problem of *ruʾyat Allāh* (the vision of God [through perception]), polemicising against the views of the Ashʿari and Muʿtazili theologians who deny or seriously qualify this possibility. He also exhorts his audience to perform good works. Consequently, he offers a poetic thanksgiving to God for sending the Prophet Muhammad and for taking him on the Night Journey. He concludes the *majlis* with an invocation (*duʿāʾ*), pleading – rather typically – that God accept his repentance and that of the Muslims and absolve him of sin.[52]

In what seems to be one of the earliest extant descriptions of the customs of the twenty-seventh day of Rajab in Arabic sources, Ibn al-Hajj al-ʿAbdari (d. 737/1336) condemns a number of phenomena. He mentions the hurried recitations of the Qurʾan, in which the words' meaning is altered; recitation that resembles singing; recitation of poetry that distracts people from listening to the Qurʾan; and the Sufi rites of *dhikr* and *samāʿ* that entail numerous repetitions of God's name with or without bodily gestures and music.[53] He severely reprimands Sufis for carrying out their supposed transgressions inside mosques,[54] criticising inappropriate behaviour that violates the sanctity of mosques and breaks all taboos in general. He especially deprecates lounging, sleeping, eating, drinking, urinating (men in the corners of the hall and women in vessels, which they later carry through the building) and, of course, the intermingling of the sexes during the festival.[55] He does not disapprove of it in principle, as he describes favourably the manner, real or imaginary, in which the *salaf* supposedly commemorated that 'noble night'. In contrast with Rajab as his contemporaries celebrate it, in the distant past the month was commemorated with lengthy prayer, abasement, weeping and other 'beautiful customs of the *salaf*, already known', he claims.

Ibn Taymiyya did not hold back his criticism of his contemporaries either. As so often, his reasoning is grounded in hadith, on the principle of differentiating the Muslims from the people of the book and the pagan infidels (*mukhālafat ahl al-kitāb wa-l-mushrikīn*), and on rational arguments. His position regarding the twenty-seventh day of Rajab, which his close disciple Ibn Qayyim al-Jawziyya presents in his *Zād al-Maʿād* (Provisions for the Hereafter), is consistent with his tendency to deny the significance of the identification and consecration of the sites of key events in the lives of the prophets, or, for that matter, their tombs:

> The fact that God has bestowed upon His Prophet a blessing (or grace; *faḍīla*) at a certain time or place, does not imply that this time or place is more blessed (or virtuous; *afḍal*) than other times and places . . . The Companions and Followers neither singled out the night of the *isrāʾ* by any act nor commemorated it, and precisely because of that its date remains unknown.[56]

Although Ibn Taymiyya regards the night journey as one of Muhammad's greatest blessings (*faḍāʾil*), he notes that the shariʿa does not call for the day's special consecration (*takhṣīṣ dhalika al-zamān*). The only exception to this rule, he notes, is *laylat al-qadr*, which the Qurʾan explicitly sets apart from other nights. In the first place, a Qurʾanic verse unmistakably bestows special status on this night, designating it as better than a thousand months (*khayr min alf shahr*), and an authentic saying of Muhammad calls for the observance of devotions thereon. As for other cases, Ibn Taymiyya contends that singling out a time or place with special rituals due to a particular occurrence should be avoided, for it is 'typical of Scriptuaries'. The Christians, for instance, have transformed the days on which Jesus was born and baptised into 'festivals and devotions (*mawāsim wa-ʿibādāt*)'.[57]

By the later Mamluk period, the twenty-seventh day of Rajab seems to have been synonymous with the Night of the Ascension. The historian Ibn Kathir (d. 774/1373) unintentionally bears witness to the annual observance of *laylat al-isrāʾ wa-l-miʿrāj* on that particular night of Rajab in mid-fourteenth-century Damascus. Summing up the events of 749/1349 in his chronicle *al-Bidāya wa-l-Nihāya* (The Beginning and End), he comments that people broke with custom (*al-ʿāda*) and did not assemble in the great mosque on the twenty-seventh of Rajab that year, owing to a deadly plague.[58] Ibn Kathir refrains from stating his opinion about this annual assembly, or about its one-time cancellation. Ibn Hajar al-ʿAsqalani (d. 852/1449), in contrast, explicitly considers the identification of 27 Rajab as the date of the night journey erroneous,[59] blaming the lies of some storytellers (*baʿḍ al-quṣṣāṣ*) for its proliferation. Be that as it may, several decades after Ibn Hajar's death, on 27 Rajab 897/1492, the Damascene Hanbali scholar Ibn ʿAbd al-Hadi presided over a reading of hadiths in praise of Rajab, based on a compilation by ʿAbd al-Karim b. ʿAbd al-Samad al-Tabari (d. 478/1085). This reading, which was performed by the Hanbali historian Ibn Tulun, was recorded on the first folio of the manuscript, in the handwriting of Ibn ʿAbd al-Hadi. According to a catalogue of his private library, ʿAbd al-Hadi also possessed and read in public Ibn ʿAsakir's *Faḍl Rajab* and Bayhaqi's *Faḍāʾil al-Awqāt*. As expected, the latter work contains a chapter on the merits of Rajab.[60]

Fasting

The Hanbali jurist Ibn Qudama al-Maqdisi (d. 620/1223) warns against singling out Rajab with constant fasting. He reminds his audience that the *mutarajjibūn* incurred the wrath of Caliph ʿUmar b. al-Khattab for this very reason. Citing the eponymous founder of his school of jurisprudence, Ibn Qudama labels fasting during Rajab a 'disapproved (*makrūh*)' practice. To begin with, he argues that the month's veneration is emblematic of the *Jāhiliyya* and that Rajab should not be likened to Ramadan. He also undermines the sanctity of Rajab by preferring other times for fasting. For example, he considers the last ten days of Dhu al-Hijja as the period 'dearest to God'. As a result, he rates fasting a day out of those days as equivalent to fasting a whole year, as well as staying awake to pray during the nights of those days 'on par with the *laylat al-qadr* vigil'. Other than Ramadan, he claims, the most propitious month for fasting is Muharram, rather than Rajab.[61] If one nevertheless fasts on Rajab, Ibn Qudama posits, he should break the fast on certain days or fast every other day.

Ibn Qudama's contemporary Ibn Dihya, the Andalusi scholar who settled in Egypt, opens his treatise on Rajab by bemoaning the dearth of valid information and sound opinion concerning the month's true status.

Against this backdrop, he concludes, the popular belief in Rajab's superior virtue (*faḍīla*) stems from confusion or error (*khabṭ*) typical of commoners (*al-ʿawāmm*).[62] Such is the misguided belief that the following hadith is authentic: 'Rajab is the month of God, Shaʿban is my month, and Ramadan is the month of my people, so whoever fasts during Rajab in pure belief and dedication is entitled to the highest tier of heaven and is the beneficiary of God's grace (*riḍwān Allāh*)'. For Ibn Dihya, it was fabricated by a notorious liar, as were other hadiths that promise absurdly exaggerated rewards for fasting.[63] To bolster this argument, he notes that ʿAbd Allah al-Ansari (d. 481/1088), a Persian Sufi known as Imam Khorasan, never fasted during Rajab and advised people against doing so.[64] Does this anecdote inadvertently reveal that people observed this fast in eleventh-century Khorasan? My hunch is that Ibn Dihya errs himself here, confusing the Sufi with the identically named Companion, as the latter is indeed on record denying the authenticity of sayings of the Prophet that promote the fast, as it were.

The thirteenth-century Shafiʿi Damascenes Ibn al-Salah al-Shahrazuri and ʿIzz al-Din al-Sulami, who sharply disagreed over the *ṣalāt al-raghāʾib* (see above), held that a Muslim may fast throughout Rajab.[65] Al-Sulami explains that marking Rajab in ways that differ from those of the *Jāhiliyya* is not tantamount to mimicking the pagans and therefore allowed. Moreover, not everything that was done in that era is forbidden: proper conduct should not be rejected only because it was performed by the people of falsehood (*ahl al-bāṭil*). Also, in his estimation, hadiths that categorically prohibit fasting during this month are false. Al-Sulami even issued a fatwa encouraging *khaṭībs* to urge the faithful to engage in 'good works (*aʿmāl ṣāliḥa*)' during Rajab. Himself a preacher, he lists three cases in which addressing calendrical and current events during Friday sermons is desirable. Prompting the performance of good works (*al-aʿmāl al-ṣāliḥa*) during Rajab is mentioned in this context, as well as incitement to jihad at times of war and rousing the devotees to recite the prayer for rain (*ṣalāt al-istisqāʾ*) when stricken by drought.[66] A third Damascene Shafiʿi of the same era, al-Nawawi (d. 676/1277), was more ambivalent on this matter, claiming that there is neither a single interdiction against nor endorsement of Rajab fasts in the reliable hadiths.[67]

The Hanbalis Ibn Taymiyya and Ibn Rajab, as well as the Maliki Ibn al-Hajj al-ʿAbdari generally condemned the Rajab fast, although Ibn Rajab

(d. 795/1392–3) acknowledges the desirability of fasting on the Prophet's birthday.[68] He ends his chapter on (or rather against) the sanctification of Rajab with an anecdote about one of the righteous ʿulamaʾ who fell ill during Rajab and implored to God to postpone his death until the month of Ramadan. Ibn Rajab likens that *ʿālim* (whose wish was granted) to the early righteous Muslims (*al-salaf*). Like them, he had hoped to keep on living for the sake of 'meritorious times (*al-azmān al-fāḍila*)' during which one performs good works and to die while fasting in Ramadan or while returning from the hajj. 'And it is said that he who dies like that is forgiven [for all his sins]', he adds. In this scheme, Rajab is merely a transitory period; a 'key' to the real months of goodness and bliss (*miftāḥ ashhur al-khayr wa-l-baraka*). The best period for voluntary fasts in Ibn Rajab's opinion, is Muharram – 'the most blessed' of the months, save for Ramadan, 'the [true] month of God'.[69]

Ibn Taymiyya also emphasises the importance of correct perceptions. He deems all hadiths in favour of fasting during Rajab to be unreliable. Similarly, he finds no evidence in the recorded behaviour of the Prophet, the Companions, or the four founders of the schools of laws, that they espoused additional ascetic practices such as refraining from speech in parallel to the fast (*ṣamt*), or seclusion in mosques (*iʿtikāf*) during the months of Rajab and Shaʿban.[70] In his response to queries on these matters, however, he appears to indicate that some people observe these rituals while others have their doubts. Abstention from speech and company during Rajab, Shaʿban, Ramadan and Dhu al-Hijja is said to have been practised by the Sufi shaykh Nasr al-Manbiji (d. 719/1319). His biographer, al-Nuwayri, explains that al-Manbiji would have preferred to live in that manner of asceticism year-round and to completely avoid 'intermingling with the great and mighty (*al-ijtimāʿ bi-l-akābir*)'. Yet, for the sake of the people he was obliged to meet with senior Mamluk officials, not least the sultan, and therefore could indulge in withdrawal from society only during the sacred months.[71]

Recalling the piety of his late brother Taqi al-Din, the Damascene historian Shams al-Din al-Jazari (d. 738/1338) notes that he used to fast on Mondays and Thursdays, most of Rajab and Shaʿban, six days in Shawwal, and on the tenth day of Dhu al-Hijja and Muharram.[72] Thereafter, he describes Taqi al-Din's immersion in communal and supererogatory prayer. Owing to this preoccupation with voluntary religious rites, so Shams al-Din al-Jazari writes, his brother was unable to adequately provide for himself and his four children, leaving the historian's nephews to the mercy of God, the Prophet and himself.[73]

Ibn ʿAbbad of Ronda (d. 792/1390), the Sufi preacher (*khaṭīb*) of the Qarawiyyin congregational mosque in Fez,[74] urged his congregants to fast during Rajab. He promised those who fast for but a single day a drink from the Rajab River in Paradise, 'whose colour is whiter than snow and water sweeter than honey'. Quoting the companion Abu Darda, Ibn ʿAbbad assures his flock that a mere day of fasting in Rajab softens God's wrath and closes one of the doors to hell. In a more mystical vein, he portrays believers who observe the Rajab fast as aspiring to encounter their Lord.[75]

In his yet unpublished *Risālat al-bayān li-mā wajab fī maʿnā niṣf shahr rajab* (A treatise on what should be known about mid-Rajab), Idris ʿImad al-Din offers an esoteric Ismaʿili interpretation of the excellence and sanctity of the month, along with an explanation of the meaning of its fasts. In obvious disagreement with the Sunni scholars ʿAbd al-Ghani al-Maqdisi and Ibn Dihya, he contemplates that although all days seem equal, the 'friends of God (*awliyāʾ Allāh*)' who know the signs and can decipher the esoteric meaning distinguish between regular and blessed days. For this reason, the month's hidden merits are the exclusive preserve of the initiated. The prophet David (*nabī* Dawud), who used to fast on the three 'white' days – also known as the purest days (*ṣafwat al-ayyām*) – and perform ablutions on the fifteenth of the month, was one of them. The number three, Idris ʿImad al-Din cares to explain, signifies the Prophet Muhammad, his legate (*al-waṣī*) ʿAli and the current imam.[76]

As we have seen, the debate did not die down during the Mamluk period. At the very end of the period, Ibn Hajar, like Ibn Taymiyya, asserts that having the right notion of a time is no less important than performing correct devotions during that time. Hence, even though he admits that voluntary fasting is a worthy deed in and of itself, a fast observed due to a misconception that certain days or months are meritorious and preferable is best avoided.[77]

ʿ*Umra* (Minor Pilgrimage) and *Ziyāra* (Visitation)

Ibn Jubayr, who visited the Levant a decade after the fall of the Fatimids, offers two accounts of Rajab in his travelogue, which is conveniently divided by month. The second Rajab of Ibn Jubayr's trip was practically uneventful, as he spent most of the time aboard a ship in the port of Acre, waiting for the autumn easterly – a prerequisite for setting sail westwards from the Palestine coast on medieval ships. The only festival that he managed to witness that month was a Christian one. It was celebrated on 1 November 1184 (24 Rajab 580) by some of his fellow passengers, who lit candles, delivered sermons and offered prayers to their Lord.[78] Ibn Jubayr does not name the occasion, which undoubtedly was the Roman-Catholic All Saints Day.

The more eventful Rajab of Ibn Jubayr's odyssey produced a long and enthusiastic account of that month's Islamic customs, which he observed in Mecca between 20 October and 18 November 1183. By way of introduction, he explains the antiquity and importance of performing the *ʿumra* during Rajab:

> This blessed month is held by the people of Mecca to be a solemn time of meeting of the pilgrims, and is their great festival. They have not ceased to observe it in times both ancient and modern, each generation inheriting it from the one before, uninterruptedly from the days of ignorance . . . the *ʿumra* of Rajab is the equivalent (*ukht*) of the 'Standing' on ʿArafat,[79] for they throng to it in multitudes . . . so great a number assembling that none could count them . . . there was no one of the people of Mecca and the *mujāwir*s [settled pilgrims] who that Thursday night did not go forth on the *ʿumra* . . . desirous of acquiring the blessing (*baraka*) of that great night.[80]

In preparation for the *ʿumra*, the streets of Mecca were well-lit. The three miles leading to al-Tanʿim, where most pilgrims don the *iḥrām* attire, were packed with decorated camels bearing ornate *hawdajs* (pavilions).[81] Ibn Jubayr was especially impressed by the colourful camels of both the emir of Mecca's principal officers and the ladies of his harem,[82] as well as by the cries of *labbayka* ('At Thy service, O God') which echoed off the hills. When the new moon of Rajab was confirmed, the emir heralded the night of the festival (*mawsim*) by giving the order to beat the drums and tymbals and sound the trumpets. The *ʿumra* got underway the next morning. The emir arrived, accompanied by mounted cavaliers and footmen who skillfully displayed their swordsmanship. Camel riders raced in front of him 'raising their voices in invocations (*duʿāʾ*) and praise'. After this bit of entertainment, the emir was the first to perform the rituals, which he did with great fanfare; thereafter, the masses, both men and women, followed suit. The streets remained crowded throughout the next day, as people dressed in their finest garments walked about wishing each other divine pardon of their sins (*al-taghāfur*).[83] Throughout 'the blessed month (*al-shahr al-mubārak*)', Ibn Jubayr adds, the devotees continued to perform the *ʿumra* on an individual basis. Moreover, they engaged in other devotions, particularly on 'the nights famous for grace (*al-shahīra al-faḍl*)' – namely the first, fifteenth and twenty-seventh day of Rajab.

Ibn Jubayr attributes the origins of this celebration to the festive reopening of the Kaʿba on 27 Rajab 63/683, following its restoration by ʿAbd Allah ibn Zubayr.[84] Reparations were necessary at that point, as the sanctuary was badly damaged when Mecca was besieged by Umayyad forces who tried to crush Ibn Zubayr's revolt. ʿAli al-Qariʾ (d. 1014/1605) admits the absence of a trustworthy hadith that teaches that the Prophet indeed recommended *ʿumra* during Rajab, a question that apparently did not bother Ibn Jubayr; yet, he finds it proper to follow the example of Ibn Zubayr in this case, as he was a Companion of the Prophet after all.[85]

Ibn Jubayr notes that the religious gathering he witnessed was accompanied by vigorous commercial activity, and this observation seems devoid of criticism or rebuke. On the contrary, he interprets the presence of thousands of Yemenites from the Sarw tribe,[86] 'combining the aims of performing the *ʿumra* and of provisioning the city with various kinds of food', as a sign of God's benevolence towards the people of Mecca. The tribesmen arrived ten days in advance and brought with them wheat and other grains, kidney beans, butter, honey, raisins and almonds. Ibn Jubayr also offers a perceptive analysis of these rugged Bedouins' worldview: 'Religious law (*al-sunan al-sharʿiyya*) does not direct them in their affairs, and you will find among them no [customary] devotional practices (*aʿmāl al-ʿibādāt*)'. And yet, the Sarw perform the *ʿumra* with extraordinary zeal, throwing themselves upon the Kaʿba, 'as children upon a loving mother'.[87] Ibn al-Mujawir, writing in the 620s/1220s, several decades after Ibn Jubayr, explains that the Bedouins of al-Sarw hold on to the striking claim that the caliph ʿUmar b. al-Khattab granted them permission to replace the hajj with the *ʿumra* at the beginning of Rajab.[88]

The fourteenth-century traveller Ibn Battuta also observed Meccans and many out-of-towners making several visits to the holy sanctuary over the course of Rajab.[89] Referring specifically to the town's residents, his contemporary Shaykh ʿAli ibn Ibrahim al-ʿAttar (d. 724/1324) said:

> One of the things that I have heard about the people of Mecca – may God increase its honour – is that they perform the *ʿumra* frequently during Rajab. This is something for which I know of no basis; all I know is that it was reported in a hadith that the Messenger of God said: 'an *ʿumra* in Ramadan is equivalent to the hajj'.[90]

On the twenty-ninth day of the month, the Kaʿba was reserved for women. Ibn Jubayr notes – approvingly, so it seems – that a great many of them took advantage of this opportunity to touch and kiss the black stone, from which they were usually barred by men. They celebrated it as their 'grandest, most splendid, and most solemn day', bringing with them their babies and young children.[91] In contrast, the Meccan Hanafi jurist Ibn al-Diyaʾ (d. 854/1450) is hostile to this practice; he complains that the women of Mecca visit the Haram and perform the *ṭawāf* on sacred nights (*al-layālī al-fāḍila*), behaving inappropriately. Complaints against Meccan women who performed the *ʿumra* during Rajab, Shaʿban and Ramadan also appear in the work of Ibn ʿAbd al-Ghaffar, an early-sixteenth-century scholar, whose unpublished work Marion Katz cites and discusses. The largest crowds of women, ʿAbd al-Ghaffar estimated – and thus inadvertently testifying to the continuity of this custom over the centuries – would gather on 27 Rajab (the Night of Ascension) and on the last ten days of Ramadan, outnumbering men by ten to one. They typically visited the sanctuary after the evening prayer, perhaps to avoid the streets in broad daylight. Still, men grumbled that the women bared their faces and that their loud voices and the tinkling of their ornaments filled the mosque with 'the noise of the marketplace'. Worse yet, some of them spent the night in the sanctuary eating sweets and would not refrain from washing their hands inside the building.[92] ʿAbd al-Ghaffar was obviously deeply upset by the blurring of distinctions between the sacred and the profane. The intrusion of noise, food, filth and female activity into sacred spaces and times was obviously experienced as sacrilegious by him, as it was by Ibn al-Hajj al-ʿAbdari.

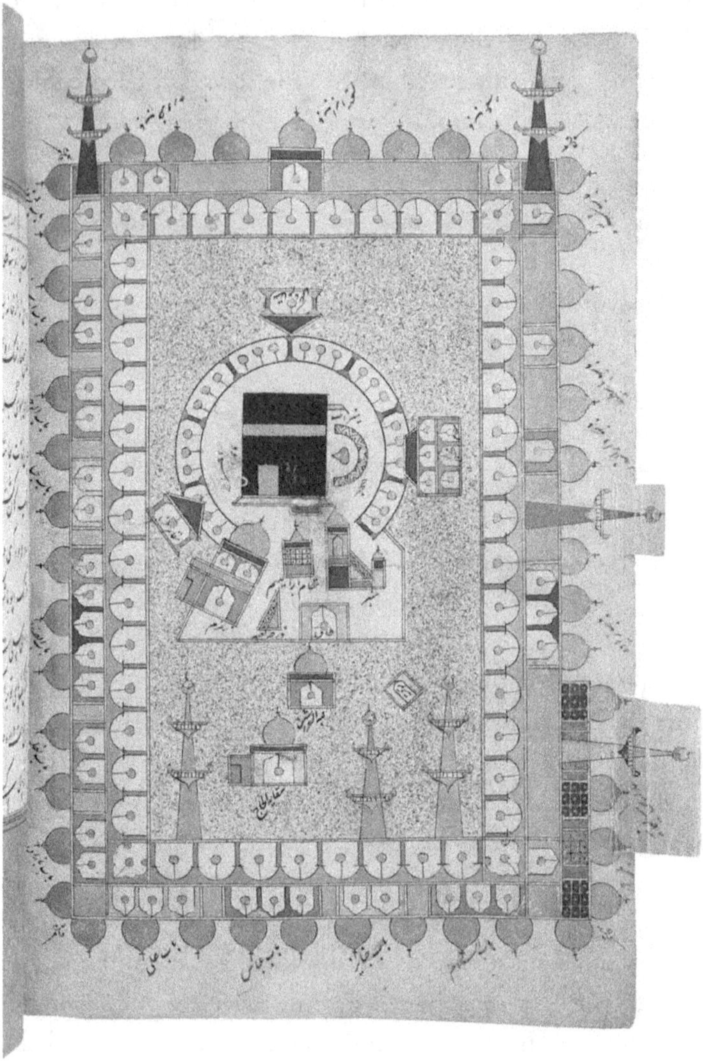

Figure 19.3 Drawing of the Ka'ba from a sixteenth-century illustrated manuscript of *Futūḥ al-Ḥaramayn* by al-Anṣarī (photo: Avshalom Avital, courtesy of the L. A. Mayer Museum for Islamic Art, Jerusalem, Israel).

Viewing the above-quoted testimonies from an etic perspective, Rajab in Mecca reveals itself as a multi-faceted 'hybrid' happening. Men and women traversed the wilderness to gather at the most sacred heart of Islam during an age-old sacred month in line with their 'great tradition' and performed formal, prescribed rites. Local authorities prepared for the festivities and took a prominent, highly visible role in them. Entertainment and commerce, as well as the display of ludic local traditions by men and women were also part and parcel of the event.

In all likelihood, there equally existed continuous medieval pilgrimage to other, more peripheral sites in Arabia during Rajab. ʿUmara al-Yamani (d. 569/1174) – the Sunni poet, jurist and chronicler whom we have encountered praising the Fatimids in Part One – mentions an annual *ziyāra* to al-Janad in the first week of Rajab. This observation turns up in his description of the local picturesque mosque, which was supposedly built by the companion and missionary Muʿadh b. Jabal. Al-Yamani does not relate the above-mentioned story about the conversion of Jews in al-Janad during Rajab, nor does he offer another explanation for the timing of this *ziyāra*. However, he confirms that the people of al-Janad equated it with the hajj.[93] Ibn al-Mujawir mentions an expensive refurbishment of the mosque in 603/1207 and a great gathering on the following first Friday of Rajab. People came from all surrounding regions, willing to pay exaggerated sums of money for the privilege of praying inside the mosque.[94]

Ahmad al-Sharji al-Zabidi (d. 893/1387), the author of a biographical dictionary on the Sufis of Yemen, reports in passing that the commoners (*al-ʿawāmm*) of Zabid and its surroundings 'prepare their saddles' for Muʿadh's venerated mosque every Rajab. In choosing these specific words, al-Zabidi seems to allude to the Prophet's well-known saying 'Do not prepare your saddles for but three mosques' (*hadīth shadd al-riḥāl*), usually interpreted as limiting Islamic pilgrimage to Mecca, Medina and Jerusalem.[95]

Al-Samhudi (d. 911/1506), a resident and historian of Medina, depicts Friday night (namely, Thursday after sunset) gatherings in his home city, as well as those of the first Friday of Rajab, the twenty-seventh of the month, mid-Shaʿban, and the twenty-seventh day of Ramadan. At these events, he complains,

> women gather in large numbers between the sundown and nighttime prayers, turning in the direction of the Noble Face [that is, the headstone of Muhammad's tomb in his mosque]. They come adorned and perfumed with various kinds of aromatic fragrances in a way that is forbidden when

> they go out [of their home]. Then a large number of men who seek corruption join them . . . Virtuous people . . . avoid visiting [the Prophet's grave] at that time.[96]

Visitation of shrines of the *ahl al-bayt* was practised by Shiʿis during Rajab; we have already quoted Ibn Tawus, recommending a visit to Mashhad al-Husayn (in Karbala) on mid-Rajab, mid-Shaʿban and the Day of al-ʿAshura.[97] He also suggests a pilgrimage to the burial place of ʿAli in Najaf, all the more so, since ʿAli was born on 14 Rajab and married his cousin Fatima, with whom he parented the line of the imams, on the fifteenth day of that month.[98]

Charitable Giving and other Devotions

To judge from Abu Shama's grievances regarding the *ṣalāt al-raghāʾib*, the gathering for the prayer in mid-thirteenth-century Damascus was accompanied by almsgiving and recitation from the Qurʾan. 'Some people, who want to establish an endowment for a good cause', he writes, 'endow the supplies of oil, candles, and food for those who spend this whole night [of the first Friday of Rajab] reciting the Qurʾan in a certain location'.[99]

The Damascene scholar ʿAli b. Ibrahim Ibn al-ʿAttar (d. 724/1324) likewise complains that in his generation, 'people donate [money] for charity especially on Rajab', despite the lack of a scriptural imperative for this timing.[100] While his Hanbali colleague Ibn Rajab agrees that this practice constitutes a deviation from the Sunna, he suggests an early source for this deviation: a sermon delivered by Caliph ʿUthman b. ʿAffan during Rajab, urging people to give their *zakāt* and return their debts during the month, for 'this is the month of your charities (*hādhā shahr zakātikum*)'.[101] In his annotated compilation of hadith *Tabyīn al-ʿAjab fī mā warada fī Faḍl Rajab*, Ibn Hajar al-ʿAsqalani (d. 852/1449) lists the following devotions of Rajab as good deeds that will be generously rewarded: Qurʾan recitation, visiting the sick, praying at funerals and kindly treating orphans. He cites Muhammad promising any devotee who completes a *khatma* (full reading of the Qurʾan) during this month the following remuneration: 'God will adorn him and his parents with crowns inlaid with pearls, and he will assuredly not be inflicted with the horrors of Resurrection Day'.[102]

Patrons would also sponsor hadith readings during Rajab, Shaʿban and Ramadan. A *samāʿ* (record of the reading of a text before an audience) in the colophon of the manuscript of *Faḍāʾil Rajab* by Muhammad b. al-Hasan al-Khallal (d. 439/1047) attests to its performance in the Madrasa al-Mustansiriyya of Mecca on 10 Rajab 668/1270.[103] A *waqfiyya* (endowment document) that was formulated in Jerusalem on 1 Rajab 838/1435 allocates part of the surplus income from the assets of a certain madrasa to celebrations during Rajab, Shaʿban and the festivals of ʿId al-Fitr and ʿId al-Adha.[104] Sultan Baybars hosted an enormous *simāṭ* (banquet) on the occasion of the dedication of a madrasa in Cairo on 11 Rajab 788/1348. We are told that, towards the end of this celebration, 'poor' and 'weak' attendees snatched up the leftovers.[105]

It should be noted that the poor were not the primary recipients of *simāṭ*s that were thrown by the Mamluks on various occasions, such as the Prophet's birthday, the nights of Ramadan, ʿId al-Fitr, and – the most extravagant occasion – ʿId al-Adha. Rather, like under the Fatimids, banquets were intended for the military and civilian elites and obviously designated to re-affirm their position and ties with the ruler.[106] When Sultan al-Nasir Hasan (r. 754/1354–61) endowed a large charitable complex incorporating a mausoleum and educational institutions, he explicitly stipulated that the *waqf* should distribute food to the poor on Fridays, Muslim festivals such as the Day of ʿAshura and throughout the months of Ramadan and Shaʿban.[107] A private *waqf* that was established in Jerusalem in 720/1320 for North-African Muslims (Maghribis) who resided in the city gives explicit precedence to the poor: 'the more needy comes before the less needy, and the one in deep debt comes before the one with less loans'. The *waqfiyya* stipulates that during the months of Rajab, Shaʿban and Ramadan the supervisor of the endowment should bake bread and distribute it at the *zawiya* of the Maghribis: two loaves for each Maghribi, male and female, who happens to be in Jerusalem at the time.[108]

Pursuant to a contract signed in Damascus in Dhu al-Hijja 885/1481, the notary Shihab al-Din Ahmad Ibn Tawq (834/1430–915/1509) undertook to read the *Ṣaḥīḥ al-Bukhārī* in the Umayyad Mosque during the three sacred months, in return for six golden Ashrafi *līra*s. He mentions the first installment of this public reading of hadith in his diary (*yawmiyyāt*), in an entry dated 1 Rajab 890/1485. The next day, which happened to be the first Thursday of the month, he attended a sermon on the merits (*faḍāʾil*) of Rajab. In an earlier entry, dated Thursday, 3 Rajab 887/1482, the notary wrote that he refrained from buying sweets, even though it was '*mawsim Rajab*'. While no explanation is forthcoming, it stands to reason that Ibn Tawq was on a tight budget due to the recurring economic crises of the time.[109] He must have fared better in 890/1485 thanks to those six golden Ashrafi *līra*s, combined with the blessings of his devotional reading in the holy mosque during the holy month.

Processions

In mid-Rajab 661/1263, more than a decade after the rise of the Mamluks to power in Egypt, a black *kiswa* – the large, elaborately-decorated cloth-covering tailor-made for the Kaʿba in Mecca – was paraded through the streets of Cairo. It was carried by mules and escorted by judges, legal scholars, Qurʾan reciters, Sufis and preachers. The procession was a state-sponsored event, advertising the piety and 'royal persona' of the new sultan, al-Malik al-Zahir Baybars. In this sense, it was reminiscent of Fatimid rituals of power.[110] The procession would become yet another way to highlight the sanctity of Rajab. Moreover, it afforded the vast majority of Egyptians who were unable to travel to Mecca a small taste of the hajj.[111] Once the new *kiswa* was installed, the guardians of the Kaʿba would bestow portions of the old covering to rulers and other dignitaries, disseminating the blessings of the sacred place throughout the Islamic world.[112]

The delivery of a *kiswa* from Egypt, adorned with Qurʾanic verses and pious phrases, probably goes back to the third/tenth century.[113] Baybars added a new Rajab element to the mix several years after his ascent to power: a decorated empty palanquin, the *maḥmal*, joined the *kiswa* procession. It resembled a tent made of embroidered yellow silk (yellow was the official colour of the Mamluks), crowned with a spherical finial made of gilded silver.[114] Until the demise of this tradition in 1953, the *maḥmal* remained the centrepiece of the *rajabiyya*, a parade marking the advent of the yearly caravan to Mecca.[115]

Leaving Cairo three or four months before the hajj allowed pilgrims to spend more time at the holy sites, to complete an *ʿumra* before the prescribed

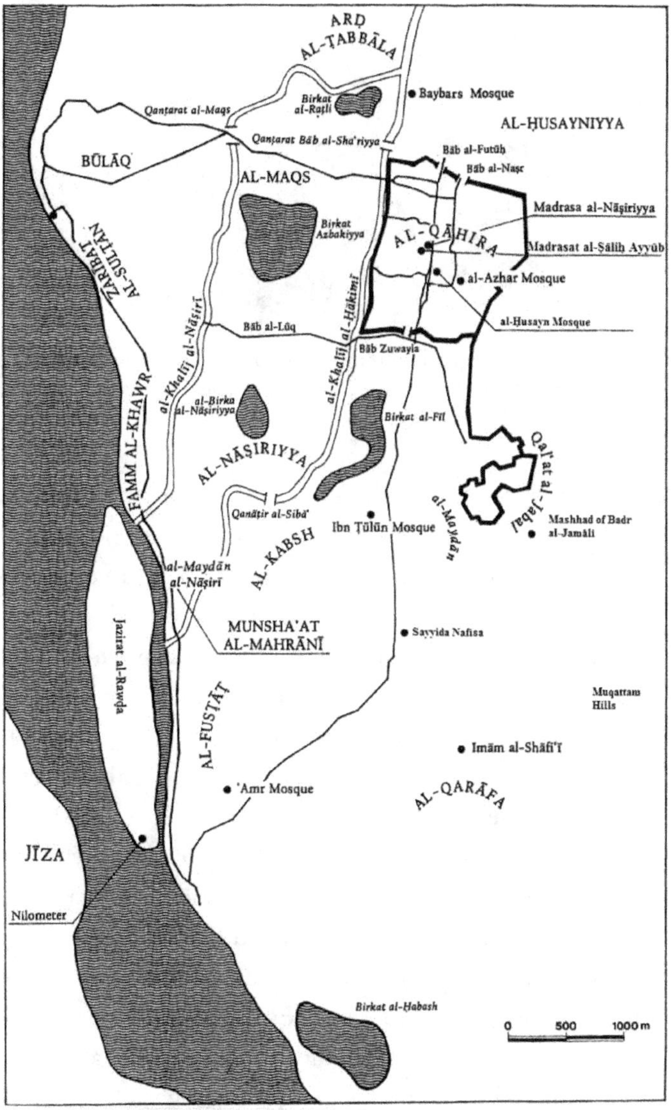

Figure 19.4 Map of Mamluk Cairo (Amalia Levanoni, *A Turning Point in Mamluk History*, Leiden: Brill 1995, p. 159, with minor modifications. Courtesy of the author).

time of the hajj, preferably during Ramadan, thereby willingly taking upon themselves the extra burden of fasting. For the most part, the participants departed from Mecca together with the bulk of the other pilgrims, after the Holiday of the Sacrifice, which marks the end of the hajj. Upon arriving back

Figure 19.5 Muslim pilgrims departing from Egypt for Mecca, followed by a camel carrying the ornate yellow *maḥmal* (stencil-printed lithograph, British Museum, AN1321871001, © The Trustees of the British Museum).

in Cairo during the month of Muharram, they would once again parade the *maḥmal* through the city's streets. Members of the religious establishment and the Sufi orders, as well as state officials and soldiers, used to gather by the citadel where the returning *amīr al-ḥajj* greeted the crowd.

To judge from the intermittent reports of Egyptian chroniclers, the *rajabiyya* was conducted sporadically during the late Mamluk period.[116] In the fifteenth century, the Mamluks integrated extravagant martial and equestrian displays into the *maḥmal* procession. Mamluk units known as *aṭlāb* preceded the *maḥmal* along the route in full attire. Rare and exotic curiosities from the Egyptian provinces (*kull mā bi-l-diyār al-miṣriyya min al-tuḥaf wa-l-gharāʾib*) were displayed, projecting the Mamluk sultanate as a rich and far-flung empire.[117] The soldiers were parodied by carnivalesque clowns and accompanied by musicians, attracting the enthusiastic participation of the Cairene crowd and people from all over Egypt.[118] Spectators used to spend two days and a night on the streets on those occasions. On al-Rumayla Plaza, the festivities continued until the morning in the light of bonfires. In Rajab 825/1422, the *muḥtasib* (superintendent of public mores) prohibited women from watching the procession from the streets or shops. The ascetic Sultan al-Zahir Sayf al-Din Jaqmaq (r. 842/1438–857/1453), who had terminated gaudy displays of royal authority (*shiʿār al-mamlaka*) such as hunting parties, public receptions and parades,[119] took this measure even further. He abolished the Rajab *maḥmal* procession altogether. To the relief of many Cairenes, however, the ban on these revelries was soon lifted. Al-Maqrizi and al-Biqaʿi (d. 885/1480) report that the celebrations continued in their times and that on the occasion of the *rajabiyya* men and women, young and old, used to stay up all night playing games, singing, dancing and amusing themselves.[120] Soldiers dressed up in frightening costumes also took part in the procession, until the sultan curtailed this practice because the troops' behaviour had gone out of control.[121]

For Mamluk-era critics, such as the scholars Ibn Taymiyya and Ibn al-Hajj al-ʿAbdari, all these festivities were a far cry from the proper etiquette for marking sacred time. Al-ʿAbdari sadly compares how the *salaf* observed Rajab – concentrating on the improvement of deeds (*tazkiyyat al-aʿmāl*) – with the way in which his contemporaries indulged in eating, dance and wasteful spending.[122] In a similar vein, Ibn al-ʿAttar exclaims: 'There is no recompense (*thawāb*) for kindling lights, eating sweets, and the like'. [123] The participation of women added to their grim appraisal of the popular celebrations of Rajab in Cairo, as in Mecca and Medina.

From the sultanate's perspective, temporarily allowing controlled rowdiness and loosening of strict social stratification ultimately might have helped reinforce the existing hierarchy. In other words, such events may have constituted a 'safety valve' against disruptive conflict.[124] But what was the outlook of the rank-and-file spectators themselves? From their point of view, were they observing religious rites in virtuous time or merely having fun? A sympathetic, albeit contemporary observer of such phenomena, the anthropologist Samuli Schielke, rejects the Durkheimian 'abyss' between sacred and profane, and inadvertently also argues against the dichotomy between pious devotion and unadulterated pleasure, as drawn by medieval (and current) Muslim authorities.[125]

Schielke attended many *mūlids* (colloquial for *mawālid*, birthdays of revered figures) in present-day Cairo. Based on his observations, he argues for a category of 'festive time' expressing piety concurrently with joy and characterised by a deeply ambivalent nature: simultaneously profound and joking, spiritual and commercial, conservative and subversive. According to his understanding of the convictions held by participants in colourful *mūlid* events, the *baraka* that is embedded in consecrated time temporarily transforms ordinary social practices, such as eating and wearing festive clothes, into lofty pursuits, thus suspending the barrier between the religious and the profane.[126]

Notes

1. Translated in El-Toudy and Abedlhamid, *Selections*, p. 235.
2. See Stewart, 'Popular Shiʿism', pp. 35–6, 66. See also Lev, *State and Society*, p. 152; ibid. *Saladin*, pp. 124–50.
3. Katz, *Birth of the Prophet*, pp. 1, 5, 113. See also Friedman, *Shiʿis*, on Shiʿism in Palestinian folklore.
4. Sayyid, *Topography*, p. 19.
5. Humphreys, 'The emergence', pp. 85–6. See al-Qalqashandi's description of al-Malik al-Muʿazzam (r. 515/1221–624/1227 in Damascus) as lacking royal pretense to the degree that he wore a simple turban and 'walked through the markets with no-one before him to clear the roads' (El-Toudy and Abedlhamid, *Selections*, p. 236).
6. See, for example, Berkey, 'The Mamluks'; ibid. 'Mamluk religious policy'.
7. Hirschler, *Medieval Damascus*, p. 106.
8. See Talmon-Heller and Ukeles, 'The lure', pp. 152–6. For additional no longer extant treatises that were housed at al-Ashrafiyya Library in Damascus, see Hirschler, *Medieval Damascus*, pp. 255, 272, 368.
9. See above, p. 169.
10. Abū Shāma, *al-Bāʿith*, p. 158.
11. Ḍiyāʾ al-Dīn Ibn al-Athīr, *al-Mathal al-Sāʾir*, vol. 2, p. 150; al-Qalqashandī, *Ṣubḥ al-Aʿshā*, vol. 11, pp. 67–70. For a commentary on this text, see Goldziher, *Muslim Studies*, vol. 1, p. 235.
12. Ibn al-Jawzī, *Kitāb al-Mawḍūʿāt*, vol. 2, p. 48.
13. ʿAbd al-Ghanī al-Maqdisī (d. 600/1203), *Kitāb al-Targhīb fī al-Duʿāʾ*, ed. Fawwāz Aḥmad Zamarlī (Beirut: Dār Ibn Ḥazm, 1995), 63 and ff. None the less, a couple of those *ḥadīth*s do mention a special time, such as the nights of Ramadan, mid-Shaʿbān and Fridays.
14. See below.
15. For example, Ibn ʿAbd al-Salām, '*Risāla*', pp. 55–8; al-Subkī, *Ṭabaqāt al-Shāfiʿīyya*, vol. 8, pp. 251–5.
16. Al-Yāfiʿī, *Mirʾāt al-Jinān*, vol. 4, p. 118. Stressing the importance of differentiating obligatory prayers that should be recited in public from other prayers, many Muslim scholars recommend performing supererogatory prayers in solitude; see Katz, *Prayer*, p. 26.
17. Abū Shāma, *al-Bāʿith*, pp. 149–50, 158.
18. Ibn Diḥya, *Adāʾ mā wajab*, p. 16.

19. Al-Subkī, *Ṭabaqāt al-Shāfiʿīyya*, vol. 8, p. 255. During his brief rule over Damascus, al-Kamil also intervened with the daily prayer schedule at the Umayyad Mosque. See Abū Shāma, *Tarājim*, p. 166; Ibn Kathīr, *al-Bidāya*, vol. 13, p. 173.
20. On al-Salih Ismaʿil, see Humphreys, *From Saladin to the Mongols*, pp. 266–7. In 639/1241, al-Sulami moved to Egypt, where he was appointed *khaṭīb* and qadi by the rival Ayyubid ruler al-Malik al-Salih Ayyub. See Abū Shāma, *Tarājim*, pp. 170–1.
21. Ibn Rajab, *al-Dhayl*, vol. 1, p. 318.
22. Al-Nawawī, *Fatāwā*, p. 35.
23. Ibn al-Jawzī, *Kitāb al-Mawḍūʿāt*, vol. 2, p. 51.
24. Ibn Diḥya, *Adāʾ mā wajab*, pp. 19–22.
25. Abū Shāma, *al-Bāʿith*, p. 209.
26. Ibid. pp. 223–5.
27. Ibid. p. 238.
28. Al-Albānī, *Musājala ʿIlmiyya*, pp. 14–18. For a more detailed discussion of this debate and the principles behind it, see Ukeles, *Innovation*, pp. 87–199. See also the earlier discussion on al-Ghazzali's stance on p. 168.
29. Ibn Ṭāwūs, *al-Iqbāl*, vol. 3, pp. 185–6. A contemporary Shiʿi polemicist against the prayer, Shaykh Hasan al-Khashn, attributes it to Sunni sources, finding Ibn Tawus to be the first Shiʿi author to embrace it (www.al-khechin.com/article/230; last accessed on 26 May 2019). On the website DUAS.ORG it appears with an English translation and is recommended for the remittance of 'a great number of sins'.
30. Ibn al-Ḥājj al-ʿAbdarī, *al-Madkhal*, vol. 1, pp. 291–8. Also see Ukeles, *Innovation*, pp. 107, 252; Colby, 'The rhetoric', p. 35.
31. *Fatāwā al-Imām al-Nawawī*, pp. 34–5. See also in Ibn al-ʿAṭṭār, *Tuḥfat al-Ṭālibīn*, pp. 222–4 (in a section devoted to al-Nawawi's warning against *bidaʿ* that were prevalent in his times).
32. Ibn al-ʿAṭṭār, in al-Albānī, *Musājala ʿIlmiyya*, pp. 54–6.
33. Al-Yāfiʿī, *Mirʾāt al-Janān*, vol. 4, p. 118.
34. This small enclosure in the Prophet's Mosque in Medina, which extends from Muhammad's tomb to his pulpit, is supposedly mentioned in a Prophetic hadith, as follows: 'The area between my house and my minbar is one of the gardens of Paradise' (*Ṣaḥīḥ al-Bukhārī*, *Faḍl al-Ṣalāt fī Masājid Makkah wa-l-Madīna*, 1204). An illustration of this space can be found at http://en.wikipedia.org/wiki/Al-Masjid_al-Nabawi. For an analysis of the concentric

circles of the shrine's sanctity, see Marmon, *Eunuchs and Sacred Boundaries*, p. 13.

35. Al-Sakhāwī, *al-Tuḥfa al-Laṭīfa*, vol. 2, pp. 328–31.
36. See also *Muhaj al-Da'awāt*, pp. 543–4, where Ibn Tawus refers the reader to a more detailed account in his *Mukhtaṣar Ibn Ḥabīb* (no longer extant). For additional references, see Kohlberg, *Muslim Scholar*, pp. 52, 89, 66, 135, 184, 236, 281, 314, 372.
37. Ibn Ṭāwūs, *al-Iqbāl*, vol. 3, pp. 170, 235. Ibn 'Arabi also speaks of secrets in his discussion of the spiritual dimension of the days of the week. He links each day to one of seven prophets, 'from whom descends a secret upon the heart . . . in which he takes delight during his day and by which he knows something of that which requires to be known'. For example: 'If your day is Sunday, then Idris is your Companion . . . ' See Ibn 'Arabī, *The Seven Days*, pp. 13–14.
38. On three as 'the embracing synthesis', especially in Shi'i Islam, see Schimmel, *Numbers*, pp. 58–85, 67.
39. Ibn Ṭāwūs, *al-Iqbāl*, vol. 3, p. 230.
40. Kohlberg, *Muslim Scholar*, pp. 22–3.
41. This is typical of Ibn al-Jawzi, Ibn Dihya, Abu Shama and Diya' al-Din Ibn al-Athir, as cited above. Ibn al-'Attar, for example, attributes the combination of the hajj with a visit to Jerusalem and Hebron, a custom based upon inauthentic hadith in his judgement, to 'the commoners of Syria (*'awāmm ahl al-Shām*)'. See his *Tuḥfat al-Ṭālibīn*, pp. 215–16.
42. For a discussion and critique of the 'two-tiered' model of culture in general and regarding religion under the Ayyubids and Mamluks in particular, see Berkey, 'Popular culture;' Marmon, 'Quality of mercy', pp. 128–9; Talmon-Heller, *Islamic Piety*, especially pp. 24–6, 248; and ibid. '*'Ilm, Shafā'ah*', pp. 25–30.
43. Talmon-Heller, *Islamic Piety*, pp. 65–6.
44. Ibn Taymiyya, *al-Fatāwā al-Kubrā*, vol. 2, pp. 358–9; ibid. *Iqtiḍā' al-Ṣirāṭ al-Mustaqīm*, vol. 2, p. 122.
45. Idrīs 'Imād al-Dīn, MS 39/909, p. 17, p. 50. There are three other manuscripts of this text in the Zahid 'Ali Collection: MS1168 (ArI, ZA); MS 1190 (ArI, ZA); MS 1257 (ArI, ZA); see Cortese, *Arabic Ismaili Manuscripts*, pp. 6–8, 149–50; ibid. *Ismaili and Other*, pp. 23, 25; and Sayyid, *Fatimids*, vol. 7, pp. 9–16. I am grateful to Delia Cortese for bringing these manuscripts to my attention and to Wafi Momin, the head of the Ismaili Special Collections Unit at the Institute of Ismaili Studies.

46. Sayyid, *Fatimids*, pp. 14–15. Idrīs ʿImād al-Dīn, MS 39/909 fl. 26. On *Ṣalāt Umm Dāwūd*, see pp. 191–2 above.
47. The number eight is also connected with Paradise in Islam (Schimmel, *Numbers*, p. 157).
48. Idrīs ʿImād al-Dīn, MS 39/909, pp. 17, 25, 24, 43.
49. Katz, *Birth of the Prophet*, p. 165.
50. See the introduction to Ibn Ḥajar, *Tabyīn al-ʿAjab*, pp. 9–19; Jones, *Power of Oratory*, p. 115.
51. Ibn Shaddad, *Rare and excellent*, pp. 77–8.
52. Ibn al-Jawzī, *al-Nūr*, pp. 151–68.
53. Colby, 'The rhetoric', p. 40; Ibn al-Ḥājj al-ʿAbdarī, *al-Madkhal*, vol. 3, p. 297. On how to properly recite the Qur'an, see Karen Nelson, *Art of Reciting*; Fierro, 'The treatises', pp. 211–16.
54. Ibn al-Ḥājj al-ʿAbdarī, *al-Madkhal*, vol. 3, pp. 107, 252.
55. Colby, 'The rhetoric', pp. 37–9; Ibn al-Ḥājj al-ʿAbdarī, *al-Madkhal*, vol. 3, pp. 291–14. For Ibn al-Hajj's ambivalence towards the celebration of Mawlid al-Nabi, see Ukeles, *Innovation*, pp. 216–20.
56. Ibn Qayyim al-Jawziyya, *Zād al-Maʿād*, vol. 1, p. 59.
57. Ibid.
58. Ibn Kathīr, *al-Bidāya*, vol. 14, p. 263.
59. Ibn Ḥajar, *Tabyīn al-ʿAjab*, p. 23.
60. I am grateful to Konrad Hirschler for these references to his *Book Culture in Late Medieval Syria: The Ibn ʿAbd al-Hādī Library of Damascus* before its publication. For more details on these treatises, see the excursus below.
61. Ibn Qudāma, *al-Mughnī*, vol. 4, pp. 429, 445.
62. Ibn Diḥya, *Adāʾ mā wajab*, p. 15.
63. Ibid. pp. 46–53.
64. Ibid. p. 56.
65. Megan Reid found that, from the end of the 1100s onwards, ascetic circles developped a favourable attitude towards long and onerous fasts, including the controversial *ṣawm al-dahr* ('continuous fast'); Reid, *Law and Piety*, pp. 57, 62.
66. Al-Sulamī, *Fatāwā*, pp. 326, 335–6, 481–5.
67. Al-Nawawī, *Sharḥ Ṣaḥīḥ Muslim*, vol. 8, p. 287; al-Jīlānī, *al-Ghunya*, vol. 2, p. 729, n. 63.
68. Ibn Rajab, *Laṭāʾif*, pp. 77–81, 228, 234. On fasting on that day as means of '*shukr al-niʿma*' – that is, thanking God for his favour of sending the Prophet of Islam – see Katz, *Birth of the Prophet*, p. 64.

69. Ibn Rajab, *Laṭāʾif*, p. 234. See also Ibn Ḥajar, *Tabyīn al-ʿAjab*, pp. 37–8, where the wish to die while performing the most meritorious devotions is attributed to the Prophet. For al-Jilani's contrasting presentation of the relationship between the months, see p. 171.
70. Ibn Taymiyya, *Majmūʿat al-Fatāwā*, vol. 25, p. 290. Refraining from speech during a fast (a practice based on Zakariyya and Maryam's oaths in Q. 19: 10 and 26, respectively) was a controversial practice, attributed by its Sunni opponents to the customs of the Jahiliyya, or to Jews and Christians (see Ibn Rajab, *Jāmiʿ al-ʿUlūm*, vol. 1, p. 375).
71. Al-Nuwayrī, *Nihāyat al-Arab*, vol. 32, p. 306. I owe this reference to Or Amir. Such 'secular intercession' or intercession between men was indeed expected from those 'whose word is accepted before a person in power' and considered as praiseworthy as religious devotions (Marmon, 'Quality of mercy', pp. 133–4).
72. Those very days are also recommended for fasting in Chittick, *Faith and Practice*, p. 146.
73. Reid, *Law and Piety*, p. 61; Ibn al-Jazarī, *Ḥawādith al-Zamān*, vol. 3, p. 638.
74. Jones, *Power of Oratory*, p. 175.
75. Ibid. pp. 103, 105.
76. Idrīs ʿImād al-Dīn, MS 39/909, pp. 4–7.
77. See, for example, Ibn Ḥajar, *Tabyīn al-ʿAjab*, pp. 70–1, 82.
78. Ibn Jubayr, *Riḥla*, pp. 311–13; ibid. *The Travels*, trans. Broadhurst, pp. 326–8.
79. This is the most important rite of the hajj, performed some 20km southeast of Mecca on 9 Dhu al-Hijja.
80. Ibn Jubayr, *Riḥla*, pp. 128–9.
81. For a description of the monuments along this road, see Ibn Jubayr, *Riḥla*, pp. 111–19; trans., *The Travels*, pp. 107–10.
82. Ibn Jubayr, *Travels*, pp. 129–30. On the 'fascination associated with the image of the royal lady as pilgrim', see Behrens-Abouseif, 'Mahmal', pp. 93–6.
83. Ibn Jubayr, *Riḥla*, pp. 130–2; trans., *Travels*, pp. 129–31.
84. Ibn Jubayr, *Riḥla*, p. 136; repeated in Ibn Baṭṭūṭa, *Riḥla*, pp. 179–80; trans. in *Travels of Ibn Battuta*, pp. 235–6. The only other source that dates the completion of Ibn Zubayr's reconstruction likewise, which I could find, is al-Najm ʿUmar Ibn Fahd (d. 885/1480), *Itḥāf al-Warā*, vol. 2, p. 75. Be that as it may, after the re-conquest of Mecca by the Umayyads, Ibn Zubayr's changes were dismantled according to the sources (Shalem, 'Clothing the sacred house', p. 178).
85. ʿAwda, '*Risālāt al-Adab*', p. 131.

86. The Sarw are a group of the Banu Sulaym, inhabiting Wadi Kulayyah in western Hijaz.
87. Ibn Jubayr, *Riḥla*, p. 133; trans. *Travels*, p. 133.
88. Ibn al-Mujāwir, *Bilād al-Yaman*, vol. 1, p. 26. Residents of villages north of Aden, such as Lahij, also made the pilgrimage on the first day of Rajab; ibid. *A Traveller*, p. 128. I thank Zacharie M. de Pierrepont for bringing this source to my attention.
89. Ibn Baṭṭūṭa, *Riḥla*, pp. 178–81; for an English rendering, see ibid. *Travels*, pp. 233–8.
90. Al-Albānī, *Musājala ʿIlmiyya*, p. 56.
91. Ibn Jubayr, *Riḥla*, p. 137–8; trans. *Travels*, pp. 137–8. Repeated in Ibn Baṭṭūṭa, *Riḥla*, pp. 179–80.
92. Katz, *Women in the Mosque*, pp. 222–4.
93. Al-Yamanī, *Taʾrīkh al-Yaman*, p. 7 (trans. to English, ibid. p. 10). See also Lecker, 'Judaism', p. 639.
94. Ibn al-Mujāwir, *Bilād al-Yaman*, vol. 2, pp. 165–6.
95. Al-Sharjī, *Ṭabaqāt al-Khawāṣṣ*, p. 43. In another entry, al-Sharji refers to a book on the merits of Rajab, Shaʿban and Ramadan by the Zabidi Sufi and scholar Muhammad b. Abi al-Sayf (d. 609/1212–13). I am indebted to Zacharie M. de Pierrepont for both of these references.
96. Marion Katz, *Women in the Mosque*, pp. 218, 353, n. 53. On Medina as the 'charismatic center of the Mamluk Empire', see Marmon, *Eunuchs*, pp. 28–9, 85–6.
97. Ibn Ṭāwūs, *al-Iqbāl*, vol. 3, pp. 236–7; Kohlberg, *Muslim Scholar*, p. 391.
98. Ibn Ṭāwūs, *al-Iqbāl*, vol. 3, pp. 231, 254.
99. Abū Shāma, *al-Bāʿith*, p. 238.
100. Ibn al-ʿAttār, in al-Albānī, *Musājala ʿIlmiyya*, pp. 54–6.
101. Ibn Rajab, *Laṭāʾif*, p. 231. According to Ibn Rajab, the proper time to pay *zakāt* is Muharram, rather than Rajab, because it is the beginning of the year.
102. Kister, 'Rajab is my month', p. 214. He draws on Ibn Ḥajar, *Tabyīn al-ʿAjab*, pp. 25–6.
103. Al-Khallāl, *Faḍāʾil*, p. 43.
104. Mujīr al-Dīn, *al-Uns al-Jalīl*, vol. 2, pp. 43, 275; al-ʿAsalī, *Maʿāhid al-ʿIlm*, pp. 213, 215.
105. Compare with the description and discussion of a similar occurence under the Fatimids, as on p. 162 above.

106. Lev, *Charity*, pp. 42, 129. On the social classification of the beneficiaries of the Ottoman Sultans, see Singer, *Charity*, pp. 184–5.
107. Sabra, *Poverty*, pp. 52–3, 88.
108. Frenkel, 'Muslim pilgrimage', pp. 80–81. I thank Or Amir for this reference.
109. Ibn Ṭawq, *al-Taʿlīq*, vol. 1, pp. 35, 174, 492. On the swings in the production and price of sugar in the eighth/fifteenth century, see Lewicka, *Food*, p. 301.
110. Frenkel, 'Public projection', p. 40; van Steenbergen, 'Ritual, politics', pp. 231–3, 245.
111. Richard McGregor calls this the 'scattering' of the *Kaʿba* and hajj; ibid. 'Dressing the Kaʿba'. For scholarly and popular explanations of this tradition, see Behrens-Abouseif, 'The *Maḥmal* legend', pp. 90–6.
112. El-Toudy and Abedlhamid, *Selections*, p. 387.
113. On the Fatimid *kiswa*, see p. 165 above.
114. Behrens-Abouseif, 'The *Maḥmal* legend', p. 89. For a closer look, see Qalqashandī, *Ṣubḥ al-Aʿshā*, vol. 4, p. 57.
115. McGregor, 'Dressing the Kaʿba', p. 248. McGregor claims that from the sixteenth century onwards, the procession was held only two to three weeks before the hajj caravan embarked for Mecca. At the beginning of the twentieth century, the procession began in front of the citadel and moved on to the Masjid al-Husayn. The *kiswa* was hung up on its walls for two weeks; people touched it and even cut off small pieces for *baraka* (ibid. p. 260).
116. Jomier found six references to *rajabiyya*s in the fourteenth century and seven in the fifteenth century; ibid. *Le maḥmal*, pp. 83–4. In all likelihood, Ibn Battuta's detailed and lively account of Cairo's 726/1326 *maḥmal* procession, which goes unmentioned by Jomier, is not drawn from personal experience, as he actually spent that Rajab elsewhere. His second visit to Cairo took place in 749/1348, after the departure of the Rajab caravan. See Elad, 'The description', pp. 256–72; Ibn Baṭṭūṭa, *The Travels of Ibn Battuta*, vol. 1, p. 59, n. 181.
117. Ibn Shāhīn, *Kashf al-Mamālīk*, p. 67.
118. Meloy, 'Processions', p. 643; Turner, 'Processions, religious', ibid. p. 644.
119. Van Steenbergen, 'Ritual, politics', p. 229, n. 3.
120. Shoshan, *Popular Culture*, pp. 70–4; Meloy, 'Celebrating the *Maḥmal*', pp. 412, 419. See also Sanders, 'Mawākib;' Elbendary, *Crowds and Sultans*, p. 173.
121. McGregor, 'Dressing the Kaʿba', p. 259.
122. Ibn al-Ḥājj al-ʿAbdarī, *al-Madkhal*, pp. 294–8.

123. Al-Albānī, *Musājala ʿIlmiyya*, pp. 54–5.
124. Stephenson, *Ritual*, p. 47.
125. Durkheim, *Elementary Forms*, pp. 53, 347, 356–61.
126. Schielke, *Perils*, pp. 42–52. See also Zerubavel, *Hidden Rhythms*, p. 127. Compare with Abraham Joshua Heschel's take on the Jewish Sabbath, emphasising that the Sabbath is for body as well as soul, hence that comfort and pleasure are an integral part of this holy day. See Heschel, *Sabbath*, p. 19.

20

Excursus: Arabic Treatises in Praise of the Sacred Months

The following is a preliminary list of works dedicated to the merits of Rajab, or to the three sacred months (Rajab, Shaʿban and Ramadan), or to the merits of all months, and all meritorious times (*Faḍāʾil al-Awqāt*). It is arranged in chronological order of the date of the authors' death. Shiʿi authors are marked SH, Sunni authors SU, and unidentified authors feature two question marks (??).

- Ibn Bābawayh al-Qummī (d. 381/991), *Faḍāʾil al-Ashhur al-Thalātha* (The Merits of the Three Months), ed. Mīrzā ʿArfāniyān, Beirut 1992. SH
- Abū ʿAbd Allāh b. ʿAyyāsh al-Jawharī (d. 401/1010–11), *ʿAmal Rajab wa-Shaʿbān wa-Ramaḍān* (The Good Works of Rajab, Shaʿban and Ramadan). SH
- Al-Iṣbahānī, Abū Saʿīd Muḥammad (d. 414/1023), *Faḍl al-Ṣiyām* (The Virtue of Fasting) ??
- Al-Khallāl, Muḥammad b. al-Ḥasan (d. 439/1047), *Faḍāʾil Shahr Rajab* (The Merits of the Month of Rajab), ed. ʿAbd al-Raḥmān Muḥammad, Beirut 1996. SU
- Al-Bayhaqī, Abū Bakr Aḥmad b. al-Ḥusayn (d. 458/1066), *Faḍāʾil al-Awqāt* (The Merits of Times), ed. Khallāf Maḥmūd ʿAbd al-Samīʿ, Beirut 1417/1997.[1] SU
- Al-Kattānī, ʿAbd al-ʿAzīz b. Aḥmad (d. 466/1074), *Faḍāʾil Shahr Rajab* (The Merits of the Month of Rajab). SU
- Al-Ṭabarī, ʿAbd al-Karīm b. ʿAbd al-Ṣamad (d. 478/1085), *Ḥadīthān fī Faḍl Rajab*[2] = *Ḥadīthān Aḥadhumā fī Faḍl Rajab li-Abī Muʿashshar*

al-Ṭabarī (Two Hadiths in Praise of Rajab = Two Hadiths, one in praise of Rajab by Abu Muʿashshar al-Tabari), ed. Jamāl ʿAzūn, Beirut 2000. SU (most likely)

- Al-Ḥākim al-Ḥasakānī (fifth/eleventh century), *Faḍāʾil Shahr Rajab* (The Merits of the Month of Rajab). Bound with: *Shawāhid al-Tanzīl li-Qawāʿid al-Tafḍīl: fī al-Āyāt al-nāzila fī Ahl al-Bayt*, ed. Muḥammad al-Maḥmūdī, Tehran 1990, 3 vols. SU[3]
- ʿAbd al-Qādir al-Jīlānī (d. 561/1166), *al-Ghunya li-Ṭālibī Ṭarīq al-Ḥaqq* (The Sufficient [Guide] for the Seekers of the Way of Truth), ed. Ṣallāḥ b. ʿUwayḍa, Beirut 1997, 2 vols. SU
- Al-Madīnī, Abū Mūsa, *Faḍāʾil al-Ayyām wa-l-Shuhūr* (The Virtues of Days and Months) ??
- Ibn ʿAsākir, ʿAlī b. al-Ḥasan (d. 571/1176), *Faḍl Rajab* (Virtues of Rajab).[4] SU
- Ibn al-Jawzī, Abū al-Faraj (d. 597/1200), *al-Nūr fī Faḍāʾil al-Ayyām wa-l-Shuhūr* (The Light of the Virtues of Days and Months), ed. ʿAbd al-Ḥakīm al-Anīs, 2018 SU
- Muḥammad b. Abī al-Sayf al-Zabīdī (d. 609/1212–13), *Faḍāʾil Rajab, Shaʿbān and Ramaḍān.* ??
- Al-Qazwīnī, ʿAbd al-Qāsim al-Rāfiʿī (d. 623/1226), *Faḍāʾil Rajab wa-Shaʿbān wa-Ramaḍān.* ??
- Ibn Diḥya al-Kalbī (d. 633/1235), *al-ʿAlam al-Manshūr fī Faḍāʾil al-Ayyām wa-l-Shuhūr* (A Propagation of the Merits of Days and Months). SU
- Ibn Ḥajar al-ʿAsqalānī (d. 852/1449), *Tabyīn al-ʿAjab bi-mā warada fī Faḍl Rajab* (An Enthusiastic Demonstration of the Virtue of Rajab), ed. Muḥammad al-Dīn and Aḥmad al-Namkī, al-Dūḥa 1989. SU
- Idrīs ʿImād al-Dīn (d. 872/1471), *Risālat al-Bayān li-mā wajab fī Maʿna Niṣf Shahr Rajab* (An Expalanation of what needs to be known [or: done] about the Meaning of Mid-Rajab), MS. SH
- Ibn al-Mibrad, Yūsuf (d. 909/1503), *Maʿārif al-Inʿām wa-Faḍl al-Shuhūr wa-l-Ayyām* (Knowing the Favours and Virtue of Months and Days), ed. Nūr al-Dīn Ṭālib et al., Damascus, 2011. SU

Notes

1. For details on another edition, see Works Cited.
2. Ibn ʿAbd al-Hadi Library of Damascus, MS D 3750/11, fols 151–5. See Hirschler, *Monument*, p. 426. The text was read in public on 27 Rajab 879/1992.
3. Bound together with a much larger Shiʿi work.
4. Ibn ʿAbd al-Hadi Library of Damascus, MS D 3807/11, fols 107–14. See Hirschler, *Monument*, p. 347. Mentioned in Kister, 'Rajab is the month', p. 208. See reference to Ibnʿ Asakir also in the excursus on *Faḍāʾil ʿAsqalān*, on p. 85 above.

21

Summary

Rajab was celebrated on the Arab Peninsula before the rise of Islam, as one of four sacred months of travel to fairs and pilgrimage to shrines. Resort to arms was considered taboo during these periods. Some early Islamic authorities assert that Islam has only enhanced Rajab's merit, while others claimed that the month's veneration was terminated by the Prophet Muhammad. The debate remained unsettled for centuries (and carries on today on multiple websites). Undeterred, Muslims of all classes developped many and manifold creative ways, formal and informal, private and public, to continuously sanctify Rajab, adapting to changing historical contexts.

With the repeal of intercalation and the transition to the hijri calendar, Rajab lost its connection to the springtime festivities of Arabia. The ban against warfare during the four holy months, which was tied to the region's pagan sacred enclaves and their pilgrimage routes, as well as to the pre-Islamic socio-economic order, had also lost its force.[1] Rajab visits to the sites of fairs in Arabia seem to have persisted for several generations and then faded away. The Rajab visitation of Mecca (known as *ʿumra*) persevered, supported by ruling authorities. Most of our early source material, however, appears to refer to individual or familial rites, such as fasting, domestic ritual slaughter, *iʿtikāf* in mosques, supererogatory prayer and invocation.

The *terminus post quem* of the formal public commemoration of Rajab in Egypt and in Northern Syria seems to fall into the first half of the tenth century, when the Fridays of the month were marked by special sermons in the presence of the ruler.[2] The Fatimids, who wrested control over Egypt in 358/969 and transferred their seat of government to their newly established 'ritual city' al-Qāhira in 362/973, celebrated Rajab on a whole new scale. They developped a new repertoire of public rituals and state festivals, with a distinct Isma'ili imperial flavor. Rajab became an occasion for displaying the imam-caliph's power and generosity to all his subjects on the one hand, while on the other hand promoting his veneration as the supreme *walī-Allāh* (friend of God) for the initiated Isma'ili elite. At this stage, the palace was the focal point of official ceremonies in which the imam-caliph and his representatives assumed a dominant role.[3] As Isma'ili Cairo became integrated into a metropolis that included also Fustat (Misr) and al-Qarafa, and as the position of the imam-caliph was contested, the formal events spread beyond the walled royal city to Sunni mosques and to the streets. Additionally, the great cemetery of al-Qarafa was the scene of informal popular gatherings, a mixture of religious devotions, leisure and commercial activity, which the authorities occasionally tried to suppress.[4]

Late in the eleventh century, a new communal Rajab devotion, the prayer of great rewards (*ṣalāt al-raghā'ib*), surfaced in the politically peripheral, yet religiously vibrant town of Jerusalem. It was an arduous supererogatory nocturnal ritual (preferably performed after a day's fast), based on Muhammad's putative custom as recorded in what experts widely considered an unreliable hadith. Despite the reservations of scholars who considered it an unwarranted innovation, the ritual drew legions of believers from various walks of life and was repeated annually. The concentrated effort that this ritual demanded seems to have made it all the more satisfying, empowering and full of promise. Its communal and repetitive nature, as well as the prospect of the intercession of angels and of 'transferring' rewards to dear ones must have added to its allure.

With the rise of the *iḥyā' al-sunna* movement during the Zangid and Ayyubid periods, the prayer of great rewards seems to have become a genuine expression of the commoners' piety. Although conceived in the sacred esplanade of Jerusalem, it was obviously not tied to the holy place. It could be successful proliferated elsewhere, as long as it was performed at the right time – that is, during an exceptionally potent night of Rajab, between the first Thursday and first Friday of the sacred month.

The Rajab *'umra* in Mecca, in contrast, conflated the territorial and temporal dimensions of the sacred, producing an especially powerful religious experience, as vividly reflected in travelogues.[5] It was held in a place that combined features typical of Mircae Eliade's 'center of the world' or '*axis mundi*', and Victor Turner's 'center out there', perhaps best defined by Erik Cohen's 'continuum' between the two. For non-Arabian pilgrims, its location demanded a risky venture into the wilderness and distancing oneself from centres of political and economic power. The rites of the *ʿumra* and the ceremonial opening of the door to the Kaʿba at sunrise (performed daily only during Rajab, allegedly), as described by eleventh- and twelfth-century pilgrims,[6] were conducted in a formal and decorous manner. The *ʿumra* was controlled by political authorities and orchestrated by religious dignitaries; yet, it was accompanied by intermittent outbursts of messy enthusiasm (of both men and women), as well as lively commerce and various kinds of entertainment. Food shipped in from more fertile regions, spectacular lighting, colourful processions, fancy attire for men and beasts of burden, displays of swordsmanship, camel races and the music of 'drums, tymbals, and trumpets'[7] were all integral parts of the festivities. Some rites were reserved for particular blessed days of the month – the first, fifteenth and twenty-seventh days of Rajab.

While there were varying opinions about its correct date, in the Mamluk period Muhammad's night journey and ascension to heaven was usually commemorated on the twenty-seventh day of Rajab. Allusions to several significant events in the biography of the Prophet recur in works in praise of Rajab, but only the anniversary of the night journey appears to have evolved into a widely celebrated annual festival. Since the twelfth or thirteenth century it was observed by Sunnis and Shiʿis alike.

In the second half of the thirteenth century, the Mamluk Sultan Baybars brought in new formal celebrations of Rajab and incorporated the *maḥmal* into the annual caravan that left Cairo for Mecca during that month. The Mamluks aptly demonstrated their role as protectors of the Hijaz by funding the Rajab procession of the *kiswa* and the *maḥmal*, assigning their soldiers a prominent role in the parade. Religious diginitaries, men of the administration and the multitudes joined in, or at least came to watch. The spectacle was known as al-Rajabiyya. From the stern perspective of fourteenth- and fifteenth-century Sunni advocates of 'the way of the Prophet and the first Muslims (*al-sunna wa-l-salaf*)', the somber religious dimension of the Rajab vigils was thus sadly overshadowed by celebrations and inappropriate merrymaking on extravagantly illuminated streets, in bazars, cemeteries, mosques and shrines.[8]

At this stage, the Rajab events in Cairo, which were initially orchestrated 'from above' and demonstrated the sovereign's piety and power, had apparently taken on a life of their own. We can speculate, however, that most participants did not hold a dichotomous outlook that separates between religious and pleasurable pastimes. They may have experienced the Rajabiyya as simultaneously entertaining *and* spiritual, as suggested by Samuli Schielke, or, as suggested by Marion Katz, as an occasion that naturally combined rejoicing with giving thanks for God's bounty.[9]

Hostility to revelries was voiced by scholars who endorsed the month's sanctity, yet deplored the use of sacred time for leisure and merriment at the expense of 'proper' religious devotions. Scholars who utterly opposed the elevated status of Rajab and considered it an 'error (*khabṭ*)' typical of 'commoners (*al-ʿawwām*)' criticised also conventional and consensual devotions such as invocations, almsgiving and fasting, if performed with the intention to sanctify the month. They were especially opposed to communal rites, as their regular performance may create the wrong impression regarding their legal status. A few of these critics underscored the pre-Islamic roots of Rajab customs. Others labelled them *bidaʿ* that lack any foundation in Qurʾan or in authentic hadith and impinge on the unique canonical status of Ramadan and of several other days, truly designated by the shariʿa for annual commemoration.

These concerns seem to characterise Sunni discourse; throughout my survey, I did not encounter any medieval Imami figures who voiced such apprehensions. To the contrary, Shiʿi authorities wholeheartedly recommended special devotions for each day of the month: fasts, invocations, almsgiving, visits to the graves of the imams and the annual celebration of signposts in Shiʿi sacred history. The notion that Rajab was a sacred time meriting special rites seems to have been accepted in ʿAlid circles without reservation from early on, in line with Marion Katz's observation that the ʿAlids probably preceded the Sunnis in filling their religious calendar with celebratory commemoration.[10] Typically, the Shiʿi works rely more heavily on ʿAli ibn Abi Talib, Fatima, al-Husayn and the first imams, while the Prophet and his Companions are a major source of aphorisms in Sunni compilations.[11]

This is probably true also regarding the production of liturgical texts for those occasions. Moving personal invocations for Rajab are ascribed to pivotal ʿAlid figures, such as the fourth imam ʿAli Zayn al-ʿAbidin (d. 95/713) and the sixth imam Jaʿfar al-Sadiq (d. 148/765). The appeal of these prayers was not limited to ʿAlid communities, however. According to my provisional inventory,[12] these sorts of texts were included in compilations of prayers for special times by Sunni as much as by Shiʿi authors from the third/ninth century onwards, and they became part of a popular living tradition that would endure for centuries to come. Rajab is portrayed in those manuals as a privileged time for seeking pardon (*istighfār*) and intercession (*shafāʿa*), typically that of the angels, and for performing incredibly rewarding devotions.

Medieval sources that argue against the sanctity of Rajab and against the notion that it is an especially rewarding occasion for virtuous deeds are cited currently in twenty-first-century online debates. In line with prevalent fundamentalist discourse – captured by the saying that innovation is the most dangerous sin after polytheism (*al-bidʿa akhṭar al-dhunūb baʿd al-shirk*) and by the catchy slogan 'we are followers, not innovators (*li-annanā naḥnu muttabiʿūn wa-lasnā mubtadiʿūn*)' – multiple websites denounce the sanctification of Rajab. More generally, they insist that all the seemingly pious practices that designate some days as 'special' and more meritorious than other days are innovative, misguided and wrong.[13]

Majallat al-Jundī al-Muslim (*The Journal of the Muslim Soldier*), for example, also devoted a short article to the clarification of the matter. Fourteen hadiths extolling the virtues of Rajab are quoted and dismissed as inauthentic, and six practices – sacrificial slaughter, the celebration of *laylat al-isrāʾ* on 27 Rajab, the prayer of great rewards (*ṣalāt al-raghāʾib*), fasting, almsgiving and the minor pilgrimage to Mecca (*al-ʿumra al-rajabiyya*) – are briefly described and likewise repudiated.[14] The authoritative Saʿudi Permanent Committee for Scholarly Research and *Iftāʾ* headed by Ibn al-Baz published a fatwa against the visitation of graves and cemeteries on certain days, referring specifically to the first and last days of Rajab, as well as Fridays.[15] In contrast, contemporary Shiʿi websites encourage the performance of the *duʿāʾ* of Ibn Tawus on the first Friday night of Rajab, nowadays called *laylat al-raghāʾib* , and suggest plenty of other texts for recitation throughout the month.[16]

Notes

1. See above, p. 136.
2. See above, pp. 145–7.
3. See above, p. 157.
4. See above, p. 166.
5. See especially the descriptions of the Rajab *ʿumra* in the travelogues of Nasir Khusraw and Ibn Jubayr, as cited above.
6. See above, pp. 164–5, 200–1.
7. See above, p. 199.
8. See above, p. 209.
9. For a fuller presentation of Schielke's 'festive time' see above, p. 210; Katz, *Birth of the Prophet,* pp. 106–10.
10. Katz, *Birth of the Prophet*, p. 5.
11. As reflected, for example, in the index of the Qumm 1414H edition of *al-Iqbāl bi-l-Aʿmāl al-Ḥasana*, vol. 3, pp. 383–5.
12. See the excursus on p. 218.
13. An article posted on 13 Rajab 2008 online at http://ar.islamway.net/article/3671 is a good example.
14. Ibid.
15. Al-Darwīsh, ed. *Fatāwā al-Lajna al-Dāʾima*, vol. 9, pp. 113–14 (no. 8818/3).

Final Comments: Spacial and Temporal Sanctity

> I implore by the sanctity (*bi-ḥurmat*) of the sacred month and the sacred house
>
> (The Prayer of Umm Dawud)[1]

Making the shift from the 'microscopic' investigation of the history of the shrine(s) of the head of al-Ḥusayn and the rites of the month of Rajab to 'macroscopic' observations of the medieval Islamic construction of the sacred, I found marked similarities between the understanding of holy days and holy places. From the etic perspective it may be said that there were common strategies for the consecration of places and times and for the 'invention of tradition', as well as a common Islamic vocabulary by which to describe them.

Both were imagined as channels of enhanced accessibility to God, wherein his mercy is exceedingly bountiful, or as settings that promise especially rewarding transactions: the remission of sins and the incredible multiplication of recompenses for the performance of a wide variety of religious devotions. Some medieval Islamic scholars warned that this increase was coupled with harsher divine retribution for sinning and desecration – typically associated with bloodshed, the 'excessive' presence of women, intermingling of the sexes, violation of a prescribed code of conduct and rowdy behaviour of sorts. Rarely, however, do we get an explicit emic view of the juxtaposition of the sanctity of places and time from the medieval sources. Ibn Taymiyya, who often voices singular views, stands out in this context as well, by distinguishing between rituals of place and time, and by defining the first as more offensive to the Islamic conception of *tawhid* (monotheism) than the latter (to the exclusion of the prescribed hajj), as they more closely resemble pagan rites. He is one of very few scholars to make such a comparison[2] and to ciriticise so vehemently the very sanctification of times and places, other than those explicitly pronounced as sacred in the Qur'an. Most Muslims of his generation held a very different view of sacred topography and of the religious calendar, identifying multiple noble and blessed settings in both.

Clearly, sacred place and time were not competing categories in the religious experience of Muslims in the medieval Middle East. To the contrary, they were regarded as complimentary and even as enhancing each other's effect. Hence, when Ibn Tawus recommends the visitation of al-Husayn's shrine on the fifteenth day of Rajab in his compilation of good works for special dates, *al-Iqbāl bi-l-A'māl al-Ḥasana*, he encourages believers to reap the merits inherent in the sacred place and during the sacred time simultaneously, thereby exponentially multiplying their rewards, both spiritual and material.[3] Seemingly, the *baraka* of a geographical location, be it a town or a shrine, was restricted in comparison to that of a universally recurring hour, day or month; it had to be actively sought by travel to the sacred place and physical access to its shrine. In the understanding of medieval Muslims, however, blessings could be transferred by objects that had been there and had touched it, such as a shred cut off from the *kiswa* or other cloth-covering. Alternatively, the blessings of the place were held to be available and effective way beyond its confines, thanks to the power of intercession (*shafā'a*), earned by those who practised their religious devotions there.

The intercession of angels and their benevolent presence is a recurrent theme in texts that construct the sacredness of both sites and times, denoting the enhanced presence of God and his attentiveness to human devotions.[4] On holy days, the angels supposedly increase their ritual activity near the divine throne, showing the way to humans (according to al-Ghazzali's interpretation[5]), or imploring on behalf of sinful men. Angels descend on places such as the grave of the Prophet,[6] the mosques of Mecca, Medina and Jerusalem,[7] and al-Sham (Syria), marking their noble standing and protecting them.[8] Shi'i texts depict groups of angels greeting pilgrims at al-Husayn's tomb in Karbala, escorting and guarding them, and interceding on their behalf.[9]

While the spilling of blood in sanctuaries and during sacred months was taboo in pre-Islamic Arabia, the blood of saints and martyrs sanctified places as well as great events that were later celebrated annually, and its miraculous fresh appearance indicated or reaffirmed their acquired status. Other common features that constituted the holiness of sacred places in the medieval Islamic religious imagination were the apparitions of righteous men or prophets, footprints or relics of such men, light, the smell of perfume (rather than decay), and other wonders laden with hidden meanings and 'secrets (*asrār*) that are beyond the comprehension of ordinary human beings'.

Miraculous light, such as the columns that pointed to the location of al-Husayn's head in all the narratives of its peregrinations after its transferal from the battlefield of Karbala and the ritualised kindling of light in preparation for and during festivities are also prevalent markers of sacred times and places. So much so that scholars who disapproved of the performance of special rites on particular nights often voiced their dismay at the huge cost of extravagantly lit mosques, shrines and streets.

Holy places and times were 'storied' settings. They were often identified as loci of sacred history – that is, of key events in the lives of prophets and saints, based on the 'great' and 'little' traditions: scriptures, early myths and local folklore. More often than not, several signifiant and/or auspicious events were said to have occurred on the same day or in the same place. The claim of the Hanbali Sufi ʿAbd al-Qadir al-Jilani that God chose al-ʿAshuraʾ (the tenth day of Muharram) for al-Husayn's martyrdom – because it was 'the noblest, greatest, most glorious day in his eyes'[10] – is an attempt to explain and articulate the connection between sacred time and history. It appears to have been generally believed that 'great events (*ḥawādith aẓīma*)' occur during inherently auspicious times,[11] rather than vice versa, and that such events sanctify time and make it holy thereafter. Ibn Taymiyya – who argues that identifying the sites of signposts in the lives of prophets and remembering the location of their graves are insignificant acts devoid of religious value[12] – once again voices a highly atypical opposition to the idea of remembering and commemorating the dates of such occurrences as well.

Marion Katz, who pointed out the central role of the Prophet as key to salvation in medieval Islam, suggests that the celebrations of the *mawlid* and *laylat al-miʿrāj* in honour of the Prophet 'had a circular component which cyclically brought close the blessings of [those] great events' to all. Hence, she claims, the enthusiastic celebration of the *mawlid* as a '"little path" to salvation by commoners, who knew that their fulfillment of religious obligations is wanting, and were terrified of the result'.[13] I found a more hopeful attitude towards the efficacy of *istighfār* and the remittance of sins, playfully articulated in the 'tables' calculating the multiplication of rewards for distinct devotions. Moreover, looking at a wider range of sources that deal with sacred times and places, I found a more varied repertoire of paths for the achievement of salvation, or at least God's mercy.

A few Islamic scholars draw a correlation between the performance of religious rites and the promotion of sanctity. The notion that men complement the divine enterprise undergirds Ibn Nubata's claim that, while God is partial to Rajab and made it the first of the months of merits (*awwal shuhūr al-faḍāʾil*), it is incumbent upon us humans to glorify it (*awjaba ʿalaynā taʿzīmuhu*).[14] Al-Ghazzali articulates the dual, namely divine-human, nature of sanctification in a slightly different fashion. Upon compiling an inventory of 'noble times (*awqāt sharīfa*)' and 'noble circumstances (*aḥwāl sharīfa*)' for supererogatory prayer, he explains that the loftiness of these days is further increased by the intentions and hearts of the faithful who join together at these particular times to evoke God's abundant mercy.[15] Even the virtues of the holiest cities of Mecca and Medina are enhanced by the arrival of pilgrims and the amassment of their prayers,[16] as the performance of religious rites augments holiness and is elevated by them at one and the same time.[17]

The main ritual that was conducted in holy places and during sacred times, both on an individual and communal basis, by Sunnis and Shiʿis, men and women, is undoubtedly prayer. Supplications come first in the list of devotions that the newly consecrated shrine in Ascalon was expected to host, based on the foundational inscription on Badr al-Jamali's *minbar*. Putting their faith in the blessings (*baraka*) of the holy site, devotees uttered fervent and on occasion tearful prayers and private invocations at shrines,[18] or circumambulated the tombstone amidst an enthusiastic loud crowd.[19] The notion that the saint was present at the place was expressed in the formulas uttered upon entering.[20] Some visitors strengthened their supplication by a tomb or relic by touching the cover or silver railing that protected it; taking an oath (which may have included a promise to return to the *mashhad*);[21] and reciting an appropriate poem.[22] Rites performed in a *mashhad* at a special time, ranging from any Friday night to *Laylat al-Qadr*, were expected to be all the more effective.[23]

Deeming sacred time in and of itself to be as efficacious as holy places, believers spent certain days and nights reciting special prayers and executing a strenuous number of prostrations, often at the end of a day's fast. Some added a short invocation to their regular prayers on each such day (that is, throughout the month of Rajab).

Probably starting from the third/ninth century, liturgical texts for special occasions were assembled into devotional manuals entitled *Faḍāʾil al-Awqāt* (The Merits of Times). Some (or parts) of these texts describe intense religious emotions, while others display poetic acumen, incorporating rhymes, allusions to well-known Qurʾanic figures and vivid images of rewards in the afterworld. Treatises on the merits of places were likewise compiled from laudatory hadiths, anecdotes about the pious and recommendations for highly rewarding good works. The proliferation of treatises of both kinds may be regarded as both an expression of the growing popularity of the veneration of sacred days and places, and a catalyst of this trend.[24] Sunni and Shiʿi manuals bear a close resemblance to each other; both express shared Islamic perceptions and like-minded individual hopes for approaching the divine, in words that sit well with Ismaʿilis, Imamis and Sunnis. The manner of the calculation of rewards for these practices (the 'economy of requital') and the colourful lists of incredibly lush material and spiritual prizes expecting practitioners are also very much alike in all those texts.[25]

Sacred spaces and times, and the festivities associated with them create ample opportunities for philanthropy, ranging from the donation of candles for a single session of Qurʾan recitation, to the funding of grand public banquets and the establishment of monumental shrines. Almsgiving, a highly recommended devotional practice under all circumstances, was widely thought to secure exponentially increased recompense if performed at a holy site or during a sacred time, such as Rajab, although more than a few esteemed jurists noted the absence of *sharʿī* evidence for that conviction.[26] Large-scale patronage of sacred space and time necessitated the political power of rulers and members of the elites. Great resources were recruited for royal processions and audiences, as well as the preparation, distribution and consumption of special foods on holy days and at venerated shrines.

As noted by theorists of ritual, such occasions usually displayed social hierarchies and power relations, and manifested the wealth, dominion and pious devotion of the ruling authorities.[27] Even when the streets were so crowded that 'no one could tell the chiefs from the subjects' anymore, things were usually under control, and order was maintained. On occasion, however, the precarious status quo and social unity – the bolstering of which is often regarded by sociologists and anthropologists as the very purpose of rituals[28] – was jeopardised by unforeseen vandalism or violence.[29] Occasionally, ceremonies 'went wrong' and religious rites were disrupted by undecorous and even violent behaviour, in contrast to theories determining the constructive functions of rituals as social glue, or, in a more critical eye, as mechanism of social control.[30] The intersections of sacred time *and* place, such as experienced in Mecca during Rajab, or at a Husayni shrine on the day of Ghadir Khumm, intensified religious feeling, giving rise to collective joy and expressions of social solidarity on the one hand, while on the other hand exposing conflicting discourses and producing occasional outbursts of intra- and inter-communal strife.

Still, Rajab's veneration and the sanctification of the Husayni martyries in Ascalon and Cairo, our 'secondary' case studies of holiness, were perpetuated for centuries. As I hope to have demonstrated in the two parts of this book, such continuity is due to the adaptability of local traditions to changing historical circumstances and to active promotion by rulers. As the need for places and times that are set apart from and elevated above the routine and mundane seems to be universal, adjusting old beliefs and practices regarding such expanses to new contexts is, generally, more rewarding than extracting them from the landscape and the calendar. It also better serves local aspirations and marks communal idetities.[31]

The majority of the scholars who argued against the sanctity of shrines in honour of the head of al-Husayn attempted to disprove the authenticity of the relic associated with them. They neither denied the potency of the remains of a holy figure, nor did they reject the idea that places touched by such relics are repositories of *baraka*. Likewise, very few scholars either refuted the notion that there are especially meritorious hours, days and months in the religious calendar (besides those explicitly mentioned in the Qur'an), or dismissed the 'sacred months' by unequivocally claiming that their pre-Islamic sanctity was abrogated by the revelation of Islam and the special status accorded to Ramadan. For all Muslims, the non-learned faithful included, 'secondary' sacred places and times, such as Husayni shrines and the nights of Rajab, offered ample accessible and affordable opportunities to participate in supererogatory devotions, to come closer to the great transcendent God, and to partake in His mercy (*raḥma*), individually as well as communally.

Notes

1. *Bi-ḥurmat al-shahr al-ḥarām, bi-ḥurmat al-bayt al-harām, wa-l-mashʿar al-ḥarām wa-l-rukn wa-l-maqām wa-l-mashāʿir al-ʿuzzām wa-qabr Nabyyika Muḥammad ʿalayhi al-salām* (al-Hasakānī, *Faḍāʾil*, p. 506).
2. Memon, *Ibn Taymīya's Struggle*, pp. 15, 258.
3. See Katz, *Birth of the Prophet*, esp. pp. 153–68.
4. Burge, 'Angels', pp. 232–3, 239; Padwick, *Devotions*, pp. 67–8.
5. Al-Ghazzali generally regards the angels as role models for humans, see Reynold, 'Angels'. On the imitation of the angels by Adam, who seeks forgiveness for his sin, and during the *hajj*, see Katz, 'Hajj', pp. 111, 123.
6. See Katz, *Birth of the Prophet*, p. 157.
7. Mujīr al-Dīn, *al-Uns al-Jalīl*, vol. 1, p. 353.
8. Cited in al-Asyūṭī, *Faḍāʾil*, p. 239; and in Olesen, *Culte*, pp. 204–5.
9. Sindawi, 'Visit', p. 252; Ibn Qawlawayh, *Kāmil al-Ziyārāt*, pp. 223–6, 231–6.
10. Katz, *Birth of the Prophet*, p. 114.
11. Ibid. p. 144.
12. See above, p. 115.
13. Katz, *Birth of the Prophet*, pp. 167–8.
14. See Ibn Nubāta, *Khuṭab Minbariyya*, pp. 45.
15. Al-Ghazzālī, *Iḥyāʾ ʿUlūm al-Dīn*, vol. 1, pp. 403–4. I find this strikingly reminiscent of Turner's 'secularised' idea of communitas.
16. Lazarus-Yafeh, 'Mecca and Jerusalem', p. 205.
17. For contemporary debates on the nature of the relationship between ritual acts, times and places, see Grimes, *Craft*, pp. 259–61.
18. See, for example, Ibn Taymiyya, *Majmūʿat al-Fatāwā*, vol. 27, p. 54.
19. See above, pp. 88, 121.
20. See above, p. 89.
21. Al-ʿImrānī, *Sīrat Shaykh al-Islām*, pp. 95, 103.
22. See pp. 81, 109 above.
23. Al-Fāriqī, *Taʾrīkh*, pp. 33–4.

24. See above, pp. 25, 218.
25. For a typical example, see al-Jīlānī, *Ghunya*, vol. 2, pp. 738–9.
26. See above, pp. 204, 224.
27. Stephenson, *Ritual*, p. 43.
28. Stephenson depicts and critiques this idea in ibid. *Ritual*, pp. 36, 42.
29. See pp. 162 and 205 above.
30. Stephenson, *Ritual*, pp. 38–48.
31. For a discussion of the uninterrupted sanctity of Jerusalem, see Limor, Reiner, and Frenkel, *Pilgrimage*, pp. 26–7.

Works Cited

Ababsa, Myriam, 'Shi'i Mausoleums of Raqqa: Iranian proselytism and local significations', in Fred Lawson (ed.), *Demystifying Syria*. London: Saqi Books, 2009: 85–104.

Al-ʿAbdarī, Ibn al-Ḥājj. *Kitāb al-Madkhal*, 4 vols. Cairo: al-Maktaba al-Tijāriyya al-Kubrā, 1929.

Al-ʿAbdarī, Muḥammad. *Al-Riḥla al-Maghribiyya*, ed. Muḥammad al-Fāsī. Ribat: Jāmiʿat Muḥammad al-Khāmis, 1968.

Al-Abṭaḥī, Muḥammad b. al-Muwaḥḥid (ed.). *Al-Ṣahīfa al-Sajjādiyya*. Qumm: Muʾassasat al-Imām al-Mahdī, 1411/1990.

ʿAbd al-Nāṣir, M. ʿA. (ed.). *Al-Majālis al-Muʾayyadiyya li-l-Muʾayyad al-Dīn al-Shīrāzī*. Cairo: Dār al-Thaqāfa li-l-Ṭibāʿa wa-l-Nashr, 1975.

Abū Shāma. *Al-Bāʿith ʿalā Inkār al-Bidaʿ wa-l-Ḥawādith*, ed. Mashhūr Ḥasan Salmān. Riyad: Dār al-Raya li-l-Nashr wa-l-Tawzīʿ, 1410/1990.

Abū Shāma. *Tarājim Rijāl al-Qarnayn*, ed. M. Z. al-Kawtharī. Beirut: Dār al-Jīl, 1974.

Abū Ṭālib al-Makkī. *Qūt al-Qulūb*, ed. Saʿīd Nusayb Mukārim. Beirut: Dār Ṣādir, 1995.

Afsarruddin, Asma. *The First Muslims: History and Memory*. Oxford: Oneworld Publications, 2008.

Al-Albānī, M. N. *Musājala ʿIlmiyya bayna al-Imāmayn al-Jallālayn al-ʿIzz b. ʿAbd al-Salām wa-Ibn al-Ṣalāḥ*. Damascus: al-Maktab al-Islāmī, 1960–1.

Alexandrin, Elizabeth R. *Walāyah in the Fāṭimid Ismāʿīlī Tradition*. Albany: State University of New York Press, 2017.

Allan, James W. *The Art and Architecture of Twelver Shiʿism: Iraq, Iran and the Indian Sub-Continent*. London: Azimuth Editions, 2012.

Alliata, E. 'The legends of the Madaba Map'. In Michele Piccirillo and Eugenio Alliata (eds), *The Madaba Map Centenary, 1897–1997: Travelling through the Byzantine Umayyad Period. Proceedings of the International Conference held in Amman, 7–9 April 1997.* Jerusalem: Franciscan Printing Press, 1999: 47–101.

Anabseh, Ghalib. 'The sanctity of the city of ʿAsqalān in the "Merits Literature" of Palestine: An examination of Mamluk and Ottoman sources'. *Journal of Holy Land and Palestine Studies* 5 (2006): 187–98.

Anonymous. *Akhbār al-Dawla al-ʿAbbāsiyya*, ed. ʿAbd al-ʿAzīz al-Dūrī and ʿAbd al-Jabbār al-Mūṭlibī. Beirut: Dār al-Ṣādir, 1971.

Antrim, Zayde. *Routes and Realms: The Power of Place in the Early Islamic World.* Oxford University Press: New York, 2012.

al-ʿArif, ʿArif. *Al-Mūjaz fī Taʾrīkh ʿAsqalān*. Jerusalem: Maṭbaʿat Bayt al-Maqdis, 1943.

ʿArrāf, Shukrī. *Ṭabaqāt al-Anbiyāʾ wa-l-Awliyāʾ fī al-Arḍ al-Muqaddasa*. Tarshīḥa: Maṭbaʿat Ikhwān Makhūl, 1994.

ʿAsalī, Kāmil Jamīl. *Maʿāhid al-ʿIlm fi-l-Bayt al-Muqaddas*. Amman: Jamʿiyyat ʿUmmāl al-Maṭābiʿ al-Taʿāwūniyya, 1981.

Asani, Ali S. 'Devotional practices'. In Farhad Daftary, Amyn B. Sajoo and Jiwa Shainool (eds), *The Shiʿi World: Pathways in Tradition and Modernity*. London and New York: I. B. Tauris and The Institute of Ismaili Studies, 2015: 150–68.

Al-Asyūṭī, Shams al-Dīn. *Faḍāʾil al-Shām,* ed. Abū ʿAbd al-Raḥmān ʿĀdil b. Saʿd. Beirut: Dār al-Kutub al-ʿIlmiyya, 2001.

Al-Asyūṭī, Shams al-Dīn. *Itḥāf al-Akhiṣṣā bī Faḍāʾil al-Masjid al-Aqṣā*, ed. Aḥmad R. Aḥmad. Cairo: al-Hayʾa al-Miṣriyya al-ʿĀmma li-l-Kitāb, 1982–4.

Attou, Noria. *Los Sermones de Ibn Nubata, según el manuscrito hallado en Almonacid de la Sierra*. Unpublished PhD diss., Madrid 2004.

Aubin-Boltanski, Emma. 'Salāh al-Dīn, un héros à l'épreuve: Mythe et pèlerinage en Palestine'. *Annales: Histoire, Sciences Sociales* 1 (2005): 91–107.

Avi-Yonah, M. *The Madaba Mosaic Map, With Introduction and Commentary.* Jerusalem: Israel Exploration Society, 1954.

ʿAwda, ʿA. A. '*Risālāt al-Adab fī Rajab* by ʿAlī al-Qārī'. *Jerusalem Studies in Arabic and Islam* 18 (1994): 128–45.

Ayoub, Mahmoud. ʿArbaʿīn'. In Ehsan Yar-Shater (ed.), *Encyclopaedia Iranica.* London: Routledge and Keagan Paul, 1989: vol. 3, pp. 275–76; available at www.iranicaonline.org

Ayoub, Mahmoud. 'Cult and culture: Saints and shrines in Middle Eastern popular piety'. In Richard G. Hovannisian and George Sabagh (eds), *Religion and*

Culture in Medieval Islam. Cambridge: Cambridge University Press, 1999: 103–15.

Ayoub, Mahmoud. 'The Excellences of Imam Husayn in Sunni hadith tradition'. In *Imam Husayn in Muslim Tradition*. London: Routledge and Keagan Paul, 1986: 58–70.

Ayoub, Mahmoud. *Redemptive Suffering in Islam*. The Hague: Mouton, 1978.

Ayyad, Essam S. *The Making of the Mosque*. Piscataway, NJ: Gorgias Press, 2019.

Azad, Arezu. *Sacred Landscape in Medieval Afghanistan: Revisiting the Faḍāʾil-i Balkh*. Oxford: Oxford University Press, 2013.

Bābā, ʿAbduh M. *Al-Majmūʿa al-Mubāraka fī al-Ṣalawāt al-Maʾthūra wa-l-Aʿmāl al-Mabrūra*. Nablus: Maktabat Khālid b. al-Walīd, 1990.

Al-Baghawī, Abū Muḥammad b. al-Ḥusayn. *Tafsīr Maʿālim al-Tanzīl*, ed. Muḥammad ʿA. al-Nimr et al. Riyad: Dār Ṭayba, 1411/1989.

Al-Baghdādī, Abū Manṣūr. *Al-Nāsikh wa-l-Mansūkh*, ed. Ḥilmī ʿAbd al-Hādī. Amman: Dār Adawī, 1407/1987.

Bağlı, Hümanur. 'Material Culture of Religion: New Approaches to Functionality in Islamic Objects', *The Design Journal* 18 (2015): 305–25.

Bahādur, Shihāb Allāh. *Muʿjam mā ullifa fī faḍāʾil wa-taʾrīkh al-Masjid al-Aqṣā wa-1-Quds wa-Filasṭīn wa-mudunihā min al-qarn al-thālith ilā nakbat Filasṭīn sanat 1367 h. / 1948 m*. Dubbai: Markaz Jumʿat al-Majid li-1-Thaqāfa wa-1-Turāth, 2009).

Al-Bakrī, Abū ʿUbayd. *Al-Masālik fī Taʾrīkh al-Mamālik*, ed. A. Ferre and A. Van Leeuwen. Tunis: al-Dār al-ʿArabiyya li-l-Kitāb 1992.

Barghūthī, ʿUmar Ṣāliḥ and Khalīl Ṭūṭaḥ. *Taʾrīkh Filasṭīn*. Jerusalem: Maṭbaʿat Bayt al-Maqdis, 1923.

Bashear, Suliman. 'Apocalyptic and other materials on Early Muslim-Byzantine wars: A review of Arabic sources'. *Journal of Royal Asiatic Society* 1 (1991): 173–207.

Bauden, Frederic. 'Maqriziana XII: Evaluating the sources for the Fatimid period: Ibn al-Maʾmun al-Bataʾikhi's history and its use by al-Maqrizi'. In Bruce D. Craig (ed.), *Ismaili and Fatimid Studies in Honor of Paul E. Walker*. Chicago: Middle East Documentation Center, 2010: 33–85.

Al-Bayhaqī. *Kitāb Faḍāʾil al-Awqāt*, ed. ʿAdnān al-Qaysī. Mecca: Maktabat al-Manāra, 1410/1990.

Behrens-Abouseif, Doris. 'The *maḥmal* legend and the pilgrimage of the ladies of the Mamluk court'. *Mamlūk Studies Review* 1 (1997): 87–96.

Behrens-Abouseif, Doris. *The Minarets of Cairo*. Cairo: I. B. Tauris, 2010.

Berg, C. C. 'Ṣawm'. In P. Bearman, Th. Bianquis, C. E. Bosworth, E. van Donzel and W. P. Heinrichs (eds), *Encyclopaedia of Islam*, 2nd edn, available at http://dx.doi.org/10.1163/1573-3912_islam_COM_1008 (last accessed 8 May 2019).

Berkey, Jonathan. 'The Mamluks as Muslims'. In Ulrich Haarmman and Thomas Phillip (eds), *The Mamluks in Egyptian Politics and Society*. Cambridge: Cambridge University Press, 1998: 163–73.

Berkey, Jonathan. 'Mamluk religious policy'. *Mamluk Studies Review* 13/2 (2009): 7–22.

Berkey, Jonathan. 'Popular culture under the Mamluks: A historiographical survey'. *Mamlūk Studies Review* 9 (2005): 133–46.

Berkey, Jonathan. 'Tradition, innovation, and the construction of knowledge in the medieval Near East'. *Past and Present* 146 (1995): 38–65.

Berkey, Jonathan. *The Transmission of Knowledge in Medieval Cairo: A Social History of Islamic Education*. Princeton: Princeton University Press, 2014.

Bierman, Irene. *Writing Signs: The Fatimid Public Text*. Berkeley: University of California Press, 1998.

Bilu, Yoram. 'The role of charismatic dreams in the creation of sacred sites in present-day Israel'. In Benjamin Z. Kedar and R. J. Zwi Werblowski (eds), *Sacred Space: Shrine, City, Land*. Jerusalem: Palgrave Macmillan, 1998: 295–315.

Al-Birūnī. *The Chronology of Ancient Nations*, trans. and ed. C. E. Sachau. London: Pub. for the Oriental Translation Fund of Great Britain & Ireland by W. H. Allen, 1879.

Blair, Sheila S. 'On giving to shrines: "Generosity is a quality of the people of Paradise"'. In Linda Komaroff (ed.), *Gifts of the Sultan: The Art of Giving at the Islamic Courts*. New Haven: Los Angeles County Museum of Art, 2011: 51–74.

Blair, Sheila S. *Text and Image in Medieval Persian Art*. Edinburgh: Edinburgh University Press, 2014.

Bloom, Jonathan M. *Arts of the City Victorious*. Cairo: Yale University Press, 2007.

Bloom, Jonathan M. 'Ceremonial and sacred space in Early Fatimid Cairo'. In Amira K. Bennison and Alison L. Gascoigne (eds), *Cities in the Pre-Modern Islamic World*. London and New York: Routledge, 2007: 96–114.

Bloom, Jonathan M. *The Minaret*. Edinburgh: Edinburgh University Press 2013.

Bloom, Jonathan M. 'Woodwork in Palestine, Syria, and Egypt during the 12th and 13th centuries'. In Robert Hillenbrand and Sylvia Auld (eds), *Ayyubid Jerusalem: The Holy City in Context, 1187–1250*. London: Al Tajir-World of Islam Trust, 2009: 129–46.

Bonner, Michael. '"Time has come full circle": Markets, fairs and the calendar in

Arabia before Islam'. In A. Q. Ahmed, B. Sadeghi and M. Bonner (eds), *The Islamic Scholarly Tradition: Studies in History, Law, and Thought in Honor of Professor Michael Allan Cook*. Leiden and Boston: Brill, 2011: 15–48.

Borrut, Antoine and Paul M. Cobb. 'Introduction: Toward a history of Umayyad legacies'. In Antoine Borrut and Paul M. Cobb (eds), *Umayyad Legacies: Medieval Memories from Syria to Spain*. Leiden: Brill, 2010: 1–22.

Bowman, Glenn. 'Popular Palestinian practices around holy places and those who oppose them: An historical introduction'. *Religion Compass* 7 (2013): 69–78.

Böwering, G. 'Time'. In Jane Dammen McAuliffe (ed.), *Encyclopaedia of the Qur'ān* (Leiden: Brill, 2006), vol. 5; available at www.brillonline.com

Brett, Michael. *The Fatimid Empire*. Edinburgh: Edinburgh University Press, 2017.

Broadhurst, R. C. J. (trans.). *A History of the Ayyubid Sultans of Egypt, Translated from the Arabic of al-Maqrizi with Introduction and Notes*. Boston: Twayne Publishers, 1980.

Brown, Peter. *The Cult of the Saints: Its Rise and Function in Latin Christianity*. Chicago: University of Chicago Press, 1981.

Brunschvig, Robert. 'Le culte et le temps dans l'Islam classique'. *Revue de l'histoire des religions* 177/2 (1970): 183–93.

Burge, S. R. 'Angels, ritual and sacred space in Islam'. *Comparative Islamic Studies* 5 (2009): 221–45.

Burke, Peter. *History and Social Theory*. Ithaca, NY: Cornell University Press, 1992.

Burnaby, Sherrard Beaumont. *Elements of the Jewish and Muḥammadan Calendars*. London: G. Bell, 1901.

Burnett, Charles. 'Astrology'. In Kate Fleet, Gudrun Krämer, Denis Matringe, John Nawas and Everett Rowson (eds), *The Encyclopaedia of Islam*, 3rd edn, available at www.brillonline.com.

Al-Būṣīrī, Aḥmad b. Abī Bakr. *Itḥāf al-Khayra al-Māhira bi-Zawā'id al-Masānid al-'Ashara*, 9 vols, ed. Abū Tamām Y. Ibrāhīm. Riyad: Dār al-Waṭan li-l-Nashr, 1999.

Canard, M. 'Ibn Nubāta'. In P. Bearman, Th. Bianquis, C. E. Bosworth E. van Donzel and W. P. Heinrichs (eds), *The Encyclopaedia of Islam*, 2nd edn, available at www.brillonline.com.

Canard, M. 'al-'Azīz Bi'llāh'. In P. Bearman, Th. Bianquis, C. E. Bosworth E. van Donzel and W. P. Heinrichs (eds), *The Encyclopaedia of Islam*, 2nd edn (Leiden: Brill, 1965), vol. 1, p. 825; available at www.brillonline.com

Carlebach, Elisheva. *Palaces of Time: Jewish Calendar and Culture in Early Modern Europe*. Cambridge and London: Harvard University Press 2011.

Chittick, William C. (trans., intr. and ann.). *Psalms of Islam: Zayn al-ʿĀbidīn ʿAlī ibn al-Ḥusayn, al-Ṣaḥīfāt al-Kāmilat al-Sajjāddiyya*. London: Muhammadi Trust of Great Britian, 1988.

Christ, Georg. *Trading Conflicts: Venetian Merchants and Mamluk Officials in Medieval Alexandria*. Leiden: Brill, 2012.

Cobb, Paul M. 'Virtual sacrality: Making Muslim Syria sacred before the Crusades'. *Medieval Encounters* 8 (2002): 35–55.

Cohen, Erik. 'Pilgrimage centers, concentric and eccentric'. *Annals of Tourism Research* 19/1 (1992): 33–50.

Colby, Frederick S. 'The rhetoric of innovative tradition in the festival commemorating the night of Muḥammad's Ascension'. In Steven Engler and Gregory P. Grieve (eds), *Historicizing 'Tradition' in the Study of Religion.* Berlin: De Gruyter, 2005: 33–50.

Conder, Claude Reignier. *Tent Work in Palestine: A Record of Discovery and Adventure.* London: R. Bentley, 1887.

Connerton, Paul. *How Societies Remember.* Cambridge: Cambridge University Press, 1989.

Contadini, Anna. *Fatimid Art at the Victoria and Albert Museum.* London: V&A Publications, 1998.

Cook, Michael. *Commanding Right and Forbidding Wrong in Islamic Thought.* Cambridge: Cambridge University Press, 2000.

Cortese, Delia. *Arabic Ismaili Manuscripts: The Zāhid ʿAlī Collection in the Library of The Institute of Ismaili Studies.* London: I. B Tauris and The Institute of Ismaili Studies 2003.

Cortese, Delia. *Ismaili and Other Arabic Manuscripts: A Descriptive Catalogue of Manuscripts in the Library of the Institute of Ismaili Studies.* London: I. B. Tauris and The Institute of Ismaili Studies, 2000.

Cortese, Delia and Simonetta Calderini. *Women and the Fatimids in the World of Islam.* Edinburgh: Edinburgh University Press, 2006.

Crone, Patricia and Martin Hinds. *God's Caliph.* Cambridge: Cambridge University Press, 1986.

Crow, Karim Douglas. 'Imam Jaʿfar al-Sadiq and the elaboration of Shiʿism'. In Farhad Daftary, Amyn B. Sajoo and Jiwa Shainool (eds), *The Shiʿi World: Pathways in Tradition and Modernity.* London and New York: I. B. Tauris and The Institute of Ismaili Studies, 2015: 56–77.

Cubitt, Catherine. 'Sites and sanctity: Revisiting the cult of murdered and martyred Anglo-Saxon royal saints'. *Early Medieval Europe* 9 (2000):53–83.

Cureton, William (ed. and trans.). *History of the Martyrs in Palestine by Eusebius Bishop of Caesarea*. Paris: Gorgias Press LLC, 1961.

Dadoyan, Seta B. *The Fatimid Armenians: Cultural and Political Interaction in the Near East*. Leiden: Brill, 1997.

Daftary, Farhad. *Ismaili History and Intellectual Tradition*. New York: Routledge, 2018.

Daftary, Farhad. *The Ismāʿīlīs: Their History and Doctrines*. Cambridge: Cambridge University Press, 1992.

Daftary, Farhad. *A Short History of the Ismailis: Traditions of a Muslim Community*. Edinburgh: Edinburgh University Press 1998.

Dallal, A. 'Calendar'. In Jane Dammen McAuliffe (ed.), *Encyclopaedia of the Qurʾān*. Leiden: Brill, 2001: vol. 1, pp. 272–3; available at www.brillonline.com

Al-Darwīsh, Aḥmad b. ʿAbd al-Razzāq (ed.). *Fatāwā al-Lajna al-Dāʿima li-l-Buḥūth al-ʿIlmiyya wa-l-Iftaʾ bi-l-Mamlaka al-Suʿūdiyya*. Riyad: al-Idāra al-ʿĀmma 1416/1996, vol. 9.

Dauphin, Claudine, Mohamed Ben Jeddou and Jean-Marie Castex. 'To Mecca on pilgrimage on foot and camel-back: The Jordanian Darb al-Hajj'. *Bulletin for the Council for British Research in the Levant* 10/1 (2015): 23–36.

De Smet, Daniel. 'Les fête chiites en Égypte fatimide'. *Acta Orientalia Belgica* 10 (1995): 187–96.

De Smet, Daniel. 'La translation du *raʾs al-Ḥusayn* au Caire fatimide'. In Urbain Vermuelen and Daniel De Smet (eds), *Egypt and Syria in the Fatimid, Ayyubid and Mamluk Eras II*. Leuven: Peeters, 1998: 29–44.

Denny, Frederick M. 'Islamic ritual: Perspectives and theories'. In Richard C. Martin (ed.), *Approaches to Islam in Religuous Studies*. Tuscon: University of Arizona State, 1985: 63–77.

Dhahabī, Shams al-Dīn. *Siyar Aʿlām al-Nubalāʾ*, ed. Bashār ʿA. Maʿrūf and Muḥī al-Dīn H. Sirḥān. Beirut: Muʾassasat al-Risāla, 1985.

Dhahabī. *Taʾrīkh al-Islām wa-Wafayāt al-Mashāhīr wa-l-Aʿlām*, ed. ʿUmar ʿAbd al-Salām Tadmurī. Beirut: Dār al-Kitāb al-ʿArabī, 1993.

Dickinson, Eerik. 'Ibn al-Ṣalāḥ al-Shahrazūrī and the *Isnād*'. *Journal of the American Oriental Society* 122 (2002): 481–505.

Drory, Joseph. 'Balawi's impressions of Palestine'. In Urbain Vermeulen et als. (eds), *Egypt and Syria in the Fatimid, Ayyūbid and Mamlūk Eras* VII. Leuven: Peeters, 2013: 381–91.

Drory, Joseph. 'Some observations during a visit to Palestine by Ibn al-ʿArabī of Seville in 1092–1095'. *Crusades* 3 (2004): 101–24.

Duri, Abd al-Aziz. 'Jerusalem in the Early Muslim period, 7th to 11th centuries AD'. In K. J. Asali (ed.), *Jerusalem in History*. New York: Olive Branch Press, 2000: 105–29.

Durkheim, Emile. *The Elementary Forms of the Religious Life*, trans. J. W. Swain. New York: Free Press, 1965.

Eade, John and Sallnow, Michael J. 'Introduction'. In John Eade and Michael J. Sallnow (eds), *Contesting the Sacred: The Anthropology of Christian Pilgrimage*. London: Routledge, 1991: 1–29.

Ebstein, Michael. *Mysticism and Philosophy in al-Andalus*. Leiden: Brill, 2014.

Eddé, Anne-Marie. *Saladin*, trans. Jane Marie Todd. Cambridge, MA: Belknap Press of Harvard University Press, 2011.

Elad, Amikam. 'The coastal cities of Palestine during the Early Middle Ages'. *The Jerusalem Cathedra* 2 (1982): 146–67 [in Hebrew].

Elad, Amikam. 'The description of the travels of Ibn Battuta in Palestine: Is it Original?' *Journal of the Royal Asiatic Society* 2 (1987): 256–72.

Elad, Amikam. 'The historical value of *Faḍāʾil al-Quds* literature'. *Jerusalem Studies in Arabic and Islam* 14 (1991): 41–90.

Elbendary, Amina. *Crowds and Sultans: Urban Protest in Late Medieval Egypt and Syria*. Cairo: The American University in Cairo Press, 2015.

Eliade, Mircae. *Patterns in Comparative Religion*, trans. by Rosemary Sheed. New York: Sheed and Ward, 1958.

Eliade, Mircae. *The Sacred and the Profane: The Nature of Religion*, trans. W. R. Trask. New York: Harcourt, Brace and World 1959.

Elisséeff, Nikita. 'Ibn ʿAsākir'. In P. Bearman, Th. Bianquis, C. E. Bosworth E. van Donzel and W. P. Heinrichs (eds), *The Encyclopaedia of Islam*, 2nd edn. Leiden: Brill, 1979, vol. 3, available at www.brillonline.com

Ephrat, Daphna. 'The shaykh, the physical setting and the holy site: the diffusion of the Qadri path in late medieval Palestine'. *Journal of the Royal Asian Society*, Third Series, 19 (2009): 1–20.

Ephrat, Daphna. *Spiritual Wayfarers, Leaders in Piety: Sufis and the Dissemination of Islam in Medieval Palestine.* Cambridge, MA: Harvard University Press, 2008.

Ergin, Nina. 'The Fragrance of the Divine: Ottoman Incense Burners and Their Context'. *The Art Bulletin* 96 (2014): 70–97.

Ethington, Philip J. 'Placing the past: "Groundwork" for a spatial theory of history'. *Rethinking History* 11 (2007): 465–95.

Fahd, T. 'Ikẖtiyārāt'. In P. Bearman, Th. Bianquis, C. E. Bosworth, E. van Donzel and W. P. Heinrichs (eds), *The Encyclopaedia of Islam*, 2nd edn, available at www.brillonline.com.

Al-Fākihī. *Akhbār Makka*. Beirut: Dār Khiḍr, 1998.

Al-Fāriqī. *Taʾrīkh Ibn al-Azraq al-Fāriqī*, ed. ʿUmar ʿAbd al-Salām Tadmurī. Sidon: al-Maktaba al-ʿAṣriyya, 2017.

Feldman, Jackie. 'Introduction: Contested narratives of storied places – The Holy Lands'. In *Religion and Society: Advances in Research* 5 (2014): 106–27.

Fierro, Maribel. 'Caliphal legitimacy and expiation in al-Andalus'. In Muhammad Khalid Masud, Brinkley Messick and David Powers (eds), *Islamic Legal Interpretation: Muftis and their Fatwas*. Cambridge, MA: Harvard University Press, 1996: 55–62.

Fierro, Maribel. 'The treatises against innovation (*kutub al-bidaʿ*)'. *Der Islam* 69 (1992): 204–46.

Fierro, Maribel. 'Al-Turtushi and the Fatimids'. In Farhad Dafatry and Jiwa Shainool (eds), *The Fatimid Caliphate: Diversity of Traditions*. London: I. B. Tauris, 2017: 118–63.

Frankfurter, David. 'Introduction: Approaches to Coptic pilgrimage'. In David Frankfurter (ed.), *Pilgrimage and Holy Space in Late Antique Egypt*. Leiden: Brill, 1998: 3–50.

Frenkel, Miriam. 'Constructing the sacred: Holy shrines in Aleppo and its environs'. In Urbain Vermuelen and K. De Hulster (eds), *Egypt and Syria in the Fatimid, Ayyubid and Mamluk Eras* VI. Leuven: Peeters, 2010: 43–78.

Frenkel, Yehoshua. 'Islamic education institutions in Mamlūk Jerusalem (1250–1516)'. In Rivka Feldhay and Immanuel Etkes (eds), *Education and History: Cultural and Political Contexts*. Jerusalem: The Zalman Shazar Center, 1999: 113–46 [in Hebrew].

Frenkel, Yehoshua. 'Muslim pilgrimage to Jerusalem in the Mamluk period'. In B. F. Le Beau and M. Mor (eds), *Pilgrims and Travelers to the Holy Land*. Omaha, NE: Creighton University, 1996: 63–88.

Frenkel, Yehoshua. 'Popular culture (Islam, early and middle periods)'. *Religion Compass* 2 (2008): 1–31.

Frenkel, Yehoshua. 'Public projection of power in Mamluk Bilād al-Shām'. *Mamlūk Studies Review* 11/1 (2007): 39–53.

Friedman, Yaron. '"Kūfa is better": The sanctity of Kūfa in early Islam and Shiʿism in particular'. *Le Muséon* 126 (2013): 203–37.

Friedman, Yaron. *The Shīʿīs in Palestine. From the Medieval Golden Age until the Present*. Leiden: Brill, 2019.

Fuchs, H., de Jong, F. and J. Knappert. 'Mawlid (a.), or Mawlūd'. In P. Bearman, Th. Bianquis, C. E. Bosworth E. van Donzel and W. P. Heinrichs (eds), *The Encyclopaedia of Islam, 2nd edn*, available at www.brillonline.com.

Ganneau, Clermont. 'The Arabs in Palestine', in *SWP Special Papers*. London: Committee of the Palestine Exploration Fund, 1881: 315–30.

Gardet, L. 'Muslim views of time and history, an essay in cultural typology'. In *Cultures and Time*. Paris: Unesco Press, 1976: 197–227.

Al-Ghazzālī, Abū Ḥāmid. *Al-Ghazālī's Invocations and Supplications, Kitab al-Adhkār wa'l-da'awāt, Book IX of The Revival of the Religious Sciences Iḥyā' 'Ulūm al-Dīn*, trans. and ed. K. Nakamura. London: Islamic Texts Society, 1999.

Al-Ghazzālī, Abū Ḥāmid. *Iḥya' 'Ulūm al-Dīn*, 6 vols, ed. 'Abd al-Raḥīm b. al-Ḥusayn al-'Irāqī et al. Beirut: Dār al-Khayr, 1414/1994.

Al-Ghazzālī, Abū Ḥāmid. *Worship in Islam: Al-Ghazzālī's Book of the Iḥyā' on the Worship*, trans. Edwin Elliot Calverley. London: Luzac & Co. and School of Oriental Studies, American University at Cairo, 1925.

Gil, Moshe. *A History of Palestine, 634–1009*, trans. Ethel Broido. Cambridge: Cambridge University Press, 1992.

Giladi, Avner. 'History and emotions'. *History* 23 (2009): 23–41 [in Hebrew].

Gleave, Robert. 'Prayer and prostration: Imāmī Shi'i discussions of *al-sujūd 'alā al-turba al-Ḥusayniyya*'. In Pedram Khosronejad (ed.), *The Art and Material Culture of Iranian Sh'ism*. London: I. B. Tauris and Iran Heritage Foundation, 2012: 233–53.

Goitein, S. D. and O. Grabar. 'al-Ḳuds'. In P. Bearman, Th. Bianquis, C. E. Bosworth E. van Donzel and W. P. Heinrichs (eds), *The Encyclopaedia of Islam*, 2nd edn.

Goitein, Shelomo Dov. 'Ramadan and the Muslim month of fasting,' in S. D. Goitein (ed.), *Islamic Religious and Political Institutions*. Leiden: Brill, 1966: 90–110.

Goitein, Shelomo Dov. 'The sanctity of Jerusalem and Palestine in Early Islam'. In ibid. 135–48.

Goldziher, Ignàc. *Muslim Studies*, trans. S. M. Stern and C. R. Barber. London: G. Allen & Unwin, 1967, 2 vols.

Golmohammadi, J. 'Minbar (B.)'. In P. Bearman, Th. Bianquis, C. E. Bosworth E. van Donzel and W. P. Heinrichs (eds), *The Encyclopaedia of Islam*, 2nd edn. Leiden: Brill, 1993: vol. 7, p. 77; available at www.brillonline.com

Goodman, Lenn E. 'Time in Islam'. In Anindita Nyogi Balslev and Jitendra Nanh Mohanty (eds), *Religion and Time*. Leiden: Brill, 1993: 162–83.

Grehan, James. *Twilight of the Saints*. Oxford: Oxford University Press, 2014.

Grimes, Ronald L. *Beginnings in Ritual Studies*. N.p.: University Press of America, 1982.

Grimes, Ronald L. *The Craft of Ritual Studies*. Oxford: Oxford University Press, 2014.

Haider, Najam, *The Origins of the Shiʿa: Identity, Ritual, and Sacred Space in Eighth-Century Kufa*. Cambridge: Cambridge University Press, 2011.

Halm, Heinz. 'The Ismaʿili oath of allegiance (*ʿahd*) and the 'Sessions of Wisdom' (*majalis al-hikma*) in Fatimid times'. In Farhad Daftary (ed.), *Medieval Ismaʿili History and Thought*. Cambridge: Cambridge University Press, 1996: 91–115.

Halm, Heinz. *The Fatimids and their Traditions of Learning*. London: I. B. Tauris and The Institute of Ismaili Studies, 1997.

Al-Hamadhānī, ʿAbd al-Jabbār. *Tathbīt Dalāʾil al-Nubuwwa*, ed. ʿAbd al-Karīm ʿUthmān. Beirut: Dār al-ʿArabiyya, 1382/1966.

Hamdani, Sumaiya Abbas. *Between Revolution and State: The Path to Fatimid Statehood: Qadi al-Nuʿman and the Construction of Fatimid Legitimacy*. London: I. B. Tauris and The Institute of Ismaili Studies, 2006.

Hamdani, Sumaiya Abbas. 'Ismaʿili studies on Fatimid Egypt: Review article'. *Journal of the Economic and Social History of the Orient* 56 (2013): 514–22.

Al-Ḥārithī, Huwayda (ed.). *Kitāb Waqf al-Sulṭān al-Nāṣir Ḥasan bin Muḥammad bin Qalāwūn ʿalā Madrasatihi bi-l-Rumayla*. Beirut: In commission at United Distributing Co., 2001.

Al-Ḥasakānī. *Faḍāʾil Shahr Rajab*, ed. Muḥammad al-Maḥmūdī. Tehran: Muʾassasat al-Ṭabʿ wa-l-Nashr, 1990.

Heddrick, T. L. and Nina Ergin. 'A Shared Culture of Heavenly Fragrance: A Comparison of Late Byzantine and Ottoman Incense Burners and Censing Practices in Religious Contexts'. *Dumbarton Oaks Papers* 69 (2015): 331–54.

Heschel, Abraham Joshua. *The Sabbath: Its Meaning for Modern Man*. New York: Farrar, Straus and Young, 1951.

Al-Hibri, Tayeb. 'The Abbasids and the relics of the Prophet'. *Journal of Abbasid Studies* 4 (2017): 62–96.

Hillenbrand, Carole. *The Crusades: Islamic Perspectives*. Edinburgh: Edinburgh University Press, 1999.

Hillenbrand, Carole. 'Some aspects of al-Ghazali's views on beauty'. In A. Giese and J. C. Bürgel (eds), *Gott is Schön: Festschrift Professor Annemarie Schimmel*. Bern: Peter Lang Verlag, 1994: 249–65.

Hillenbrand, Robert. 'The uses of light in Islamic architecture'. In Jonathan Bloom and Sheila Blair (eds), *God is the Light of the Heavens and the Earth*. New Haven: Yale University Press, 2015: 86–121.

Hirschler, Konrad. *Medieval Damascus: Plurality and Diversity in an Arabic Library*. Edinburgh: Edinburgh University Press, 2016.

Hirschler, Konrad. *A Monument to Medieval Syrian Book Culture: The Library of Ibn ʿAbd al-Hādī*. Edinburgh: Edinburgh University Press, 2020.

Hiyari, Mustafa A. 'Crusader Jerusalem, 1099–1187 AD'. In Kamil Jamil Asali (ed.) *Jerusalem in History*. New York: Olive Branch Press, 2000: 130–76.

Hobsbawm, Eric and Terence Ranger (eds). *The Invention of Tradition*. Cambridge and New York: Cambridge University Press, 1983.

Hoch, Martin. 'The Crusaders' strategy against Fatimid Ascalon and the "Ascalon Project" of the Second Crusade'. In Michael Gervers (ed.), *The Second Crusade and the Cistercians*. New York: St. Martin's Press, 1992: 119–28.

Hofer, Nathan. *The Popularization of Sufism in Ayyubid and Mamluk Egypt, 1173–1325*. Edinburgh: Edinburgh University Press, 2015.

Hollenberg, David. *Beyond the Qurʾān: Early Ismāʿīlī Taʾwīl and the Secrets of the Prophets*. Columbia, SC: University of South Carolina Press, 2016.

Humphreys, R. Stephen. 'The emergence of the Mamluk army'. *Studia Islamica* 45 (1977): 67–99.

Humphreys, R. Stephen. *From Saladin to the Mongols: The Ayyūbids of Damascus, 1193–1260*. Albany: State University of New York Press, 1977.

Hunsberger, Alice C. *Nasir Khusraw the Ruby of Badakhshan: A Portrait of the Persian Poet, Traveller and Phillosopher*. London: I. B. Tauris and The Institute of Ismaili Studies, 2000.

Hunsberger, Alice C. (ed.). *Pearls of Persia: The Philosophical Poetry of Nasir-i Khusraw*. London and New York: I. B. Tauris and The Institute of Ismaili Studies, 2013.

Ḥusayn, M. K. (ed.). *Al-Majālis al-Mustanṣiriyya li-l-Dāʿī ʿAlim al-Islām Thiqat al-Imām*. Cairo: Dār al-Fikr al-ʿArabī, n. d.

Huster, Yaakov. *Ashkelon 5: The Land behind Ashkelon*. Winona Lake, IN: Eisenbrauns, 2015.

Ibn ʿAbd al-Ẓāhir. *Al-Rawḍa al-Bahiyya fī Khiṭaṭ al-Muʿiziyya*, ed. A. F. al-Sayyid. Cairo: Maktabat al-Dār al-ʿArabiyya li-l-Kitāb, 1996.

Ibn ʿArabī. *The Seven Days of the Heart: Prayers for the Nights and Days of the Week*, trans. Pablo Beneito and Stephen Hirtenstein. Oxford: Anqa, 2000.

Ibn al-Athīr, Ḍiyāʾ al-Dīn. *Al-Mathal al-Sāʾir fī Adab al-Kātib wa-l-Shāʿir*, ed.

Muḥammad Muḥī al-Dīn ʿAbd al-Ḥamīd. Egypt: Muṣṭafa al-Bābī al-Ḥalabī, 1358/1939.

Ibn al-Athīr. ʿIzz al-Dīn. *Al-Kāmil fī al-Taʾrīkh*, ed. Muḥammad Y. Daqqāq. Beirut: Dār al-Kutub al-ʿIlmiyya, 1987.

Ibn ʿAsākir. *Taʾrīkh Madīnat Dimashq*, ed. Muḥibb al-Dīn A. ʿUmar b. Gharāma al-ʿUmari. Beirut: Dār al-Fikr li-l-Ṭabāʿa wa-l-Nashr wa-l-Tawzīʿ, 1998, vol. 69.

Ibn al-ʿAṭṭār. *Tuḥfat al-Ṭālibīn fī Tarjamat al-Imām Muḥyi al-Dīn*, ed. M. H. Salmān. Riyad: Dār al-Samiʿi, 1414.

Ibn Bābawayh. *Faḍāʾil al-Ashhur al-Thalātha*, ed. Ghulām Riḍāʾ ʿArfāniyān. Beirut: Dār al-Maḥajja al-Bayḍāʾ, 1412/1992.

Ibn Baṭūṭṭa. *Riḥlat Ibn Baṭūṭṭa: al-Mussamā Tuḥfat al-Nuẓẓār fī Gharāʾib al-Amṣār*, ed. Ṭallāl Ḥarb. Beirut: Dār al-Kutub al-ʿIlmiyya, 1413/1992.

Ibn Baṭūṭṭa. *The Travels of Ibn Battuta*, trans. and ed. H. A. R. Gibb et al. Cambridge: Hakluyt Society, 1958, vol. 1.

Ibn Diḥya. *Adāʾ mā wajab fī Bayān waḍʿ al-Waḍḍāʿīn fī Rajab*, ed. Muḥammad al-Albānī and Zuhayr al-Shāwīsh. Beirut, Damascus and Amman: al-Maktab al-Islāmī, 1419/1998.

Ibn Fahd, ʿUmar. *Itḥāf al-Warā bi Akhbār Umm al-Qurā*, ed. Fahīm Muḥammad Shaltūt. Mecca: Jāmiʿat Umm al-Qurā, 1983.

Ibn al-Faqīh. *Kitāb al-Buldān*, ed. Yūsuf al-Hādī. Beirut: ʿAlim al-Kutub, 1997.

Ibn Ḥabbān. *Mashāhir ʿUlamāʾ al-ʾAmṣār wa-Aʿlām Fuqahāʾ al-Aqṭār*, ed. Marzūk ʿAlī Ibrāhīm. Beirut: Muʾassasat al-Kutub al-Thaqāfiyya, 1408/1987.

Ibn Ḥajar. *Tabyīn al-ʿAjab bi-mā warada fī Faḍl Rajab*, ed. Ṭāriq b. ʿA. al-Darʿī. Cairo: Muʾassasat Qurṭuba, n.d.

Ibn Ḥanbal. *Musnad Aḥmad b. Ḥanbal*, ed. Aḥmad Muḥammad Shākir. Cairo: 1958.

Ibn Ḥawqal. *Kitāb Ṣūrat al-Arḍ*. Cairo: Sharikat Nawābigh al-Fikr, 1340/2009.

Ibn Ḥayyan. *Akhbār al-Quḍāt*, ed. ʿAbd al-ʿAzīz al-Murāghī. Cairo: al-Maktaba al-Tijāriyya al-Kubra, 1947, vol. 2.

Ibn al-ʿImrānī. *Al-Inbāʾ fī Taʾrīkh al-Khulafāʾ*, ed. Qasim al-Samarrai. Leiden: Brill 1973.

Ibn Iyās. *Badāʾiʿ al-Zuhūr*, ed. M. Mustafa. Wiesbaden: Harrassowitz, 1975.

Ibn al-Jawzī, Abū al-Faraj. *Kitāb al-Muntaẓam*, ed. M. ʿAṭā. Beirut: Dār al-Kutub al-ʿIlmiyya, 1992, vol. 15.

Ibn al-Jawzī, Abū al-Faraj. *Al-Nūr fī Faḍāʾil al-Ayyām wa-l-Shuhūr*, ed. ʿAbd al-Ḥakīm al-Anīs. N.P. Idārat al-Buḥūth, 2018.

Ibn al-Jawzī, Sibṭ. *Kitāb al-Mawḍūʿāt*, ed. Tawfīq Ḥamdān. Beirut: Dār Al-Kutub al-ʿIlmiyya, 1415/1995.

Ibn al-Jawzī, Sibṭ. *Mirʾāt al-Zamān fī Tawārīkh al-Aʿyān*, ed. M. Ḍ. ʿIrqasusī. Damascus: al-Risāla al-ʿIlmiyya, 2013.

Ibn al-Jazzarī. *Taʾrīkh Ḥawādith al-Zamān*, ed. ʿUmar ʿAbd al-Salām Tadmurī. Beirut: al-Maktaba al-ʿAṣriyya, 1419/1998, vol. 3.

Ibn Jubayr. *Riḥla*, ed. William Wright. Leyden: Brill, 1907.

Ibn Jubayr. *The Travels of Ibn Jubayr*, trans. R. J. C Broadhurst. London: J. Cape 1952.

Ibn Kathīr. *Al-Bidāya wa-l-Nihāya*. Beirut: Dār Iḥyaʾ al-Turāth al-ʿArabī, 1993.

Ibn Khallikān, Shams al-Dīn. *Wafayāt al-Aʿyān wa-Anbāʾ Abnāʾ al-Zamān*, ed. Iḥsān ʿAbbās. Beirut: Dār al-Thaqāfa, 1968–72, 8 vols.

Ibn Manẓūr, Muḥammad b. Mukarram. *Lisān al-ʿArab*, ed. ʿAbd Allāh al-Kabīr. Cairo: Dār al-Maʿārif, 1987, 6 vols.

Ibn Manẓūr, Muḥammad b. Mukarram. *Mukhtaṣar Taʾrīkh Dimashq li-Ibn ʿAsākir*, ed. Rawḥiyya al-Naḥḥās. Damascus: Dār al-Fikr, 1984.

Ibn al-Mujāwir. *Ṣifat Bilād al-Yaman wa-Makka wa-Baʿḍ al-Ḥijāz al-Musammā Taʾrīkh al-Mustabṣir*, ed. O. Löfgren. Leiden: Brill, 1951.

Ibn al-Mujawir. *A Traveller in Thirteenth-Century Arabia: Ibn al-Mujawir's Taʾrīkh al-Mustabṣir*, trans. G. R. Smith. Aldershot: Ashgate, 2008.

Ibn al-Murajjā. *Kitāb Faḍāʾil Bayt al-Maqdis wa-l-Khalīl wa Faḍāʾil al-Shām*, ed. Ofer Livne-Kafri. Shefarʿam: Dār al-Mahriq, 1995.

Ibn al-Muyassar. *Akhbār Miṣr*, ed. H. Masse. Cairo: Maṭbaʿat al-Maʿhad al-ʿIlmī al-Faransī, 1919.

Ibn Nubāta, ʿAbd al-Raḥīm b. Muḥammad. *Diwān Khuṭab Minbariyya*. Beirut: Dār al-Najm 1994.

Ibn Qawlawayh. *Kāmil al-Ziyārāt*. Beirut: Nashr al-Faqāha, 1997.

Ibn Qayyim al-Jawziyya. *Al-Ḍawʾ al-Munīr ʿalā al-Tafsīr*, ed. ʿAlī Ḥammād al-Ṣāliḥī. Dukhna and Riyad: Muʾassasat al-Nūr and Dār al-Salāṃ, n. d.

Ibn Qayyim al-Jawziyya. *Zād al-Maʿād fī Hudā Khayr al-ʿUbbād*, ed. Shuʿayb al-Arnāʾūṭ and ʿAbd al-Qādir al-Arnāʾūt. Beirut: Muʾassasat al-Risāla, 1998.

Ibn Qudāma. *Al-Mughnī*, ed. ʿAbdallāh al-Turkī and ʿAbd al-Fattāḥ al-Ḥulw. Cairo: Hajr li-l-Ṭabāʿa wa-l-Nashr, 1987.

Ibn Rajab. *Al-Dhayl ʿAlā Ṭabaqāt al-Ḥanābila*, ed. Muḥammad al-Fiqī. Cairo: Maṭbaʿat al-Sunna al-Muḥammadiyya, 1952.

Ibn Rajab. *Jāmiʿ al-ʿUlūm wa-l-Ḥikam*, ed. Abū al-Nūr. Cairo: Dār al-Salām, 2004.

Ibn Rajab. *Laṭā'if fī mā bi-l-Mawāsim min al-Waẓā'if*, ed. Y. M. al-Sawas. Damascus: Dār Ibn Kathīr, 1992.

Ibn Sa'd. *Kitāb al-Ṭabaqāt al-Kabīr*, ed. 'Alī Muḥammad 'Umar. Cairo: Maktabat al-Khanjī, 2001.

Ibn Sa'īd al-Maghribī. *Kitāb al-Mughrib fī hulā al-Maghrib*, ed. K. L. Tallqvist. Leiden: Brill, 1899.

Ibn Shaddād, Bahā' al-Dīn. *The Rare and the Excellent History of Saladin or al-Nawādir al-Sulṭāniyya wa'l-Maḥāsin al-Yusūfiyya by Bahā' al-Dīn Ibn Shaddād*, trans. D. S. Richards. Aldershot: Routledge, 2002.

Ibn Shāhīn. *Zubdat Kashf al-Mamālik wa-Bayān al-Ṭuruq wa-l-Masālik*, ed. 'Umar 'Abd al-Salām Tadmurī. Sidon and Beirut: al-Maktaba al-'Aṣriyya, 2011.

Ibn Taghrī Birdī. *Al-Nujūm al-Zāhirah fī Mulūk Miṣr wa-l-Qāhira*, ed. Fahīm Muḥammad Shaltūt et al. Cairo: Dār al-Kutub al-Miṣriyya, 1963, vol. 4.

Ibn Ṭawq. *Al-Ta'līq: Yawmiyyāt Shihāb al-Dīn Aḥmad b. Ṭawq 834–915* AH*/1480–1502 AD*, ed. Ja'far al-Muhājir. Damascus: al-Ma'had al-Faransī li-l Dirāsāt al-'Arabiyya bi-Dimashq, 2000.

Ibn Tāwūs. *Al-Iqbāl bi-l-A'māl al-Ḥasana*, ed. Jawād al-Qayyūmī al-Isfahānī, Qumm: Maktab al-A'lam al-Islāmī, 1993–5, 3 vols.

Ibn Ṭāwūs. *Al-Malhūf 'alā Qatlā al-Ṭufūf*, ed. Faris Tabrizyan. Tehran: Dār al-Uswa li-l-Ṭibā'a wa-l-Nashr, 1993.

Ibn Tāwūs. *Muhaj al-Da'awāt wa-Manhaj al-'Ibādāt*. Beirut: Al-Mu'assasa al-Islāmiyya Li-l-Nashr, 1987.

Ibn Taymiyya. *Daqā'iq al-Tafsīr: al-Jāmi' li-Tafsīr Ibn Taymiyya*, ed. Muḥammad al-Sayyid al-Julaynid. Jadda and Beirut: Dār al-Qibla li-l-Thaqāfa al-Islāmiyya, 1406/1986, vol. 3.

Ibn Taymiyya. *Al-Fatāwā al-Kubrā*, ed. Muḥammad 'Abd al-Qādir 'Aṭā' et al. Beirut: Dār al-Kutub al-'Ilmiyya, 1408/1987, vol. 2.

Ibn Taymiyya. *Al-Fatwā al-Ḥamawiyya al-Kubrā*, ed. Ḥamad al-Tawījrī. Riyad: Dār al-Tawījrī, 1419/1998.

Ibn Taymiyya. *Iqtiḍā' al-Ṣirāṭ al-Mustaqīm li-Mukhālafat Aṣḥāb al-Jaḥīm*, ed. Nāṣir b. A. al-'Aql. Riyad: Maktabat al-Rushd, n. d., vol. 2.

Ibn Taymiyya. *Majmū'at al-Fatāwā*, 3rd edn, ed. 'A al-Jazzār and A. al-Bāz. Mansura/ Riyad: Dār al-Wafā', 2005, 35 vols.

Ibn Taymiyya. *Al-Qā'ida fī Ziyārat Bayt al-Maqdis*. In C. D. Matthews, 'A Muslim iconoclast on the "merits" of Jerusalem and Palestine'. *Journal of the American Oriental Society* 56 (1936): 1–21.

Ibn Taymiyya. *Tafsīr Shaykh al-Islām Ibn Taymiyya*, ed. Iyād b. al-Qaysī. Dammām: Dār Ibn al-Jawzī, 1432/2011, vol. 3.

Ibn Ṭuwayr. *Nuzhat al-Muqlatayn fī Akhbār al-Dawlatayn al-Fāṭimiyya wa-l-Ṣallāhiyya*, ed. Ayman Fu'ād Sayyid. Beirut: Dār al-Nashr, 1412/1992.

Ibn ʿUthmān. *Murshid al-Zuwwār ilā Qubūr al-Abrār*, ed. Muḥammad Fatḥī Abū Bakr. Cairo: al-Dār al-Miṣriyya al-Lubnāniyya, 1995.

Ibn Ẓafar al-Siqillī. *Kitāb Anbā' Nujaba' al-Abnā'*, ed. Lajnat Ihyā' al-Turāth al-ʿArabī. Beirut: Dār al-Āfāq al-Jadīda, 1980.

Ibn al-Zayyāt, Muḥammad. *Al-Kawākib al-Sayyāra fī Tartīb al-Ziyāra fī al-Qarāfatayn al-Kubrā wa-l-Ṣughrā*, unknown editor. Cairo: Al-Maṭbaʿa al-Amīriyya, 1325/1907.

Al-Ibrashy, May. 'Cairo's Qarafa as described in the *ziyara* literature'. In Richard McGregor et al. (eds), *The Development of Sufism in Mamluk Egypt*. Cairo: Institut français d'archéologie orientale, 2006: 269–97.

Al-Ibrashy, May. 'Death, life and the barzakh in Cairo's cemeteries: The place of the cemetery in the sacred geography of late medieval Cairo'. October 2004, https://international.ucla.edu/institute/article/15501 (last accessed 5 June 2019).

Idrīs ʿImād al-Dīn. *Risālat al-Bayān li-mā wajaba min Maʿrifat al-Ṣalāt* (or *Risālat al-Bayān li-mā Wajaba fī Maʿnā Niṣf Shahr Rajab*) MS 39/909 50 ff.; MS 1190, 69 ff.; Institute of Ismaili Studies, Special Collections.

Idrīs ʿImād al-Dīn. *ʿUyūn al-Akhbār; Ta'rīkh al-Khulafā' al-Fāṭimiyīn bi-l-Maghrib: al-Qism al-Khāṣṣ min Kitāb ʿUyūn al-ʿAkhbār*, vol. 4, ed. Muṣṭafā Ghālib; vol. 5, ed. Muḥammad al-Yaʿlāwī. Beirut: Dār al-Gharb al-Islāmī, 1973, 1985.

Imad, Leila S. *The Fatimid Vizierate, 969–1172*. Berlin: K. Schwarz, 1990.

Ioh, Hideyuki. 'The calendar in pre-Islamic Mecca'. *Arabica* 61 (2014): 471–513.

Irwin, Robert. 'Mamluk history and historians'. In Roger Allen and D. S. Richards (eds), *Arabic Literature in the Post-Classical Period*. Cambridge: Cambridge University Press, 2006: 159–70.

Al-Iṣfahānī. *Kitāb al-Aghānī*, ed. Iḥsān ʿAbbās, Ibrāhīm al-Saʿāfīn and Bakr ʿAbbās. Beirut: Dār Ṣādir, 2008, vol. 17.

Al-Jabartī, ʿAbd al-Raḥmān. *ʿAjā'ib al-Athār fī al-Tarājim wa-l-Akhbār (The Marvelous Chronicles: Biographies and Events)*, ed. Shmuel Moreh. 5 vols. Jerusalem: The Max Schloessinger Memorial Foundation, 2013.

Al-Jamil, Tariq. 'Ibn Taymiyya and Ibn al-Mutahhar al-Hilli: Shiʿi polemics and the struggle for religious authority in medieval Islam'. In Yossef Rapoport and Shahab Ahmed (eds), *Ibn Taymiyya and his Times*. Karachi: Oxford University Press, 2010: 229–46.

Al-Jīlānī, ʿAbd al-Qādir. *Al-Ghunya li-Ṭālibī Ṭarīq al-Ḥaqq*, ed. Faraj Tawfīq al-Walīd. Baghdad: Maktabat al-Sharq al-Jadīd, 1988, 3 vols.

Jiwa, Shainool. *Towards a Shiʿi Mediterranean Empire: Fatimid Egypt and the Founding of Cairo*. London: I. B. Tauris and The Institute of Ismaili Studies, 2009.

Jomier, Jacques. *Le mahmal et la caravane égyptienne des pèlerins de la Mecque, XIIIe–XXe siècles*. Cairo: Institut français d'archéologie orientale, 1953.

Jones, Linda G. *The Power of Oratory in the Medieval Muslim World*. Cambridge and New York: Cambridge University Press, 2012.

Jwaideh, Wadie. *The Introductory Chapters of Yāqūt's Muʿjam al-Buldān*. Leiden: Brill, 1959.

Al-Jundī, Abū ʿAbd Allāh. *Al-Sulūk fī Ṭabaqāt al-ʿUlamāʾ wa-l-Mulūk*, ed. Muḥammad M. al-Ḥiwānī. Sanʿa: Maktabat al-Irshād, 1414/1993, vol. 1.

Kahle, Paul and Hans Spoer. *Palestinian Life, Customs and Practices: German Articles from the Late 19th and Early 20th Centuries*, ed. and trans. Robert Schick. Amman: Dāʾirat al-Maktaba al-Waṭaniyya, 2010.

Kaplony, Andreas. *The Ḥaram of Jerusalem, 324–1099: Temple, Friday Mosque, Area of Spiritual Power*. Stuttgart: F. Steiner, 2002.

Kaptein, N. J. G. *Muḥammad's Birthday Festival: Early History in the Central Muslim Lands and Development in the Muslim West until the 10th/16th Century*. Leiden: Brill, 1993.

Kassam, Zayn and Bridget Blomfield. 'Remembering Fatima and Zaynab: Gender in Perspective'. In Farhad Daftary, Amyn B. Sajoo and Jiwa Shainool (eds), *The Shiʿi World: Pathways in Tradition and Modernity*. London and New York: I. B. Tauris and The Institute of Ismaili Studies, 2015: 210–27.

Katz, Marion Holmes. *The Birth of the Prophet Muḥammad: Devotional Piety in Sunni Islam*. London and New York: Routledge, 2007.

Katz, Marion Holmes. 'The hajj and the study of Islamic ritual'. *Studia Islamica* 98/99 (2004): 95–129.

Katz, Marion Holmes. *Prayer in Islamic Thought and Practice*. New York: Cambridge University Press, 2013.

Katz, Marion Holmes. *Women in the Mosque: A History of Legal Thought and Social Practice*. New York: Columbia University Press, 2014.

Kedar, Benjamin Z. 'Holy Men in a Holy Land. Christian, Muslim and Jewish Religiosity in the Middle East in the Time of the Crusades', *Hayes Robinson Lecture Series* no. 9, London 2005.

Kenneth, Cragg. 'Constance E. Padwick, 1886–1968'. *Muslim World* 59 (1969): 29–39.

Khalek, Nancy. *Damascus after the Muslim Conquest*. Oxford: Oxford University Press, 2012.

Khalidi, Rashid. *Palestinian Identity: The Construction of Modern National Consciousness*. New York: Columbia University Press, 1997.

Al-Khallāl, Muḥammad b. al-Ḥasan. *Faḍāʾil Shahr Rajab*, ed. ʿAbd al-Raḥmān Muḥammad. Beirut: Dār Ibn Ḥazm, 1996.

Khusraw, Nasir-i. *Naser-e Khosraw's Book of travels (Safarnama)*, trans., intr. and ann. by W. M. Thackston. Costa Mesa, CA: Mazda Publishers, 2001.

Kimber, Richard. 'Qibla'. In Jane Dammen McAuliffe (ed.), *Encyclopaedia of the Qurʾān*, available at www.brillonline.com.

Kister, M. J. 'Radjab'. In P. Bearman, Th. Bianquis, C. E. Bosworth E. van Donzel and W. P. Heinrichs (eds), *The Encyclopaedia of Islam*, 2nd edn. Leiden: Brill, 1995: vol. 8, pp. 373–5; available at www.brillonline.com

Kister, M. J. '"Rajab is the month of God . . . ": A study in the persistence of an early tradition'. *Israel Oriental Studies* 1 (1970): 191–223; repr. In M. J. Kister (ed.), *Studies in Jāhiliyya and Early Islam*. London: Variorum Reprints, 1980, no. XII.

Kister, M. J. 'Sanctity joint: On holy places in the Islamic tradition'. *Jerusalem Studies in Arabic and Islam* 20 (1996): 18–65.

Kister, M. J. 'Shaʿbān is my month . . . : A study of an Early Tradition'. In *Studia Orientalia: Memoriae D. H. Baneth Dedicate*. Jerusalem: Institute of Asian and African Studies at the Hebrew University and Max Schloessinger Memorial Foundation, 1979: 15–34.

Klemm, Verena. *Memoirs of a Mission: The Ismaili Scholar, Statesman and Poet, al-Muʾayyad fiʾl-Din al-Shirazi*. London: I. B. Tauris and The Institute of Ismaili Studies, 2003.

Knott, Kim. 'Religion, space, and place: The spatial turn in research on religion'. *Religion and Society: Advances in Research* 1 (2010): 29–43.

Knysh, Alexander. 'Months'. In Jane Dammen McAuliffe (ed.), *Encyclopaedia of the Qurʾān*, available at www.brillonline.com.

Kohlberg, Etan. *A Medieval Muslim Scholar at Work: Ibn Ṭawūs and his Library*. Leiden: Brill, 1992.

Kugle, Scott. *Sufis and Saints' Bodies: Mysticism, Corporeality and Sacred Power in Islam*. Chapel Hill: University of North Carolina Press, 2007.

Larson, Frances. *Severed: A History of Heads Lost and Found*. London: Granta, 2014.

Lazarus-Yafeh, Hava. *Interwined Worlds: Medieval Islam and Bible Criticism*. Princeton: Princeton University Press, 1992.

Lazarus-Yafeh, Hava. 'Mecca and Jerusalem'. *Judaism: A Journal of Jewish Life and Thought* 46 (1997): 197–205.

Lazarus-Yafeh, Hava. *Some Religious Aspects of Islam: A Collection of Articles*. Leiden: Brill, 198.

Lecker, M. 'Judaism among Kinda and the *Ridda* of Kinda'. *Journal of the American Oriental Society* 115 (1995): 635–50.

Leisten, Th. 'Dynastic tomb or private mausolea: Observations on the concept of funerary structures of the Fatimid and Abbasid caliphs'. In Marianne Barrucand (ed.), *L'Égypte fatimide, son art et son histoire*. Paris: Presses de l'Université de Paris-Sorbonne, 1999: 465–79.

Lev, Yaacov. 'Charity and social practice: Egypt and Syria in the ninth-twelfth centuries'. *Jerusalem Studies in Arabic and Islam* 24 (2000): 472–507.

Lev, Yaacov. *Charity, Endowments, and Charitable Institutions in Medieval Islam*. Gainseville: University Press of Florida, 2005.

Lev, Yaacov. *Saladin in Egypt*. Leiden: Brill, 1999.

Lev, Yaacov. *State and Society in Fatimid Egypt*. Leiden: Brill, 1991.

Levanoni, A. ''Askalān'. In Kate Fleet, Gudrun Krämer, Denis Matringe, John Nawas and Everett Rowson (eds), *The Encyclopaedia of Islam*, 3rd edn, available at www.brillonline.com.

Lewicka, Paulina. *Food and Foodways of Medieval Cairenes: Aspects of Life in an Islamic Metropolis of the Eastern Mediterranean*. Leiden: Brill, 2011.

Limor, Ora. *Holy Land Travels: Christian Pilgrims in Late Antiquity*. Jerusalem: Yad Yitzhak Ben Zvi, 1998 [in Hebrew].

Limor, Ora, Elchanan Reiner and Miriam Frenkel (eds). *Pilgrimage*. Raanana: The Open University Press, 2005 [in Hebrew].

Lindsay, James E. 'Caliphal and moral exemplar? Ibn 'Asākir's portrait of Yazīd b. Mu'āwiya'. *Der Islam* 74 (1997): 250–78.

Livne-Kafri, Ofer. 'Jerusalem and the sanctity of the frontier cities in Islam'. *Kathedra* 94 (1999): 77–8 [in Hebrew].

Livne-Kafri, Ofer. 'The Muslim traditions "in praise of Jerusalem" (*Faḍā'il al-Quds*): Diversity and continuity'. *Annali* 58/1–2 (1998): 165–92.

Lucas, Scott C. *Constructive Critics: Ḥadīth Literature and the Articulation of Sunni Islam*. Leiden: Brill, 2004.

M. G. 'Review'. *The Journal of the Royal Asiatic Society* of *Great Britain and Ireland* (1902): 183–84.

Mahfouz, Naguib. *Palace Walk*, trans. William M. Hatchins and Olive E. Kenny. Cairo: American University in Cairo Press, 1989.

Al-Malījī, Abū al-Qāsim. *Al-Majālis al-Mustanṣiriyya li-l-Dāʿī ʿAlam al-Islām Thiqat al-Imām*, ed. Muḥammad Kāmil Ḥusayn. Cairo: Dār al-Fikr al-ʿArabī, 1947.

Al-Maqrīzī. *Ittiʿāẓ al-Ḥunafāʾ bi-Akhbār al-Aʾimma al-Fāṭimiyyīn al-Khulafāʾ*, ed. M. H. M. Aḥmad. Cairo: al-Majlis al-Aʿlā li-l-Shuʾūn al-Islāmiyya, 1973.

Al-Maqrīzī. *A History of the Ayyubid Sultans of Egypt, Translated from the Arabic of al-Maqrizi with Introduction and Notes*, trans. R. C. J. Broadhurst. Boston: Twayne Publishers, 1980.

Al-Maqrīzī. *Al-Mawāʿiẓ wa-l-Iʿtibār bi-Dhikr al-Khiṭaṭ wa-l-Athār*, ed. Ayman Fuʾād Sayyid. London: Muʾassasat al-Furqān li-l-Turāth al-Islāmī, 2002–5.

Marmon, Shaun. *Eunuchs and Sacred Boundaries in Islamic Society*. New York: Oxford University Press, 1995.

Marmon, Shaun. 'The quality of mercy: Intercession in Mamluk society'. *Studia Islamica* 87 (1998): 125–39.

Masarwa, Yumna. 'Transforming the Mediterranean from a highway to a frontier: The coastal cities of Palestine during the Byzantine and Early Islamic periods'. In Antoine Borrut et al. (eds), *Le Proche-Orient de Justinien aux Abbasides: Peuplement et dynamiques spatiales*. Turnhout: Brepols, 2011: 149–68.

Mayerson, Philip. 'Urbanization in Palestina Tertia: Pilgrims and paradoxes'. In Philip Mayerson (ed.), *Monks, Martyrs, Soldiers and Saracens: Papers on the Near East in Late Antiquity (1962–1993)*. Jerusalem: Israel Exploration Society and New York University, 1994: 232–49.

McGregor, Richard. 'Dressing the Kaʿba from Cairo: The aesthetics of pilgrimage to Mecca'. In David Morgan (ed.), *Religion and Material Culture: The Matter of Belief*. London and New York: Routledge, 2010: 247–61.

McGregor, Richard. 'Notes on the literature of Sufi prayer commentaries'. *Mamlūk Studies Review* 17 (2013): 199–211.

Meloy, J. L. 'Celebrating the maḥmal: The Rajab festival in fifteenth century Cairo'. In Judith Pfeiffer, Sholeh A. Quinn and Ernest Tucker (eds), *History and Historiography in the Post-Mongol Central Asia and the Middle East: Studies in Honor of John E. Woods*. Wiesbaden: Harrassowitz, 2006: 404–26.

Meloy, J. L. 'Processions: Military'. In J. Meri et al. (eds), *Medieval Islamic Civilization: An Encyclopedia*. New York: Routledge, 2006, vol. 2, pp. 642–3.

Memon, Muḥammad Umar. *Ibn Taymīya's Struggle against Popular Religion, with an Annotated Translation of his Kitāb Iqtidā as-Sirāt al-Mustaqīm*. The Hague: Mouton, 1976.

Meri, Josef W. 'Aspects of *baraka* (blessings) and ritual devotion among medieval Muslims and Jews'. *Medieval Encounters* 5 (1999): 46–69.

Meri, Josef W. *The Cult of Saints among Muslims and Jews in Medieval Syria*. Oxford: Oxford University Press, 2002.

Meri, Josef W. 'A late medieval Syrian pilgrimage guide: Ibn al-Ḥawrānī's *al-Ishārāt ilā Amākin al-Ziyārāt* (Guide to Pilgrimage Places)'. *Medieval Encounters* 7 (2001): 3–78.

Meri, Josef W. (ed. and trans.). *A Lonely Wayfarer's Guide to Pilgrimage: ʿAlī ibn Abī Bakr al-Harawī's Kitāb al-Ishārāt ilā Maʿrifat al-Ziyārāt*. Princeton: Darwin Press, 2004.

Mir, Mustansir. 'Names of the Qurʾān', in Jane Dammen McAuliffe (ed.), *Encyclopaedia of the Qurʾān*. Leiden: Brill, 2012, vol. 3, p. 512b.

Mol, Arnold Yasin. '*Laylat al-Qadr* as Sacred Time: Sacred Cosmology in Sunnī Kalām and Tafsīr'. In Majid Daneshgar and Walid A. Saleh (eds), *Islamic Studies Today: Essays in Honor of Andrew Rippin*. Leiden and Boston: Brill, 2017: 74–97.

Morgan, David. 'Sacred space'. In Lindsay Jones (ed.), *The Encyclopedia of Religion*, 2nd edn. Detroit: Macmillan Reference, 2005, vol. 12, pp. 978, 985.

Mourad, Suleiman and James Lindsay. *The Intensification and Reorientation of Sunni Jihad Ideology in the Crusader Period: Ibn ʿAsākir of Damascus (1105–1176) and His Age, with an Edition and Translation of Ibn ʿAsākir's The Forty Hadiths for Inciting Jihad*. Leiden and Boston: Brill, 2012.

Mouton, Jean-Michel. *Damas et sa principauté sous les Saljoukides et les Bourides (468–549/1076–1154): Vie politique et religieuse, Textes arabes et études islamiques*. Cairo: Institut français d'archéologie orientale, 1994.

Mouton, J.-M. 'La presence chrétienne au Sinaï à époche fatimide'. In Marianne Barrucand (ed.), *L'Égypte fatimide, son art et son histoire*. Paris: Presses de l'Université de Paris-Sorbonne, 1999: 613–24.

Muḥammad, Suʿād Māhir. *Masājid Miṣr wa-Awliyāʾuhā al-Ṣāliḥūn*. Cairo: al-Majlis al-Aʿlā li-l-Shuʾūn al-Islāmiyya, 2010.

Muḥammad, Suʿād Māhir. *Mashhad al-Imām ʿAlī fī al-Najaf wa-mā-bihi min al-Hadāyā wa-l-Tuḥaf*. Cairo: Dār al-Maʿārif, 1388/1969.

Mujīr al-Dīn al-Ḥanbalī. *Al-Uns al-Jalīl fī Taʾrīkh al-Quds wa-l-Khalīl*, ed. ʿAdnān Y. Abū Tabana. Hebron: Dandis 1999.

Mulder, Stephennie. 'Shrines in the Central Islamic lands'. In Richard A. Atlin (ed.), *The Cambridge World History of Religious Architecture*. New York: Cambridge University Press, 2014.

Mulder, Stephennie. *The Shrines of the ʿAlids in Medieval Syria: Sunnis, Shiʿis, and the Architecture of Coexistence*. Edinburgh: Edinburgh University Press, 2014.

Munt, Harry. *The Holy City of Medina: Sacred Space in Early Islamic Arabia*. New York: Cambridge University Press, 2014.

Munt, Harry. 'Pilgrimage in Pre-Islamic Arabia and Late Antiquity'. In Eric Tagliacozzo and Shawkat M. Toorawa (eds), *The Hajj: Pilgrimage in Islam*. Cambridge: Cambridge University Press, 2016: 13–30.

Al-Muqaddasī. *Aḥsan al-Taqāsīm fī Maʿrifat al-Aqālīm*. Leiden: Brill, 1906.

Al-Muqaddasī. *The Best Divisions for Knowledge of the Regions*, trans. Basil Anthony Collins. Reading: Garnet, 1994.

Al-Nābulsī, ʿAbd al-Ghanī. *Al-Ḥaqīqa wa-l-Majāz fī Riḥlat Bilād al-Shām wa-Miṣr wa-l-Ḥijāz*, ed. R. A. Murad. Damascus: Dār al-Maʿrifa, 1989.

Al-Nawawī. *Fatāwā al-Imām al-Nawawī*, ed. Maḥmud al-Arnāʾūṭ. Damascus: Dār al-Fikr, 1419/1999.

Al-Nawawī. *Sharḥ Ṣaḥīḥ Muslim*, ed. Khalīl al-Mayyis. Beirut: Dār al-Qalam, 1987.

Al-Naysābūrī, al-Fattāl. *Rawḍat al-Wāʿiẓayn*, ed. Ḥusayn al-Aʿlamī. Beirut: Muʾassasat al-ʿAlamī li-l-Maṭbūʿāt, 1986.

Nelson, Karen. *The Art of Reciting the Qurʾan*. Austin: University of Texas Press, 1985.

Netton, Ian R. 'Ibn Jubayr: Penitent pilgrim and observant traveler'. In Ian R. Netton (ed.), *Islamic and Middle Eastern Geographers and Travelers*. London: Routledge, 2008, vol. 2, pp. 83–88.

Newman, Andrew J. *Twelver Shiism: Unity and Diversity in the Life of Islam, 632 to 1722*. Edinburgh: Edinburgh University Press, 2013.

Nol, Hagit. 'Cities, Ribāṭs and Other Settlement Types in Palestine from the Seventh to the Early Thirteenth Century: An Exercise in Terminology'. *Al-Masāq*, 2020. doi: 10.1080/09503110.2019.1692555.

Al-Nuwayrī. *Nihāyat al-Arab fī Funūn al-Adab*, vol. 20, ed. M. R. Fatḥ Allāh and I. Muṣṭafā; vol. 32, ed. Fahīm M. Shaltūt. Cairo: Dār al-Kutub al-Miṣriyya, 1975–98.

Ohtoshi, Tetsuya. 'The manners, customs, and mentality of pilgrims to the Egyptian City of the Dead: 1100–1500 AD'. *Orient* 29 (1993): 19–44.

Ohtoshi, Tetsuya. '*Taṣawwuf* as reflected in *Ziyāra* Books and the Cairo Cemeteries'. In Richard McGregor et al. (eds), *The Development of Sufism in Mamluk Egypt*. Cairo: Institut français d'archéologie orientale, 2006: 299–330.

Olesen, Niels Henrik. *Culte des Saints et Pèlerinages chez Ibn Taymiyya*. Paris: Librairie orientaliste P. Geuthner, 1991.

Padwick, Constance E. *Muslim Devotions: A Study of Prayer Manuals in Common Use*. London: SPCK, 1961.

Paret, R. and Chaumont, E. ''Umra'. In P. Bearman, Th. Bianquis, C. E. Bosworth, E. van Donzel and W. P. Heinrichs (eds), *The Encyclopaedia of Islam*, 2nd edn, available at www.brillonline.com.

Pedersen, J. 'Minbar (A.)'. In P. Bearman, Th. Bianquis, C. E. Bosworth, E. van Donzel and W. P. Heinrichs (eds), *The Encyclopaedia of Islam*, 2nd edn. Leiden: Brill, 1993, vol. 7, pp. 74–5; available at www.brillonline.com

Peers, Glenn. 'The church at the Jerusalem Gate of Crusader Ascalon: A rough tolerance of Byzantine culture?' *Eastern Christian Art* 6 (2009): 67–86.

Piccirrillo, M. 'Ascalon in mosaics from Transjordan'. In Naftali Arbel (ed.), *Ashkelon: 4000 years and another Forty*. Ascalon: Ha'Amuta LeMoreshet Ashkelon 1990: 166–71 [in Hebrew].

Prawer, Yehoshua. 'Ascalon and the Ascalon strip in Crusader politics'. In ibid. 181–220.

Pringle, Denis. *The Churches of the Crusader Kingdom of Jerusalem: A Corpus*. Cambridge: Cambridge University Press, 1993.

Pringle, Denis. *Secular Buildings in the Crusader Kingdom of Jerusalem: An Archaeological Gazetteer*. Cambridge: Cambridge University Press, 1997.

Shablanjī, Muʾmin. *Nūr al-Abṣār fī Manāqīb Bayt Āl al-Mukhtār*, ed. Maḥmūd Ḥalabī. Beirut: Dār al-Mʿarifa, 2005.

Al-Qalqashandī. *Selections from Subḥ al-Aʿshā by al-Qalqashandī: Clerk of the Mamluk Court*, ed. Heba al-Toudy and Tarek Gala Abdelhamid. London and New York: Routledge, 2017.

Al-Qalqashandī. *Ṣubḥ al-Aʿshā fī Ṣināʿāt al-Inshā*, ed. Muḥammad H. Shams al-Dīn et al. Beirut: Dār al-Kutub al-ʿIlmiyya, 1987–8.

Al-Qasāṭlī, Nuʿmān. *Al-Rawḍa al-Nuʿmāniyya fī Siyāhat Filasṭīn wa-Baʿḍ al-Buldān al-Shāmiyya*, ed. Sh. R. Hujja, ʿImād Rifʿat al-Bishtāwī and Muḥammad al-ʿAlamī. Irbid: Muʾassasat Ḥamāda, 2009.

Al-Qazwīnī. *Āthār al-Bilād wa-Akhbār al-ʿUbbād*, unknown editor. Beirut: Dār Ṣādir, 1380/1960.

Qutbuddin, Tahera. *Al-Muʾayyad al-Shirāzī and Fatimid Daʿwa Poetry: A Case of Commitment in Classical Arab Literature*. Leiden: Brill, 2005.

Ragib, Y. 'Un contract du mariage sur soie d'Égypt fatimide'. *Annales Islamologiques* 16 (1980): 31–7.

Rapoport, Yossef and Shahab Ahmed (eds). *Ibn Taymiyya and his Times*. Karachi: Oxford University Press, 2010.

Raven, Wim. 'Reward and punishment'. In Jane Dammen McAuliffe (ed.), *Encyclopaedia of the Qurʾān*, available at www.brillonline.com.

Redfield, Robert. *The Little Community and Peasant Society and Culture*. Chicago: University of Chicago Press, 1989.

Reid, Megan H. ''Ashūra, (Sunnism)'. In Kate Fleet, Gudrun Krämer, Denis Matringe, John Nawas and Everett Rowson (eds), *The Encyclopaedia of Islam*, 3rd edn, available at www.brillonline.com.

Reid, Megan H. *Law and Piety in Medieval Islam*. Cambridge and New York: Cambridge University Press, 2013.

Retsö, Jan. ''Atīra'. In ibid.

Richards, D. S. (trans.). *Egypt and Syria in the Early Mamluk Period: An Extract from Ibn Faḍl Allāh al-ʿUmarī's Masālik al-Abṣār fī Mamālik al-Amṣār*. New York: Routledge, 2017.

Rispler, Vardit. 'The 20th century treatment of an old *Bidʿa*: *Laylat al-Niṣf min Shaʿbān*'. *Der Islam* 72 (1995): 82–97.

Rodman, Margaret C. 'Empowering place: Multilocality and multivocality', *The American Anthropologist* 14 (1992): 640–56.

Sabra, Adam. *Poverty and Charity in Medieval Islam: Mamluk Egypt, 1250–1517*. Cambridge: Cambridge University Press, 2000.

Ṣafadī, Ṣalāḥ al-Dīn Khalīl b. Aybak. *Al-Wafi bi-l-Wafayāt*, ed. Aḥmad al-Arnāʾūṭ and Aḥmad Muṣṭafā Turkī. Beirut: Dār Iḥyāʾ al-Turāth al-ʿArabī, 2000, vol. 4.

Al-Sakhawī. *Tuḥfat al-Aḥbāb wa-Baghyat al-Ṭulāb*, ed. Maḥmūd Rabīʿ and Ḥasan Qāsim. Cairo: Maṭbaʿat al-ʿUlūm wa-l-Ādāb, 1356/1937.

Al-Sakhāwī. *Al-Tuḥfa al-Laṭīfa fī Taʾrīkh al-Madīna al-Sharīfa*. Beirut: Dār al-Kutub al-ʿIlmiyya, 1994, vol. 2.

Ṣāliḥa, Maḥmūd. *Al-Majdal Taʾrīkh wa-Ḥaḍāra*. Gaza: Al-Markaz al-Qawmī li-l-Dirāsāt wa-l-Tawthīq, 1999.

Sallnow, Michael. *Pilgrims of the Andes: Regional Cults in Cusco*. Washington, DC: Smithsonian, 1987.

Sanders, Paula. 'Claiming the past: Ghadî Khumm and the rise of Hâfizî historiography in Late Fâtimid Egypt'. *Studia Islamica* 75 (1992): 82–104.

Sanders, Paula. *Creating Medieval Cairo: Empire, Religion and Architectural Preservation in Nineteenth-Century Egypt*. Cairo: American University in Cairo Press, 2008.

Sanders, Paula. 'From court ceremonial to urban language'. In Clifford Edmund Bosworth (ed.), *The Islamic World from Classical to Modern Times: Essays in Honor of Bernard Lewis*. Princeton: Darwin Press, 1989: 311–21.

Sanders, Paula. 'Marāsim'. In P. Bearman, Th. Bianquis, C. E. Bosworth, E. van Donzel and W. P. Heinrichs (eds), *The Encyclopaedia of Islam*, 2nd edn. Leiden: Brill, 1991, vol. 6, p. 519; available at www.brillonline.com

Sanders, P., Chalmeta, P., Lambton, A. K. S., Nutku, Özdemir and J. Burton-Page. 'Mawākib'. In P. Bearman, Th. Bianquis, C. E. Bosworth, E. van Donzel and W. P. Heinrichs, *The Encyclopaedia of Islam*, 2nd edn, available at www.brillonline.com.

Sanders, Paula. *Ritual, Politics, and the City in Fatimid Cairo*. New York: State University of New York Press, 1994.

Sayyid, Ayman Fu'ād. *Al-Dawla al-Fāṭimiyya fī Miṣr: Tafsīr Jadīd*. Cairo: al-Dār al-Miṣriyya al-Lubnāniyya, 1413/1992.

Sayyid, Ayman Fu'ad (ed. and trans.). *The Fatimids and their Successors in Yaman: The History of an Islamic Community: Arabic Edition and English Summary of Idris 'Imad al-Din's 'Uyun al-akhbar*, vol. 7. London: I. B. Tauris and The Institute of Ismaili Studies, 2002.

Sayyid, Ayman Fu'ād (ed.). *Nuṣūṣ min Akhbār Miṣr*. Cairo: al-Ma'had al-'Ilmī al-Faransī li-l-Āthār al-Sharqiyya, 1983.

Sayyid, Ayman Fu'ād. *The Topography and Urban Evolution of Cairo / al-Qāhira: Ḥiṭaṭuhā wa-Taṭawwuruhā al-'Imrānī*. Cairo: al-Hay'a al-Miṣriyya al-'Āmma li-l-Kitāb, 2015.

Schick, Robert. *The Christian Communities of Palestine from Byzantine to Islamic Rule*. Princeton: Darwin Press, 1995.

Schielke, Samuli Joska. *The Perils of Joy: Contesting Mulid Festivals in Contemporary Egypt*. Syracuse, NY: Syracuse University Press, 2012.

Schimmel, Anne-Marie. *The Mystery of Numbers*. New York: Oxford University Press, 1993.

Schimmel, Anne-Marie. Review of Constance Padwick, *Muslim Devotions*, in *Die Welt des Islams*, New Series, 7 (1961): 192–94.

Schöller, Marco and Werner Diem. *The Living and the Dead in Islam: Studies in Arabic Epitaphs*. Wiesbaden: Harrassowitz, 2004.

Serjeant, R. B. 'Ḥaram and Ḥawtāh, the sacred enclave in Arabia'. In R. B. Serjeant (ed.), *Studies in Arabian History and Civilization*. London: Variorum Reprints, 1981: 41–58.

Shalem, Avinoam. 'Fountains of light: The meaning of medieval rock crystal lamps'. *Muqarnas* 11 (1994): 1–11.

Shams, Muḥammad 'Azīz and al-'Imrān 'Alī b. Muḥammad (eds). *Al-Jāmi' li-Sīrat Shaykh al-Islām Ibn Taymiyya*. Mekka: Dār 'Alām al-Fawā'id, 1420/1999.

Al-Sha'rānī, 'Abd al-Wahhāb. *Al-Ṭabaqāt al-Kubrā*. Cairo: Maktabat Muḥammad al-Malījī, 1315/1898.

Al-Sharjī. *Ṭabaqāt al-Khawāṣṣ Ahl al-Ṣidq wa-l-Ikhlāṣ*, ed. ʿA. al-Ḥibshī. Sanʿa and Beirut: al-Dār al-Yamaniyya li-l-Nashr wa-l-Tawzīʿ, 1992.

Sharon, Moshe. *Corpus Inscriptionum Arabicarum Palaestinae*. Leiden: Brill, 1997–2017, 6 vols.

Shoshan, Boaz. *Popular Culture in Medieval Cairo*. Cambridge: Cambridge University Press, 1993.

Shoshan, Boaz. *Poetics of Islamic Historiography: Deconstructing Ṭabarī's History*. Leiden: Brill, 2004.

Sindawi, Khalid. 'The head of Husayn Ibn Ali: Its various places of burial and the miracles that it performed'. In Marshall J. Breger, Yitzhak Reiter and Leonard Hammer (eds), *Holy Places in the Israeli-Palestinian Conflict: Confrontation and Co-existence*. London and New York: Routledge, 2010: 264–73.

Sindawi, Khalid. 'Al-Husain Ibn ʿAli and Yahya Ibn Zakariyya in the Shiʿite sources: A comparative study'. *Islamic Culture* 78 (2004): 37–54.

Sindawi, Khalid. 'The sanctity of Karbala in Shiite thought'. In Pedram Khosronejad (ed.), *Saints and their Pilgrims in Iran and Neighboring Countries*. Wantage: Sean Kingston Pub., 2012: 21–40.

Sindawi, Khalid. 'Visit to the Tomb of Al-Ḥusyan b. ʿAlī in Shiite poetry: First to Fifth Centuries AH (8th–11th centuries CE)'. *Journal of Arabic Literature* 37 (2006): 230–58.

Singer, Amy. *Charity in Islamic Societies*. Cambridge: Cambridge University Press, 2008.

Al-Ṣiqillī, Ibn Ẓafar. *Kitāb Anbāʾ Nujabāʾ al-Abnāʾ*, ed. Lajnat Iḥyaʾ al-Turāth al-ʿArabī. Beirut: Dār al-Āfāq al-Jadīda, 1400/1980.

Sirriyeh, Elizabeth. 'Dreams of the holy dead: Traditional Islamic oneirocriticism versus Salafi scepticism'. *Journal of Semitic Studies* 45 (2000): 115–30.

Smith, Jonathan Z. *To Take Place: Toward Theory in Ritual*. Chicago and London: University of Chicago Press, 1982.

Smith, William Robertson. *Lectures on the Religion of the Semites*. New York: Macmillan, 1927.

Stephenson, Barry. *Ritual: A Very Short Introduction*. Oxford and New York: Oxford University Press, 2015.

Stern, M. S. 'Notes on the theology of al-Ghazzālī's concept of repentance'. *Islamic Quarterly* 23 (1979): 82–98.

Stewart, Devin J. 'The Maqāmāt of Aḥmad b. Abī Bakr b. Aḥmad al-Rāzī al-Ḥanafī and the ideology of the Counter-Crusade in twelfth-century Syria'. *Middle Eastern Literatures* 11 (2008): 211–32.

Stewart, Devin J. 'Popular Shiism in medieval Egypt: Vestiges of Islamic sectarian polemics in Egyptian Arabic'. *Studia Islamica* 84/2 (1996): 35–66.

Stowasser, Barbara Freyer. *The Day Begins at Sunset: Perceptions of Time in the Islamic World.* London and New York: I. B. Tauris, 2014.

Al-Subkī. *Ṭabaqāt al-Shāfiʿiyya al-Kubrā*, ed. ʿAbd al-Fattāḥ Muḥammad Ḥulw and Maḥmūd Muḥammad al-Ṭannāḥī. Cairo: Maṭbaʿat ʿĪsā al-Bābī al-Ḥalabī, 1383/1964.

Swartz, Heller. 'Sacred time'. In Lindsay Jones (ed.), *The Encyclopedia of Religion*, 2nd edn. Detroit: Macmillan Reference, 2005, vol. 12, pp. 7986–97.

Al-Ṭabarī. *The History of al-Ṭabarī: The Caliphate of Yazīd b. Muʿāwiyah*, trans. I. K. A. Howard. Albany: State University of New York Press, 1990, vol. 29.

Ṭabbāʿ, Muṣṭafā ʿUthmān. *Itḥāf al-Aʿizza: fī Taʾrīkh Ghazza*, ed. ʿAbd al-Laṭīf Zākī Abū Hāshim, 4 vols. Gaza: Maktabat al-Yazjī, 1420/1999.

Tabbaa, Yasser. 'Originality and Innovation in Syrian Woodwork of the Twelfth and Thirteenth Centuries'. In Daniella Talmon-Heller and Katia Cytryn-Silverman (eds), *Material Evidence and Narrative Sources: Interdisciplinary Studies of the History of the Muslim Middle East*. Leiden: Brill, 2014: 188–215.

Tabbaa, Yasser. *The Transformation of Islamic Art during the Sunni Revival.* Seattle: University of Washington Press, 2002.

Talmon-Heller, Daniella. 'Charity and repentance in medieval Islamic thought and practice'. In Miriam Frenkel and Yaacov Lev (eds), *Charity and Giving in Monotheistic Religions*. Berlin and New York: W. de Gruyter, 2009: 265–79.

Talmon-Heller, Daniella. 'The Cited Tales of the Wondrous Doings of the Shaykhs of the Holy Land by Ḍiyāʾ al-Dīn Abū ʿAbd Allāh Muḥammad b. ʿAbd al-Wāḥid al-Maqdisī (569/1173–643/1245): Text, translation, and commentary'. *Crusades* 1 (2003): 111–54.

Talmon-Heller, Daniella. 'Graves, relics and sanctuaries: The evolution of Syrian sacred topography'. *ARAM* 19 (2007): 601–20.

Talmon-Heller, Daniella. 'Historiography in the service of the *Muftī*: Ibn Taymiyya on the origins and fallacies of *ziyārāt*'. *Islamic Law and Society* 26 (2019): 1–25.

Talmon-Heller, Daniella. '*ʿIlm, shafāʿah* and *barakah:* The resources of Ayyūbid and early Mamlūk *ʿulamāʾ*'. *Mamlūk Studies Review* 13 (2009): 23–45.

Talmon-Heller, Daniella. *Islamic Piety in Medieval Syria*. Leiden: Brill, 2007.

Talmon-Heller, Daniella. 'Job, (Ayyūb), al-Ḥusayn and Saladin in Late Ottoman Palestine: The memoirs of Nuʿmān al-Qasatlī, the Arab scribe of the PEF Team'. In David Gurevich and Anat Kidron (eds), *Exploring the Holy Land: 150 Years of the Palestine Exploration Fund*. Sheffield: Equinox, 2019: 124–50.

Talmon-Heller, Daniella, B. Z. Kedar and Yitzhak Reiter. 'Vicissitudes of a holy place: Construction, destruction and commemoration of Mashad Ḥusayn in Ascalon'. *Der Islam* 93 (2016): 182–215.

Talmon-Heller, Daniella and Miriam Frenkel. 'Religious innovations in Fatimid Jerusalem'. *Medieval Encounters* 25/3 (2019): 203–26.

Talmon-Heller, Daniella and Raquel Ukeles. 'The lure of a controversial prayer – *Ṣalāt al-Raghā'ib* (the Prayer of Great Rewards) in sixth/twelfth-eighth/fifteenth century Arabic texts and from a socio-legal perspective'. *Der Islam* 89 (2012): 141–66.

Tamari, Salim. *Mountain against the Sea*. Berkeley: University of California Press, 2009.

Taylor, Christopher S. *In the Vicinity of the Righteous: Ziyāra and the Veneration of Muslim Saints in Late Medieval Egypt*. Leiden: Brill, 1999.

Thomas, David. 'Apologetic and polemic in the *Letter from Cyprus* and Ibn Taymiyya's *al-Jawāb al-Ṣaḥīḥ li-man baddala Dīn al-Masīḥ*'. In Yossef Rapoport and Shahab Ahmed (eds), *Ibn Taymiyya and his Times*. Karachi: Oxford University Press, 2010: 247–65.

Thomson, Kirsten. *Politics and Power in Late Fāṭimid Egypt: The Reign of Caliph al-Mustanṣir*. London: I. B. Tauris, 2016 [e-book].

Trombley, Frank R. 'The Arabs in Anatolia and the Islamic law of war (*fiqh al-jihād*), seventh–tenth centuries'. *Al-Masāq* 16 (2004): 147–61.

Tuan, Yi-Fu. *Passing Strange and Wonderful: Aesthetics, Nature and Culture*. Chicago: Island Press, 1993.

Tuchman, Barbara. *Bible and Sword*. New York: New York University Press, 1956.

Turner, Edith. 'Pilgrimage: An overview'. In Lindsay Jones (ed.), *The Encyclopedia of Religion*, 2nd edn. Farmington Hills, MI: Macmillan, 2005, vol. 10, p. 7145.

Turner, Edith. 'Processions, religious'. In Joseph Meri et al. (eds), *Medieval Islamic Civilization: An Encyclopedia*. New York: Routledge, 2006, vol. 2, 644.

Turner, Victor W. *The Ritual Process: Structure and Anti-Structure*. Chicago: University of Chicago Press, 1969.

Turner, Victor and Edith Turner. *Image and Pilgrimage in Christian Culture*. New York: Columbia University Press, 1978.

Al-Ṭurṭūshī, Abū Bakr. *Kitāb al-Ḥawādith wa-l-Bida'*. ed. 'Abd al-Majīd Turkī. Beirut: Dār al-Gharb al-Islāmī, 1990.

Ukeles, Raquel M. *Innovation or Deviation: Exploring the Boundaries of Islamic Devotional Law*, unpublished PhD diss., Harvard University, 2006.

Al-ʿUlaymī, Mujīr al-Dīn. *Al-Taʾrīkh al-Muʿtabar fī Anbāʾ man Ghabar*, ed. Nūr al-Dīn Ṭālib. Damascus: Dār al-Nawādir, 1431/2011, 3 vols.

Al-ʿUlaymī, Mujīr al-Dīn. *Al-ʾUns al-Jalīl fī Taʾrīkh al-Quds wa-l-Khalīl*, ed. ʿAdnān Abū Tabbāna. Hebron: Maktabat Dandīs, 1999, 2 vols.

Al-ʿUmarī, Ibn Faḍl Allāh. *Masālik al-Abṣār fī Mamālik al-Amṣār*, ed. ʿAbd Allāh b. Yaḥyā al-Sarīhī. Abu Dhabi: al-Majmaʿ al-Thqāfī, 2003.

Vaglieri, L. V. 'Ḥusayn b. ʿAlī b. Abī Ṭālib'. In P. Bearman, Th. Bianquis, C. E. Bosworth, E. van Donzel and W. P. Heinrichs (eds), *The Encyclopaedia of Islam*, 2nd edn. Leiden: Brill, 1979, vol. 3, p. 612; available at www.brillonline.com

Van Berchem, Max. 'La chaire de la mosquée d'Hébron et le martyrion de la tête de Husain à Ascalon'. In Gotthold Weil (ed.), *Festschrift Eduard Sachau zum Siebzigsten Geburtstage gewidmet von Freunden und Schülern*. Berlin: G. Reimer, 1915: 298–310. Repr. In Max van Berchem (ed.), *Opera Minora*. Genève: Slatkine, 1978.

Van Steenbergen, Jo. 'Ritual, politics and the city in Mamluk Cairo: The Bayna al-Qaṣrayn as a Mamluk "*lieu de mémoire*", 1250–1382'. In Alexander Beihammer, Stavroula Constantinou and Maria Parani (eds), *Court Ceremonies and Rituals of Power in Byzantium and the Medieval Mediterranean: A Comparative Perspective*. Leiden: Brill, 2013: 225–76.

Vincent, L. H. and E. J. H. Mackay. *Hébron: Le Ḥaram el-Khalîl. Sépulture des Patriarches*. Paris: E. Leroux, 1923.

von Grunebaum, G. E. 'The sacred character of Islamic cities'. In ʿAbd al-Raḥmān Badawī (ed.), *Mélanges Taha Husain*. Cairo: Dār al-Maʿārif, 1962: 25–37.

Wagtendonk, K. *Fasting in the Koran*. Leiden: Brill, 1968.

Walker, Paul. 'Purloined symbols of the past: The theft of souvenirs and sacred relics in the rivalry between the Abbasids and Fatimids'. In Farhad Daftary and Josef W. Meri (eds), *Culture and Memory in Medieval Islam: Essays in Honour of Wilfred Madelung*. London: I. B. Tauris and The Institute of Ismaili Studies, 2003: 364–87.

Walker, Paul. *Orations of the Fatimid Caliphs: Festival Sermons of the Isamaili Imams*. London and New York: I. B. Tauris and The Institute of Ismaili Studies, 2009.

Walker, Paul. 'Egyptian Popular Festivals in the Fatimid Period'. In Obada Kohela (ed.), *History and Islamic Civilisation: Essays in Honour of Ayman Fuʾād Sayyid*. Cairo: al-Dār al-Miṣriyya al-Lubnāniyya, 2014: 69–91.

Wensinck, A. J., Gimaret, D. and A. Schimmel. 'Shafāʿa'. In P. Bearman, Th. Bianquis, C. E. Bosworth, E. van Donzel and W. P. Heinrichs (eds), *The Encyclopaedia of Islam*, 2nd edn, available at www.brillonline.com.

Wheeler, Brannon. *Mecca and Eden: Rituals, Relics, and Territory in Islam*. Chicago: University of Chicago Press, 2006.

Wilkinson, John. *Jerusalem Pilgrims before the Crusades*. Warminster: Aris & Phillips, 1977.

Williams, Caroline. 'The cult of ʿAlid saints in the Fatimid monuments of Cairo, part I: The Mosque of al-Aqmar'. *Muqarnas* 1 (1983): 37–52.

Williams, Caroline. 'The cult of ʿAlid saints in the Fatimid monuments of Cairo, part II: The Mausolea'. *Muqarnas* 3 (1985): 39–60.

Williams, Caroline. *Islamic Monuments in Cairo*. Cairo: The American University in Cairo Press, 1985.

Williams, Caroline. 'The Qurʾanic inscriptions on the *tābūt* of al-Ḥusayn'. *Islamic Art* 2 (1987): 3–13.

Winter, Michael. 'The *mawlids* in Egypt from the eighteenth to the twentieth centuries'. In G. Baer (ed.), *The ʿUlama and Problems of Religion in the Muslim World*. Jerusalem: Magnes Press, 1971: 79–103 [in Hebrew].

Winter, Michael. *Society and Religion in Early Ottoman Egypt*. New Brunswick, NJ: Transaction Books, 1982.

Wishnitzer, Avner. *Reading Clocks, Alla Turca: Time and Society in the Late Ottoman Empire*. Chicago: University of Chicago Press, 2015.

Al-Yāfiʿī, ʿAbdallāh b. Asʿad. *Mirʾāt al-Jinān wa-ʿIbrat al-Yaqẓān fī Maʿrifat Ḥawādith al-Zamān*. Beirut: Dār al-Kutub al-ʿIlmiyya, 1994, vol. 4.

Yagur, Moshe. *Between Cairo and Jerusalem*, unpublished MA thesis, Hebrew University, Jerusalem, 2012 [in Hebrew].

Al-Yamanī, ʿUmāra b. Abī al-Ḥasan. *Kitāb Taʾrīkh al-Yaman*, trans. Henry C. Kay. London 1892, repub. 1968.

Yano, Michio. 'al-Bīrūnī'. In Kate Fleet, Gudrun Krämer, Denis Matringe, John Nawas and Everett Rowson (eds), *The Encyclopaedia of Islam*, 3rd edn available at www.brillonline.com.

Yaʿqūbī. *The Works of Ibn Wāḍiḥ al-Yaʿqūbī: An English Translation*, ed. Mathew S. Gordon, Chase F. Robinson et al. Leiden: Brill, 2018, vol. 2.

Yeomans, Richard. *The Art and Architecture of Islamic Cairo*. Reading: Garnet, 2006.

Zerubavel, Eviatar. *Hidden Rhythms: Schedules and Calendars is Social Life*. Chicago: University of California Press, 1981.

Index

Illustrations are indicated by page numbers in **bold**

Abbasid dynasty, 35, 36, 46, 64, 65, 76, 87, 113, 121
ʿAbd al-Rahman Katkhuda, 93
ʿAbdallah b. Muhammad (traditionist), 138
ʿAbdallah b. al-Sultan, 180–1
ʿAbdallah b. ʿUmar, 138
al-ʿAbdari, Muhammad, 91, 106
ablutions, 144, 180, 192, 198
Abraham, 63, 130, 172
Abraham's well (Ascalon), 63, 101
absolution *see* forgiveness, seeking of; sin: remittance of
Abu Bakr, 139, 152
Abu Darda, 198
Abu al-Hasan ʿAli (Cairene shaykh), 89–90
Abu Qatada, 129
Abu Shama, 184–5, 186, 187, 204
Abu Talib al-Makki, 145
Acre, 44, 71, 199
Adam, 159, 172, 173
al-ʿAdil (Ayyubid ruler), 103
Adomnan of Iona, 63
al-Afdal Shahanshah ibn Badr al-Din al-Jamali, 59, 67, 160
ahl al-bayt, 43, 50, 59, 77, 81, 88, 115, 120, 122, 204
ʿAʾisha, 137, 139
Aleppo, 36, 51, 74, 88, 91
Alexandria, 45, 49, 94
Alexandrin, Elizabeth, 174n20
ʿAli al-Asghar b. Zayn al-ʿAbidin, 43
ʿAli ibn Abi Talib, 3, 36, 50–1, 81, 130, 143–4, 161, 170, 173, 198, 204, 224
ʿAli Zayn al-Abidin, 29, 143–4, 179, 225
ʿAlids, 29, 77, 87–8, 114–15, 121, 224–5
alms *see* charity; donations
al-Amir bi-Ahkam Allah, 52, 80, 84n48, 160–1
ʿAmr ibn al-ʿAs Mosque (Cairo), 157
angels, 32, 56, 81, 141, 144–5, 170, 171, 172, 180, 222, 225, 228
al-Ansari, ʿAbd Allah, 196
Antrim, Zayde, 18
al-Anwar Mosque (Cairo), 157
apparitions (of holy figures), 4, 90, 101, 115, 143, 229; *see also* dreams
al-Aqsa Mosque (Jerusalem), 57, 72n3, 105, 167
Arculf, Bishop, 63
ʿArif al-ʿArif, 97, 99, 100
Artuqids, 44
Ascalon
  Abraham's well, 63, 101
  Ayyubid reconquest of, 64, 98–9, 102, 105
  churches, 64
  conquest by Crusaders, 3, 66, 73–4
  defenders of (*murābiṭūn*), 63–4, 113, 114, 120, 121
  demolitions of, 102–6, **104**, 120
  denominational composition, 71
  depiction on Madaba Map, 62, **63**
  depictions in travellers' accounts, 62, 105–9
  discovery of al-Husayn's head, 44, 46–9
  fortifications, 49, 73, 101, 103

Ascalon (*cont.*)
  Frankish rule, 101–2
  as frontier town, 46, 49–50, 73, 101, 103–4, 108, 113, 120, 121
  mosques, 64, 106
  pilgrimage to, 6, 71
  pre-Fatimid 63, 65
  shrine of Egyptian Christian martyrs, 62–3, 64–5, 114, 120
  shrine of al-Husayn's head *see* Mashhad Ra'sal-Husayn (Ascalon)
  strategic importance, 49–50, 73–4
  treatises in praise of, 6, 85
  Umayyad period, 63–4, 65
asceticism, 197, 213n65; *see also* fasting
al-Ashraf (Ayyubid sultan), 90
al-Ashrāf, 13, 79
Ashrafiyya Library, 183, **184**
al-ʿAshura, 79, 80, 121, 129, 204, 205, 229
al-ʿAsqalani, Abu Muhammad al-Hasan Ibn Adam, 85
al-Asyuti, Muhammad Shams al-Din, 85, 107–8
ʿAtaʾ b. Abi Rabah, 136
Ayoub, Mahmoud, 28n3
ayyām al-bīḍ (white days), 144, 173, 198
Ayyubid period
  Cairo, 87–91, 182
  madrasas, 87, 90–1
  rites of Rajab, 5, 182–209, 22–3
  shrine of al-Husayn at Ascalon, 3, 102–4, 107, 120–1
  shrine of al-Husayn at Cairo, 3, 87–91, 121–2
  see also individual Ayyubid rulers
axis mundi, 1, 10, 70, 222–3
Azad, Arezou, 18
al-Azhar Mosque (Cairo), 80, 87, 155–7, 158
al-ʿAziz (Fatimid caliph), 79, 155

Badr al-Din al-Jamali, 44–51, 61, 65, 66, 67, 71, 81, 99, 115, 119, 159
Badr al-Din minbar, 45–51, **47**, **48**, 82n8, 103, 104–5, 119, 230
Baghdad, 59, 186, 193
al-Balawi, Khalid, 107
Baldwin III, 74
Balkh, 18
banquets, 80, 160–2, 205, 231
Banu Aswad, 142
al-Baqiʿ cemetery (Medina), 114
baraka (blessings), 13, 17, 22, 77, 81, 88–90, 105, 163, 209, 228, 230, 232
al-Barghuthi, ʿUmar Salih, 97
al-Basasiri, 59
Baybars, Sultan, 103, 178n84, 205, 206, 223
al-Bayhaqi, 195, 218
Bedouins, 136, 200
Berkey, Jonathan, 90, 95n16
Bible, 63, 74
bidaʿ (innovations), 20, 93, 112–13, 116, 166–7, 186–91, 222, 224, 225
Bierman, Irene, 48
al-Biqaʿi, 209
birthdays *see mawlids*
al-Biruni, 5, 19, 32, 130, 132n22, 151
blessings (*baraka*), 13, 17, 22, 77, 81, 88–90, 105, 163, 209, 228, 230, 232
blood, 13, 29, 36, 74, 116, 135–6, 227, 228
Bloom, Jonathan, 46
Bohra Dawudiyya, 94, **99**
Brown, Peter, 3
al-Bukhari, 114, 138, 205, 211
Burke, Peter, 7
Burnaby, Sherrard, 19
Burnett, Charles, 20

Cairo
  ʿAmr ibn al-ʿAs Mosque, 157
  al-Anwar Mosque, 157
  Ayyubid period, 87–91, 182
  al-Azhar Mosque, 80, 87, 155–7, 158
  expansion of city, 45
  Fatimid period, 6, 42–5, 52, 67, 77–81, 94, 121, 155–64, **156**, **160**, 221–2
  Ibn Tulun Mosque, 43, 45
  Madrasa al-Fadiliyya, 187
  Madrasa al-Jawhariyya, 90
  madrasas, 87, 90–1, 187, 205
  Mamluk period, 6, 91–4, 206–9, **207**, 223–4
  markets, 45, 164

Mashhad al-Juyyushi, 45, **45**
Mashhad (mausoleum) of al-Sayyida Nafisa, 45, 115, 161
al-Qarafa cemetery, 18, 89–90, 157, 160, 166, 222
rites of Rajab, 6, 155–64, 186, 187, 206–9, 221–2, 223–4
Saladin seizes control of, 75–6, 87
shrine of al-Husayn's head *see* Mashhad Raʾs al-Husayn (Cairo)
shrines dedicated to *ahl al-bayt*, 43
Turbat al-Aʾimma mausoleum, 52, 78
calendars
agricultural calendars, 20
astrological calendars, 20
Christian calendar, 97
Georgian-Palestinian Calendar, 68n11
hijri calendar, 19, 97, 127, 151–2, 221
intercalation, 151–2, 221
Jewish calendar, 19, 23n10
liturgical calendars, 6, 18–20, 127–8, 151–3
lunar calendars, 6, 19–20, 127–8, 151–3
Cave of the Patriarchs (Hebron), 45–6, 104–5
cemeteries
contested status as sacred places, 18
greeting the dead, 89–90
informal gatherings at, 164, 166, 222
rites performed at, 18
as source of sanctity for cities, 64
visitation of, 18, 89–90, 106, 112–13, 166, 225
see also tombs; *and individual cemeteries*
'central' pilgrimage sites, 10–11, 17, 70, 222–3
chandeliers, 52, 55–7, **56**; *see also* light
charity, 141, 142, 160, 161, 166, 204–6, 225, 231; *see also* donations
Chittick, William C., 150n57
Christ, Georg, 94
Christian calendar, 97
Christian martyrs, 3, 62–3, 64–5, 114, 120
Christianity, 3, 32, 33, 62–3, 65, 94, 112, 114–15, 194, 199
circumambulation, 88, 122, 136, 143, 230
Cobb, Paul, 18
Cohen, Erik, 11, 17, 119, 223
commercial activity, 11, 49, 200, 203, 222
continuity, 3–5, 33–5, 61–3, 64–5, 76–7, 87–8, 120, 129
Cook, Michael, 22
Coptic Church, 94
cross-sectarian patronage, 18, 28, 51–2, 87–8, 122
Crusades, 3, 55, 66, 73–4, 98–9, 102–4, 113, 120, 192–3
Cubitt, Catherine, 120

Daftary, Farhad, 84n38
Damascus
Ashrafiyya Library, 183
Dar al-Hadith al-Ashrafiyya, 90, 91
Islamisation, 33
madrasas, 90, 187
Mosque of al-Qasb, 66
procession of al-Husayn's head to, 29–31, **31**, 36–7, **37**, 49, 65, 229
rites of Rajab, 185, 186, 187–8, 194–5, 204, 205–6
shrine of al-Husayn's head, 33, **36**, 107
shrine of Yahya b. Zakariya, 33–5, **35**, 107
tombs of the Companions, 91
Umayyad Great Mosque, 33–5, **34**, **35**, **36**, 107, 186, 205
David (Dawud), 198
Dar al-Hadith al-Ashrafiyya (Damascus), 90, 91
Dawud b. ʿIsa b. Musa, (emir Mecca) 137
De Smet, Daniel, 23, 51, 84n38
Denny, Frederick, 152
al-Dhahabi, 35
dhikr, 98, 122, 141, 193
Dhu al-Hijja, 127, 129, 138, 147, 151, 152, 195, 197
Dhu al-Qaʿda, 127, 136, 147, 151, 152, 164
divine light, 49, 57, 65
divine mercy, 129, 140, 169, 180, 227, 230, 233
divine recompense, 129, 159, 188, 209, 227, 231
Dome of the Rock (Jerusalem), 55

donations
  to the poor, 141, 142, 160, 161, 166, 205, 231
  to shrines and mosques, 52, 55–9, 161, 204–5, 231
  see also charity
dreams, 90, 101–2, 115; *see also* apparitions
Drory, Joseph, 107
du'ā' (invocation), 91–3, 136, 143–4, 170, 189, 193, 225, 231
Durkheim, Emile, 9–10, 21, 209

Eade, John, 80
Elad, Amikam, 110n24
Eliade, Mircae, 1, 9, 12, 70, 119, 222–3
Encyclopedia of Religion, 10
Epiphanius the Monk, 63
Eusebius of Caesarea, 62

Faḍā'il (merits) literature, 6, 14, 22, 63, 85, 123, 169, 218–19, 231
Fahd, Tawfik, 20
fairs (*sūqs*), 137, 152–3, 164, 221; *see also* markets
al-Fa'iz (Fatimid caliph), 77, 79
al-Fakihi, 137
famine, 44, 160, 162, 164–5
Farewell Sermon (*khuṭbat al-wadā'*), 127, 129, 151
al-Fariqi, Ibn al-Azraq, 66, 67, 74, 122
fasting
  Ayyubid and Mamluk periods, 195–8
  donation of food to the poor in lieu of, 141
  during Muharram, 197
  during Rajab, 139–41, 142, 146, 171–3, 185, 195–8, 225
  during Ramadan, 2, 127, 139, 171, 197
  Fatimid period, 171–3
  hadiths on, 139–41, 146, 171, 196, 197
  obligatory fasts, 19, 139
  pre-Islamic and early Islamic period, 139–41
  rewards for, 139–41, 146, 171–2, 196, 198
Fatima, 33, 36, 42, 51, 106, 114, 119, 130, 204, 224
Fatima Umm Dawud, 144
Fatimid dynasty, 42–52, 65–7, 73–81, 106, 113, 114, 119–21, 154–65, 182–3, 221–2
Fatimid period
  banquets, 80, 160–2
  caliphal audiences, 158
  Cairo, 6, 42–5, 67, 77–81, 94, 121, 155–64, **156**, **160**, 221–2
  civil war, 44
  food distributions, 155, 157, 161–3
  formal rituals, 79–81, 155–64, 221–2
  imam-caliphs, 42–4, 46–8, 52, 77, 79–81, 121, 154–65, 222; *see also individual names*
  processions, 155–7, 159, 161, 163–4
  rites of Rajab, 5, 6, 154–73, 221–2
  shrine of al-Husayn at Ascalon, 45–52, 65, 66–7, 73–4, 119–20
  shrine of al-Husayn at Cairo, 66, 74–81, 121
  veneration of *ahl al-bayt*, 43, 50, 77–9, 120
al-Fattal al-Naysaburi, 140
food
  banquets, 80, 160–2, 205, 231
  distributions of, 80, 121, 155, 157, 161–3, 205, 231
  donated to the poor, 141, 142, 205
  sweets, 155, 161–2, 164, 206
forgiveness, seeking of (*istighfār*), 6, 143–4, 146, 170–1, 179–81, 200, 225, 230
formal pilgrimage sites, 11, 17, 202–3
formal rituals, 21, 79–81, 97, 121, 155–64, 183, 206–9, 221–2, 223
Frankfurter, David, 4
Frenkel, Yehoshua, 18, 19–20
Friday sermons (*khuṭba*), 43, 59, 81, 87, 142, 196
Friedman, Yaron, 18
frontier towns (*thughūr*), 46, 49–50, 73, 101, 103–4, 108, 113, 120, 121
Funeral Prayer (*ṣalāt al-janā'iz*), 180
Fustat (Misr), 43, 46, 55, 73, 87, 145, 157, 161, 222

Ganneau, Clermont, 102
Gaza, 62, 71

Ghadir Khumm, 50–1, 79, 81, 121, 232
al-Ghayani, Ibrahim b. Ahmad, 93, 115
al-Ghazzali, Abu Hamid, 5, 12, 22, 57, 95n7, 142, 167–8, 187, 188, 228, 230
Goldziher, Ignaz, 3–4
Grehan, James, 37–8

hadiths
  cited on Badr al-Din minbar, 50–1
  encouraging love for al-Husayn, 80
  false or fabricated, 64, 113, 129, 169, 185, 187, 189, 196, 197, 222, 225
  on fasting, 139–41, 146, 171, 196, 197
  in praise of Rajab, 195, 225
  on prayer, 144–5, 146, 180, 185, 222
  readings of, 205–6
  referring to Ascalon, 63, 64
  on ritual slaughter, 138
  on sacred months, 128–9, 147, 195, 196
  on veneration of tombs, 112
al-Hafiz (Fatimid caliph), 81
Haider, Najm, 117n7
hajj, 2, 81, 127, 128, 134, 152, 164, 170, 206–7
al-Hakim bi-Amr Allah, 43, 55, 79, 157
al-Hakim al-Hasakani, 219
al-Hamadhani, al-Qudat ʿAbd al-Jabbar, 71
Hamdanid dynasty, 6, 79
al-Harawi, 35, 40n29, 76, 91, 101–2, 106, 122
al-Harbi, Abu Ishaq Ibrahim, 132n22
al-Hasan, ʿAli b. ʿAbd Allah b. Jahdam, 169
al-Hasan b. ʿAli, 43, 44, 51, 61, 76, 114, 144
Hatim al-Taʾi, 137
Hebron (al-Khalil), 45–6, 59, 82n3, 103, 104–5, 169, 212n41
Heschel, Abraham Joshua, 217n126
hijri calendar, 19, 97, 127, 151–2, 221
Hirschler, Konrad, 183, 213n60
Hobsbawm, Eric, 61–2, 167
Horns of Hattin, battle of, 102
hospitality, 134, 155
Hubasha fair, 137
Hülegü Khan, 107
hunting, 13, 135, 208

al-Husayn
  accounts of whereabouts of head, 32–6, 38, 61, 65–7, 119
  comparison with Jesus, 114–15
  discovery of head at Ascalon, 44, 46–9
  hadiths encouraging love for, 80
  Ibn Taymiyya on veneration of the head of, 112–16
  martyrdom, 3, 29–32, **30**, **31**, 49, 65, 88, 119, 229
  miracles associated with head, 29, 49, 65, 74–6
  in Palestinian folklore, 97–9
  procession of head to Damascus, 29–31, **31**, 36–7, **37**, 49, 65, 114, 229
  revered by both Shiʿi and Sunni Muslims, 28, 88, 119, 122
  shrines commemorating processions of head, 36–7, **37**, 51, 76
  shrines of the head of *see* Mashhad al-Husayn (Damascus); Mashhad Raʾs al-Husayn (Ascalon); Mashhad Raʾs al-Husayn (Cairo)
  tomb at Karbala, 80–1, 117n7, 204, 228
  transfer of head to Cairo, 3, 66, 67, 74–81, 121
  visitation of associated shrines during Rajab, 1–2

Ibn ʿAbbad of Ronda, 198
Ibn ʿAbbas (companion), 129
Ibn ʿAbd al-Ghaffar, 201
Ibn ʿAbd al-Hadi, 195
Ibn ʿAbd al-Zahir, 74–5, 91, 178n84
Ibn Abi Dawud, 175n37
Ibn Abi al-Hamra, 167, 169–70
Ibn Abi Tayy, 155
Ibn al-ʿArabi, Abu Bakr, 71, 212n37
Ibn ʿAsakir, 32, 35, 74, 85, 195, 219
Ibn al-Athir, Diyaʾ al-Din, 185, 186
Ibn al-ʿAttar, ʿAli b. Ibrahim, 137–8, 186, 188–9, 201, 104, 209
Ibn Babawayh, 140, 141, 144, 218
Ibn Battuta, 106, 201, 216n116
Ibn Dihya al-Kalbi, 128, 134, 137, 186, 187, 195–6, 198, 219
Ibn al-Diyaʿ, 201

Ibn Fahd, al-Najm ʿUmar, 214n84
Ibn Hajar al-ʿAsqalani, 138–9, 195, 198, 204, 219
Ibn al-Hajj al-ʿAbdari, 188, 193, 196–7, 201, 209
Hanbalis, 5, 122, 138, 142, 185, 191, 193, 195, 196, 204, 229
Ibn Hawqal, 33, 60n16
Ibn al-Hawrani, 35
Ibn al-ʿImrani, 65–6, 122
Ibn Iyas, 74
Ibn al-Jawzi, 169, 185, 187, 193, 212n41, 219
Ibn Jubayr, 35, 43, 88–9, 101, 122, 198–201
Ibn Kathir, 93, 122, 194–5
Ibn al-Maʾmun al-Bataʾihi, 43, 52, 73, 159–60, 161
Ibn Manẓūr, 15n28
Ibn al-Mibrad, 219
Ibn al-Mujawir, 200, 203
Ibn al-Murajja, 169
Ibn al-Muyassar, 43, 66–7, 122
Ibn Nubata al-Fariqi, 145–7, 192, 230
Ibn Qalawun, Muhammad, 93
Ibn Qatana (grammarian), 37
Ibn Qawlawayh, 81, 83n35, 117n7
Ibn Qayyim al-Jawziyya, 136, 194
Ibn Qudama al-Maqdisi, 173, 195
Ibn Rajab, 5, 128, 196–7, 204
Ibn al-Salah al-Shahrazuri, 85, 196
Ibn Shaddad, Bahaʾ al-Din (biographer of Saladin), 102, 110n21, 192–3
Ibn Shaddad, ʿIzz al-Din (geographer), 73, 107
Ibn Shahin, 76
Ibn Taymiyya, 5, 6, 10, 32, 40n30, 56, 61, 91–3, 112–16, 122–3, 152, 182, 191, 194, 196–7, 209, 227–9
Ibn Tawq, 205–6
Ibn Tawus, 1–2, 5, 13–14, 188, 189–91, 204, 225, 228
Ibn Tughj al-Ikhshid, 145
Ibn Tulun, 195
Ibn Tulun Mosque (Cairo), 43, 45, **160**
Ibn Tuwayr, 55, 80, 163–4
Ibn ʿUthman, 89, 118n20
Ibn al-Zayyat, 89
Ibn Zubayr, 200
Ibn Zulaq, 42
Ibrahim b. ʿAbd Allah (rebel), 76
Ibrashy, May, 18
ʿId al-Adha, 129, 138, 154, 205
ʿId al-Fiṭr, 154, 162, 205
Idris ʿImad al-Din al-Qurashi, 5, 32, 36, 67, 78, 122, 191–2, 198, 219
Ifriqiya, 78
iḥyāʾ al-sunna movement, 222
iḥrām (attire for pilgrimage), 13, 170, 199
Ikhshid dynasty, 6, 145
imam-caliphs, 42–4, 46–8, 52, 77, 79–81, 121, 154–65, 222; *see also* Fatimid dynasty; *and individual names*
innovations (*bidaʿ*), 20, 93, 112–13, 116, 166–7, 186–91, 222, 224, 225
intercalation, 151–2, 221
intercession (*shafāʿa*), 49, 81, 140, 141, 171, 180, 222, 225, 228
invented traditions, 61–2, 66, 119, 167, 227
invocation (*duʿāʾ*), 91–3, 136, 143–4, 170, 189, 193, 225, 231
Ioh, Hideyuki, 136, 152
Irwin, Robert, 42
ʿIsa *see* Jesus
al-Isbahani, Abu Saʿid Muhammad, 218
al-Isfahani, ʿImad al-Din, 103, 105
Islamisation, 33, 59, 64, 65
istighfār (seeking of forgiveness), 6, 143–4, 146, 170–1, 179–81, 200, 225, 230
iʿtikāf (seclusion in mosques), 142, 157, 197

al-Jabarti, ʿAbd al-Rahman, 95n15
Jaʿfar al-Sadiq, 79, 114, 139–40, 144, 191–2, 225
Jaffa-Tel ʿAjul Treaty, 103
Jāhiliyya see pre-Islamic period
Jamal al-Din b. Yaghmur, 91
Janad, 142, 203
al-Jawhari, Abu ʿAbd Allah b. ʿAyyash, 145, 218
al-Jazari, Shams al-Din, 197–8
Jerusalem
  al-Aqsa Mosque, 57, 72 n3, 105, 167
  Bayt al-Maqdis, 12

conquest by Crusaders, 55, 73, 74
Dome of the Rock, 55
Fatimid period, 169
food distributions, 205
Gate of Mercy (*Bab al-Rahma*), 169
Gate of Pardon (*Bab al-Tawba*), 169
al-Haram al-Sharif (Temple Mount; Noble Sanctuary), 13, 57, 169, 176
ʿIsa's cradle, 91
Mamluk period, 205
pilgrimage to, 123, 170
prayer in 14, 116, 166–9, 222
rites of Rajab, 166–9, 205, 222
Saladin's reconquest, 59, 105, 192–3
travel guides, 169
Wailing Wall, 72 n3
Jesus (ʿIsa), 32, 114–15, 130, 194
Jewish calendar, 19, 23n10
jihad, 46, 63, 73, 97, 178n84, 196
al-Jilani, ʿAbd al-Qādir, 5, 134, 142–3, 170–3, 219, 229
John the Baptist (Yahya b. Zakariya), 33–5, 107
Jomier, Jacques, 216n116
Jones, Linda, 58
Judaism, 19, 23n10, 32, 57, 63, 72n3, 74, 112, 115, 142, 151, 203, 217n126
Jumada al-Akhira, 127, 136, 151, 163, 165

Kaʿb al-Ahbar, 128
Kaʿba (Mecca), 2, 13, 136, 138, 143, 165, 200, 201, **202**, 206, 223
al-Kamil Muhammad b. Ghazi (Ayyubid ruler), 107, 186
Karbala, 3, 29, 32, 36, 49, 54n43, 65, 81, 84n38, 114, 117n7, 204, 228
al-Kattani, ʿAbd al-ʿAziz b. Ahmad, 218
Katz, Marion, 20–1, 22, 166, 182, 192, 224, 229–30
Kedar, B. Z., 23
Khadija, 137
Khalek, Nancy, 18, 33
Khalid b. ʿAbdallah al-Qasri, 138
Khalidi, Tarif, 130–1
al-Khallal, Muhammad b. al-Hasan, 205, 218
al-Khashn, Shaykh al-Husayn, 191, 211n29
Khorasan, 40n35, 196
Khusraw, Nasir, 43–4, 55, 64, 71, 164–5, 176n47
al-Kindi, Shurayf ibn al-Harith, 142
Kister, Meir, 22, 138
kiswa (cloth cover for the Kaʿba), 165, 206, 223, 228
Knott, Kim, 17–18
Kohlberg, Etan, 191
Kufa, 18, 142, 144

layālī al-wuqūd (nights of kindling lights), 55, 157, 161
laylat al-isrā wa-l-miʿrāj (Night Journey and Ascension), 130, 146, 169, 192–5, 223, 225, 229
laylat al-qadr (Night of Power), 12, 145, 180, 194, 231
Lazarus-Yafeh, Hava, 20, 152
Lev, Yaacov, 51, 76, 161, 182
light
divine light radiating from Shiʿi imams, 49, 57, 65, 229
lighting of shrines and mosques, 52, 55–7, **56**, **58**, **89**, 157, 161, 229
lights as part of festivities, 55, 138, 155–7, 161, 163, 223, 229
nights of kindling lights *see layālī al-wuqūd*
in the Qurʾan, 56–7
symbolic meanings, 56–7
liturgical calendars, 6, 18–20, 127–8, 151–3
lunar calendars, 6, 19–20, 127–8, 151–3

McGregor, Richard, 216n111, 216n115
Mackay, E. J. H., 23
Madaba Map, 62, **63**
al-Madaʾini, Abu al-Hasan, 85
al-Madini, Abu Musa, 219
Madrasa al-Fadiliyya (Cairo), 187
Madrasa al-Jawhariyya (Cairo), 90
Madrasa al-Mustansiriyya (Mecca), 205
madrasas, 87, 90–1, 185, 187, 205
Mahfouz, Naguib, 27–8
al-Mahfuzi, Qadi, 90
maḥmal, 206, **208**, 208, 223
al-Majālis al-Muʿayyadiyya, 158, 159

al-Majālis al-Mustansiriyya, 173n20
Majallat al-Jundī al-Muslim, 225
Majdal, 98, 110n14
al-Maliji, ʿAbd al-Hakim, 173n20
Mamluk period
  banquets, 205
  Cairo, 6, 91–4, 206–9, **207**, 223–4
  formal rituals, 206–9, 223
  patronage of religious institutions, 183, 204–5
  processions, 206–9, 223–4
  rites of Rajab, 5, 6, 182–209, 223–4
  shrine of al-Husayn at Ascalon, 3, 103–9, 121
  shrine of al-Husayn at Cairo, 3, 91–4, 121–2
al-Manbiji, Nasr, 197
al-Mansur (Abbasid caliph), 76, 144
al-Mansur bi-Allah (Fatimid caliph), 78
Mansuriyya, 42
Maqam al-Husayn, 97–8; *see* Mashhad al-Husayn; Mashhad Raʾs al-Husayn
Maqam Ibrahim (Aleppo), 91
al-Maqdisi, ʿAbd al-Ghani, 185, 198
al-Maqdisi, Abu Muhammad, 167
al-Maqrizi, 5, 42–3, 54n43, 67, 103–4, 122, 161, 166, 208–9
Mark the Evangelist, 94
markets, 164; *see also* fairs
Marmon, Shaun, 22
martyrdom
  Anglo-Saxon martyrs, 120
  Christian martyrs, 3, 62–3, 64–5, 114, 120
  of al-Husayn, 3, 29–32, **30**, **31**, 49, 65, 88, 119, 229
  of al-Kamil, 107
  of *murābiṭūn*, 63
  of Shiʿi imams, 51
Mary, 114, 115, 214n70
Mashhad al-Husayn (Damascus), 33, **36**, 107
Mashhad al-Juyyushi (Cairo), 45, **45**
Mashhad al-Muhassin (Aleppo), 74
Mashhad al-Sayyida Nafisa (Cairo), 45, 161
Mashhad Raʾs al-Hasan wa-l-Husayn (Hamah), 82n20
Mashhad Raʾs al-Husayn (Ascalon)
  Abbasid period, 46, 64, 65, 121
  Ayyubid period, 3, 102–4, 107, 120–1
  and the Badr al-Din minbar, 45–51, 103, 104–5, 119, 230
  contested authenticity of relic, 61–2, 65–7, 108, 114, 122, 232
  cross-sectarian patronage, 51–2
  during Frankish rule, 101–2
  embellishment of, 52
  establishment of, 3, 49–50, 65–7, 119
  Fatimid period, 45–52, 65, 66–7, 73–4, 119–20
  Ibn Taymiyya on, 112–16
  lighting of, 52
  Mamluk period, 3, 103–9, 121
  marble dais in location of, 94, **99**
  as mausoleum for al-Kamil's head, 107
  Ottoman period, 3, 109
  as pilgrimage destination, 71, 120
  reconstruction of, 109
  rites performed at, 49, 65, 230–1
  in travellers' accounts, 105–9
  Umayyad period, 63–4, 65, 121
  upkeep of, 49, 109, 121
  visitation of, 49, 65, 101–2, 113, 119, 120, 122
Mashhad Raʾs al-Husayn (Cairo)
  Ayyubid period, 3, 87–91, 121–2
  building of, 28, 66, 67, 77
  casket for head, 77–8, **78**, 121
  cenotaph, **89**
  circumambulation of relic, 88, 122
  contested authenticity of relic, 91–3, 114, 122–3, 232
  cross-sectarian patronage, 28, 122
  Fatimid period, 66, 74–81, 121
  Ibn Taymiyya on, 112–16
  lattice screen (*mashrabiyya*), 94
  lighting of, **89**
  literary depictions, 27–8
  madrasa and minaret attached to, 91, **92**, 94
  Mamluk period, 3, 91–4, 121–2
  as meeting place for jurists, 90
  as meeting place for mystics, 90, 121
  oath-taking, 93

Ottoman period, 3, 93–4
pilgrimage to, 87–8, 90
restoration and renovation of, 28, 93–4
rites performed at, 79–81, 88–9, 93, 121–2
transfer of head to, 3, 66, 67, 74–81, 121
in travellers' accounts, 88–9, 91
al-Maturidi, Abu Mansur, 14
mausolea *see* shrines; tombs
Mauss, Marcel, 175n41
mawāsim (annual festivals), 97–8, 161
mawlid al-nabī (birthday of the Prophet), 20–1, 22, 197, 205, 229–30
mawlids (birthdays of holy figures), 20, 51–2, 130, 209
al-Mawsili, Muhammad, 98–9
Mecca
Ka'ba, 2, 13, 136, 138, 143, 165, 200, 201, **202**, 206, 223
Madrasa al-Mustansiriyya, 205
pilgrimage to, 2, 13, 112, 116, 123, 136–9, 164–5, 170, 199–203, 206–8, 221, 222–3, 225
prayer in, 14, 116
rites of Rajab, 123, 136–9, 164–5, 199–203, 206–8, 221, 222–3, 225
sanctity, 12–13, 116, 136, 230
Zamzam Well, 130
Medina, 12, 13, 14, 18, 33, 36, 56, 61, 79, 88, 114, 116, 123, 139, 186, 203–4, 230
memory, 4, 65, 107, 120
Meri, Joseph, 18
Meron, 72n3
Merv, 36–7
Meshullam of Volterra, 57
minbars
Badr al-Din minbar, 45–51, **47**, **48**, 82n8, 103, 104–5, 119, 230
donated to shrines and mosques, 57–9
function and symbolism of, 58–9, 93
Muhammad's minbar, **190**, 211
Nur al-Din Zangi's minbar, 83n23, 105
miracles, 29, 46, 49, 65, 74–6, 98, 228–9
mi'rāj (ascension of Muhammad), 146, 192–5, 223, 229
Mishna, 15n10
Misr *see* Fustat
Mohammad, Soad Maher, 40n30
Mongols, 107, 183
Moses (Musa), 32, 91
Mosque of 'Umar (Ascalon), 106
Mosul, 29, 36, 99
Mouton, Jean-Michel, 51, 60n18
Mu'adh b. Jabal, 142, 203
Mu'awiyya I (Umayyad caliph), 130, 138, 165
Mu'awiyah II (Umayyad caliph), 66
al-Mu'azzam (Ayyubid ruler), 210n5
Muhammad, Prophet
birthday (*mawlid*), 20–1, 22, 51, 197, 205, 229–30
commemoration of life events, 20–1, 50–1, 81, 130, 192–5, 223, 229–30
Farewell Sermon (*khuṭbat al-wadā'*), 127, 129, 151
fasting, 139
intercession by, 180
mosque and tomb at Medina, 22, 56, 211, 228
Night Journey and Ascension (*laylat al-isrā' wa-l-mi'rāj*), 130, 146, 169, 192–5, 223, 225, 229
prayers taught by, 170–1
raids against enemies, 136
sandal of at Damascus, 90, 91
'umra during Rajab, 137–8
Muharram, 127, 129, 147, 151, 195, 197, 208, 229
Mu'in map, 63
al-Mu'izz li-Din Allah, 43, 78–9, 155
Mujir al-Din, 55, 108, 122
Mulder, Stephennie, 18, 23, 33, 40, n24, 51, 52, 57, 87–8
Munt, Harry, 15n22, 18
al-Muqaddasi (geographer), 64
al-Muqtadir, 64
murābiṭūn (defenders), 63–4, 113, 114, 120, 121
Musa, 32, 91
al-Musabbihi, 42, 157
Muṣḥaf 'Uthmān, 82n11
music, 166, 168, 193, 208, 209

al-Mustansir (Fatimid caliph), 43–4, 46–8, 49–50, 158–9, 164–5
mysticism, 37, 120
mystics, 12, 64, 89, 90, 121–2, 142, 145, 188, 192, 198; *see also* Sufis

Nabi Musa, 72n3, 91
Nabi Samuel, 72n3
al-Nabulsi, ʿAbd al-Ghani, 82n20, 122
Nafisa bint Hasan b. Zayd, 114–15
Najaf, 36, 205
al-Nasir Hasan (Mamluk sultan), 205
nationalism, 97–8
al-Nawawi, 186, 187, 188–9
Netton, Ian, 88
Night Journey and Ascension (*laylat al-isrāʾ wa-l-miʿrāj*), 130, 146, 169, 192–5, 223, 225, 229
Night of Power (*laylat al-qadr*), 12, 145, 180, 194, 231
nights of kindling lights (*layālī al-wuqūd*), 55, 157, 161
Nile rites, 154
Noah (Nuh), 130, 159
Nur al-Din Zangi, 105
al-Nuwayri, 93, 122, 197

oath-taking, 93, 230
Ohtoshi, Tetsuya, 18, 90
Ottoman period, 3, 19–20, 93–4, 109

Padwick, Constance, 12, 22, 143, 179–80
Palace Walk (Mahfouz), 27–8
Palestinian folklore, 97–9
Palestinian nationalism, 97–8
pardon *see* forgiveness
patron saints, 73, 102, 122
patronage, 18, 48, 56, 83n23, 162, 175n41, 183, 186, 204–5, 231
ʻperipheral' pilgrimage sites, 10–11, 17, 70, 120, 121, 203, 223
pilgrimage
  to Ascalon, 6, 71
  ʻcentral' pilgrimage sites, 10–11, 17, 70, 222–3
  and crossing of wilderness, 70, 120, 202, 223
  during Rajab, 136–9, 164–6, 198–204, 206–8, 221, 222–3, 225
  during Ramadan, 201, 207–8
  formal pilgrimage sites, 11, 17, 202–3
  hajj, 2, 81, 127, 128, 134, 152, 164, 170, 206–7
  to Jerusalem, 123, 170
  to Karbala, 80–1, 117n7, 204
  to Mecca, 2, 13, 112, 116, 123, 136–9, 164–5, 199–203, 206–8, 221, 222–3, 225
  to Medina, 203–4
  ʻperipheral' pilgrimage sites, 10–11, 17, 70, 120, 121, 203, 223
  pre-Islamic and early Islamic period, 134, 136–9
  Turner on, 6, 10–11, 70–2, 120, 223
  ʿumra, 128, 136–9, 164–6, 198–204, 206–8, 221, 222–3, 225
  wearing of *iḥrām*, 13, 170, 199
  by women, 11, 201, 203–4
poetry, 11, 80–1, 121, 156, 160, 193, 230
popular rituals, 20–2, 164, 166, 183–91, 222
prayer
  Ayyubid and Mamluk periods, 183–92
  change of prayer direction, 130
  comparative efficacy at different places, 14, 115–16, 230–1
  comparative efficacy at different times, 22, 116, 180, 230–1
  during Rajab, 1–2, 22, 141–5, 146, 157, 166–71, 179–81, 183–92, 222, 225
  during Ramadan, 145
  early Islamic period, 141–5
  Fatimid period, 157, 166–71
  hadiths on, 144–5, 146, 180, 185, 222
  invocation (*duʿāʾ*), 91–3, 136, 143–4, 170, 189, 225, 231
  neglect of, 146
  participation of angels, 144–5
  prayer assemblies, 22, 142, 145, 166–70, 180, 183–7, 204
  prayer manuals, 22, 179–81, 183, 224–5, 231
  repetition of, 141, 168, 180, 190
  rewards for, 22, 116, 170–1, 188, 231

ṣalāt al-istisqāʿ, 196
ṣalāt al-janāʾiz, 180
ṣalāt al-raghāʾib, 166–70, 171, 183–91, 204, 222, 225
Ṣalāt Umm Dāwūd, 191
and seeking of forgiveness, 6, 143–4, 146, 170–1, 179–81, 200, 225, 230
and seeking of intercession, 49, 81, 180, 222, 225
at shrine of al-Husayn at Ascalon, 49, 65, 230–1
at shrine of al-Husayn at Cairo, 81, 121
supererogatory prayer, 1, 141, 166–9, 183–91, 222, 230
Prayer for Great Rewards (*ṣalāt al-raghāʾib*), 166–70, 171, 183–91, 204, 222, 225
pre-Islamic period
conceptions of time, 11, 127–8, 129
rites of Rajab, 5, 134–47
processions, 155–7, 159, 161, 163–4, 206–9, 223–4, 231
Prophet's Mosque (Medina), 56, 189, **190**

al-Qalqashandi, 49–50, 55, 73, 74–5, 77, 155, 182
al-Qarafa cemetery (Cairo), 18, 89–90, 157, 160, 166, 222
al-Qariʿ, ʿAli, 200
al-Qasatli, Nuʿman, 98–9
al-Qasb Mosque (Damascus), 66
Qays b. ʿAbbad, 140
al-Qazwini, ʿAbd al-Qasim al-Rafiʿi, 219
al-Qazwini, Zakariya b. Yahya, 105
Qurʾan
on abstention from warfare, 135–6
allegorical interpretations, 106, 158
on angels, 145
conceptions of time, 11–12, 20, 127, 152
conceptions of space, 12
on forgiveness, 179
on intercalation, 151
on *laylat al-qadr*, 194
mapping onto the landscape, 106, 120, 169
professional recitation of, 80, 121, 156, 157, 163, 204, 231
recitation during Rajab, 156, 157, 163, 193, 204
recitation during Shaʿban, 128
on sacred months, 127, 151, 152
stories of Adam and Noah, 159
story of Solomon in Wadi al-Naml, 106, 120–1
symbolism of light, 56–7
verses inscribed on casket for al-Husayn's head, 77
Quraysh, 134, 136
Qutbuddin, Tahera, 174n20

Rabiʿ al-Awwal, 192
Rajab
abstention from speech, 197
abstention from warfare, 5, 127, 135–6, 221
academic literature on, 22–3
appelations for, 134
Ayyubid period, 5, 182–209, 222–3
banquets, 160–2, 205
caliphal audiences, 158
charity, 141, 142, 160, 161, 166, 204–6, 225, 231
contested sanctity of, 5–6, 22, 128, 195–7, 221, 224, 225
designation as sacred month, 127, 128–9, 147, 151
etymologies of, 171
fasting, 139–41, 142, 171–3, 185, 195–8, 225
formal and state rites, 155–64, 183, 206–9, 221–2, 223
Fatimid period, 5, 6, 154–73, 221–2
food distributions, 155, 157, 161–3, 205
hadiths in praise of, 195, 225
hadith readings, 205–6
Mamluk period, 5, 6, 182–209, 223–4
Night of Ascension, 192–5, 201, 223
nights of kindling lights, 55
pilgrimage, 136–9, 164–6, 198–204, 206–8, 221, 222–3, 225
poetry recitation, 156, 160, 193
prayer, 1–2, 22, 141–5, 146, 157, 166–71, 179–81, 183–92, 222, 225

Rajab (*cont.*)
pre-Islamic and early Islamic period, 5, 134–47
processions, 155–7, 159, 161, 163–4, 206–9, 223–4
Qur'an recitation, 157, 163, 193, 204
remittance of sin, 129, 140, 141, 142–3, 170, 227
rewards for devotions, 129–30, 139–41, 146, 159, 188, 204, 225
ritual slaughter, 136–9, 225
seclusion in mosques, 142, 157, 197
sermons, 145–7, 157, 158–9, 193, 221–2
treatises in praise of, 6, 195, 218–19
Umayyad period, 6, 138, 142
'umra, 136–9, 164–6, 198–204, 206–8, 221, 222–3, 225
white days, 144, 173, 198
ziyāra, 1–2, 165–6, 203–4, 225

rajabiyya processions, 206–9, **208**, 223–4
Ramadan, 2, 13, 127, 128, 139, 145, 147, 155, 171, 197, 201, 205, 207–8, 232
Ramla, 71
Ranger, Terence, 61–2, 167
Raqqa, 36
Ra'uf Basha, 109
Redfield, Robert, 119
Reid, Megan, 22, 213n65
Reiter, Itzhak, 23
religious festivals, 19, 20, 54, 79–81, 97–8, 121, 145, 154, 161, 188, 193-4, 199, 205, 223
repentance, 22, 141, 146, 180, 193; *see also* forgiveness, seeking of
rewards
during Rajab, 129–30, 139–41, 146, 159, 171–2, 188, 204, 225
for fasting, 139–41, 146, 171–2, 196, 198
for good deeds, 116, 129–30, 139–41, 159, 204
greater at certain times, 22, 116, 129–30, 139–41, 146, 159, 171–2
and prayer, 22, 116, 170–1, 188, 231
Richard the Lionheart, 102, 103
Rightly Guided Caliphs, 51, 65, 87; *see also individual caliphs*
ritual performance
formal and state rituals, 21, 79–81, 97, 121, 155–64, 183, 206–9, 221–2, 223
popular rituals, 20–2, 164, 166, 183–91, 222
rewards for, 129–30
rites of Rajab *see* Rajab
as sanctifying time and place, 14, 88–9, 230
at shrines, 49, 65, 79–81, 88–9, 93, 121–2, 230–1
social functions of, 232
ritual slaughter, 129, 136–9, 162, 225
robes of honour (*khila'*), 163
Rodman, Margaret, 17
Roman Catholic Church, 94, 199
rope of God (*ḥabl Allāh*), 1
al-Ruhawi, 'Abd al-Qadir (imam), 187

sacred months
abstention from warfare, 5, 127, 135–6, 221
comparative weight of sins and good deeds, 129–30, 140–1, 227
in the Farewell Sermon, 127, 129, 151
hadiths on, 128–9, 147, 195, 196
in the Qur'an, 127, 151, 152
set of four sacred months, 5, 127–8, 151, 221
set of three sacred months, 128–9, 147, 155
treatises in praise of, 6, 195, 218–19
see also sacred time; *and individual months*
sacred place
and apparitions, 101, 115, 229
and comparative weight of sins and good deeds, 14, 115–16, 134, 227, 230–1
continuity of, 3–5, 33–5, 61–3, 64–5, 76–7, 87–8, 120
discontinuity of, 9
hierarchies of sacredness, 15n10, 17
Ibn Taymiyya's polemics on, 6, 112–16
and miracles, 228–9
in the Qur'an, 12

re-dedication of, 4, 61–3, 64–5, 76–7, 120
relationship to sacred time, 21, 165, 227–33
sancitified by ritual performance, 14, 88–9, 230
storied nature of, 229–30
terminology for, 12–14
sacred–profane continuum, 10–11
sacred–profane dichotomy, 9–10, 209
sacred terminology, Arabic roots, 12–14
sacred time
and comparative efficacy of prayer, 22, 116, 180, 230–1
and comparative weight of sins and good deeds, 116, 129–30, 140–1, 159, 227
pre-Islamic conceptions of, 11, 127–8, 129
in the Qur'an, 11–12, 20, 127, 151, 152
relationship to sacred place, 21, 165, 227–33
and rewards received for devotions, 22, 116, 129–30, 139–41, 146, 171–2, 227
sanctified by ritual performance, 14, 230
storied nature of, 229–30
terminology for, 12–14
see also sacred months
sacrifice *see* ritual slaughter
al-Safadi, 107
al-Ṣaḥīfa al-Sajjādiyya, 143
St. Catherine's monastery, 59
saint veneration, 3–4, 17, 33–5, 37–8, 51, 113
al-Sakhawi, 189
Saladin, 59, 75–6, 87, 88, 90–1, 97–9, 102–5, 121, 182, 192–3
ṣalāt al-istisqā' (Prayer for Rain), 196
ṣalāt al-janā'iz (Funeral Prayer), 180
ṣalāt al-raghā'ib (Prayer for Great Rewards), 166–70, 171, 183–91, 204, 222, 225
Ṣalāt Umm Dāwūd, 191, 227
al-Salih Isma'il (Ayyubid sultan), 186
al-Salih Najm al-Din Ayyub, 103
Saliha, Mahmud, 97
Sallnow, Michael, 61, 80
Salman al-Farisi, 170–1
al-Samhudi, 56, 203–4
al-Samarrai, Qasim, 69n21
Sanctuary of Abraham (Hebron), 45–6, 104–5
Sanders, Paula, 21, 51, 81, 154–5, 162
Sarw tribe, 200
Sa'udi Permanent Committee for Scholarly Research and *Iftā'*, 225
Sayf al-Din Jaqmaq (Mamluk sultan), 208
Sayyida Ruqayya, 40n24
Schielke, Samuli, 4, 209, 224
Schimmel, Anne-Marie, 168
seclusion in mosques (*i'tikāf*), 142, 157, 197
second *fitna*, 63
Seljuks, 44, 49, 59, 67, 177n63
sermons
during Rajab, 145–7, 157, 158–9, 193, 221
at Fatimid sessions of wisdom, 158–9
Friday sermons, 43, 59, 81, 87, 142, 196
pre-Islamic and early Islamic period, 145–7
sessions of wisdom (*majālis al-ḥikma*), 158–9, 163
Sha'ban, 20, 22, 55, 103, 127–8, 145, 147, 155, 158, 161, 166–7, 171, 185, 197, 203–5
shafā'a (intercession), 49, 81, 140, 141, 171, 180, 222, 225, 228
al-Shafi'i, 138
al-Shahrazuri, Ibn al-Salah, 187–8
al-Sha'rani, 'Abd al-Wahhab, 76, 122
shari'a (Islamic law), 19, 20–1, 87, 113, 115–16, 122, 128, 185, 194, 224, 231
al-Sharji al-Zabidi, Ahmad, 203
Sharon, Moshe, 23
al-Shatibi, 187
Shawwal, 197
al-Shirazi, al-Mu'ayyad fi al-Din, 158–9, 160
shrines
catchment area of, 70–1
commemorating procession of al-Husayn's head, 36–7, **37**, 51
commemorating transfer of al-Husayn's head to Cairo, 76

shrines (*cont.*)
cross-sectarian patronage, 18, 28, 51–2, 87–8, 122
dedicated to *ahl al-bayt*, 43, 88, 204
desecration of, 74, 102
donations to, 52, 55–9
dreams or visions occurring at, 101–2
embellishment of, 6, 52, 55–9
founded by Saladin, 97
of al-Husayn's head *see* Mashhad al-Husayn (Damascus); Mashhad Ra'ʾs al-Husayn (Ascalon); Mashhad Raʾs al-Husayn (Cairo)
Ibn Taymiyya's polemics on, 6, 112–16
lighting of, 52, 55–7, **56**, **58**, **89**, 157, 161, 229
multiple shrines for the same figure, 3 7–8
oath-taking at, 93, 230
as places of safety, 102
re-dedication of, 4, 61–3, 64–5, 76–7, 120
rites performed at, 49, 65, 79–81, 88–9, 93, 121–2, 230–1
visitation of, 1–2, 49, 50, 65, 71, 112–16, 119, 120, 122–3, 165–6, 203–4, 228
Sibt ibn al-Jawzi, 32, 37, 66, 122
Sinai, 59, 62
Sindawi, Khalid, 23
sins
comparative weight of at different places, 134, 227
comparative weight of at different times, 116, 129–30, 159, 227
remittance of, 129, 140, 141, 142–3, 170, 227, 230
repentance for, 22, 141, 180, 193
seeking forgiveness for, 6, 143–4, 146, 170–1, 179–81, 225
Siraj al-Din, al-Shafiʿi, 189
Smith, Jonathan Z., 106, 167
Smith, William Robertson, 9
Solomon, 106
spatial turn, 17–18
speech, abstention from (*ṣamt*), 197
Stewart, Devin, 182
Stowasser, Barbara, 19
al-Subki, Taqi al-Din, 186
Sufis, 5, 13, 87, 95n15, 98, 122, 141, 142, 169–70, 172–3, 182, 183, 189, 192–3, 196–8, 203, 208, 215n95, 229
al-Sulami, ʿIzz al-Din ibn ʿAbd al-Salam, 186, 196
Sulayman b. ʿAbd al-Malik, 33, 138
Sunni hegemony, 87–8, 91, 121, 182
supererogatory prayer, 1, 141, 166–9, 183–91, 222, 230
supplication *see* invocation; prayer
sweets, 155, 161–2, 164, 206

al-Tabari (historian), 31–2, 69n21
al-Tabari, ʿAbd al-Karim b. ʿAbd al-Samad, 195, 218
al-Tabbaʿ, ʿUthman Mustafa, 108–9
Tabbaa, Yasser, 46
Tamari, Salim, 97
Tamim al-Dari, 56
Tawus b. Kaysan al-Yamani, 143–4
Taylor, Christopher, 18
thughūr (frontier towns), 46, 49–50, 73, 101, 103–4, 108, 113, 120, 121
al-Tibr Mosque, 76–7
tombs
contested authenticity of, 91–3
multiple tombs associated with same figure, 37–8
as source of sanctity for cities, 64
visitation of, 18, 33, 50, 80–1, 112–13, 191, 225
see also cemeteries; shrines
Torah, 74
Turbat al-Aʾimma mausoleum (Cairo), 52, 78
Turner, Victor, 6, 10–11, 70–2, 119, 223
al-Turtushi, 116, 122–3, 166–7
Tutakh, Khalid, 97
Tyre, 49, 71

ʿUbayd Ibn Maʿali, 77
ʿUmar ibn al-Khattab, 127, 138, 139, 142, 195
al-ʿUmari, Ibn Fadl Allah, 61, 62, 107, 122
Umayyad dynasty, 29–32, 49, 65, 114

Umayyad Great Mosque (Damascus), 33–5, **34**, **35**, **36**, 107, 186, 205
Umayyad period, 6, 63–4, 65, 121, 138, 142
Umm al-Rassas map, 63
ʿ*umra* (minor pilgrimage), 128, 136–9, 164–6, 198–204, 206–8, 221, 222–3, 225
ʿUthman, Caliph, 36, 136, 204

van Berchem, Max, 23
vigils, 183, 189, 195, 223
Vincent, L. H., 23
visitation (*ziyāra*)
  of the Cave of the Patriarchs, 104–5
  during Rajab, 1–2, 165–6, 203–4, 225
  Ibn Taymiyya on, 112–16
  of shrines, 1–2, 49, 50, 65, 71, 112–16, 119, 120, 122–3, 165–6, 203–4, 228
  of tombs or cemeteries, 18, 33, 50, 80–1, 89–90, 106, 112–13, 166, 191, 225
von Grunebaum, Gustave, 14, 17, 20, 64

Wadi al-Naml (Valley of the Ants), 97, 99, 100, 106, 120–1
Wagtendonk, K., 23, 139
al-Walid (Umayyad caliph), 33
warfare, abstention from, 5, 127, 135–6, 221
white days (*ayyām al-bīḍ*), 144, 173, 198
wilderness, 70, 120, 202, 223
William of Tyre, 74
Williams, Caroline, 23, 77
Wishnitzer, Avner, 19, 20
women
  at cemeteries and pilgrimage sites, 11, 166, 201, 203–4
  intermingling with men, 135, 166, 193, 227
  in Mecca, 199, 201–2
  participation in processions, 157, 163–4, 208, 209
  seclusion in mosques, 142

al-Yafiʿi, 189
Yahya b. Zakariya (John the Baptist), 33–5, 107
al-Yamani, ʿUmara, 162, 203
al-Yaʿqubi, 134, 135
Yaqut al-Hamawi, 115, 148n20
Yazid (Umayyad caliph), 31–3, 36, 65, 93, 114

al-Zabidi, Muhammad b. Abi al-Sayf, 215n95, 219
al-Zahir, Ahmad Jaqmaq (Mamluk sultan), 208
al-Zahir b. al-Hakim bi-Amr Allah (Fatimid caliph), 157
al-Zahir, al-Malik (Ayyubid ruler) 88
Zamzam Well (Mecca), 130
al-Zanbur shrine, 76
Zangid dynasty, 105, 114, 183, 222
Ziyad ibn Abihi, 142
Ziyad Ibn ʿUbayd Allah, 29, 32, 65
ziyāra see visitation

EU representative:
Easy Access System Europe
Mustamäe tee 50, 10621 Tallinn, Estonia
Gpsr.requests@easproject.com

www.ingramcontent.com/pod-product-compliance
Lightning Source LLC
Chambersburg PA
CBHW050210240426
43671CB00013B/2275
* 9 7 8 1 4 7 4 4 6 0 9 7 2 *